ADVENTURE TOURISM AND SPORTS
Risk and Challenges

ADVENTURE TOURISM AND SPORTS
Risk and Challenges

PART–1

JAGMOHAN NEGI
&
G. MANOHER

Himalayan Tourism and Recreation in Mountains
New Delhi

KANISHKA PUBLISHERS, DISTRIBUTORS
NEW DELHI-110 002

KANISHKA PUBLISHERS, DISTRIBUTORS
4697/5-21 A, Ansari Road, Daryaganj
New Delhi-110 002
Phones : 2327 0497, 2328 8285
Fax : 011-2328 8285
E-mail: kanishka_publishing@yahoo.co.in

First Published 2001
Second Edition 2010
© Jagmohan Negi & G. Manoher
ISBN 81-7391-350-1 (Set)

Editorial Assistance:

G. Manoher: An outstanding adventure tourist, sportsman and nature lover.

Ritushka: Cultural conscious and environmentalist.

Suniti Negi: Social and environmental conscious, and adventurist on Himalayan region.

Renu Bisht: Adventure tourism and trekking lover.

PRINTED IN INDIA

Published by Madan Sachdeva for Kanishka Publishers, Distributors, 4697/5-21A, Ansari Road, Daryaganj, New Delhi-110 002, Typeset by Sunshine Graphics, Delhi, and Printed at Rajdhani Printers, Delhi.

Preface

It is a recognised fact that there is a large international segment of tourists interested in adventure activities, sports and rail tourism etc. With this end in view, a number of new tourism concepts may be developed and promoted to make India a competitive tourists destination in the world. India is increasingly becoming popular destination for adventure travellers and combined efforts are required to promote the same.

The book entails the efforts, the government is planning to create infrastructural facilities for trekking, mountaineering and winter/water related sports. Tented accommodation may be provided for setting up of adventure camp sites. Camp tourism provides a unique opportunity to live in the natural surrounding and enjoy the thrills of adventure and nature tours, sightseeing and other activities. Arrangement may be made for camping at distant regions. Efforts be made to encourage caravan tourism. Camping sites may be developed and trekker's huts may be put up at high altitudes, specially in the hilly regions. Together with these activities, skiing may also be actively promoted. Training at different levels be imparted. For the promotion of winter sports, recently a centre has been set up at Auli (Uttaranchal). To promote adventure tourism through winter sports more Winter Sports Projects be initiated.

Skiing on a infinite stretch of snow is a real adventure experience. New adventure destinations required to be identified, planned and promoted. Some of the state governments extend financial assistance for procuring equipment for aero sports, paragliding and hang gliding.

Another area in adventure sports which required to be explored is the water-sports. The Department of Tourism has set up a National Institute of Water Sports in Goa (1990) to promote water-sports throughout the country. The state governments assist in procuring water-sport equipment, viz. canoeing, kayaking, hover craft, wind surfing, yachting, water scooter, river rafts etc. The institute is set up under the Ministry of Tourism on an 18 acre beachside plot near NIO Circle, Caranzalem, Panaji, Goa. The institute is envisaged as a pioneer "mother" training establishment and resource centre in the field of water-sports tourism. It is proposed to carry out an over-all assessment of the existing and anticipated requirements of water-sports activities in the country and formulate this project with selective private sector participation in non-training aspects, etc. so as to make it financially self-sufficient over a period of three years. The institute will ensure linkages with state level and other water-sports centres, establish standardisation and certification of safety norms and ensure that facilities in the private sector are not duplicated.

Yet another important area for adventure tourism is India's wildlife sanctuaries and national parks. Cruise boats, launches etc. have been provided at wildlife centres with water frontage to view wildlife from close quarters. These include cruise boats to watching dolphins, fibre glass boats, launches, cruise vessels, mini buses with spot lights etc. Enchanting forest trails provide a very eco-friendly experience.

Sports tourism has also given an impetus to tourism in India. Financial help is being extended to improve the greens at the existing sites or to develop new areas for golf. Mountain hiking in remote valleys of Lahaul, Laddakh, Kullu, Sikkim, Garhwal and Kumaon Himalayas and the eastern part of the Himalaya is very popular. Jeep safaris and photography tours are quite popular. The mountain road from Leh in

Laddakh to Manali provides one of the greatest road journeys in the world. Linking Buddhist Laddakh and the tribal areas of Lahaul with the fertile Kullu Valley, the road traverses the Greater Himalayan over a series of famous passes, with the Tanglang La at 5,360 m. being the second highest in the world. Driving through some unbelievably breathtaking scenery, the views from the top of these passes are truly stunning.

The Garhwal and Kumaon regions in the eastern corner of India's Northern Himalayas, close to the borders of Tibet and Nepal, contain one of the finest mountain of the Himalayas and yet this is an area surprisingly ignored by the western trekkers. The pristine valleys of this area opened for trekking since 1994 and have been explored after decades of isolation. The attraction of Garhwal and Kumaon lies in the fact that dense forest still cover the slopes and the trails offer outstanding views of high peaks like Nanda Devi from as close as 3 km.

Sone et lumiere (flood lighting) has been formulated by Department of Tourism and Archaeological Survey of India in order to make some of the tourist destination very attractive. The department extends financial assistance to state governments/union territories to meet the equipment cost of such facilities.

Ministry of Railways has introduced several fast air-conditioned trains, connecting tourist centres in the country. Special trains have been introduced such as the Palace-on-Wheels and the Royal Orient. Palace-on-Wheels train with historical charm and modern conveniences, takes the tourist as a royal odyssey. This train is designed to suit modern needs with central airconditioning, soothing four channel music, inter-connected telephone system, a separate pantry and lounge in each coach and comfortable coupes with the privacy of attached bathrooms.

The Royal Orient is are of the few extravaganza left of an epoch of grandeur. The train includes 13 wondrous gold embossed saloon cars that recreate the resplendent life-style of the times of yore.

The luxurious lounge, central airconditioning, library, television and radio entertainment, soft channel music are some of the special features of this train.

SECTION III: ADVENTURE ON SNOW
Soft and Hard

PART: TWO

SECTION IV: ADVENTURE IN WATER
White Pure and Crystal

SECTION V: ADVENTURE IN SPACE AND AIR
Variety, Clarity and Dedication

SECTION VI: PILGRIM TOURISM
(Tirth Yatras/Holy Yatras)

PART : 1

SECTION I

INTRODUCTION

1

Adventure Tourism and Sports:
An Introduction

India's vast geographical diversity provides a wealth of outdoors adventure. All tastes are catered for from the gentlest to the fast placed and there is something for every level of competence the beginner and the expert. Not only does India have an immense variety of outdoor thrills, but prices here are extremely low by international standards.

Travel agents and tour operators very often specialise in certain fields, offering package deals for groups and individuals.

In summer the focus is on the mountains in the northern most region. Jammu and Kashmir, Himachal, Garhwal and Kumaon, Sikkim, Bhutan, North-East and Napal Himalayas all lie in the lap of the great Himalayan range, where the trekking season is roughly from July to mid October, August and September being the best months.

Altitudes range from 9,000 feet to 14,500 feet above sea level, and trekkers need only a reasonable degree of physical fitness, prior experience not being necessary. In Laddakh, the lowest altitudes is 11,000 feet above sea level and with the shortage of oxygen, acclimatisation is compulsory, some passes commonly encountered during a trek being as high as 18000 feet above sea level.

The majority of *trekking trails* in India are well within the "inner line" which falls within a certain distance of the external boundaries of the country. In the rare even that a trekker wishes to cross the inner line, prior permission must be obtained.

Trekking is such a popular sport in the region that equipment can very easily be hired. Equipment includes kerosene stoves, carry on mats, tents, even waterproof jackets. Would be trekkers need only bring trekking boots and sun screen lotion in addition to specialised equipment. If required, this can include all materials and all weather storage drums in the case of extended treks hiring of ponies, porters, guides and cooks is simple and can be arranged in a matter of minutes at the starting point of the trek.

For the first time trekker, all this is pre-arranged by trekking agencies who usually charge per person per day on the basis of luxuries offered: such as a constant supply of hot water for bathing, riding ponies throughout and varied menus.

Also in focus all through summer is *river running* in precisely those states which offer trekking. However, the most popular stretch for this sport is on the Ganga near Rishikesh. Here again, specialised agencies offer guides, trained personnel and the hire of equipment that includes inflatable rafts and crash helmets. Camping arrangements range from the modest to the luxurious and are included in the services provided. The advantages of making arrangements through an agency that specialises in river running are manifold. It completely obviates the necessity for carrying bulky equipment to India, routes are well planned and grades of difficulty for the river are precisely marked. The best season for river rafting is from April to September.

Heli skiing in Manali provides an enormous variety of ski runs and routes as complicated or as straight forward as the individual can tackle. A helicopter treks a group of advanced skiers up onto any one of the numerous peaks that surround the resort from where they make their descent.

For six months of the year between October and March, India's coastline thousands of miles long, provides perfect *beach holidays*. These range from secluded, seldom visited beaches ideal for those wanting a quiet holiday, to internationally renowned resorts, complete with several luxury resort to choose from, and yet others where the accent is on water sports.

Each of India's coastal states, Gujarat, Maharashtra, Goa, Karnataka, Kerala, Tamil Nadu, Andhra Pradesh and Orissa have choice of beaches. Those in Goa are all popular, many offer luxury resort hotels on the beach itself, a few offer wind surfing and yachting. Gopalpur-on-sea in Orissa, Chorwad and Ahmedpur Mandvi in Gujarat are but two examples of relatively quiet beaches. Lakshadweep offers excellent wind surfing, snorkelling and scuba diving in the crystal clear waters of the lagoons which surround each island.

The desert state of Rajasthan offers an exotic encounter with the outdoors in the form of *camel safaris*. The Thar desert in western Rajasthan is the locale for an age old adventure. Camels—one per rider—are used as a unique form of sightseeing which can last one day, leaving early morning and returning by nightfall. Camel safaris can be undertaken over a period of several days in which case camping equipment is necessary. Whatever the duration, agencies in Jaisalmer organise trips to wind sculpted sand dunes, ornate Jain temples and tiny villages in the middle of the wilderness. Charges include the hiring of a guide (absolutely necessary) and camping equipment. Camel safaris are commonly organised in the relatively cooler months of winter.

Developing on the same theme, *horse safaris* have become enormously popular in Udaipur and its environs. The part of Rajasthan that lies in the Aravalli hills are geographically distinct from the rest of the desert state. Here, erstwhile titled landlords built lavish castles and imposing forts in the villages that were parcelled out to them. It is these palaces, among the less known and visited in the country, that are the destination of a horse safari. A party is taken through thickly wooded hills, through colourful villages and into a stately home which usually forms the focus of the safari. Horse safaris can also be arranged to forts, wildlife sanctuaries and lakes that dot the surroundings of Udaipur.

The adventure sports reflect to great range and diversity of the modern adventure travel vacation. It includes everything from ballooning to ski diving and the entire world in between. Adventure travel in by its nature mutlifaceted. Some trip may specialise in rafting, trekking, cycling and the like. Most sailing trips include some diving. Many overlanding trips feature to hiking to scenic vistas or historic sites. Some trips bade so many different types of adventure into their itinerary.

Unlike the conventional mould of visiting a hill station or a beach there relaxing and just relaxing in a comfortable, secluded place, these adventure freaks try for anything tagged innovative or thrilling. India is the destination for the fitness freaks and nature lovers all rolled into one, the choice of sporting holidays abounds here.

Over the last decade there has been a change in the concept of holidaying in India. An increasing number of people want a little more to their holiday than visiting overcrowded hill stations or viewing monuments. They now want activity-oriented vacations with a chance to commune with mother nature and breathe a dash of fresh air.

Why people pursue adventure activities? The joy and thrill of being out of doors, the captivating beauty of mother nature, the marvellous camping experience, the strong camaraderie and the sense of achievement on finishing a climb or negotiating a rapid all add up to make a strong case for pursuing adventure sports.

Adventure sports can be broadly divided into two—specialised and non-specialised. Almost anyone can take part in non-specialised adventure sports primarily *trekking* and *river rafting.* To get initiated into trekking, take on a trek which is relatively easy in order to get to know your ability. You can either venture into the mountains with an experienced trekker or join an adventure club or go through any reputed adventure travel company. It is a good idea to get as much information as possible about the area to be visited—the people, their culture, the geography, terrain and weather conditions. A basic knowledge of first aid is essential. Never venture out alone.

There is no dearth of opportunities in the country, but it requires a spirit of adventure and a willingness to meet challenges on the part of youth leaders, teachers and professors, social servants and grown-up people in the services and the professions, to give guidance and encouragement and programmed help to the boys and girls of our schools and universities and to all non-student youth who do not have schooling facilities or have not been able to utilise them.

For a developing nation like ours, with over half the population under the age of 25 and facing an acute crisis in basic necessities like food, shelter and clothing, widespread unemployment and many areas of darkness in education, youth programmes even fundamental and essential one like adventure training and exposure to physical challenge—must justify any expenditure of resources.

We must grow our own programmes and our own policies on the native soil. There is no gain-saying that training in mountaineering, rock-climbing, trekking, orienteering, study and conservation of wildlife, conservation service in National Parks and Sanctuaries, sea-sports and water sports, life-saving and community services, drought, and famine and flood relief programmes for youth are meaningful in the development of not only qualities of head and heart among our youth, but also in encouraging a national character which will stand the country in good stead in times of crisis and also of prosperity.

What we need in the country is a programme of Adventure Training which will be able to offer an exposure to all those aspects of the wilderness, not to tens and hundreds, but to thousands and eventually hundreds of thousands of young men and women all over India. This requires a massive organisational effort. The need for low-cost programmes and stringent economy makes this a big challenge to our teachers and others who would like to help.

Surging waves, and soaring mountains is a challenge to your courage. There is an endless challenge to man's courage and his spirit of adventure. Mountaineering on the Himalayan heights, trekking enchanting forest trails, skiing on an infinite stretch of snow, rafting on the turbulent waters of the upper Ganges, wind-surfing on the surging waves of the seas, sailing, fishing, scuba-diving, hang gliding, India has it all. What you need is an urge for adventure and a zeal to travel.

India have great beauty ranging from the mighty peaks of Himalayas to the golden sand beaches of Goa. With the Himalayas therefore multitude of rivers, waterfalls, lakes, wild life sanctuaries, national parks, glaciers, mountain peaks of exceptional heights and variety of flora and fauna which not only attract the people of distant places but also provide the glimpses of adventure activities of local inhabitants.

Adventure sports has been a part of our ancient culture. Initially it was connected with religion. The great Shankara-charya had thought number of pilgrim centres in India at Badrinath (North-Garhwal), Dwaraka (West), Jagannath Puri (East) and Rameshwaram (South). Visit to these centres brings happiness and inner satisfaction. Seeking the unknown, carving for the forbidden, getting attracted towards mystery are all basic human instincts to add a touch of colour to otherwise black and white life. This leads to the needs for excitement, thrill and fear in one's life.

The wealthy landscape, outstanding geographical features, flora and fauna of the land are diverse in every region and therefore, offer a varied range of exciting and exhilarating sports and activities for adventurous and nature loving tourists and travellers. We have endless possibilities to offer to the tourists, explorers, and fun, excitement and adventure seekers. It is up to the adventure seekers to decide which part they would like to explore or pursue their hobbies in.

India is full of dancing rivers, virgin beaches, serene and deep seas, the beautiful proud mountains, deep green forests, flora and fauna, wildlife, the vast deserts, sloping valleys, places and snow and ice covered region offers and invites you for trekking, mountaineering, rock climbing, ice skating, hand gliding, heli skiing, river rafting, motor rally and close encounter with the rich and unique world life. The choice is unlimited.

Geography sets the outer limits of not only our experiences

but of our imaginations as well. To free ourselves from these limits, to challenge our own notions about ourselves and the world, we need to be exposed to a myriad cultures, places, people. The best way to do that? By travelling, of course!

Men like Christopher Columbus, Amerigo Vespucci, Marco Polo travelled widely—and somewhat wildly. The odds against these people were extremely high, but what motivated these journeys was dreams, the excitement of charting unknown territory, the sheer joy, as Star Trek would have it, of going where no man has gone before.

Beyond the thrill of adventure, travelling exposes us to new ways of thought, values, cultures and notions of beauty. It broadens our horizons and allows us to view our own culture from a more objective distance.

A good example of how travel combines both relaxation and learning was the custom of the grand tour. On reaching the age of 18, the children of the English aristocracy were packed off with their chaperones to tour the classical capitals of Europe. Paris, Vienna, Berlin, St. Petersburg, Geneva; some time in all these cities was considered essential to round off their education. They heard concerts and the opera, saw the best ballet and were acquainted with the work of the best artists. What better coming of age present could a young person ask for?

Our less romantic age does not, of course, give us the same avenues for exploration as theirs did but travelling is still about dreams. One dreams of going places, works at realising this dream and then matches the reality of it with one's expectations. In the process, we learn lessons that secondary knowledge just cannot provide.

Sometimes, what we see in the course of our travels makes us realise how very mundane our dreams are. Imagine, for instance, all of us who crave to go to USA, Land of Hope and Glory. Many of us imagine a vast overflowing Disney-world of 30 types of breakfast cereal, 80 types of sugar free chewing gum, shopping at the Banana Republic.

Travel allows one to test the limits of one's imagination and in that process, it lets us belong more closely to a place that is not our own. In this world, which they say, is without barriers, this feeling of knowing and loving other lands, cultures and people, is surely much more important than that silly-sci-fi fantasy of push button virtual travel.

Today, we must have about 25,000 kms. of road travel shaking hands with our past, and the year gone by has been such a nonstop trip of crisscrossing highways, lanes, bylanes, interstates.

Thank the lord, for he has given you the good fortune to see in this lifetime lakes that change colour, tantric dances, meeting with the most important lama after the Dalai, Kashmir, Amarnath, Buddha's bones in Andhra Pradesh, short north-eastern elephants just like the people there, the blues of Cherrapunji's falls, Arunachal's thick as fog No. 1 forest cover in India thanks to the Army, a flock of geese holding up the traffic most endearingly, a backwaters ride through dunking kids, men in bed, in the bed of the backwater that is, fishing nonchalantly, a sudden deep red of chilli fields, with us laid out in the middle of it, or modelling by some passing sunflower fields.

A billion moments and more that come back to soothe you, take you over when the city smog chockes out the imagination, and help shatter a couple of million myths which any sheltered upbringing carefully inculcates, and give a ready answer to your parents, to everyone who asks what can travelling aimlessly possibly give you.

Today, we all love an India we know, but seeing more of it just deepens the bond in a totally sweeping way, beyond your own understanding till you come very close to sounding like an overconfident.

Today, India is such an amazing amalgam of landscapes, each giving of its own steam, incense and colour. Hearing the *ektara* on the sand dunes in Jaisalmer is as cool as cool can be, you do not lust after a holiday in Europe for one. The highest inhabited village in Asia, the oldest monasteries this side of Tibet, cool palace floors made of fruit juice and egg yolks, shaking minarets, the second oldest cave paintings known to man, waterfalls in the shape of honeycombs, the largest banyan tree in the world, the only place in the world to see double-humped camels, Aryan tribes that speak no language known to us.

Before your next holiday abroad, go be a part of the India that sends foreigners in a tizzy. What touches you, holds you, reaches out to you and talks you out of your conditioned ways has been the different Indias, all the way. And cynicism has been ditched for this lifetime. And yet it's not been a silk route so to speak.

Like the time, senior Army officers come close to trying to act fresh. It shatters another myth. That people from good families don't do these things. Everybody from any background could be nice. A driver relaxing in his bus to Leh offers a sweet to lessen the discomfort of the seat, and tells you that nice people are nice.

And when you spend a blissful day, drowning the eyes in wild, wild flowers in Gulmarg when the world shunned Kashmir, made you take a second look at days. As the day rolled in such easy camaraderie, and wild horses, wild flowers and a couple of snowy mountains, cheering from the background, you knew the fuss you have get used to is needless.

And you know what, as you traverse lands, sometimes weary, or suddenly faced with a bump on the car, one knew that the new found bond forged with destiny is being tested.

When you think you are too much in control, you are tested and your arrogance is put in place. It may take its own time, but it acts up. So you see, it makes you a philosopher of sorts. And you suffer the pains of attachment.

Then a time comes after a real hard day's trek, you sat down to eat. The food you gorge is simply delicious because you are hungry and not because it is some exotic foreign cuisine. Till date you have never relished a meal so completely and you must have fed yourself a couple of hundred cuisines. It is great fun discovering snacks, making your own combinations, trying out restaurants looking for fish and rice on the cheap.

In Bijapur, just about known as the Agra of the South,

the Gol Gumbaz has the second biggest dome on earth and inside that dome, when you climb up this tomb of Adil Shah, is a whispering gallery where one thump of your feet sounds like the entire American Army. Yes, our country is strewn with monuments which add oodles of charm to the landscape they inhabit, they defy logic, they arouse the sense and the breeze, and make you believe again, unabashedly so.

Thus, adventure travel could be divided into following categories:

1. Rafting
2. Kayaking
3. Canoeing
4. Trekking
5. Backpacking
6. Safaris—wildlife and natural history
7. Adventure cruises
8. Adventure touring
9. Camel safaris
10. Mountaineering expeditions and seminars
11. Inn to Inn/Hotel to Hotel Hiking
12. Ski adventure
13. Seminars in wilderness medicine
14. Overland journeys
15. Camping
16. Pilgrims travel
17. Beach and Island tourism
18. Adventure Sport
19. Bungee Jumping

Adventure Travel

If you are in good health, have an open mind, enjoy the outdoor of doors, go to explore remote areas and meet your neighbourhood on planet earth, you qualify for trekking. All participants must be aware of the stresses of climate, altitudes and remoteness, and in some cases a medical certificate from your doctor certifying a clean bell health is requested. Age limits are generally up to the individual. Certain exertions and activities are not appropriate for small children, but the top end of the age spectrum is highly flexible, if you have been living a life of action and curiosity, there is no reason to stop now. Adventure travel provides safe opportunity for the traveller to step outside normal routines, challenge expectations and rest mettle. You don't have to be He-man or Sheena. You just have to be yourself.

The companies which offer trips have explored the remotest regions, worked out the logistics, found the best and the most efficient ways of running their trips—and kept the motivation for being in the adventure travel business in the forefront of their minds. Their job may be rugged and hours long, but the rewards for doing something they like, and of introducing new people to the pleasure that spark their own enthusiasm, are many and tangible. It is a tough job.

Trekking

Trekking on the mountains is fully organised long distance walk with porters or pack animals carrying all equipment, tents, food and your personal gear for the entire trip. Each treck should he staffed by a leader and a local manager who directs a cook, camp assistants, porters or animal handlers. In most of the treks in India use horses, and mules and in Nepal trekking yaks are used for the purpose. The kitchen staff should be trained in hygiene. Suitable provision should be made of toilet tents, a dining tent, hot washing water and hot tea.

Backpacking

Backpacking means carrying on year back all you need to survive in the wilderness—your personal gear such as: sleeping bag, foam pad, clothes and equipment, plus a share of a community gear such as tents, food, stove, fuel, etc.

Wildlife

For nature lovers, who love to commune with flora and fauna, the state's wildlife sanctuaries and game reserves provide ample opportunity. One can have once in a life time opportunity to see the rare sub-Himalayan region's species, not visible anywhere. The leopard, the monal, the kalij pheasant, the Himalayan ibex, the Thar, wild bear, rhesus monkeys, Thar ibex, brown bear, serow, black bear, monal, koplaz and many others.

Trekking Rafting and Wildlife Encounter

For these treks moderate physical preparation is important, but a background of outdoor pursuits is not necessary. You should have provision of the back-up required to ensure you fulfil your 'Spirit of Adventure'. Himalayas, a land of spectacular contrasts, is accessible to all who wish to enjoy it. The programmes capture these exciting opportunities without placing major demands on you. They are exciting and satisfying but have been designed to allow those with less time to spare, the opportunity to savour the many delights Nepal has to offer.

Adventure Touring

Adventure touring means a sightseeing trip with travel by vehicle and optional hiking. Accommodations are available on small hotels and supplementary accommodation units. Even though there is no camping and no required hiking, adventure tours are special. They visit locations which are well off the beaten path of standard tours.

Mountaining Expeditions and Seminars

These seminars are conducted by experienced alpinists. They offer you the opportunity to learn the complete range of mountaineering skill including basic knots, belaying, basic rope handling, self arrest, glissading, snow climbing techniques glacier travel, crevase rescue and mountain safety. Usually, you do not receive any prior experience, but all participants must be very fit.

Each mountain expedition vary widely in scope and skill received. Most commercial expedition climb peaks that are more physically than technically demanding.

Hotel-to-Hotel/Inn-to-Inn Hiking

This is a popular sport among mountain enthusiasts, especially in areas where a system of inns and alpine 'huts' has been built throughout mountain region to accommodate hikers and climbers. This called the developed on whole Himalayan region. Since food and bedding is provided at these accommodation, hikers need not carry sleeping hags, tents, fuel, stove or food. You can enjoy the beauty of very remote mountain regions. You need to carry are your personal hiking clothes. Depending upon what you would like to bring with you in the way of clothing, your pace might weigh between 15 and 20 lbs.

Accommodations in these huts vary widely in the amenities is they offer. Some are luxurious, others are very rustic and offer just bare basis. Many hiking trips spend more nights in delightful mountain hotels than in these huts. No matter what the accommodation, a wide variety of hearts local cuisine is served including wine.

Traits of varying sleepiness connect the accommodations, which are usually a day's hike (four to six hours) apart. These trips are escorted by a leader who knows the area well and is with the group at all times.

Seminars in Wilderness Medicine

You can combine some of the most popular adventure with seminars for health professionals in topics ranging from high altitude to tropical medicine, from orthopedics to wilderness travel. Each itinerary allow direct participation in an environment relevant to the seminar. Faculty are chosen not only for their outstanding academic backgrounds but for their in the field experience and their ability to choose. Camp size is limited to 15 or fewer to maximise faculty contact.

Overland Journeys

Overlanding in trekking terms means travelling in graded dirt roads in remote places through rugged terrain, often by four-wheeled drive vehicle. Overland journeys usually visit places with few tourist facilities, camping accommodation. Stay in guest house or spontaneous accommodation such as a village school houses are used by these trips. A range of easy to moderate day hikes could be structured into the trips as an integral feature, but there is no required hiking.

Camping

Many people love being in the nature lap. Those of you cherish to observe nature right from the crack of dawn to dusk and listen to the mysterious silence of the jungle at night; camping on a hilltop or on the banks of a river is a dream in reality. You may join the new band wagon of nature loving thriller freaks and wear the badge of adventure sport.

Pilgrim Travel

Pilgrim-tourism and the development of *tirthas*, the places of pilgrimages, is now in the news. In India, since time immemorial, tourism has been inextricably associated with places of pilgrimage strewn all over the country, mostly in conjunction with tanks, rivers, seas, forests, hills and mountains, presenting, rich panorama of variegated environment and cultural fare. Pilgrim-trail in those days was known as *Yatra* and it occupied a significant place in the lives of the people. It is no less significant today hence the talk of developing *tirthas* acquires great importance in the national context.

The thinking in this regard is mostly confined to some areas like preserving local monuments, cleansing the waters or providing transport and adequate accommodation facilities to the visitors of the *tirthas.*

A tourist wants reasonably good transport system to reach the place of destination, comfortable accommodation to stay for a couple of days, clean water to take a dip into and well maintained monuments to see.

Bungee-Jumping

The Bangalore bungee-tower at 120 ft. is considered just a moderate jump when compared with those around the world. A Swiss bungee-jump structure at a height of 700 ft. is the tallest.

Once an individual jumps, he or she experiences free fall which is the most exhilarating. The jumper dives face down as the bungee is tied to the ankle. As the earth rushes to meet the diver, the bungee comes into play. It gradually retards the fall and the jumper bounces up before experiencing free fall once again. This is repeated a couple of times before the individual gently lands on the ground.

It is like in a dream where you fall off a balcony but never land on the ground.

The venture is the brainchild of Ozone, a Bangalore-based adventure sports outfit and Midas, an event management company. Set up at the cost of a "few lakh rupees", it will act as a barometer to the adventure mindedness of the Indian, as until now such a project had never been undertaken before in the country. If it succeeds, the organisers plan to take bungee-jumping to other Indian cities as well. Bungee-jumping, started in New Zealand in the '50s was later popularised in the United States and today is a much-sought after sport around the world.

One version has that on the small Pacific island of Pentacost, an angry housewife fresh after an argument with her husband tied vine to her feet and jumped off the window. She came bouncing back, thus igniting a new sport.

Ever felt like jumping off the cliff in frustration? You can do so in Bangalore now, at a price. And, the best part: You will be safe after the jump. Welcome to bungee-jumping, for the first time in India as a commercial venture.

Pay Rs. 350, and jump from a height of 120 ft. tied to a bungee cord. "Safety is guaranteed", says a French bungee-jump expert John Pascal who is overseeing the venture.

Of course, it is not for those with a weak heart, or for people with cardiac problems, or for that matter any other physical ailment like slipped disc. A doctor on the spot will ensure that the jumper is fit for it. In fact, one doctor will be present throughout the period of the jump.

Pascal who has over 3,000 jumps to his credit says he has never experienced any problems. The only theoretical weak link could be the bungee cord itself. But, the chances of the bungee breaking is extremely remote as it is made from the finest quality latex. Moreover, a bungee is used only for 200 jumps which it is routinely discarded.

The Spirit of Adventure

"The road is more important than the inn". This is the essence of adventure travel. Trekking offers you the opportunity to witness natural beauty, to observe other peoples and experience different societies first hand. Adventures can lead you knowledgeably and safely through the great Himalaya, introducing you to exotic places along trails.

King of Sports: Football

Football is one of the world's most popular game. As many as 16 men's and 8 women's teams will play matches during the Atlanta Olympics. Women's football is being introduced for the first time in the Olympics. And for the first time, there will be an age limit on the men's competition. All players must be 23 or younger, though each team will be allowed three wild cards of any age.

Football also known as soccer was added to the Olympics in 1900 and, despite some violent on-field troubles which have plagued the game at all levels, has been a regular at every Olympics except 1932 in Los Angeles.

Football has been played for hundreds of years in Europe. During the second century in Greece and Rome, the game's popularity was such that authorities began to view the game as a riotous nuisance and a serious threat to national security. In 1314, King Edward II of England outlawed football because he considered the sport to be an "unforgivable" waste of time?

Though modern football continues to be rough and football fans are known for their frenzy and riotous behaviour, the sport's popularity has only grown. Latin American countries were dominant in the early Olympic competitions, but an European country has won every gold medal since 1936. Spain is the defending champion.

India, twice Asian champion, had participated in Olympic football from 1948 to 1960. At the 1956 Melbourne Olympics, India had defeated host Australia and was the first Asian country to reach the semifinals. Selan Manna, Chunni Goswami and P.K. Banerjee have been world famous Indian players.

Boxing: Brute Sport

Boxing has most often been denounced for its violence. It was removed from the first Olympics in 1896 for its brutal form. Sweden had outlawed the sport before the 1912 Games. Scoring has also been a bone of contention in boxing. Since 1989, scoring of points has been handled by a computer.

At the ancient Greek Olympic Games, boxing was a barbaric sport. In those days, boxers came to the ring wearing a leather helmet and spiked metal gloves. It was much, much later in 1867 that padded gloves were introduced in boxing to protect the participants from injury. Yet boxing remains one of the most intriguing and most-watched sports on the Olympic schedule. Some of the world's best known boxers were born in the Olympic boxing competitions. Floyd Patterson won a gold medal in 1952. Cassius Clay (now Mohammad Ali) in 1960; Joe Frazier in 1964; George Foreman in 1968; Sugar Ray Leonard in 1976; Oscar de la Hoya in 1992—all became household names as professional boxers later. But, though, Teofilo Stevenson of Cuba won three straight heavyweight gold medals, he never turned professional.

Cuba, which won seven of 12 golds in Barcelona, would be a favourite at Atlanta. Led by heavyweight Felix Savon, who hasn't lost an international bout since 1989 and had won the gold at both Barcelona and the 1995 World Championships, the Cubans have dominated virtually every competition they entered. Germany, Russia and France also have strong teams. Indian boxers trained in Cuba are being sent to Atlanta which has risen some medal hopes for India.

Gymnastics: Elastic Heroes

Gymnastics has been a star attraction of Olympic Games. Top gymnasts have often become more popular than film stars. In 1972, in Munich, 17 year old Olga Korbut of Soviet Union became a household name throughout the world. In 1976, in Montreal, it was Nadia Comaneci of Romania ... in 1984, in Los Angeles, it was Mary Lou Retton.... Among the men, Vitali Scherbo of Belorus had given an extraordinary performance at Barcelona. He would be keenly watched by fans at Atlanta.

In ancient Greece, gymnastics was a part of school education. Later, it developed as a sport and was an important event of the ancient Olympics. The sport almost disappeared when ancient Olympics was stopped being organised in 393 A.D. It was revived in the 19th century in Germany by Frederick John. Later, Peter Henrick of Sweden refined the sport.

There are six events for men and four events for women in gymnastics. The competition is inevitably tense and compelling. Once again, in Atlanta, gymnastics will be in the centre ring, and a host of new heroes and heroines will emerge from the competition of capture hearts and imagination of millions. Competition will be held in the team event, individual allaround, and individual apparatus finals. Gymnastics-rhythmic will feature two events: the individual allaround, in which athletes compete with four apparatus (rope, ball, clubs and ribbon), and the group event in which eight groups will compete in two exercises: one with five hoops, and the other with three balls and two ribbons.

A total of 304 athletes are expected to compete at the Georgia Dome and the University of Georgia Coliseum in gymnastics-artistics and gymnastics-rhythmic.

Badminton: Swift Shuttle

Badminton makes its second Olympic appearance in Atlanta after its inaugural medal tournament in Barcelona. Earlier, exhibitions matches were held in 1972 in Munich and 1988 in Seoul. Though popular as a leisurely sport, international-calibre badminton is a fast-paced, highly-skilled game where the shuttlecock can fly as fast as 200 miles per hour.

Though, badminton began in Britain in the 19th century, it developed as a sport in India during the colonial period. The standard rules of the games were also first evolved in India by the Britishers. Badminton is unique among racket sports for two reasons. It uses a shuttlecock instead of a ball, and the shuttlecock can't touch the ground during a rally. The shuttlecock is made from 16 goose & duck feathers, fixed in a cork base with a thin leather lining. The lightweight rackets (less than four ounces) used by tournament players are made from blends of carbon, graphite, boron, aluminium and steel.

Indonesia, Korea, China, Sweden and Malaysia have dominated the sport since 1970. Indonesia won both Olympic singles titles in 1992; Korea won both doubles titles. Mixed doubles is being introduced for the first time in 1996.

India has also produced world-class players like Prakash Padukon and Syed Modi. Prakash Padukon had won the All-England Badminton Championship in 1980 and he remained No. 1 in the world ranking till 1981. Syed Modi had won the gold at the Commonwealth Games. National champion Dipankar Bhattacharya had achieved the 8th ranking, and had missed the bronze at Barcelona by just one rank number.

Baseball: America's 'Cricket'

Baseball is to America what cricket is to India and Britain. Yet, the USA have won only once in the 1988 Seoul Olympics where it was played as a demonstration game. Baseball gained medal status in Barcelona Olympics in 1992.

It is a game played between two teams with a bat and ball. Though it looks somewhat like cricket, it is a very different game. In baseball, the batsman is known as batter and the bowler as pitcher. Played on a square field with four bases, the competing teams take turns in batting and fielding. The batting base, a pentagonal white slab of rubber, is known as the home base. To score a run, the batter has to touch the other three bases and return to his home base. Much like cricket, the batter can be caught-out or run-out while trying to score a run. Besides, the batter is considered out if a fielder touches him with the ball in his hand or reaches the home bases before the batter returns. The team scoring maximum runs in nine innings is considered the winner.

The baseball is made of rubber and cork covered with white leather. At the Atlanta Olympics, eight teams from Australia, USA, Cuba, Italy, Japan, Korea, Nicaragua and Holland will compete for medals. Though baseball has been played in Olympics as a demonstration game since 1904, it had to try very hard to gain full recognition at Olympic games. Cuba won the first gold medal at the first full-medal competition held at Barcelona.

Basketball: Cage Craze

Basketball was introduced in 1891 by James Naismith, a physical education instructor in Springfield, USA, in 1896. The first match was played at Iowa city. During the 1930s, many rules were changed to speed up the game. Tall players have a big advantage in the game. Most top teams of the world thus comprise very tall players.

Basketball is played with an inflated ball between two teams of six players each on a rectangular court, usually indoors. Each team tries to score by losing the ball through the opponent's goal which is an elevated horizontally mounted hoop and net called a basket. In basketball, fouls are caused by physical contact between players when one player puts another at a disadvantage. After certain fouls, the play is momentarily stopped and the fouled player awarded one or two unhindered free throws from beyond a 15 foot line in front of the basket board.

After its induction in 1936 Olympics in Berlin, America won all the Olympic titles until 1972 when they were upset by Soviet Union in Munich. But in the last Olympics at Barcelona, America claimed yet another gold. Women basketball made its debut at Montreal in 1976.

2

Himalayas: An Attraction for Adventure

Uncover the age old wonders of the Karakoram and Kashmir, the mountain jewels of India and Pakistan. Here on the deep blew ice of the Batura Glacier, thrill to the myriad 20,000+ ft. peaks of the Karakoram, and marvel at the temples and places of the ancient Indian emperors. Extend your stay in the valleys of Swat and Chitral, where the people bazaars, and natural wonders keep cameras clicking.

Himalaya is a trekker's paradise. There are varied routes through challenging passes and *en-route* meadows lushed with bursting and blooming flowers, dense forests of pine and cedar, crystal clear lakes and rivulets meandering through the countryside.

Himalayas invites you for trekking all the year around. A trekking experience in Himalaya offers a myriad range of opportunities for the nature lover. It offers an incredible variety. Each area has its own unique character, terrain, vegetation, climate, people and custom.

There is the high attitude plateau of Laddakh, known as 'little Tibet'. To the south of the Kashmir and Himachal with their emerald green valleys, alpine meadows, pine forests, clear mountain streams and lakes.

Further south east lies Garhwal Himalayas, a spectacular region containing many peaks over 20,000 ft. (6,096 mtrs.). Nestling in the Garhwal valleys are some of the most venerated temples and shrines such as Badrinath, Kedarnath and Gangotri, all located near the source of the sacred Ganges.

The trekking areas in Sikkim resemble the middle hills of Nepal. Vegetation is lush on the southern slopes and the rhododendron forests display a riot of colours in springtime. There are over 400 varieties of orchids in this tiny state.

Himalayas, the most glorious mountain ranges of the world have been a perennial source of delight and inspiration both for the adventurers and spiritualists. Grand and majestic, each step brings forth of picturesque valleys, overbidding peaks and deep crevices which bring to mind the folklore of an era.

Just say the world 'Himalayas', and the response it evokes is almost universal. You have a feeling of awe and excitement, of reverence and spirituality, of mystery and majority and of sheer magnitude and invisibility that compels humility yet challenges the human spirit.

This magnificent sweep is spread over five Indian states from Kashmir to the west to Darjeeling in the east. More than half of the Himalaya are within India's border. 2,400 km. long, 400 km. wide, and with an astonishing mean elevation of 6,000 metres at their central axial range, the Himalayas are the greatest physical features of the earth. They contain the highest peaks, the highest pass, the highest living animals, the highest fossils and the deepest gorge.

The Himalayas can be overflown but not tunnelled, climbed but not tamed. No railways cross them and only a few roads. And the entire range of the world's climate, its flora and fauna, are compressed within 5 vertical miles of those astounding mountain.

For sheer natural beauty, too the Himalayas are unsurpassed. The silent snow bound height guard secret valleys of unbelievable loveliness that give the seeker and 'the pilgrim a glimpse of paradise'.

Himalayas are the world's youngest and loftiest mountains. Geologically, the Himalayas are still young and growing. It has been formed only, 60 million years ago when a travelling crust of earth from the south pole collided with

Laurasia, folding up the Himalayas. Stretching for almost 1,000 miles, it is a treasure house of life. Remote civilizations and unique floral and faunal system thrive here protected by folds of the mountains and preserved from the onslaught of modernization. Through the ages, travellers from India as well as abroad, ascetics and sages have established a network of mountain trails connecting remote parts of these fascinating mountain to the rest of the world.

To day, this great mountain system plays an invaluable role in determining the quality of life on the Indian subcontinent. The mountain range controls the climate of India, Nepal, Pakistan and Bhutan, by holding the monsoons till the appropriate and protecting the land from the cold Siberian winter. The snow from the Himalayas feed the perennial northern rivers assuming water and farmland irrigation.

The climate and geological diversity of the Himalayas has led to the creation of an unique ecosystem which holds a rich wealth and natural resources, both living and non-living. The sharp zoning in vegetational types and the resultant habitats are the home of a large assemblage of birds and animal life. Himalayan flora is unique. It encompasses forests of all types—tropical swampy forests, decidious forests, coniferous forests, rhododendron forests, alpine meadows and even hot and cold deserts.

There could be no better way of exploring the natural wonders of the Himalayas than in the most natural way—on foot. Well developed infrastructure facilities now offer these trails to all those who have the will to go, the university to peak and the ability to walk.

The Himalayas are a biological wonderland. It encompasses variety of forest types and founal assemblages. Within the Himalayas there are number of vertical and horizontal zones which result in a distinctive habit for a variety of birds and animals. Horizontal zoning occurs primarily due to the early monsoon that moves north west ward from the Bay of Bengal, rapidly dissipating moisture. Consequently, animal and plant life vary from one part of Himalayas to the other, even though they are at the same elevation.

Vertical zones result from the changes in temperature and moisture with increasing elevation. In general, the temperature drops about 6°C for every 3,400 ft. rise in elevation.

Plant and animal life is also determined by the location of the permanent snow line, the height of which depends on summer temperatures, amount of snow fall and exposure, fluctuating generally even within the same zonal range.

The whole Himalayas could be divided into five zones:

1. Aeodian zone
2. Alpine zone
3. Sub-alpine zone
4. Temperate zone
5. Tropical and subtropical zones.

Aeodian Zone (above 15,000 ft.)

This zone occurs above 15,000 ft. and covers the area above the snow line. Because of the harsh climate condition, flowering plants are absent here. The life is limited to bacteria, fungi, insects and crustaceans that subsist upon airborne food particles. Much of the ground is exposed to this zone as snow seldom accumulates here.

Alpine Zone (9,000-15,000 ft.)

This zone is found between 9,000 to 15,000 ft. It covers the belt between the temperline and snow line and is characterised by harsh winters, short summers, shallow soils, strong winds and lack of moisture. In the upper limit of this zone a few pioneering rock plants like stone crop, rock jasmine and primroses manage to brave the lack of moisture. Plants like eidelweiss and snow's car are also found in this upper half.

The pride of the alpine zones are its meadows. Covered with lush grass, they support a profession of coloured wild flowers. The spectacle is most evident in grassy meadows where snow melt collects and where deeper soil has developed over the ages. Some of the flower plants of the Himalayan alpine meadows are: buttercups, anemones, la kspurs, everlasting flowers, asters, dandelions thistles, saxifrages, cinqufoils, louise worth, geranicous and genetians. A flower worth looking for in the meadows is the magnificent blue poppy, also referred to as the Queen of the Himalayan flowers.

Alpine scrub is usually found around streams and U-shaped valleys. The main plant species here are rose, mormon tea, juniper and several species of rhododendrons.

Animals in the alpine zones are mostly Eurasian species that have the ability to adapt to the severe conditions of the northern latitudes. Mammalian species include, bharal, pikas, marmots, red fox, weasel, moles, mice, lynx, wolf, brown bear and ibex. Many species of birds also breed in the grassy alpine meadows.

Sub-Alpine Zone (9,000 to 12,000 ft.)

This zone is between 9,000 ft. to 12,000 ft. It is a transient buffer between temperate coniferous forests and the alpine belt. Short, stunted and windblown birch, juniper and rhododendron plants dominate this area. On the north western Himalayan side rhododendron are replaced by sage brush, popular and willow trees while the rest of the area has a distribution of fir, pine or spruce trees.

The main mammalian species of this zone are the rapidly dwindling music deer and the abreal mouse found in birch forests.

Temperate Zone (6,000 to 10,000 ft.)

The temperate zone between 6,000 to 10,000 ft. is a continuous forest belt. The flora and fauna of this zone is truly Himalayan in composition.

The upper areas of this belt are characterised by conifers such as fir, hemlock pine, cyprus and cedar. Undergrowth is mainly sparse comprising of rhododendrons bamboo and other scrub species.

Temperate green forests are found between an elevation of 3,000-5,000 ft. in some Himalayan areas. Evergreen oaks interspersed with laurels, chestnut, maples and mangolias are found here. New streams and revines where water is available in plenty, numerous wild flowers, ferns and orchids grow.

Forests in the temperate region in Kumaon and parts of Kashmir consist mainly of oak and blue pine and in the Garhwal Himalayas of fir with deodar. Take Garhwal Himalayas are arid to semi-arid at this attitudinal zone. As you climb higher, conifers become more abundant. In the western Himalayas coniferous forests are dominated by the fine needled blue pine and the west Himalayan fir. Other tree species include the magnificent deodar and the west Himalayan spruce. East Himalayan fir grows from Kashmir to Bhutan in an almost continuous belt. Another pine species which thrives in the central and western Himalayas is the chir-pine.

The fauna of the temperate zone is diverse and unique. Large mammals that inhabit this belt include the goral, scrow, and the Himalayan tahr. Langur, monkeys, Himalayan black bear, yellow throated martens, leopards, red pandas and a variety of smaller cats are also found in large numbers. The greatest variety is in the faunal assemblage of this region from the forest flow to the top of the canopies, a managerie of birds thrive. Laughing thrushes, munias, net hatchers, tree creepers, tits and warblers are present in abundance.

Tropical and Sub-Tropical Zones (150 to 6,000 ft.)

Between 150 to 6,000 ft., you will find tropical and sub-tropical forest zones. They occupy the hills bundering the lowlands of the eastern and central Himalayas. The canopies in these forests are made of many deciduous and evergreen hard woods like sat, teak and bauhinia. Sal is however, the major species and forms an almost continuous belt at the base of the Himalayas.

At an elevation of about 4,500 ft., tropical forests are

taken over by sub-tropical mountain forests. Common trees in the area include chestnut, schina, horse chestnut and walnut. Oaks are also in plenty and alders grow along drainages.

Sub-tropical fauna is also common to the grasslands and includes some Indian species such as cheetal, tiger, water buffalo, hog deer and elephant.

If you are an adventure sports freak, the majestic Himalayas is the best place for you to be in. Adventure tourism in our country is one of those few sectors where a little investment can earn big foreign exchange. From the majestic Himalayas to the vast ocean wealth, the country has a lot to offer to promote itself as the destination of the 21st century. Be it skiing, trekking, rock climbing, peak climbing, scuba diving, snorkelling in the rivers or ocean waters, paragliding in open skies, white water rafting, kayaking, canoeing in the rapids of various rivers etc., every activity is quite popular.

A trip to the Himalayas will excite even the most jaded amateur photographer in the world. The earth's extreme environment at the mountains offer the most dramatic landscapes. But why should we limit our contact with the Himalayas to a few hill stations only? The possibilities of exploring more and more of the region by delving deep into unknown frontiers should also be an option to the tourists.

The Himalayas, the abode of snows, encompass a region of deep religious and cultural traditions and an amazing diversity of people. To travel in the remote areas of the Himalayas offers much more than superb landscapes. It is like taking a ride in the time machine to travel back in time and meet people, who still lead life like their ancestors did.

The Himalayas are the ultimate destination for lovers of adventure. It offers almost every known form of activity for the adventure seeker. The very mention of mountains makes one think about *trekking.* A trek is a special and rewarding mountain holiday. It is a known fact that, the best way to enjoy any place is on foot. In the Himalayas, on display are the awesome grandeur of the mountains, various villages, monasteries, locals and other worthy facets of the mountain life. The trekking opportunities vary from the beautiful alpine pastures of Himachal Pradesh to the spectacular gorges in Zanskar or the high altitude desert of the Tibetan plateau in Laddakh, the regular pilgrim treks and other treks in Garhwal and Kumaun Himalayas in Uttaranchal. Rock climbing is the other form of adventure which is very popular in the mountains. Rock climbing today is not just a necessity to obtain a qualification in mountaineering. More and more adventure seekers are taking to rock climbing.

The Himalayas are soon going to become the world's premier area for *aerosports*. Good thermal soaring effects during summer and almost year round hill soaring make India the ultimate destination for lovers of the sport. Some of the major sites are the Kashmir valley, Sanasar in J&K, major stretches of the Western Ghats, Nilgiri hills in Tamil Nadu, and the hills of the north eastern states.

Paragliding, the latest aerosport to take the world by storm is a major activity in aerospace. Visitors at places like Auli in Uttaranchal, Sanasar in J&K, Bilaspur, Solang Nalla (Manali), Bir-Billing in Himachal can regularly enjoy the sight of Paragliders flying in the sky. It is like a bag full of wonders when the pilots take off for the flights. The skies turn into a painted canvas with all the colourful paragliders flying.

India is the cheapest *ski* destination of the world. Indian Himalayas have plenty of slopes which can provide the ultimate in winter tourism. Skiing is the most popular from the sport during the winters. The alternatives offered at the time were hampered by the lack of infrastructure and equipment, but have gradually developed into good skiing resorts. Solang Nalla and Narkanda in H.P., Auli in Uttaranchal etc. have all shown tremendous potential. In fact today Auli has all the infrastructure needed.

Heli skiing and speed skiing have already been tried on the upper reaches of the mountains and if developed properly can turn out to be the best foreign exchange earners for the country.

Angling or *fishing* is a sport with wide dimensions in the Himalayas and an unparalleled variety. Though we vast fishing panorama stretches from the coastal regions of the

Arabian Sea to the Bay of Bengal, some of the very best catches are made in the snow fed streams and high altitude lakes of the Himalayas.

Water sports, like white water rafting, canoeing, and kayaking are some of the major water sports which attract a lot of attention both in India as well as abroad. River rafting is a rapidly growing activity all over the world. India offers some spectacular stretches down many a rivers in the hilly areas. The thrills provided by the river waters during rafting and kayaking are unparalleled. The snow fed Himalayan rivers descend from great heights across cliffs and boulder strewn beds before they enter the planes, and are the major rafting destination in India. The most popular waters for rivers running are the Indus river and the Zanskar river in Laddakh, the Ganges in Garhwal Himalayas in Uttaranchal, the four rivers of H.P., river Teesta in Sikkim etc.

For the nature lovers India offers some of the best flora and fauna in the world. *Wildlife* Sanctuaries are spread all over the country and offer enthusiasts a wide range of animal sighting opportunities including several endangered species. The most famous sanctuary, situated on the foothills of the Himalayas, is the Jim Corbett park in Uttaranchal, which provides some of the best tiger sighting in the world. The park also has leopards, panthers, and several species of deer and antelopes. Himalayas is the home of the famous snow leopard and some of the most exotic bird life.

In the Himalayas, grow a wide variety of wild flowers. The valley of flowers in Uttarakhand/Uttaranchal and other Bugyals in the mountain valleys are home to over hundreds of wild flowers. Brilliant clusters of these flowers light up the way, and provide with some of the most memorable moments. Varieties of colours, varieties of unknown flowers, sweet fragrance makes human mind ecstatic. Bursts of Alpine Calendula, Cobra flowers, Kasturi Kamals, the scented Bramha Kamals, and many other varieties—blossom all around and makes one forget himself.

SECTION II

ADVENTURE ON LAND

UNIQUENESS AND VARIETY IN
MOUNTAINS, VALLEYS AND DESERTS

3

Trekking and Tours

Trekking has come a long way since the days it meant a tedious journey on foot or gruelling hours of travel by ox-cart. In the modern sense trekking means walking on foot in the hills and mountains for pleasure and recreation. Today trekking conjures up visions of the spectacular northern and eastern Himalayas or the mid strewn western ghats or the blue tranquility of the Nilgiri Hills. In a environment free of depredation of modern city life, you as a young trekker would like to commune with Nature, savouring it awe inspiring bounties.

The purpose of trekking is different to different persons, which mainly depends upon their interest. In India people usually trek to most difficult places as pilgrims and to the holy shrines in the mountain where Rishis, Yogis and sages have meditated. Such a trekking is performed by thousands of devotees every year to holy shrines of Bandrinath, Kedarnath, Amarnath, Triloknath, Vaishno Devi, and many far of places where religious temple are located.

People has also been trekking for various purposes like trade, hunting, surveying and geological purposes. There is yet another purpose of trekking. Many people trek to study the tribal people, their way of living, the customs, working conditions, origin and their relation with the rest of the world.

There are yet another group of trekkers who are adventurists and are interested to explore new routes and treks, cross high passes and find the hiker to unexplored valleys and caves.

After the conquest of Mt. Everest in 1951, trekking gained importance for trekking experience is necessary before joining any expedition in the Himalayas. Trekking in the Himalayas, fulfils the interest of every type of trekker, whether you are young or old, beginner or experienced and whether you go for pleasure and recreation or for an adventure. It creates the spirit of adventure among participants, provides opportunity to come in contact with nature. See the country-side and its people, channelise the energy to the direction, enrich the experience, builds the character by making you live with follow travellers away from the comfortable life and bearing difficulties and discomforts together.

Trekking satisfied childrens, young boys or of man's basic impulses—the urge to travel forth and seek adventure. An urge that cannot be satisfied by young and old alike. A trekking is comparatively undemanding, requiring only stamina for walking and long hours, and mental ability to adapt to a changing environment.

Trekking brings home the fundamental truth that man needs very little to lead a full and joyous life. Most treks traverse uninhabited areas where modern amenities are not just available. The trekker learns to prune his needs to the bare necessities of life and discovers that it all fits into a mere rucksack. Ask any traveller and he will tell you of the exhilaration of travelling light and get the source that all his life's need are at hand.

In India, you will find joys of getting close to nature. We have rugged faced hills, and mountains, green slopes carpeted with wild flowers, scarlet rhododendrons, and blue gentians, Banks of dancing marigolds and peonies. Cool breeze whistling through spreading trees, ice cold streams, merrily gurling over boulders and grounded pebbles, high above the aerobatic wheeling birds, eagles dotting the azure sky full of billowing clouds, golden avioles, scarlet minivets and white cheeked bulbuls piercing the pure air with their sweet calls. Down below, valleys of quaint town and sturdy hamlets, carefree laughter echoing in meadows and orchards, the songs of poetry, song and legend and many more of year interest.

India is the ultimate destination for a trekking enthusiast-offering routes from the short and easy to the long distances of snowy peaks. The spectacular Himalayas, abode of snow, evokes a feeling of reverence and excitement which is universal. It is their sheer magnitude and invincibility that both compel humility and challenge the human spirit.

Trekking in India means going to the Himalayas. Sprawling 2,500 km. long over an area covering 5,00,000 sq. km., with an astonishing mean elevation of 6,000 metres at their central axial range, with the highest peak and the deepest gorge, the Himalayas are the greatest physical feature of the earth. Their incredible between has made the seeker and the pilgrim believe that he has glimpse of paradise.

Peninsular India offers natural beauty, of another kind, clothed in green woodland and fragrant orchards. The Western Ghats, the Aravalli Hills, the Satpura Range and the Nilgiri Mountain have a rich heritage of flora and fauna, each with a special lure of his own.

We require a proposal which envisages not static, top-heavy establishments like mountaineering institutes, but rather adventure itineraries. We could begin with, for example, a location like the Tungabhadra Dam and the surrounding hills and forests and the lake, where rudimentary barrack accommodation for 1,000 young people at a time could be provided. Groups of these would converge at Tungabhadra either Statewise or from all parts of the country, by the cheapest form of transportation, to receive programmed itineraries in all the activities mentioned above, under the guidance of trained personnel. The group of 1,000 which is an arbitrary figure, would be made up of smaller groups of 20 or even 10, each under the charge of a school-teacher or a college lecturer or some such guidance personnel from their institution or yuvak kendras or youth clubs.

They would subsist on most economical rations and the

most simple and hardy of kits, which they would naturally have to carry themselves. They would need to take 10-day or fortnight-long itineraries and programmes in different parts of the location and then return to their respective homes. Certificates or badges could be offered as achievement incentives. The training would have to be imparted more to the group-in-charge, the teachers and the supervision personnel, rather than direct to the young as this would bring about a closer relationship between the teachers and the youth in circumstances of close companionship and mutual self-reliance.

Similar itineraries can be worked out for selected coastal areas and for forested hills in Kerala, Orissa, Gujarat and West Bengal. Mountain itineraries in high elevations, in locations like Kulu-Manali, beyond Chakrata, Arunachal, Kashmir and Rajasthan, could also be developed, based on a system of mountain-huts. All this is perfectly feasible. To begin with the Central Government would have to give the lead and work through the Education Departments of the States. Eventually the entire programme and organisation would have to develop upon State Governments with expert Central assistance.

Trek Grading

For your understanding trekking trips could be divided into different categories. Usually there are two methods of grading at international level. Based on the whitewater rafting of class I to class V with class V being the most difficult, the scale is an added guideline choosing your adventure. Some of them grade them from 'A' to 'E', 'A' being the easiest and 'E' the hardest (technical mountaineering skills required). Since different people have different tolerance for altitude, remoteness and like, these scales cannot be exact. It is intended for use in making general distinction between the offerings.

Following is a distinction between two different methods of grading.

Grade I to V

Class I: Easy

These trips emphasise the scenic or cultural value of a particular region, using hotel accommodations and travel by comfortable van or bus. Short hikes and gentle river floats may be included. These trips are suitable for all ages and inclination.

Class II: Moderate

Mild outdoor programmes which immense the participation a bit more fully in the world of adventure. Camping is often involved, and longer day hikes and/or river trips with white water are usually included. However, the degree of exertion is optimal, making these trips suitable for all ages as well.

Class III: Average

Camping is the normal means of overnighting on a class III trip, hikes and river trips may be longer and more difficult. However, some hotel, or lodge nights are often included for convenience. Generally treks of shorter duration (up to 10 days) and/or lower altitudes (below 3000 m.) are considered of this class. Good health is the only physical requirement, though a minimum age of 12 years is usually requested.

Class IV: Difficulty

Trips of longer duration farther from population centres, including physically demanding activity—such as trekking above 3,000 metres or rafting a class IV-V river are considered class trips. Previous outdoor experience (camping, hiking, etc.) is helpful, and a physician's certificate of health is generally required. Age limits vary with individual trips, operations and participants, but most class IV trips have an 18 years age minimum.

Class V: Strenuous

When previous technical experience and skills are required, the trips are classed a strenuous, to make their restriction clear. Generally these trips are of an extraordinary nature, in sparsely populated areas, and they may demand previous whitewater, rock climbing or similar skills. Treks of long duration (as month or more) which reach an altitude of over 5,500 metres are included in this category.

Grade 'A' to 'E'

Grade A

Generally sightseeing trips or safaris with no sustained walking involved. Most utilize hotel and/or lodge accommodation, instead of camping tents. Suitable for all ages.

Grade B

These are least strenuous treks, usually comprising 4-8 days on trail with maximum elevation in the 9,000-12,000 ft. range. Walking per day is usually in the 4-8 hours range, with maximum daily ascents of 1,500 ft. Suitable for 'weekend athletes' who do not have the time during the work to exercise.

Grade C

Treks of two weeks or longer, with maximum elevation of 17,000 to 18,000 ft. Daily ascents and descents of up to 3,000 ft. Suitable for people who are accustomed to regular exercise or have previous backpacking and hiking experience.

Grade D

These are the most strenuous treks. Numerous daily ascents and descents, sustained at higher altitudes. Pass crossings in the 14,000-18,000 region. These are trips for people in good physical condition who want a challenge.

Grade E

Implies top physical condition, and mountaineering skills.

Different types of treks are offered in Europe. Some are based on village inns, some on camping. Some trips enjoy vehicle support so that you need to carry only a day pack. Others enjoy partial vehicle support, usually because it is impossible to get a vehicle into the particular area you are using a camping site on these occasions you will have to carry what you need for one or two nights. The plus side of the situation is that on these occasions you are getting deep into the mountains then there are hotel to hotel treks with vehicle support and a high degree of comfort.

All these trek characteristics are mentioned in the trip description, and will influence your choice of vacation. Some of the treks in the Himalayas are easier as they have a full trek crew who do absolutely everything for you. There are guides, cooks and porters, tea in bed, no camp chores, just the luxury of strolling through the highest mountains in the world. There is a description for each country on how the trekking is organised, which will further help you make your choice.

Planning and General Information

Who Travels?

Age is not the most important priority. The oldest trekkers are up to 76 years old. They enjoy a 15-day trek looking for rare flowers. Most, however are between 20 and 55 years and from varied background. All have a common interesting desire experience more than just the ordinary. It is voyage through the nature and remain alive in the memories of any one who takes it. Beginners should remember that there is also a psychological commitment involved in walking in the mountains.

Lovely images of sun set and dawn, memories of evenings spent around the camp fire and of splendid view from cols and peaks, conceal in your memory and those of your friends the fact that these are also radically different moments.

Exhaustion from the merciless sun. Descents, sometimes in driving rain, when the town or hut never seems to arrive. In whole of the Himalayas the problem is great considering the vastness of these mountains, and the distance from home. Your trails could be difficult by mud or snow, high altitudes fords and landing strips can be used only when the weather allows. A willingness to deal with the delays, confer seem developments, and can comfortable situations is essential if you wish to walk on these trails.

When Should You Go?

Most of the trips are scheduled at best times of the year; when the weather is usually clear. Take account of spring and summer flowers, birds and animals migrations and religious festivals. Generally you can expect good conditions and plenty of extras to add to your experience!

How Fit You Need To Be?

Read trip description, for they will help you. Be aware that even your easiest trips place some demands—coping with officialdom, the higher altitudes, an occasional long day, a sudden storm.

Physical preparation is important for all treks. The longer the trek the more participation. But remember you are on a holiday and you want to enjoy yourself, so the pace is moderate, you should take it slowly to gain full benefit. There are rest days for acclimatization, relaxation and exploration.

If you regularly walk, climb or practice any other 'endurance' sport, such as jogging or cross country skiing, you will have no problem dealing with physical demand of walking. For others, it is advisable to get into training, and perhaps to have a full check up. Before you go for walking in the Himalayas, it is best to get into shape by walking on the hills and mountains wherever you like. If the weather allows it, it is best to climb high altitudes, sleeping overnight in huts at about 3,000 metres. Even if you regularly run or walk at low altitudes you are advised to undertake training that involves some climbing; the muscles and lungs work very differently than they do on a level surface. Some trekking or tours may require some familiarity with ice axe, crampons, harness and rope. Prepare by taking a climbing cause offered by a local maintain instructor or outdoor centre, or by choosing an organised work accompanied by guides.

Which Route to Choose

The main factors to be considered in choosing a route are— elevation, the type of natural and human environment, geographic location, degree of technical and physical challenge. Contrasts may be great and extreme in the Himalayan region. The length of the possible routes also varies from a few days to a month or more.

Will You Have Altitude Problems?

All of the high altitude treks should be carefully planned to minimise any discomfort or inconvenience due to the rarefied atmosphere. Most people will notice minor effects of high altitude. You will walk a little slower and stop more frequently. All treks have rest days on the approach to high altitudes, so you will acclimatise as well as possible.

The Trip

Setting out for the Himalayas means travelling to one of the most interesting natural and human environment on the earth. There are differences in climate, in smells and in all the impressions you experience. This makes he leap to a new world exciting and stimulating. Two decisive factor in planning a trip to the Himalayas are:

(1) *The Season*

A decisive feature of the Himalayan climate is the monsoon, which hits the range from June to September. Daily this season, it is impossible to walk along the routes of the eastern Himalaya (Bhutan, Sikkim and Khumba) and those along the southern slopes of the central and western Himalayas. The occasional thunder storm should not really interfere with walking in the Garhwal Himalayas, around Nanga Parvat, and in the rest of the western Himalayas. There are no problems, on the other hand, in Tibet, Laddakh, Karakoram and the Hindukush area that are sheltered against the monsoon's force by the main chain of the Himalayas.

(2) *The Visa*

Visa for Pakistan and Nepal can be obtained without difficulty, but those for Tibet, India, and Bhutan require more time and more effort. In addition you may require a walking permit on a special authorization, if your destination is near troubled borders.

What is the Food Like?

Adventures enjoy their food. Good food helps make good trips. You will enjoy fresh food, prepared in style by well trained local cooks. Book Indian and western cuisine are prepared under hygienic conditions. For trekking and rafting substantial breakfasts, lunches and dinners are provided. Special diets are also catered.

'Haute' cuisine is quite difficult in high places, but the ingenuity of cook often has to be seem to be believed. Some cooks can produce birthday cake, complete with dedication in icing, using only a camp fire!

Food is included while on trek and, depending on the area, there will be fresh local food, or a blend of local food and ingredients imported. There are obvious limitations in remote areas, but food should nutritious and there should be plenty of it.

But remember not all treks are camping tours. On hotel to hotel treks you can enjoy good local dishes and wines every evening.

Vegetarian diets are welcomed on trekking. If you have a really strict diet, you must carry some additional supplies of your own. In major towns and cities only breakfast is supplied. You are free to explore local restaurants and sample local dishes.

What Do You Carry?

Your personal gear is carried by porters, yaks or ponies, with the support of vehicles. Generally, all you need a day pack in which you will keep your camera, water bottle and perhaps a pullover or jacket. At higher altitude you all need to pack gloves, hat and a warm jacket. Of course, the joy of trekking is getting deep into the mountains and sometime those is no vehicle concern. Therefore, the basic principle is to trek when and wherever possible without a large backpack, which happen most of the time.

What Size Groups?

The average group size is 10 and the maximum 15. If there are too few on a trip (which rarely happens), you may be offered the choice of an alternative tour or the right to cancel without a full refund.

Alone or with a Guide

The Himalaya pose organisational and psychological problems due to distance, difference in history, language and culture from the mountains. Travelling with an organised group have some undeniable advantages. You will meet new travelling companions, some are else takes care of your aeroplane reservations, visas, permits and the on-site organisation, and on the presence of a qualified guide you can safely cross glaciers.

The baggage could be entrusted to porters and you carry only a day pack with wind breakers, camera, and a little food. The problems in this system is a high price and your contacts with the local people will be fairly limited.

Another alternative is an independent walking, carrying your own provisions and cooking equipment. This of curse is appropriate only for walkers trained to the fatigue routine of American style 'backpaking' and it greatly limits all sorts of accessories.

The third alternative solution, involves, reading the Himalayas on your own, without contacting an agency, and then to here porters and perhaps a *sirdar* and a cook on your arrival. This is more economical and suggested for those who have some experience of walking in the mountains. Porters, cooks and *sirdars* can be easily found at the beginning of nearly all the more popular rates and they can also be contacted through little agencies in the local area.

Porters

In case you prefer to hire a porter, it is advisable to keep in mind a series of rules and customs, established by common sense and tradition. The load, contained in a plastic bag or tub should never weigh more than 20 kg. (44 pounds). Each porter will add his own possessions to your load, along with food for himself and other porters. Walks have a certain number of set days and porters are owed to each of these days. As part of the cost of hiring porters, add the days of road travel plans the cost of public transportation, the food during the walk and a tip or gift of clothing or some other part of the equipment. A pair of running shoes or a plastic sheet for the kitchen may be enough for a low-elevation walk, for walker that involve high altitude stretches, and glaciers, you should count on spending more, and in some cases you must provide the porters with the necessary equipment— ice-axe, crampons heavy boots, sunglasses.

How For Do You Walk Each Day?

There are many factors to consider, climate, altitude, the terrain and availability of fuel, water and good level camp sites with the finest view. As a rate of trend you may cover around 10 to 12 miles a day in deal conditions and six to eight miles where altitude (acclimatization) or temperature dictate. One must also consider that a pack animal a porter cannot move at the same pace as someone with a light day pack!

Many of you are photographers, sketchers, botanists and bird watchers, so treks are paced to allow time to enjoy these interests, but the occasional long day is sometimes unavoidable.

Do You Need Boots?

Certainly, for treks about 2,500 m. your feet are doing all the work so invest in them. Ask staff a reputable gear shop to advise you. Make sure your boots have good ankle support and a non-slip and break them in before you leave. For shorter, lower-altitude treks (e.g. Annapurna explorer) strong but lighter weight footwear is an acceptable alternative.

What Class of Hotel is Used?

Select hotels that reflect the local character and style, but which meet high standards. Choose hotels which are clean, neat and centrally located.

Which is the Best Place to Go?

It does not matter which trek you choose from the scenic standpoint because the sheer scale of the mountains as is so grand you cannot be disappointed. Another question is which are the less crowded areas? The most important decision is to choose a trek which suits your experience and physical capabilities.

How Safe is it to Trek in Remote Area?

On trek it is completely safe providing simple common sense prevails. After all you are walking not climbing. A major concern is altitude sickness which can occur over 10,000 ft. No one can predict susceptibility to mountain sickness, your itineraries should be carefully planned to allow for acclimatization. Most people suffer no more than a headache, and a slight loss of performance.

Stomach upsets can never be eliminated and occur on much more prosaic vacation. Again good camp hygiene and common sense precaution like using to iodine to purify vegetables and water, training camp helpers etc. and a generally professional approach are the best form of preventive medicine.

What Can Go Wrong?

The only truthful answer is many things—but that is where expertise comes in. However, one can not control everything and delays can and do occur, specially when flying to tiny airstrips in the mountains. You will also encounter worked out trails or bridges, and a myriad of situations that call for quick thinking and improvisation. Commonsense will tell you that mountainous terrain can be difficult. These problems are by no means everyday occurrences, but sometimes itineraries are to be changed and delays do occur.

Do You Need Insurance?

Comprehensive travel insurance covering medical expenses and emergency evacuation is essential. LIC offers a selection of suitable policies to your perusal.

What about More Detailed Information?

Trekking and touring organisations will forward to you detailed trip notes of any adventure on request. Information guides, notes on visas, vaccination and insurance are forwarded on receipt of deposit. You will be well prepared long before you set off on your adventure.

Do You Need a Lot of Special Equipment and Clothing?

People already have most of what they need at home for the trek. Especially if they already do a little hill walking. You only need expensive sleeping bags and denim jackets for high altitude treks. These can be hired if you are not likely to use them again.

Clothing and Equipment

Lightness and comfort are the most important qualities in walking clothing. Pack your bags according to the altitude of the route chosen and the season of the year. While walking in the Himalayas, you will be exposed to extreme of climate and sun. In first a few days, you may pass from ±40°C or over 100°F of the lower valleys to the icy climate of the glaciers. At a high altitude the contrasts between day and night are extreme.

At average altitudes in the Himalayas (2,000 to 4,000 metres), the best solution is to wear a pair of heavy cloth trousers (preferably looser and more comfortable the jeans), with a pair of shorts to be worn during the hotter haws of the day, and with some padded trousers for the colder hours of the day. Classic breeches are always comfortable, and can be worn with thermal underwear when things get chilly. A wool or pile sweater can be worn over a standard wool shirt or a more modern pullover made of synthetic material.

At all altitudes you must have complete raingear (jacket and leggings) made of Gore-text or similar material. The list must include a wool cap and a canvas hat against the sun, a pair of wool or pile gloves, and a pair of sunglasses.

Among the accessories, one must carry a water bottle, spare laces and a multipurpose knife (Swiss Army knife).

It is essential to carry a torch the best being a head-torch. Choose a sleeping bag with a view to the colour days of the route.

The rucksack is yet another fundamental component of equipment. If you prefer to walk carrying most of the luggage, choose a suitable model with considerable capacity (from 70 litres up). A 'day pack' can be much smaller, if you are travelling with an organised walk. The decisive feature is the boots you wear. A mistake on this crucial factor can ruin an otherwise memorable walk. It is very important to break in your boots in the months before leaving walking boots made of synthetic materials are the best solution.

For the stretches at high altitudes, and to avoid problem in case of sudden blizzard, it is best to have a pair of plastic climbing boots with one. Ice axes and compasses are necessary in only a few special cases. Ski poles especially adjustable ones are also very useful.

What Gear or Equipment is Provided by Trekking Organisations?

On Himalayan treks, most of these trekking organisations provide warm and roomy sleeping tents, insulated mats, mess tents, toilet tents, cooking equipment, cutlery and crockery, kit bags, food, comprehensive medical kits on all treks, pack animals, transport, porters, guides and leaders. Just about everything in fact, except personal items. What you need to bring, and it is not a lot, is all carefully outlined in trip information. For treks in Himalayas, a top quality sleeping bag, inner sheet thermal duret jacket, waterproof jacket and water bottle is provided.

Climbing Equipment

For challenging walk you need not to have the technical equipment used by rock climbers or high altitude Himalayan climbers. If your routes involve crossing snow covered glaciers, where it is possible to find hidden crevasses, you will require adequate clothing and equipment such as ice-axes, crampons, harness, scope and the occasional length of hope and karabiners.

Are There Special Trips for Clubs and Schools?

Yes, many trekking companies organise a trip for a group of friends or a social organisation, perhaps even to shoot a film in some far flung place. They not only help with practical advice on the feasibility of your places but also put together your itinerary in the most economical way. They also give substantial discounts to private groups.

Medical Problems

Hiking in the Himalaya poses a series problems. Blisters and cramp, frostbite and sprains are as common among those who walk to Everest.

A rapid change in climate, food and environment and specially the rapid rise in altitude, create a different set of problems. Typhoid vaccinations and, in some cases measures against malaria are standard procedures for those who travel through Asia, and the same is true of normal ailmentary precautions. One should drink boiled or distilled water and wash fruit and vegetables. It is quite normal to suffer about or two of malaria especially when visiting the Himalaya for the first time. In case of bad fever or persistent dysentery, it is best to consult a doctor.

Those who suffer from respiratory or heart problems should not climb so high. A gradual acclimatization is recommended to all. You should increase altitude gradually, descend whenever possible to steep at lower altitude than the higher altitude reached during the stage, and be ready to change your plans or head down hill quickly in case of persistent discomfort or illness. Normal mountain sickness. which manifests itself with headaches and lethargy is not really serious, but if neglected, it can develop into pulmonary or cerebral oedema, both of which can be fatal. In this case the only safe solution is to be transported as quickly as possible downhill.

Environmental Concern

The peaks of the Himalayas are among the most spectacular natural movements on the face of the earth. But the valleys at its feet, all the way up to the pasture at 4,000-4,500 metres, are full of wilderness devoid of human presence. On the contrary the presence of woods, pastures, and springs, and of small and large caravan rates has drawn human towards the mountain for thousands of years. Today, many of the green valleys of this region are overpopulated and even the oases established over the centuries in the desert valleys of Laddakh are growing rapidly in population. It results in deforestation, pollution, soil erosion, and the declining of many species to the brink of extinction for the most heavily frequented areas, such as those around Everest, Annapurna, and K2, a considerable share of the responsibility goes to expedition of climbers and walkers. And it is in these areas that the greatest efforts to protect the environment have been concentrated, such as those enacted by the Sagarmatha National Park, Annapurna Conservation Area etc.

As a conscientious walker, you should refrain from harmful behaviour and monitor the behaviour of his/her porters, *sirdars* and cooks who are often careless about proper disposal of waste or carrying rubbish backdown, and about using gas or fuel stoves, instead of wood fires.

Your respect for the environment of the Himalaya should go beyond the woods, animals and landscapes. It is equally important to respect the traditions, culture, and faith of the peoples of these mountains. Scanty clothing is frowned upon everywhere. It can create serious problems in Islamic valleys. Everywhere you should respect the religious sites, sites and beliefs. You should refrain from acting like the typical aggressive tourist, looking for good photographs at any price. Porters and *sirdars* should be treated respectfully, keeping in mind that in the Himalayas, working for someone is far different from slavery. You should refrain from purchasing antiques and the hides or pelts, of endangered species. Those who are found with such objects in their possessions—pelts of snow leopards, bharals—risk very heavy fines.

Additional Information

Remoteness and Trip Changes

The regions in which you travel are remote. Life style and culture can differ totally from yours and you must understand and accept this. Trekking company will be responsible for postponement or delay or change of itinerary caused by delay flights, schedule changes, inclement weather or any other factor at any point in the tour. No refunds are made after the start of the trip. Leaders will solve way problems in the interests of the whole group. Efforts are made to minimise any inconvenience to each member but they are not responsible for any additional costs.

Mountain Flights

Due to the nature of the Himalayan terrain, domestic flights are occasionally delayed. On some extra days are used to allow flexibility in the event of possible delays in flight schedules. On rare occasion, it may be the necessary to re-route the trek to an alternative area. Should you be delayed, the trekking company, generally meet your accommodation and food costs on a normal trek bases. You will pay no extra. Be aware that delays are caused by weather conditions. Your safety is first priority.

Insurance

Personal travel insurance is compulsory while it is not mandatory that you purchase cancellation, evacuation and accident insurance, it is strongly recommended that you do so.

International Travel Documents

You will require a current passport and a visa. You should check the situation carefully with your travel agent or the relevant consul. Details of variations required appear in information booklets. Foreign national require a re-entry visa which should be obtained before leaving.

Wildlife Hot Spots

Though a lot of hue and cry has been raised over the threats to Indian wildlife from poaching, the more insidious threats that could dismember the contiguous forest belts and protected areas—home to wildlife—are from industrial and commercial projects, says Bittu Sahgal, member of the Indian Board for Wildlife and the Steering Committee of Project Tiger.

Here is a map of the 50 wildlife hot spots in this 50th year of India's Independence. Sanctuaries and national parks are the best water catchment areas. The water security of the sub-continent will be at risk if these areas are degraded or lost.

India's endangered wildlife species might become extinct because of the rapacity of developers, than the avarice of poachers.

Mines, dams, canals, polluting industries, new highways, thermal plant and urban constructions including tourism projects, townships and resettlement sites are coming up in protected areas with the tacit approval of the government.

There are threats to India's wildlife and forests—from the Andaman and Nicobar Islands to the Sunderbans in West Bengal, Namdapha Tiger Reserve in Arunachal Pradesh and the new threats to the Silent Valley in Kerala.

The Kerala Government, has allowed valleys, contiguous to the Silent Valley, to be deforested and there is even talk of reviving the old hydroelectric project.

In Madhya Pradesh white sandstone mining has affected the Panna Tiger Reserve. In the nearby Gangau sanctuary, diamond mining is encroaching on forest land. The park is choked with slurry and polluted water.

The wild ass sanctuary in the Rann of Kutch is now threat-
ened with shrimp ponds, chemical factories and a proposal to
construct a network of canals as part of the Narmada Project.

Planning and Preparation for Trekking

Trekking is a real joy in the unhurried pace of travel, appreci-
ating the awesome beauty of mountains and the majesty and
the might of the rivers and glaciers, enjoying the infinite
variety of colourful, fragrant flowers and the simplicity of
dignified people where the joy is in the journey and the
destination is to reach within yourself. You will have no hassles
of technical climbing nor the frenzy of race, but just the
relaxing rhythm of walking and wandering uphill and down,
along murmuring brooks—sometimes strenuous sometimes
easy—but walking nonetheless, in harmony with nature.

Trekking in India is generally done in the hilly and mountain areas as the plains are very hot. The Himalayas are criss-
crossed by a complex network of mountain trails that offer
access to remote civilization and areas of unsurpassed natural
beauty. The success of a Himalayan trek can depend largely
on your physical fitness, proper equipment and how well
prepared you are to venture into unknown areas inhabited
by people whose culture and language are foreign to you.

Preparation

Let me outline some of the areas in which you can prepare
yourself better.

Physical Fitness

You're the best judge of your fitness, but don't get too
ambitious and set off on a long, arduous route. It helps if
you have prior experience or maintained a high level of
stamina. If not, it's advisable to get some exercise or indulge
in physical activities at least 15 days before you take off. An
average trek in the Himalayas entails a walk of 6-8 hours a

day, most of the time uphill. You need to be in good physical condition for that.

Choice of Route

Beginners should go for easy or moderate treks, not extending beyond six or seven days. It is advisable to choose a well-travelled route which will have facilities along the way. Some spectacular trek routes in the Himalayas which fall in this category are Har-ki-Dun and Valley of Flowers in Garhwal, the Pindari Glacier in Kumaon, Dzongri in Sikkim and Sandakphu near Darjeeling. The maximum altitude one gains on any of these treks is about 15,000 ft. Most of these routes have the facility of trekkers' huts *en route* and a back-up of ponies and porters. Experienced trekkers could try some spectacular treks in Laddakh and the upper reaches of Garhwal and Kumaon. As far as possible, avoid trekking solo, especially in unknown terrain.

Best Season

In the Himalayas, the ideal season is summer for most routes. Some exceptions are treks in Laddakh and to the Valley of Flowers. In the Sahyadris, hikes are best during the monsoon. Treks around Pachmarhi in the Satpura hills and around the Nilgiris in the South should be ideally planned during the winter.

Good Timing

Always start early in the morning, around 7 a.m., so that a good part of the trek is done before the midday sun hots up. Aim to end around 4 p.m. or 5 p.m., well before the sun sets, so that even if there are delays, you can be safely home before dark.

Group Dynamics

If you are travelling in a group, it is best to appoint a front guard and a rear guard. The former is generally the group leader, who is familiar with the terrain. He needs to be prudent because he sets the pace of the trek. The rear guard has an equally important role to play, for he is invariably burdened with the laggers, who he is supposed to cheer and proud on every now and then, so that they reach the destination before sundown. Predictably, he is not very popular.

Knapsack Essentials

Trekking is perhaps the most inexpensive adventure sport as far as equipment goes. You would need a haversack, sleeping bag, good walking shoes, torch, water bottle, personal medicines, sunglasses and a cap. Add some warm clothes, two pairs of trousers, three T-shirts and a pair of trackpants and socks.

Food

It is advisable to carry some food, especially on a less frequented route. Bread, baked beans, biscuits, canned food and chocolates are useful. Drinking water from mountain streams is generally safe, but adding two or three drops of chlorine to a glass of water makes it much more potable. Chlorine drops are available in small bottles at most chemist shops.

Money Matters

Budget for around Rs.300 per day for expenses on food, boarding porterage, etc. If in a group, make sure that, between all of you, you have at least Rs.10,000 for an emergency.

Healthwatch

A little breathlessness is natural on a trek, but if it is severe, one must rest and have some water. A trek is not an exercise in speed; a steady and moderate pace is ideal. That would also give you the time to smell the forest flowers and observe the flora and fauna around. Severe breathlessness, headache and nausea could also be a sign of altitude sickness. In that case, the person should be immediately shifted tc a lower altitude.

Right of Way

While on a trek, one often comes across a herd of cattle hurtling down the trail. Give way to the bovines, staying close to the mountainside—or you could be quite literally in deep trouble.

The Right Company

You could opt to go with a professional trekking outfit which will handle all the logistics, but make sure to choose an experienced one. If you form a group of your own, then make sure you have read enough about the terrain and facilities available on the trail. Carrying a map of the route is advisable. You could also hire one of the porters or guides usually available at the base.

Trekking Ethics

This is one aspect that is all too often ignored. While on a trek, one must adhere to a couple of principles.

The first is eco-awareness. Mindless commercialisation of many trek routes has left an ugly mark on many popular Himalayan trails, in the form of plastic bags, cans and bottles littered along the way. A responsible trekking organisation should strongly discourage such activities. Personal junk should be collected in a bag and disposed of later at the camp.

Secondly, one must respect the local culture and avoid confrontations with the villagers one encounters *en route*. Many trekkers don't find anything wrong in giving money or sweets to the village children but don't realise that they are actually encouraging them to beg.

Now that you're well prepared, dust your timberlands, pick up your cap and hit the trail. Despite all its physical demands, trekking is wonderfully invigorating and gratifying.

Few experiences can match the exhilaration of a walk on a jungle trail snaking through thick woods of pine and deodars, with a mountain stream gurgling in the background and intermittent glimpses of snow-covered peaks.

Besides communing with nature in its unspoilt form, you could also end up meeting some interesting people. You may even develop a lasting friendship with some of them, for the camaraderie, coupled with the fun, laughter and hardships shared along the way forge bonds that last long after the journey is over.

Climate

Climate in Himalayas is primarily dependent on two factors: elevation and time of year. In any season, you must be prepared for extremes in temperature, from the very hot to the very cold. Many trekkers come prepared only for winter conditions and sweat it out because of inadequate light clothing at the lower altitudes. Though the monsoons normally break on the sub-continent by mid July and abate by September, localised thunderstorms can occur anywhere in the mountain, particularly during spring and summer, so you should come prepared with enough waterproof clothing and protection. Autumn is the best time to trek in most areas but March, April and May are also good months.

Physical Fitness

You should be physically fit as you have to be at considerable good heights for most of the time and you may face acclimatisation problem. Most Himalayan treks demand 6-8 hours of walking everyday. At different altitudes and gradients, this can be a trying task for the physically unfit. It is therefore, best to tone up your body systems by exercising for at least an hour and a half every day for three months before you start. Short forays into trails in your neighbourhood will also help your body familiarise itself to strenuous walking.

Qualities

You require a lot of patience for adjustment as their co-trekkers, the organizers and the situation prevailing on treks.

How to Trek

You can plan to trek in four ways alone: with porter; with a guide and a crew; and through a travel agency.

Trekking alone is not usually recommended as you will be travelling in unfamiliar areas and will find it difficult to communicate with local villages without knowing their language. Porters can usually be hired from small towns and villages at the base of the trekking trails. The porter will help you carry your baggage, communicate with the locals and often enlighten you with stories and lore about the region. Hiring a guide and crew is more expensive but worth the money if you want to leave yourself free from all logistical problems. Try and find a guide who has trekking experience and testimonials to provide it. The guide will in turn hire the cook and the porters and arrange for the provisions required *en route*. Travel agencies are the most professional and expensive trek handlers. They will normally take care of all travel requirements including air ticketing and transportation leaving you totally free to enjoy your walking expedition. Your closest Government of India Tourist office, and local tourist offices in the trekking areas, will be able to help you select a reliable travel agency and also advice you on the prevailing porter and guide rates.

Trekking Permit

There is no such system of issuing a trekking permit as is done in Nepal and other countries, as long as you do not enter restricted areas across the protected area beyond the linear line. Surveys of India maps, available at office at Janpath in New Delhi, define the restricted areas and are invaluable assets to the trekkers as they clearly indicate most mountain trails, altitudes and gradients. Mark your trails on the map in advance to ensure that you do not branch of on the many subsidiary trails that radiate from the main route.

You can enter some area with special entry permits. Exact information from the concerned tourist department should be obtained prior to planning a trek as regulations are liable to change.

Equipment and Clothing

It is best to prepare your trekking kit and equipment before you arrive in India as it is not always possible to get what you want at the time that you want it. You are the best judge on what you should carry in terms of personal gear and camping equipment as this would depend largely on the area that you are trekking in. As a basic guideline, some of the items that you might consider taking are listed below.

Camping Equipment

You will not need to carry a tent or a foam pad if you are trekking in a group or plan to sleep only in houses and inns: A tent will, however, give you the option of camping on any spot close to water.

Clothing and Personal Gear

You will require clothes for yourself as well as some to give your porters. As far as possible carry only those fabrics that can be easily washed in the cold water streams *en route*. Some suggested items are:

Clothing

Underwear: 3 pairs

Swim suit:	for women to bath in village streams
Socks:	take a few linen socks in addition to three sets preferably woollen
Walking skirts for women:	Shorts can often offend local villages and skirts are a good and comfortable alternatives
Shirts/T-Shirts:	3 pairs
Light weight shirts:	2 wash and wear pairs
Walking shirts:	1 pair
Trekking paints:	1 pair of loose baggy trousers that allow freedom of movement to the legs
Down Jacket/Jacket:	1 windproof

Foot wear and Foot care

Trekking boots:	make sure they care broken in and are of good quality
Insoles:	to prevent foot fatigue
Tennis shoes:	1 pair for the time when you want to rest your feet
Gloves:	1 pair woollen
Umbrella:	1
Hat:	1
Money Belt:	1
Handkerchiefs:	3
Poncho and ground cloth:	necessary protection against wet weather

Sleeping bag
Sleeping sack
Woollen pullover/Wind Jackets/Down Jacket
Goggles/Sunglasses
Rucksack/Day pack
Walking stick
Washing kit
Sanitary towel
Towel
Washing soap

Toothpaste/brush
Make ups
Comb/brush
Toilet paper
Face/foot powder
Mirror

For Face—Cold cream, anti sun-burn cream, chap stick, shaving kit for gents, nail cutter, powder insect repellent etc.

First Aid Kit—Small first aid box, medicines prescribed by doctors, to some, sterilization tablets, chocolates, plaster and bandage, tablets for headache, diarrhoea, constipation, bad cold, stomach upset, anti sunburn cream, Tape, throat lozenges, water purification tablets, insect repellent, eye drops, lotions, lip sal zin cream and face cream.

General—Cigarettes, lighter, thermos/water bottle, sanitary towels, personal requirements of ladies, pencils, note book, knife, torch, whistle and compass, binocular if you are a bird-watcher, extra pair of boot laces, sewing kit, penknife, snow glasses, torch, batteries, cells, diary, reading and writing material, tinned and dehydrated food.

Miscellaneous—Tape recorders, binocular tapes, batteries, liquor.

The Western tourist carrying his or her possessions in a backpack is a familiar sight, and it seems that a greater number of our compatriots are emulating this mode of carrying personal luggage. While it is a simple utilitarian item, the use of the backpack has interesting implications on life as well as on values and altitudes. Perhaps the most important is that it encourages egalitarianism: carrying load is not considered to be something menial and therefore below one's dignity.

Traditionally this view is alien in our country where load is meant to be carried by coolies and servants; and even light and small objects (briefcases or tiffin carriers) are left to be carried by peons or subordinates.

Another important implication of backpacking is on fitness: while a backpack distributes load all over a greater portion of the body making it is much easier to carry, it still implies a fair degree of fitness in the person carrying it.

Backpacking also distributes responsibility within a family, as each individual has to shoulder his own load. This is specially good for younger members of a family as it builds up confidence and gives them a feeling of independence.

Backpacking also implies a somewhat yogi-like attitude to possessions, particularly clothes. Backpackers are more concerned with experiencing rather than possessing.

Backpacks also encourage mobility and a kind of freedom. One can stop and start walking more easily to bend to put down or pick up luggage. The body is vertical instead of being dragged awkwardly to one side by hand-held luggage (holding luggage on both hand achieves better balance but fatigue can step in early). It also enables direct physical contact with the natural environment as well as the human influences working on it. The experience of a region and its culture is thus richer and deeper.

The Right Backpack

Capacity and Usage

The capacity is measured in litres, such as 20 litres or more. When buying a large backpack one should keep in mind one's physical strength. Some packs are expandable, by opening or collapsing the zipped compartment, while day packs are smaller and useful to take with a larger pack. Most packs have particular straps for a sleeping bag or a ground bag.

Frame

A study frame usually concealed within the back and made up of aluminium helps keep larger packs in a straight and even form.

Materials

Synthetic fabric is popular, being sturdy, easy to store and protects against water and stains. Natural materials (cotton, jute) are options but one must consider the duration of travel, weather forecast, damage by mice, insects etc.

Locks

Some or all compartments of a backpack are lockable. Cloakrooms and luggage rooms require that all luggage kept there be locked.

Colours

Bright and catchy colours not only keep the mood upbeat but are specially useful in forested areas for signalling a human presence and warning prowling hunters or poachers. They also attract the attention of rescue missions.

Food and Accommodation

Board and lodging facilities are available on most of the routes.

Cooking Equipment

Cooking equipment will be required only if you are planning to trek on trails, that do not have food facilities and if you do not hire the services of a guide. Most cooking equipment can be bought locally though it not be a light as is available now a days in various other places. You will require the following basic equipment:

(i) Store—Kerosene stoves function best at high altitudes and fuel is easily available
(ii) Fuse container—light and sturdy
(iii) Nesting cookpots—minimum two
(iv) Stuff bags—to carry provisions

(v) Freeze direct foods.

In addition, it will be handy to carry the following items:

Backpack
Medicine kit   Can opener
Maps   Pocket knife
Note book   Scissors
Toilet kit   Flash light
Toilet paper   Water bottle
Watch   Sewing kit
Enamel cup   Boot protector
Spoon   Lip balm
Sunglasses   Suntan lotion
                                 Cord
Insect repellent bug powder.

Photography

You would like to record your trip on film. Himalayan treks offer a wealth of photographic possibilities and carry a little extra photography equipment can be worth its weight. Single reflex cameras with interchangeable lenses are most suitable for the situation you would encounter. Lenses should include a wide angle (28-35 mm) for buildings and landscapes, a telephoto (70-200) for an unobstructive portraits and close up of mountain peaks. A macro lens will help you photograph flowers and insects of Himalayas. A light tripod will be handy in situation with low light. You should carry plenty of films as you will probably end up taking more photographs than you planned (a roll a day should suffice). Make sure you have waterproof covering for your camera equipment and extra batteries. You will need an ultra-violet and polarising filter for high altitude. Then you require:

(i) Camera
(ii) Lenses
(iii) Flash units

(iv) Filter
(v) Films

Season

The season and period for trekking differ from region to another due to the geographical diversity of India. However, the general season is April-June and September-November. It is possible to undertake treks in the Valley of Lahaul, Pangi and Zanskar and in Laddakh, during the rainy season (June-August) as they receive negligible rainfall.

Additional Information

English is generally understood all over India. You must also carry a copy of Indian mountaineering foundation's booklet while in the Himalayas—Do's and Don'ts which contain instructions regarding preservation of environment.

Safari-Photography

Almost every tourist sports a camera. You all want a photograph record of your safari. For the causal photographer, there is no need to run out to buy a complete new camera system. If it is a personal remembrance you are after, any of the new automatic cameras will yield satisfactory results. Scenery companions, hotels, and public/folk are easy subject, while satisfactory wildlife shots can be taken in the game parks where animals let you come close.

Animals are challenging subjects for even the most experienced photographers. These revealing wildlife shots are not taken on casual safaris. They are the result of months patients work by professional shooting with sophisticated equipment from the variety of their own vehicles. And the shots you see are culled from thousands. That is not to say that you cannot get great shots on your safari. The opportunities are there—you should come have with lot of good pictures and a handful of great ones.

Serious photographers will carry a 35 mm SLB camera with interchangeable lenses. A good 300 mm lens is indispensable for speed and versatility in framing.

An 80 mm, 200 mm, 300 mm can get good wildlife pictures, even portraits, of most of the larger park animals. Lenses of 300 mm or larger are needed for quality bird pictures and for shots of the many small or shy mammals. A wide angle lens is fun for creative shots and forgetting close subjects in the context of their surroundings, white a standard 50 mm lens is used for scenery and for portraits (a zoom in the low 28 mm-150 mm range could serve for all those purposes). A macro lens is recommended for flower and subjects. It is obviously helpful to have some camera bodies so that you can be constantly changing lenses.

'Moving' Pictures

For speed and convenient operation from a vehicle, it is best to rely on lenses which can hand-held. Fixed focal length telephoto lenses produce great full frame shots at considerable distances, but require the stability of a tripod for good results. Long lenses are also heavy and a major problem to transport. Easier to carry are mirror lenses which at 50 mm give great magnification. But they have other disadvantages: Fixed at F8, they can be used only in highlight situations, are difficult to focus, and have an extremely shallow depth of field. In general, it is impossible to get sharp images while hand-holding any lens over 300 mm. Vehicles are unsteady shooting platform, unless all passengers are motionless and the engine turned off. A should be tripod or been bag which can be quickly set up on the roof of the car is essential for powerful telephoto work motor drive is a crucial accessory for game photography because animals are constantly moving and subtly changing their expressions, when the subject in good and the light is right; you will want to be able to fire rapidly.

Lighting

Be prepared to use a lot of film; good animal shot demand it. The excitement of the first few days will carry you away. You will shot every thing. You see, even when the light a poor, the subject for away. Afterwards, you will became more subjective and won't need a shot of every distant giraffe and warthog. It is in axiomatic that the best time for shot is in the early morning and late afternoon. The sun is then low, bathing every subject in a perfect, soft, golden light. Mid-day tend to be too bright: pictures come out with a worked at, ever exposed look. It is useful to routinely stop-down a half or even a full stop, except during those brief daily periods when the light is perfect. Travellers an extended trips have the luxury of shooting exclusively at those hours, but if, you'll be in the hush for only two weeks, you will have a shoot at the less favourable time of day, too.

A flash is very useful, not only for night shots around the lodge or camp, but for day time filler. Some people or animals or articles are hard to photograph. Their dark complexion or skin contrast strongly, with the bright sunlight. Daytime flash can correct their sometime insurmountable exposure problem.

Film Issues

It is best to shoot slides. It is much cheaper to cull slides, and select the good ones for reproduction than to shoot a lot of similar exposures with print film. When the subject matter is there, and especially when the light is good fuel free to shoot with abandon, even if you previously have taken pictures of the same animal. You won't regret the multiple exposures when you cull your slides often the dream shot you thought you took will be ruined by the flick of an ear an unnoticed tuft of glass, while other prove spectacularly expressive and well exposed.

Telephoto lenses require fast film in order to permit shooting at speeds high enough to result in sharp images.

India is rich in colour though, and the faster speed films do not give good colour saturation. There are vivid colour shots. Many professionals try to shoot with nothing else. Bring more film than you think you will need. It may not be available and caused to serve to be more expensive in India. Do not ever about the film going bad in the heat. Keep your reserve and exposed rolls buried deep in your luggage, and they will survive nicely.

Protecting Your Equipment

You do have to worry about your equipment. The bouncing and dust of safari is hard on photo gear, particularly delicate high-tech electronic cameras. Once they have a problem, they are likely to be useless for the rest of the trip.

A backup camera, preferably a manual model, can suddenly become more than just a convenience. It is wise to keep your cameras and lenses packed when not in use. Some suggest keeping them inside plastic bags for dust protection. However, keep in mind that if the camera is not early accessible and ready to use, you are going to miss many of the best shots. It is really common for a perfect shot to disappear while a photographer fumbles to organise his gear. Be ready, not over protective.

Video

More and more visitors are coming equipped with video cameras. Safari really lends itself to video. The immediacy of the experience really through. Buy a quality half inch recorder so that you can edit your work when you get home; unedited videos lose viewers' interest really fast. Video cameras require a rechargeable power back.

Whether you are bringing camera as a video recorder, learn how to use it properly before leaving home.

Finally, do not let photography detract from your experience! Some people see India exclusively through lenses. They miss a lot.

Travel Guide

The guides on adventure travel trips are frequently cited as the best part of the journey. As a rule they are intelligent, respectful, witty and tolerant. They may also be highly skilled at rafting, mountaineering or other activities, and trained in exotic languages and traditions, birding or geology, or the other aspects of travel that qualifies them to make your trip safe; enjoyable and educational. Nearly all have first-aid training, and may have other advanced emergency medical qualifications. They are in short, good company and you will find travelling with them a real pleasure.

Meals on adventure trips also rank high on passengers' evaluations—many menus, whipped up on the spot and consumed beneath a starry sky would attempt the palate of the most discriminating gourmet. In general all meals on a trip are included in trip costs, except as stated in detailed itinerary.

The equipment for the journey—rafts, on other transport, cook-ware, medical supplies, safety items and other group camping gear is also provided by the trip operator. Participants are generally expected to bring their own clothing, favourite recreational beverages, and other items of personal nature. Sleeping bags, pads and tents are also the passengers' responsibility though in many cases this gear can be rented for a nominal fee from the operator.

Adventure travel conjures up images of inflatable rafts plunging over water falls, pack laden climbers learning on their ice axes at the snowy summit, or the sore feet at the end of the day. But it emphasize its emotional and spiritual rewards, the exhilaration of achievement, the thrill of learning something new, the relaxation of rigid schedules, the satisfaction of a job well done. Adventure travel is not for everyone. It is for you.

Travel Tips

Travelling is supposed to be one of life's great pleasures. But instead if you feel sick in a car/plane, your hair feels dry and your feet swell or your skin breaks out, you may wonder why. Whether you travel by air or by road here are a few tips to help you travel beautifully.

Feel Fresh

Keep yourself cool and calm while travelling by road by placing two cotton balls on the window shelf of the car, one with a drop of eucalyptus and the other with drop of peppermint oil. These oils are not only antibiotic and antiseptic but soothe the nerves and keep you fresh.

Travel Sickness

Travel sickness is to a large extend caused by conflicting messages reaching the brain from the eyes and the balancing mechanism of the ears and stomach. It helps to close your eyes while travelling or fix your eyes on an object in the distance.

While flying the pressurised cabins air cause dehydration, dry skin, swollen feet and ankles, cramp, headaches and painful knees.

Dry Skin

Before starting out on your journey have a shower after which you use a light body moisturiser to which a few drops of any calming essential oil has been added such as lavender or geranium. Remove your make-up, splash with water and apply an emollient cream. If you prefer not to take off your make-up, use a night cream under your make-up. Spray your face regularly with mineral water. Invest in a mini plant spray bottle to carry in your hand luggage.

Eye Care

Put eye cream around your eyes. If you wear contact lens,

either take your lenses out during the flight or use special drops to avoid eye fatigue.

Hair

Shampoo and condition your hair and set it. If travelling by road tie your hair with a scarf. If you have a problem with static take a little essential oil or a little gel in your hand and smooth it on your hair.

What to Drink?

Avoid alcohol when travelling by air to ward off the exhausting effects of dehydration from alcohol. Hangovers in the air can be bad. Try to avoid coffee and tea also as these are diuretics. Instead try to have a cup of peppermint tea before you leave the house—one drop of peppermint oil mixed with a teaspoon of honey in hot water.

What to Eat?

As you take longer flights, jet lag is one of the problems you face. When you need to sleep you may crave for food at odd times or may feel too sick to eat. So the best solution is to eat less than usual and try to eat healthy food such a vegetarian or low-sodium meals. Another solution is to massage a few drops of peppermint and eucalyptus oils throughout your body, or you may even add them in your bath water after the flight.

Swollen Ankles

Sitting for long periods in a train, car, bus, or while flying the speeded-up gravitational pull of the aeroplane affect circulation and cause your feet to swell up. So try to massage your legs in an upward direction to the bottom of the calf with a few drops of pure lavender oil and try to wear loose fitting shoes.

Cramps

If you are prone to getting cramp while travelling, make a compress by using geranium oil and hold the compress over the affected area—usually the calf of the leg or the foot. Also try the old Chinese trick of holding your big toes tightly between the thumb and forefinger. This treatment will alleviate the symptoms of jet lag but for the best results it must be continued.

Before you set out on a journey make sure handbag is well-stocked with the things you need. BON VOYAGE!!

Falling ill is not a welcome happening at any time but when one is on the road, illness puts paid to one's plans effectively. Travel health depends, of course, on your day-to-day health and your ability to handle medical emergencies without losing your head.

However, adequate pre-departure preparations and information regarding health hazards in the area you are about to visit will go a long way in ensuring an illness-free stay. Making sure that you are healthy pre-travel is a must—get that carious tooth filled and keep an extra pair of spectacles with you. Looking around for a dentist or ophthalmologist in a strange place can be daunting. Also, if you are on regular medications for an ailment such as hypertension or diabetes, take adequate stocks along to cover the period of your stay. The brand of medicine you are used to may not be available everywhere.

A small, simple medical kit is wise in addition to your luggage. This should include:

- Antihistamines such as Benadryl or Cetrizine useful for colds, allergies, itching from insect bites and stings. Marzine and avomine are especially good for travel sickness. Take a tablet about 45 minutes before starting your journey. Remember that antihistamines cause drowsiness and alcohol should be avoided.
- Pain-killers and medicines to bring down fever, such as aspirin. The safest of these is Paracetamol (Crocin).

Brufen is useful in body-aches and joint pains. These medicines should never be taken on an empty stomach.

- Antibiotics—keep a full course of these handy, but only after advise from your doctor. If you are allergic to any of these (such as sulphas and penicillin), ensure that this information is carried on your person at all times. Antibiotics are necessary in case of mild infections (sore throat, infected cuts), and medical help should be sought for more serious ailments.

- Dehydration mixtures for diarrhoeas especially while travelling with children, as even seemingly mild diarrhoeas can cause serious loss of fluid in them. Follow the instructions on the packet to make up the solution. Lomotil or Imodium can be used to relieve symptoms, but only if absolutely necessary. In all circumstances, fluid replacement remains the mainstay of treatment.

- Antiseptics, such as Betadine, which are available as swabs lotion or ointment. These are used to clean cuts and grazes. Dry antibiotic powders such as Neomycin may also be sprayed on the area after cleaning well with an antiseptic.

- Calamine lotion eases irritation from stings and cuts. It also helps to soothe sunburned skin.

- Bandages, band-aids, crepe bandages (for sprains) are a must. Scissors should be carried in the kit, and tweezers often come in handy in pulling out thorns glass shards and other foreign material. A thermometer is always useful, but mercury thermometers are not permitted on aeroplanes.

- Insect repellents, especially mosquito protectants are invaluable.

- Last but not least, always carry sterilised disposable syringes of varying sizes (2 ml and 5 ml) along with needles. About two of each should be enough for a short stay. With the AIDS epidemic on us, this is a wise precaution, should an injection become mandatory.

Additional Tips

Make sure that your blood group is clearly written on a card
carried on your person at all times. Any allergies should also
be mentioned on this card.

Care in what you eat and drink is vital. Most travellers suffer from stomach upsets, but these are mild and self-limiting.

Do not drink water as far as possible. This includes ice.
It is best to settle for bottled drinks. Even mineral water which
is supposedly sterile may have been filled from ordinary
sources. Tea and coffee are generally safe, as the water to
make them is boiled. Milk is best avoided. Water purification
tablets are available and can be used. Make sure you drink
plenty of fluids even if you are not thirsty, especially during
summer and travel to warmer climes. Not needing to urinate
or passing dark urine is an indication. 'If you can cook it,
boil it or peel it you can eat it'. This means that salads in any
form are taboo. Food which has been cooked and left to stand
may be dangerous hence it is wise to eat only at places which
have a rapid turnover of people, as stale, reheated food is
less likely to be served. Ice-cream of a reputed brand should
be alright, but locally made ones are best shunned.
Mayonnaise, often found in sandwiches, can cause severe
problems, as raw eggs are used to make it.

Sunburn is common in the desert and at high altitudes.
You can get sunburned even on a cloudy day, so protect
yourself with sunscreens, applied even on remote areas like
the feet.

Heat exhaustion/heat stroke are potentially serious and
can be fatal. Ensuring adequate fluid intake and salt
replacement (lost in sweating) helps. If you have lethargy,
headache, giddiness, confusion and fever seek medical help
immediately.

Excessive cold can be as dangerous as heat. Wear several
layers of clothing in different materials including synthetics,
which keep out the cold and breeze, reducing the wind-chill
factor. Hydration is important, for cold can 'dry' one out. A
hat is necessary, as a lot of heat is lost through the head.

Carry simple sugar-containing foods which generate heat rapidly.

Lack of oxygen at high altitudes can lead to acute mountain sickness. Ascend slowly, with frequent rest periods, to allow the body to acclimatize. Eat light meals and avoid alcohol and sedatives.

Motion-sickness is a common complaint, and eating lightly well before travel reduces the chances of it occurring. Sit near the centre of buses or near the wing on aircraft. Reading or smoking will aggravate it. Ginger is a natural preventive.

Malaria is almost synonymous with India. But the primary prevention is in the form of mosquito-avoidance measures. As mosquitoes bite usually from dusk to dawn, wear full-sleeved clothing during this time.

Trekking Tips for Beginners in Himalayan Region

Where to Go

Suggested treks for beginners are: the Pindari Glacier, Khatling glacier, Yamunotri, Gangotri, Gaumukh, Roopkund, Har-ki-dun, Hemkund Sahib. The valley of flowers, which are all in the Uttaranchal Hills of Garhwal and Kumaon. In Himachal, the best treks originate in the Kullu-Manali valley. One is from Naggar on the river Beas to Jari on the river Parvatti over the Chandrakhani Pass, via Malana, where it is alleged that the axe of Parashuram is buried. Manali is the trekking capital of Himachal as many treks can be undertaken from here. Crossing over the Rohtang pass you enter the Lahaul valley where you could do the trek to Chandratal, the Bara Lacha Pass, the Spiti valley from over the Kunzum top, or cross over to Bharmour and Chamba or cross over to Zanskar (from Darcha to Padum or from Padum to Leḥ via Lamayuru). A trek from Manikaran to Spiti via the Mantalai glacier and lake, which is the source of the holy Parvatti river (a tributary of the river Beas) and over the Pin Parvatti Pass is a route specifically for the specialist, and requires much planning and arduous climbing. Chamba,

Kangra (especially Dharam- sala), and Kinnaur also offer some lovely treks. In Kashmir a trek from Kishtwar to Padum is another beautiful trek but strictly for the professionals.

How to Go about Things

After you have decided where to go, organise and plan for all contingencies. Besides a rucksack, a sleeping bag, warm clothes, comfortable old jeans, a thick jacket and other essentials like a good detailed route map, canned food, candles, knife, chocolates (never eat your chocolates till you have reached our destination, as these are for emergency and are not a luxury!). Be careful about the selection of your shoes. Never wear new trekking shoes for a trek unless you want to come back with sore feet and blisters. Take your regular sports shoes or keds. Never over-exert the first day, or you will ruin the fun. Walk for distances which suit your constitution. Hire a lightweight tent and a local porter if you cannot carry too much weight. Walk at a leisurely pace, enjoy the scenery. If you find a lovely pasture take a breather and watch the nature take its own course, or the eagles high up in the sky, the snowcapped peaks, the apple orchards, the comely villagers and general scene at large. But do not take too long a rest (say half an hour or 45 minutes) as you may then not feel like getting up again! It is advisable to take break for a day or two if you are on a long trek (over a week or ten days).

Whom to Contact in Delhi

The Indian Mountaineering Foundation (IMF) at the Benito Juarez Marg near the South Campus, and The Youth Hostel Association (YHA) at the International Youth Centre (IYC) on the Teen Murti Marg, can be of help and guidance. Another association that can help you is the Climbers and Explorers Club (CEC) at the Jawaharlal Nehru Stadium. The Sri Aurobindo Ashram on the Sri Aurobindo Marg, too, offers some trekking opportunities for youngsters as well as old people, especially in and around Nainital and other areas. However you can always organise a trek on your own!

Trekking—Have a Walk of Your Life

For those looking for an overdose of the rugged, vast expanse of nature at its unbridled, untamed best. For those who wouldn't compromise on anything but the closest feel of the challenging terrain and the abundance of flora and fauna, try us out!

4

Wildlife and Natural Parks: The Valley of Flowers

The Valley of Flowers is nature's Ikebana in Chamoli district (Uttaranchal) of Garhwal Himalayan region. It covers about 10 sq.km. in length, 2 km. in width and is concave in shape. The total area is 82.5 sq. km. The valley is divided by a stream called the Pushpawati, a tributary of Bhyundar Ganga and several tiny streams and waterfalls rushdown from the Itawal deposits to merge with it. The Pushpawati joins with the Laxman Ganga. A massive mountain mantled with snow and called Ghoradhungi blocks the valley at one end. The valley is extending over a long area and end, on the north side, the origin of Bhyndhar river. Across the glacial pass (5,091 m.) is the traditional route of Bank Kund and the pasture lands of the Gamsali valley which eventually leads to the Niti valley, a restricted area.

Concealed among the craggy Himalayan ranges of Garhwal lies an enchanted valley of peace and perfect harmony. More than a thousand exotic varieties of flowers, ferns and herbs are massed here in all their frail beauty and scented sweetness. Exposed to the fragrance, the cool wind and the beauty of the ferns and flowers swaying on their slender stems, visitors who reach the valley are awed into silence. Ringed in by snowy, cloud-bedecked mountain summits standing sharply against the blue sky, the waterfalls flashing white against the mountain sides, nothing is more striking than the valley's absolute bloom of perfection.

Discovery

The valley in the Garhwal Himalays (Uttaranchal) was beloved of the ancients and was referred to in the Puranas as Gandhmandan Parvat. The local residents have always known of the valley, but they could not venture into it because of certain superstition—their belief that there are fairies in the valley and if they are there the fairies will take them away. The legends of the valley indicate that Nandan Kanan, the Valley of Flowers, was always known to the local Tolchha Bhotias.

Colonel Edmund Smythe, an Education Officer in the Army came to India as a major. He explored many byways of Uttarakhand in the mid-nineteenth century. He crossed Lakshman Pass in 1862 and chanced upon the Valley of Flowers. He has all praise for the floral and natural beauty for the region. He wrote about it in many newspapers and periodicals. His views were read far and wide.

Attracted by the accounts of Edmund Smythe, the second notable Englishman to cross Lakshman Pass was Dr. Tom Longstaff who called it Smythe's Pass. Longstaff was a mountaineer of world renown and had climb Trishul in 1907. In his book, *This My Voyage*, he has said about the Valley of Flowers:

> *"Beyond these glaciers we looked down into a valley of the richest green balm to the eyes after the story desolation we have left behind. We reached it on July 13, to find the most luxuriant meadow. We have met with in this part of the Himalayas. We waded through flowers up to our waists, ferns, yellow lilies and anemones, green fritillaries, people monks-hood, blue dwarf iris, masses of forget-me-nots with yellow king cups by the stream. Innumerable butterflies of alpine forms, including atleast two species of large swallow tails, with many singing birds, were*

about us on all sides. We found a plot of grassy sward for tents. The charms of the place were so irresistible that we spent a whole day there."

It was however, Frank Smythe, who first christened this region the Valley of Flowers. The credit for the discovery of Valley of Flowers goes to R.L. Holdsworth and Frank Smythe. Richard L. Holdsworth a botanist and member of Smythes successful Kamet expedition was, thus the real discoverer of this valley. Officially, the credit of having discovered the Valley of Flowers, in 1931 has been given to Frank Smythe, a British explorer and mountaineer. Mr. R.L. Holdsworth, Maunth Meson and Dr. John Down has also given description of this valley.

R.L. Holdsworth, wrote about this rich field of *primulas* growing wild as flowers:

"All of a sudden I realised that I was simply surrounded by primulas. At once the day seemed to brighten perceptibly. Forgotten were all pains and cold and lost porters. And what a primula it was: its leek-like habits proclaimed it a member of the rivalis section. All over the little shelves and terraces it grew, often with its roots in vanning water. At the most it stood six inches heights but its flowers were enormous for its stature, and ample in number—sometimes as many as thirty to the beautifully, proportioned umbel, and in colour of the most heavenly French blue, sweetly scented.

In 1931, six British mountaineers were returning from the successful Kamet expedition (7,756 m. 25,447 ft.) in Garhwal Himalayas. After the climb they descended to Ghamsali village, lying at the confluence of the Dhauli Ganga and Amrit Ganga rivers. Rather than returning to Joshimath by the foot track along the river Dhauli Ganga, they decided to cross the Lakshman Pass (5,086 m./16,688 ft.) also called the Bhyunder Pass--with the intention of exploring the mountains near the sources of Alaknanda and Bhagirathi, the two tributaries of the Ganga.

After a successful expedition to the Kamet peak, Frank Smythe and some other mountaineers had chanced upon the Bhyndar Valley to take shelter from a blizzard. On seeking the rich floral wealth of this beautiful meadow, he and his friend R.L. Holdsworth called it the 'Valley of Flowers'. Smythe visited this valley once again in 1937 and had been camping there for a few months collecting the numerous species of flowers and seeds and climbing the neighbouring mountain peaks. His books, *Kamet Conquered* and *The Valley of Flowers* present highly interesting accounts of his adventures.

Today, from mid-July till the end of August, this dazzling assembly of flowers plays host to dainty butterflies and tiny whirring creatures by day; to millions of glow worms by night.

Frank Smythe chanced upon a fairy land, an alpine pasture in blossom and fragrant with innumerable flowering plants. This pasture of *bugyal* as it is locally known, was full of rare species of vegetation.

Frank Smythe went back to the valley to collect seeds and pods in 1937. He camped here for three months to collect material for his book *The Valley of Flowers* and the seeds for the Botanical Garden in Edinburgh Scotland. On his second visit he has recorded:

"*It was my privilege to undertake this work and the reader, while remembering, and I hope generously, my ignorance, must judge for himself whether the Bhyunder Valley deserves its title 'the Valley of Flowers'. Others will visit it, analyse it and probe it, but, whatever their opinions, to me it will remain the Valley of Flowers, a valley of place and perfect beauty where the human spirit may find repose.*"

He has written:

"*In all my mountain wanderings I had not seen a more*

beautiful flower than this primula, the fine raindrops clung to it soft petals tiles of galaxiers of seed pearls and forsted it leaves with silver. Lower where we camped near a moraine, were androsaces, saxifrages, sedums, yellow and red potintillas, geums, geraniums, asters, gentians, to mention but a few plants. and it was impossible to take steps without crushing a flower. Next day we descended to lush meadows. Here our camp was embowered amidst flowers, snow-white drifts of anemones, golden lily-like namocharis, marigolds, globe flowers, delphiniums, violets, eritrichiums, blue corydalis, wildroses, flowering shrubs and rhododendrons, many of these flowers with homely sounding English names. The Bhyunder Valley was the most beautiful valley that any of us had seen. We campled in it for two days and we remembered it afterwards as the Valley of Flowers."

Upon seeing it for the first time, Frank Smythe, wrote in his book:

"In my mountaineering wanderings I have not seen a more beautiful valley than this. Others would come and analyse, but to me it could remain a valley of peace and perfect beauty where the human spirit may find repose".

In the year 1939, the Botanical Garden of Edinburgh send Miss Joan Margaret Legge to collect seeds of some of the rare varieties. She camped there for a while, but unfortunately lost her life when she slipped from a rock whilst picking flowers on 4th July 1939. She was cremated by the local resident of Bhyunder. Her sister got her grave constructed at the exact spot of her death. To remind one of the great love she had for the Himalayas, inscribed on her marble tomb stone are the words,

"IN LOVING MEMORY
OF
JOAN MARGARET LEGGE
FEB. 21st 1885-JULY 4th 1939
I WILL LIFT MINE EYES UPTO THE HILLS
FROM WHENCE COMETH MY HELP"

Near Anta Khal Pass there is a *Samadhi* of this British lady. The *Samadhi* reminds her love and affection towards the valley. The grave of this brave lady who is referred to as the Quen of Flowers by the local residents, is visited by all with reverence and respect.

Since then this beautiful valley has fascinated naturalists, tourists, hikers and pilgrims from all over the world ever since the rapid development of transport linkages in the Garhwal Himalayas and the emergence of Hemkund as an important religious place. Situated at a height of 3,658 m. the valley is a great attraction for the tourists. In the ancient time it was known as Nandan Kanan and is still called as Munghyar Valley.

On your visit to the Valley of Flowers, you will have to probe her hidden glencs and dells to enjoy its outstanding and astonishing beauty. After you cross the leg bridge over the river Hem Ganga, the road to the Laxman Pass bifurcates to the left. After half of kilometre trekking you enter to a region where there are every where flowers mainly canditufts, calendulas, larkspeur and potentillas in ever increasing numbers. You will find flowering bushes and creepers, *plumago, ariculate,* Jasmine, *Cichorauim, entibus, Caesalpina, pulcherrema,* Golden chain, *Saxifraga mivalias, nelumbicem,* pomgranade, *Gloriosa, Superba, Hygrophila* Spinesa, *Digitalis peerpuria, Polygoncom,* Clerodendram, curcuma, papaver, artimisia, *Betula nana,* butterfly bush, trumpet flower, clematis, golden blue–and pink bells, Himalayan honeysuckle, and lush honey suckle, among a host of other flowers welcoming you.

The multi-coloured flowers on the branches of the same tree is the charm of the valley. From June to September the valley is in its full cham and form. Thousands of alpine flowers and mlti-coloured butterflies increase the beauty of the valley. The *buransh* a dark coloured flower gives an unique look in the different flowers is a great satisfaction and relaxation to the tired tourists who have reached there to see this inquisitive place.

Flowers

Some of the flowers which can be seen in the valley are:

- Anemones–Creamy
- Androsace–White
- Balsam
- Birch
- Bleeding heart
- Bovage–blue
- Brahmkamal–Heavily perfumed
- Caesalpinia
- Calendula
- Candytuft
- Cassiope
- Chaulai
- Chichory
- Chir
- Crane's bill
- Crysanthemum
- Cypripedium–rosy petalled
- Daffodils .
- Elephant ear plant
- Fern
- Forget me not–blue
- Fox glove
- Fritillaries green and chequered
- Geraniums–pink
- Gladiolus

- Glory Lily
- Haldi
- Himalayan honey suckle
- Hygrophila spinosa
- Irises—purple and dwarf
- Jasmine
- Knot weed
- Lad's Love
- Larksur—dwarf
- Lotus
- Meadow Daisy
- Mecanopsis—The blue poppy petals as blue as the ocean
- Nanda teres
- Namo chairs
- Pansics—blue and yellow
- Patuniasp
- Plumbago auriculata
- Polemomiums—mauve
- Poppy—Opium white
- Potentila
- Primulas—pink and blue
- Rhodendron
- Ranunculus—deepest purple
- Rock Jasmine
- Rose
- Saxifrage nivalis
- Snapdragon
- Stone crop or pot herb
- St John's Wort
- Tansy
- Thistle
- Trumpet Flower
- Virgin bower.

The early varieties of these flowers can be seen in the month of May and June. A visit to valley during this period is enchanting sight. During this period it is a land of blaze with bewildering variety of flowers fluttering in the gentle intermitent breeze which wafts their fragrance abroad. By September the flowers have withered and died.

The motor head for the Valley of Flowers is Govind Ghat which is 20 km. from Joshimath and 270 km. from Rishikesh. The trak between Govind Ghat to the valley is one of varied scenic beauty. One crosses the suspension bridge over the Alaknanda, the zig-zag mountain path with the gurgling Laxman Ganga stream, past dense vegetation forests, views of the Kak Bhusandi Valley, Govind Ghat (Govind Dham) is the base for the Valley of Flowers. Half km. from one has to cross the Ram Ganga. As the path from Ghangaria gradually ascend to the Valley of Flowers, glaciers, snow bridges, alpine flowers and wildlife appears all along the route.

The delicate patch as well as the whole valley need protection and conservation. Unlike sanctuaries and national park, it has not yet a legal status. While tourists are welcome they must not be allowed to trample the beauty they come to see. Efforts are needed to conserve life as and where it is, so that the future generations can have a glimples of how it used to be in their ancestor's days.

Yet despite the publised attraction of the most spectacular gathering of flowers in the world, there are no bustling sightseers. The short flowering season coinciding with the monsoon ensures that only the most determined or venturesome brave the landslide that often bar the way to the Valley of Flowers—10,800 feet above sea level. For those who respond to the valley's soft appealing call, the journey to savour the feast of flowers means township which welcomes the Ganges as it emerges from the foothills, begins a 270 kilometre winding drive. Slate-roofed mountain villages and foaming, holy rivers provide good company all the way upto Govindghat at 5,487 feet.

Porters, ponies *dandies* (wooden palanquins) and *kandis*

(wicker baskets to carry people of *coolie's* backs) await the traveller at Govindghat which marks the beginning of a challenging 19 kilometre trek to the famed valley. The sight of the surging Alaknanda river is usually enough to inspire the majority to cross the suspension bridge and take to the mountain path on their own feet. The scenery becomes more rugged and magnificent with every passing kilometre. The steep climb is enlivened by cheerful Bhotia women carrying huge bundles of grass on their backs. One encounters bands of beaming Sikhs returning from Hemkund, the highest Sikh pilgrimage centre at 14,500 feet. "*Sat Sri Akal, Sat Sri Akal . . .*", they cry triumphantly.

14 kms. of about 9 hours of climbing ahead—pass the hamlet of Pulna, through the village of Bhyundar, lies Ghangaria. Resthouses, a *gurdwara,* and several teashops make up this last halting point at 9,147 feet. A stiff five kilometres away, atop a mountain, is the glacial lake of Hemkund. Five kilometres of gentler climbing in the other direction lies the Valley of Flowers.

To see the valley in all its radiance, one must start from Ghangaria at dawn, before the sun ascends the mountain crags. The dim light is just sufficient to walk carefully, safely across the treacherous glaciers on the narrow trail to the valley. By the time one nears the entrance the mist rises high with the warmth of the sunrise and drifts away in wreaths. Below lie the freshly awakened, still dewy flowers—a miracle revealed.

As far as the eye can see, down the length of the valley, up the lower mountain slopes, there are flowers and flowers, and more flowers. Deep red thyme, yellow and red daisies, potentillas and geraniums, golden nomocharis. Yellow buttercups and blue delpiniums. The rare, strongly scented *brahma kamal* and even rarer nocturnal plant that flowers into a phosphorescent green light at midnight. . . . The sparkling snowfed Pushpawati Ganga (river of flowers) runs through the entire length of the 10 kn. long, two kilometer wide valley. In the background, at 12,900 ft. is the Lari Bank glacier. Beyond lie perennial snow fields.

Ages ago, it is said, Ram and Lakshman, the heroes of the *Ramayana* passed through this valley, known as Nandan Kanan. Shabari, a devout Bhil nun, collected and offered them berries from the valley. In her simplicity, she tasted the berries first to make sure they were sweet. Lakshman threw away the half eaten berrie. From each berry that was thrown away, there sprang and flourished a plant called *sanjivini*. Years went by. Then, Lakshman was wounded in the epic battle against Ravana. Only the herb *sanjivini* applied on the wound could save him. Hanuman, set out for the valley to fetch the life-saving herb. After a futile search, unable to identify the plant, Hanuman picked up an entire mountain in desperation and carried it, with all its plant life, to the battle site on the shores of Lanka. Lakshman recovered and the gods, pleased with Hanuman, showered flowers from heaven. The divine flowers, it is related, fell and took root in Nandan Kanan, transforming it into a valley of flowers.

A gap of a great many centuries separates this mythical history and the present. Yet, except for the humming of bees, the buzzing of gay butterflies and insects unseen, and the occasional happy gurgle of the Pushpawati, there are no sounds to bring back the passage of time. A subtle air fo leisure and repose, a romantic indefinable charm pervades the Valley of Flowers. But to those who care to listen, the valley and its flowers speak of the very real joy of beauty. It isn't just the colour and the fragrance. Like its many flowers, there are many dimensions of beauty in the valley.

In the life-giving morning, there is the vivid transparency of fresh opening flowers. After a sudden monsoon shower, a delicate film of glistening rain drops veils the flowers while beyond against a background of dark purple clouds the mountains stand more exquisite than ever. Through the sunny hours, the flowers lean over gracefully to soften the wedges of the meltwater streams that cut through the valley. When a light breeze springs up, the flowers nod and bow their heads. Evening brings with it the exciting chance of sighting a Himalayan bear or musk deer.

In the last hour before daylight dies, the grey mist steals in softly over the valley.

The valley which was filled with snow and seasonal glaciers is left with huge chunks of ice here and there. With the seeds of flowers and plants which have been hidden and preserved by nature for many months begin to germinate, spring across from the earth and breaks into a riot of colours. This process is slow yet steady. Sprouting begins as soon as thaw sets in. You will notice colour splashes from the middle of June and the peak period is normally reached between the third week of July and the end of August. In the higher regions where the snow melts later, some varieties remain till about the middle of September. During a mild summer, you may witness many varieties till the middle of October. If you want to enjoy there are experience of the valley, the peak period in the time of intense rains. At the peak period, colours of dawn, the rainbow and the setting sun are all mingled in the valley in unmatched beauty. Wandering in the valley will reveal the existence of flowers right upto Laxman Pass of even upto 18,000 feet. The varieties which boon in June in lower region may be encountered higher up in September for the climatic conditions are the same.

In middle of June, some flowers have already blossomed at places, while the snow helds on to some others, from which numbers stream ran down. These water channels are fully formed only by the late afternoon and glisten in the fading light, offering a lovely spectacle. You will find this as the contained Himalayan scenery of magnificent primeval beauty. At times, you will observe that the entire spectacle is softened by the clouds floating over the apls and resting on slopes of the surrounding peaks. Blinding snow-glare is slowly soothened. The birds start joining the exquisite orchestra of nature. The bushes and trees all around come alive with the newly arrived birds chirping and jumping from twig to twig. The entire scene is repeated every year the seasonal glaciers slowly started receding and snow become patchy. The earth becomes soaked with water. The ground drives. It erupts in a startling exposition of colour from millions of flowers coming into blossom.

At midday, you may enjoy the distant peaks wearing their purple most caps. The revine down below are dark, mysterious and cool. In the golden, honeyed silence of the afternoon and the humming of the bees is heard.

The sun tilts towards the west and sun shine, now mellowed by the cloud cover, melts into the early evening's chill air. A soft breeze has started blowing. As the evening approaches, the wind velocity is increased. It reaches its height and thereafter it becomes gentle. Suddenly, on the distant peaks you will find a streak of lightening. With the result the blue sky turns grey and moisture-laden within minutes. You reach for shelter. The raindrops come down heavy and cold. These clouds will recede suddenly and the limpid evening sunshine will light up a trillion rain drops into sparkling pearls. Soon it is all clear and the peaks are glistening in the evening sun. You are fortunate to see this nature activity while walking all round the valley. Here on these moment you feel the presence of God.

This is time for sun to set and for you to move back to the tent, where you can muse and meditate.

The morning seems to break open this Valley of Flowers. The rays of the sun move steadily. They get strong by reflection on the snow. You will find a flood of light. You move out of your tent. You will observe that plants on the lower plain have withered and some new ones have come up a little higher. This is the fleeting beauty of the flowers. The valley is flooded with flowers during spring. It is a valley to witness the elaborate costumes of swirling colours.

You will be enchanted by this fairly land, specially because of the flowers, herbs, butterflies, wild animals, flora and fauna found here.

Flora and Fauna

Flowers

Corn flowers, petunias, begonias, pansies, gladioli, daffodils, phlox, gerberas, clematis, roses, lillies, larkspurs and countless other flowers.

Herbs

Aconite, belladonna, arnica and calendula.

Thumma

A tiny creeper considered an effective aphroadisiac in Ayurveda.

Hathajari

The root of this herb look like a clenched fist. It is a sweet tasting root and effective in stomach ailments and food poisoning.

Rudravanti Jari

It is known as weeping herb. It is a flowering herb with plenty of small golden yellow flowers. It is believed to be a panacea for many ailments. A viscous substance comes out from its stem like oil from pines. This is called the tears of the herb

Deep Jari

It has fluorescent roots that shines with a bluish light at night. The reference of this Jari has been made by Kalidas in Kumarasambhavam.

In this play the capital of the Himalayan Aushadhi Prast is described to have *deep jari* growing all over the place.

Tree: Bhojpatra

At a height of 4,145 meters, bhojpatra is the only tree that grows here. These trees have excellent bark which was used for all writing purposes till the discovery of paper. The old trees are called brahmabhoj. The older the tree, the better the bark.

Juniper Bushes

These are called Talu-jari. Among about 35 centimeters in height, the bush spread, around like a thick meshed net. The oil contents in its wood is quite high and it burns while wet. The wood has a sweet aroma and form the base for the incense industry. The bark of the bush is also used in brewing country liquor.

Birch Trees

The rocky outcrop descending from the cover slopes of Nilgiri Parvat seems to serve as a testing place for many birds. A head lies the Rataban and Ghori Parvat massifs. The peaks cast a peculiar spell on you.

To your right in the shinning stream of the Lakshman Ganga River, across it lie the lower slopes of the Hath Parvat Massif which are thickly wooded right upto the left bank of the river from whence descends a gurgling boisterous stream, a tributary of the Lakshman Ganga. Near this stream, you will find exotic birds and at times bear and bharal living together in peaceful harmony.

While walking in the valley, you may notice a Himalayan mouse hare grazing peacefully. This animal lives on the few blades of grass that grow in higher regions. The grass is considered to be very nutritious but difficult to digest. The rabbit generally pass out the half digested food and quickly eats his own droppings so as to subject them to another cycle of digestion.

Flowers and butterflies exit side by side. Many butterflies have developed colours and wings that closely resemble the flowers. The butterflies of the valley are gorgeous and some of the species are very pretty. The snow Appollo parassius butterfly which inhabits the high Himalayas is plentiful in the valley. Some of the other varieties seen are:

- Cabbage White
- Satyrids or Browns
- Amatheslids.

Nymphalids such as leaf butterfly, white and red admiral the terrorise-shell purple emperor.

There are large number of Royal's vole who move in and out.

Wildlife

While around Lakshman Ganga you may sometimes see a pair of Himalayan Thar, standing majestically on rock viewing with much keenness. Goral, Nayan and serow herds are also seen it times drinking water.

On the other slopes of Nilgiri Parvat you may be lucky to notice the probing eyes of the musk deer. The musk deer lives at a height upto 12,000 feet. Its coat has brittle hair, and is hornless. It has the musk pod (Kasturi Kanabba). The quantity of musk contained in a musk pod varies from 5 to 15 grams. Musk is dark purple as brownish in colour. It has a remarkable stability and performance of orders. Its scent is pleasantly penetrating and persistent. Hence its importance for perfume industry. It is also used in many Ayurvedic medicines mainly aphrodisiacs.

Around the valley you may also notice pug marks of the snow leopard near the Lakshman Pass and hear its calls. The snow leopard is a dweller of the higher mountain and a haunter of the wild silences its call is shriller. In stealthy, stalking, skill and speed, grace and agility, the beast is unmatched. It has the longest tail among the feline species.

Mating takes place in February-March and the litter is born in May-June offer a gestation period of approximately fourteen to sixteen weeks. The litter consists of 4-5 cubs and live for about fifteen years.

Birds

There are plentiful birds in the valley. The Tibetan raven, yellow billed chough, red billed chough, wall creeper, brown dipper, white breasted dipper, collared bush chart, Indian redstart, Himalayan gold finch, scarlet finch, Ruby-throat, Blue rock trough, robin, hedge-sparrow, Garhwal hedge-sparrow, willow-warbher, rosy pastor, great rose-finch, red breasted rose finch, gold finch, gold fronted finch, rock-sparrow, red necked, snow finch, crag matlin, pied wagtail, yellow headed wagtail, long billed calandra lark, hoope, swift owl, little owl, Himalayan griffon, vulture, lammergeger, or bearded vulture, shahin falcon, eagle, tawny-eagle, buzzard, Turkistan hili pigeon, pintail, monal pheasant, Himalayan golden eagle, and many others, like rock sparrow, the mountain cousin of the house sparrow. Their feathers are flutter, soft and fuzzy and also cover their eyes.

- Barret owlet
- Blue magpie (Red billed)
- Chough Red billed
- Eagle-Himalayan golden
- Eagle-Tawny
- Forktail-Himalayan
- Forktail-spotted
- Gold finch-Himalayan
- Griffore Vulture
- Hoopoe
- Laughing thrush white crested
- Oriole golden
- Paradise flycatcher
- Parakeet
- Partridge
- Pheasant-Kaleej

- Pheasant-Koklas
- Pheasant-monal
- Pheasant-peacock
- Pigeon-rock
- Pigeon-snow
- Ram Chakor
- Scarlet finch
- Shahin falcon
- Tragopan
- Tree pie
- Wagtail-white
- Woodpecker.

Alaknanda Valley

The Alaknanda, more ancient than the mountains themselves, dominates the Garhwal landscape. The stormy river cuts deep gorges through the mighty Himalayas till it tumbles into the muted, clear green waters of the Bhagirathi to form the placid Ganga. The narrow Alaknanda valley is broadest, perhaps a kilometre across, at Srinagar, once capital of the old Garhwal kingdom. The grey silt brought down by the 1970 floods still stands nearly a meter high near the roadside. Half the town had been swept away in the early 1800s and again 70 years later.

About 500 years ago, according to local tradition, the Alaknanda valley had been divided up into over 50 chieftainships, each with a fortress or "garh"—giving the country its name.

Srinagar itself, however, is growing into a bustling town with the Garhwal University. Orchards are being developed and the Malta orange thrived in the valley, besides apples, peaches and wild apricots in the hills.

The lower slopes are tinged a delicate red, for the forest trees had sprouted new leaves. April in these mountains is a beautiful season: the searing orange spikes of the Indian coral and the crimson flowers of the majestic silk cotton are in full bloom. The lower forests, now badly denuded, were once tiger country. At Rudraprayag, immortalised by Jim Corbett, you are stopped by simple stone slab which marks the spot where Corbett slew "the dreaded man-eater".

The roads are good and in April there is not much traffic. But contrary to the hill-driving rule of down-going traffic giving way to up-coming traffic here all vehicles give way to the army. An angry defence official is perhaps feared even more than the furious Alaknanda. But this apart, on the hill roads everyone is a friend and anyone's trouble is your trouble. You have a breakdown, truck drivers stop, offer help, loan equipment, give you a free ride.

The journey up the Alaknanda is marked by the confluences of its tributaries. The villages are at these "sacred" confluences and on the banks of the tributaries.

Approach to the Valley

Wanting an unusual holiday, you set off for the Bhyundar valley in the Himalayas known as the Valley of Flowers, the beauties of which have been extolled by the famous British mountaineer, Frank S. Smythe. The journey there, though long and arduous, is interesting.

Arrive Rishikesh and reach Joshimath, the next day you resume overnight journey from Joshimath enroute to Badrinath. The summer rush for Badrinath almost over in September and the few pilgrims bound for the holy place. The metalled road in excellent shape along the gorge of the river Alaknanda and in about an hour reach Gobind Ghat; nearby the confluence of the Alaknanda and the Lakshman Ganga (also called the Bhyundar) descending from the region of the Valley of Flowers about 15 km. away.

It is dusk when you got to Chamoli, 200 km. from Rishikesh and about 1,100 m. high. It is still very much a "chatti", a small cluster of houses, Gopeshwar, is the district headquarters, across the river and up the next hill. Off-season accommodation is no problem; there are Government dak bungalows, forest department and private rest-houses along the pilgrim routes. You may carry your own rations, stove, fuel and all. But at Chamoli, as everywhere else you are inundated by the local people's hospitality, for in the hills a stranger is as welcome as one's closest friend.

Dropping off to sleep the surging sound of the Alaknanda becomes such a habit. Many images come to mind: an early, early morning walk, watching the sunrise.

Sprawling Gopeshwar with avenue trees and cultivated gardens and spacious buildings.

The drive up from Chamoli to Joshimath and beyond is a chilling experience as you passed the twisted Belakuchi bridge, devastated in the 1970 floods, and places where trucks and buses had gone careening off the road or where landslides had come hurtling down.

Across the Alaknanda is an elephant-shaped mountain, the Hathi ka Pahar which people believe will collapse, cutting of the road to Badrinath. In a temple just below, the deity's wrist is slowly wearing away. When it breaks, the mountains will descend, the legend says. And for that future, already at Joshimath, there are two mini-shrines, the Bhavishya Kedar and Bhavishya Badri.

Better facilities will be available to tourists visiting the world acclaimed Valley of Flowers in the Garhwal hills after some years hence.

A tourist lodge offering 24-bed accommodation is proposed to be built at different centres, an important stage of halt, on the way to the valley under the tourism promotional programme for the hills.

A couple of centres in the Garhwal region with hot water springs are also proposed to be developed.

A chain of new tourist bungalows and pilgrim sheds, is proposed to be built along the pilgrim routes to the famous Himalayan shrines of Badrinath, Kedarnath, Gangotri and Yamunotri which attract thousands of pilgrims annually. On the construction of these new tourist lodges the number of pilgrims visiting the shrines is expected to register a marked increase.

The next day you may drove up to Govind Ghat where a bridle path branches off to the Valley of Flowers and Hemkund, where Guru Govind Singh is said to have meditated. Distances are not much but the gradient is steep. Badrinath is just 35 km. away, but 1,300 m. higher. You shed much luggage at Joshimath but it took a few hours to roll, fling, push, pull, carry and almost will your things down to the hillside to the log hut on the river banks.

Gobind Ghat (1,829 mts.) is well known for its Gurdwara which a landmark on this route, from where the common hilly track to the Valley of Flowers, and Hemkund branches off from the motorable Badrinath road. The Hemkund Sahib Gurdwara on the picturesque Lokpal lake is an important Sikh pilgrim centre, a short distance from the Valley of Flowers.

As you down crossed the Alaknanda by a steel rope bridge. Your trekking started with a half kilometre long steep climb after which the slope becomes easier. The monsoon rains produced a luxuriant growth in the green forest on both sides of your way, decorated with occasional clusters of roses and rhododendrons all the way till the small slumbering village of Pulna.

From Govind Ghat you climb the steep path along the Bhyundarganga, a tributary of the Alaknanda. The hillsides are lit up by the early morning sun and the brilliant red rhododendrons. The petals are used to make a local chutney, the trees lopped for firewood. On the way are Pulna and Bhyundar, twin villages. The families move down to Pulna in Winter and go up to bhyundar when the snow has melted in May.

Pulna is the winter resort of locals in Bhyundar village situated higher up—which you reach after a 7 km. circuitous climb. It consists of a few slate-roofed huts clustered round the confluence of Kak Bhusandi Ganga. A sudden gust of chilly wind makes you realise that you are at an altitude of nearly, 2,500 mts. in the Himalayas. You continued your journey for another 3 km. reaching the forest lodge at Ghangria—your night shelter, situated at an altitude of 3,050 mts. The Garhwal Tourism Development Corporation has developed this lodge into a tourist bungalow where accommodation can be booked. The GTDC also organises conducted tours from Delhi and Rishikesh during the 'season' in the Valley, i.e., from July to October. Besides there are log huts and tent accommodation as well as the Gurdwara where pilgrims prefer to stay.

You have first taste of the snow, near Bhyundar, 2,400 m. high. Taking a tumbledown a frozen tributary of the Bhyundar Ganga. Till 1847 geologists had doubted there were any glaciers at all in the Himalayas. It took some effort to learn to walk on those snow-slopes.

From Gagaria, you trek a distance of two kilometre and cross to the right bank of Lakshman Ganga by another log bridge. you enter into an awe-inspiring gorge. Towards, the left bank of the river sheer rockfaces rise thousands of feet. There are trees and bushes have clung to this rockface at a number of places. The right bank of the river, though wooded, is fairly steep.

Six kilometres trek and gentle climb will take you to the grave of Joan Margaret Legge. Here you have clear water of streams, available for drinking as well as for cooking.

After 2 kms. from the bridge over Lakshman Ganga the hanging glacier of the Nilgiri Parvat comes into view. To the left this massif lies the Narayan Parvat belonging to the main Great Himalayan Range. The land beyond the bridge is thickly wooded. Not a sound is to be heard nor any life to be seen except an exotic bird, or if you are lucky, a must deer or a snow hare. Even the hum of insects seems to be left behind. The nurmur of the Lakshman Ganga to the right is the only sound in the early morning.

On entering the zone beyond the tree line, you will have an enchantingly beautiful view of the mountain range. This is one of the grandest sights of snowy landscape in the world. Far away in the yet dusky sky, and rising like pinnacles, the rosy twin peaks of Rataban flash into view with Arjun Peak to the left and Ghori Parvat to the right.

The rising glow of the morning sun reflects from peak to peak and then descends to the lower snow pinnacles, bathing them in a soft rosy light. As the rays of the sun touch the highest, and then in quick succession the lower peaks, these crests and crags melt away in comparative distance into amber and frosted silver against a deep blue sky. As the sun rises higher, the peaks fade into cold bluish grey massifs. If you are an early riser, you will enjoy the view. Beyond the tree line, the gorge opens perceptibly you will be passing a bare rock face. Where the winter snow of Narayan Parvat sliding down to the Laxman Ganga has left rubble and permanent marks. It is a bare spur, devoid of any trees. However, you will find plenty of flowers growing here.

You move upstream for about half a kilometre, and you will cross this rivulet over a long bridge and thereafter enter the valley. For your night half, you may use a huge rock shelter which is situated at this entry point.

When the sun rises higher, the view of the snow is magnificent. As your eyes wander over the amphitheatre of dazzling peaks, it is arrested by the towering mass of Rataban. The twin peaks glow like a red arrow of blood smeared arrow. Now you have entered a freezing paradise which thaws with summer as the sun quickens this valley to colour, exuberant verdure and a wealth of butterflies and fauna. The Valley of Flower is the land where fantasy turns into facts and lives.

From here you look downward, the views of the snow to the Nag Tibba Range. The rising clouds and mist form a vast woolly white sea, whose tide of rolling billows surges among succession ranges and tangled valleys. The higher azure ridges standout as small island in this sea of clouds.

In the valley you are as a rumbling moraine waste of seasonal glaciers surrounded by a luxury of exotic flowers reading down the slopes on all sides upto the idyllic bank of the Laxman Ganga. Tender new leaves are unfolding after a night of dew and rain. Birds are singing from twig to twig, seeking mates, you will find a new life all around.

Exactly on your front are the snow pinnacles of the Himalayas, to your right are the lower wooded slopes of the Hathi Parvat, to your left are the lower steep slopes of Nilgiri Parvat and to your rear are the Nag Tibba Ranges in the far distance.

On moving about two kilometre up along the right bank of the Laxman Ganga, you may camp near the rock shelter where the slopes of Nilgiri Parvat meet the valley.

There are two sides from where you may enter the valley. One over the Kunt Khal and the other from Niti where the valley of river Amrit Ganga across the Laxman Pass.

The Tolchha women of Niti cross over the Laxman Pass and descent to Ghagaria in the opposite direction of your approach. It is the extremely difficult route. The women take this hazardous treck annually to bathe at Laxman Kund. They do this for the good health and longevity of their menfolk.

Bhyunder or Lakshman Pass

Once you have explored the charms and beauty of the lower reaches of the valley and you are fully acclimatised, it is time to venture higher. On the northern side is the Bhyunder and to the west is Kunt Khal.

Lakshman Pass

The route to Lakshman Pass goes to along the river. First along the river of water i.e. Lakshman Ganga and thereafter, along the river of ice i.e. Lakshman Ganga Glacier. The lateral moraine of this glacier is most difficult to tread on. You will find huge boulders, precariously balanced, which might shift with the slightest of weight are strewn all along till you hit the sheer rock face where the west slopes of Ghori Parvat and the south face of Ratban massif meet. Here the Cipra glacier descends from the Ghori Parvat to merge into the Lakshman Ganga glacier. Near the confluence, there are a few ice caves.

Now you take a sharp left turn to climb on the right lateral moraine of the Lakshman Ganga glacier. A tough climb of one hair takes you to the lunar landscape of the glacier of Lakshman Ganga. To the left and right are the marks left by the mammoth glaciers of bygone eras. Ahead lies the Nilgiri massif, to the right of which is the Bhyunder Pass.

Rataban is placed further right and is not visible from here. You would now be able to see her peak near the hanging, glacier which is about five kilometres from here. Beneath the feet lies million of tonnes of centuries old ice which inexorably inches forward to the snout of the glacier.

You walk for half an hour and you will see another peak to your right—the Arjun Peak to the other. The river Amrit Ganga descends to the north of Lakshman Pass, on which lie the two Bhim Pass, rock bridges.

Now you are walking at above 16,000 ft. You should not be in a hurry. Be slow and steady. Tread on step by step. Wherever you are doubtful about the head of the rocks and age hardened ice, do not forget to test the ground with your walking stick, you will find bare ice faces appearing without the moraine matter. You find the real adventure and excitement at every step.

Now you are very near to your destination. A glacier descending from Nilgiri meets Lakshman Ganga glacier to your left. Just ahead of you lies a sheer rock face. After climbing for about half an hour through a rock slide you reach an elongated plateau which is about fifty metres wide and more than two hundred meters long. You may decide to camp here. It is a grassy patch full of flowers. You can not take a step without crashing scores of flowers growing here in wild profusion. Have a look towards the hanging glacier. These flowers are right upto the fingers of the ice.

It is strenuous pass surrounded by high peaks and flanked by perennial glaciers. It affords one of the finest views. The pass is a barren one. A descent of a few kilometres on either side transports you to a land of tremendous floral beauty. Here you will see hundreds of meters of charming profusion of primulas, potentialls, geaniums, forget me nots, anemones, irises, blue poppies, and dwarf rhododendrons.

You are in a region which is beyond the monsoons, ice-mounded by wide azure horizons. Very near to the pass are perennial snow fields, then russet cliffs and gradually the profusion of flowers emerges. The floral beauty will quicken the pulse of any naturalist or lover seclusion and beauty.

It is advisable to camp here. You may have a problem of getting the water till the scene is high. There may be some streaks of water appearing in the ice field lying ahead. As soon as the clouds lift from the valley you can see the beautiful face of Rataban. It is a pretty and awe-inspiring sight. You can see the beauty of the Garhwal Himalayas in all its manifestations in the morning when the sun rises from behind the northern slopes and in the evening when the fading, light transforms them into a mass of gold. You may spend a night over here.

The next day you may move up to the Lakshman Pass through a maze of huge boulders bared by the slow erosion of the ice. The climb to the pass will take about four hours. So much of plenty flowers that they will carpet your way—a red carpet of nature.

Now, you may make an ascent of the Arjun Peak. You may get a glimpse of the distant Mount Kailash in the trans-Himalayas, towering snow covered and serene at about 6716 metres above the sea level. Snow pinnacles of the Garhwal Himalayas lie all around. You can see the views of:

−Neelkantha, Chaukhamba
−Kamet, Abi Parvat
−Nandankanan, Uja Tirchhe
−Lampak, Hanuman

−Drona Giri, Changabang
−Bethartoli Himal, Nanda Ghunti
−Nanda Gond, Nandakhat
−Nanda Kot, Trishul
−Nanda Duri.

They all appear to be belonging to another world. Their lower ranges lie hidden in grey haze, above which tower the purple spurs of the higher peaks and ranges.

Now, is the time to return to the base camp before sunset. It is descend of four hours. While descending you can enjoy grand spectacles and the beauties of the valley. Some of the flowers and flowering bushes seen are:

— Androsace
— Anemore (wild flower)
— Asters
— Balsam
— Blue flavoured sharmrock
— Blue poppy
— Brahmakamal
— Buckler-fern
— Butter cup
— Climatis
— Cock comb
— Columbine
— Cornflower
— Corydalis
— Cyanthus lobatus
— Forget me not
— *Gerbers* languinose
— Gevanion
— Globe Flower
— Iris
— Jasmine
— Jaundice berry
— *Klobesia* laxa
— Lady Fern

- Lady's Slipper
- Larkspur
- Lily of the Valley
- Monkshood
- Moon-fern
- Oak fern
- Orchis Latifilia
- Pheleum ealpinum
- Potentilla
- Primula
- Rhodrodendon
- Rock cress
- *Saxifrage evivivela*
- Sedum
- Snow plant
- Sweet Margoran
- Violet
- Wood lily
- Wood fern.

You stay for a day at the base camp. Thereafter you move towards the Kunt Khat. Kunt Khat is also another beautiful place of immense floral charm. If you intend to descent to Hanuman Chatti, through Kunt Khat it will take a trekking of two days. This is a less frequented route. The legendary Brahmakamal grows in real of profusion on this route. The Kamet expedition of 1981 had gone this way.

In the valley have is also a small pond called Nag Tal. An antirrhinum-like blue flower grows near this pond. It exudes poisonous odour which make men giddy. If you have time, you may wander on the slopes of Nilgiri, where you will stumble on to untold floral treasures of the Garhwal Himalayas.

An undulating plain on the right bank of the river is covered by lush greenery and garlanded with the sparkling waters of Himalayan streams. Beyond it stand silvery snow-clad peaks. The steep slopes of the valley are covered by a dense Bhojpatra forest (Bhojpatra Bitula) broken by several avalanche chutes.

The upper part of the valley is badly damaged by the moraines of the Tipra bank glacier. In its middle the banks of the Pushpavati are paved with stones and coarse debris. The lower part is the actual valley of flowers. This area is almost five kilometres long and less than two kilometres wide. The valley enjoys an alpine climate with temperatures seldom approaching 25°C. The mean elevation is 3,500 m. above sea level.

The valley has fascinated naturalists, tourists and pilgrims from all over the world ever since the rapid development of transport linkages in the Garhwal Himalayas and the emergence of Hem Kund as an important religious place. Unfortunately, the increasing human intervention in the Bhyundar valley has seriously damaged its environment, which is deteriorating day by day. The Bhyundar women raised their voice against this deterioration in 1972, which caused a threat to their livelihood and culture.

Here slopes ledges, terraces, barren rocks, running water, coarse grit are all crowded with millions of flowers of numerous hues and descriptions. Calling it fondly "the Valley of Flowers–a valley of peace and perfect beauty where the human spirit may find repose".

Frank Smythe's tradition is still being followed today. Every year from June to September numerous enthusiasts trek 14 kms. from Govindghat to Ghangharia in the Chamoli district of Uttaranchal. A stiff uphill climb for another 3 kms. from Ghangharia across the turbulent Pushpawati river and a glacier leads to a humble wooden bridge from where the first view of the magnificent valley sprawling in the foothills of the lofty Rataban peak 20,231 ft. can be had. The valley is home for about 2,500 botanical species out of which the 250 flowering ones from the main attraction.

Amidst Stone Huts

It may be mid-day when you got to Bhyundar, and freezing. Your eyes watered in the wind as you searched for refuge amidst the stone huts. The village is desolate, all the people being down at Pulna. But the narrow terraces of winter wheat were green and sturdy. Sown in September-October, the sprouts are covered with snow. They begin to grow again only in April when the snow melts.

At this altitude the broad leaved trees of the lower slopes replaced by the conifers, the cypress, cedar, pine. The spidery birch trees, stripped of their bark which is used for paper and packaging, looked shorn. The crimson red flowers of the rhododendron changed to a deep pink, becoming paler and paler, the higher you go. Bare, leafless willows hung over the waterside and other trees are covered with little white flowers, rather like ethereal snow-drops.

The delicate lilac-blue primula, the pale mauve, pansy-like viola, the clear blue gentiana, are among the first flowers out, much celebrated in English literature. And birds: you spot the Himalayan whistling thrush, sprightly hill robins, some flights of swallows. The crow in these parts has a pink beak and a characteristic hoarse voice.

Ideal Setting

You may be tramped in to snow to Ghangria over 3,000 m. high, leaving enormous sunk-in foot-prints as if a yeti had been this way, sinking sometimes knee-deep and taking a toss occasionally. Your shoes soaked through, walking bare-foot, uncomfortable and painful besides. At Ghangria, which is not a village but a few rest-houses in an opening of the forest, many roofs had collapsed and there may be nearly two metres of snow at some places.

You climb perhaps to 3,6000 m. Just above is Hemkund, the famed glacial lake, the flag of its gurdwara visible through binoculars. And in front through shrubby wasteland the entrance to the Valley of Flowers. It is an ideal setting for a snowfall and there is a snowfall, little white wisps of snow covering up the fresh footprints of a musk deer and giving the shrubs and the trees below a Christmasy look.

The mighty snow mountains seem to reduce people to inarticulateness, and no words can adequately express the experience. A much quoted sentence from the Puranas comes to mind:

> *"In a hundred ages of the gods, I could not tell thee of the glories of the Himalayas; as the dew is dried up by the morning sun, so are the sins of mankind by the sight of the Himalayas."*

Ghangria is the last human habitation in this region. At a little distance from the rest house there is a wooden bridge over the stream Lakshman Ganga where the bridle path bifurcates, the route to the left leading to the Valley, while a steep climb along the right leads to Hemkund. From the bridge you have a breathtaking view of the river cascading down from a dizzy height in the form of a mighty waterfall, its source being the Hemkund lake atop the lofty mountain on your right, which is just 6 km. away. You follow the path to your goal, the Valley, that is 4 km. away at a height of 3,660 mtrs. The ascent is not very steep, though at times rather difficult since in the rains small stretches of the path had been washed away.

Half way to the Valley you have to carefully negotiate a slippery snow bridge. Your vision had been restricted to a very short distance as a dense fog had pervaded all over the narrow gorge. By now large trees had practically disappeared but for a few bushes of white birches here and there with loose skins fluttering in the air like tiny flags. At places you have to wade through shallow streams tumbling down the hills on your left and crossing your path before joining the river to the right. The chill in the air make you feel that you have gained sufficient height. Then the sky start clearing up and suddenly the veil of mist lifted and a splash of bright sunshine greet you illuminating the surroundings. It seems as if the mountains are welcoming you by opening an entrance. For at last you reach a wide open space on the top, the gateway to your cherished goal—the Valley of Flowers.

Now, in this valley you find yourself roaming in a beautiful meadow, about ten square kilometres in area, surrounded by lofty mountains. The undulating valley is covered with lush green grass and foliage and embroidered with a variety of flowers of different sizes; shapes and hues—a natural garden laid out by the Almighty, which needs no human gardener to tend it. In the backdrop of this charming garden stands the majestic snow-clad Rataban peak, and further beyond, the Nilgiri Parvat. Several mountain streams criss-cross the valley gliding down to meet the Bhyundar river a little below. There are flowers, flowers and more flowers everywhere— Anemone, Geranium, Inula, Potentilla, Lily Poppy, Gentian, Primula. One stands there speechless, overawed by this feast of colour.

Concerns: Environmental and Ecological Aspects

Conservation does not mean preservation by systematic utilization of natural resources. Unfortunately the traditions and beliefs of the local people have never been studied prior to framing of any environmental protection policy. This is what happened when the valley was declared a National Park on November 6, 1982. Prior to the mid-'70s, though it was not a protected area, a perfect interaction existed here between people and nature. This was being destroyed by the forced environmental conservation policy.

The people living in the Bhyundar Valley had over the ages developed a perfect harmony with nature, through their beliefs and superstitions. The common belief in the region is that the Garhwal Himalaya is Dev Bhoomi (land of Gods) and God loves all its creations, tiny or gigantic, animate or inanimate. That is why rivers, trees, plants, peaks and even boulders are considered sacred and are worshipped. Mythological stories are connected with many of these. The myths enshrine the conservation policy of primitive man who understood well the boons and curses of nature.

The traditional occupation of people in the valley is goat and sheep herding and trade in wool and hides was the base of their economy. The shepherds take their sheep and goats to the valley but they are conscious of harm to flowering plants. They go into the valley bare-footed and treated the flowers and creepers with great respect because of their belief that these flowers where showered from haven by the gods when Lord Hanuman crossed the valley carrying the Sanjivni booti. The plucking and trampling of flowers and plants is considered an unpardonable sing against the almighty. The flowers are plucked for the worship of their deity only after the month of September, almost at the end of the season.

The entry of cattle had been banned in order to protect the environment of the valley, in opposition to the wishes of the inhabitants and without taking them into confidence. This has caused resentment and apathy in the minds of the traditional conservators of the valley. The forced alteration in the traditional occupation of the people i.e. keeping horses for tourists instead of sheep and goats, running dingy tea and refreshment shops and the inhuman task of carrying pilgrims from Govindghat to Hemkund on their shoulders, has reversed the harmonious interaction between the people and nature and affected the economy of the whole Bhyundar Valley.

In the absence of shepherds and their cattle the valley is suffering from an amoebic growth of weeds and their octopus net has capture almost half the area of the valley. These weeds displace the undergrowth of tender flowering plants. The shepherds uprooted such weeds as the valley was directly associated with their economic and religious beliefs. Cattle dung used to be good manure, essential for the proper growth of the flowering plants. Further, the hooves of sheep and goats were instrumental in soil formation.

Water from melting ice washes the whole valley in the summer, eroding its fertile soil. The encroachment of glacial debris from all sides is another threat. Avalanches bring huge amounts of debris. Because of weathering and erosion metamorphic rocks of central crystalline are being spread in the valley by numerous swift streams. This is destroying the forest cover and the abode of wildlife, particularly of the endangered Kasturi Mrig (Musk deer). It also covers the plants in the valley. Earlier, shepherds used to prevent the spread of debris in the valley by constructing stone walls and restricting the water channels.

Some tourists do much damage to the plants. They pluck flowers indiscriminately and cruelly crush plants and creepers beneath their heavy boots. People uproot medicinal plants from the valley. Therefore, the number of species, which were estimated to be 450, have been reduced considerably and some species like the Brahma kamal (Susaria obveleta), which flourish at altitude of 4,000 m., are on the verge of extinction. Occasionally acres forests and plants are cut down to prepare helipads for VIPs who visit the area. Almost 100 tons of firewood are required every month to meet the demands of the pilgrims and tourists—this is thinning the forest canopy.

Every seasons around 2000 tourists on a average visit the valley—a major section of this crowd are Sikh pilgrims to Hemkund Sahib located at 4,650 m. where Guru Govind Singh is said to have meditated in his previous birth. According to data available from the Forest Department visitors book—the first visitors to the valley on 1-7-83 were three French tourists and 86 pilgrims from Ludhiana. By the end of that season the number of visitors totalled to 890. The attraction is so immense that visitors went up as late as the months of October and November.

Unlike now very few people used to go up then. Only 100-200 pilgrims went up then to Hemkund Sahib, in

1960. Today on an average 20,000 pilgrims visit Hemkund Sahib annually. The demand for more and more facilities by the travellers is resulting in greater denudation of forests. Besides trekkers there is a constant traffic of animals—horses, mules which carry both luggage and pilgrims through Ghangharia to Hemkund. A middle-sized horse ping it every now and then is a common sight.

"The economy of the valley is tea shop economy"— the locals fell trees for firewood and thus the forests between Govindghat and Ghangharia are being ruined. In fact the area from Govindghat itself should be declared reserved. There are gurudwaras at Govindghat and Ghangharia and one at Hemkund. It is supposed to accommodate more than 1,000 people at a time. The camping in the valley has been stopped but not in Hemkund after all that too was a part of the protected forest area located on the Forest Map, guided by the Forest Conservation Act, but under strange circumstances has been leased out for 99 years."

The number of visitors in the past 10-20 years has been steadily increasing but their quality is not good. Seeing does not suffice, they don't walk across laid out paths, people pluck flowers, uproot plants and this depredation has caused havoc. The Hemkund region is rich in flora fields of wine red and yellow potentiallas, wild roses, geraniums, gualtheria and above all blue poppy. Mecnopsis aculeata and Brahmakamal or Saussurea Obvellata can be seen profusely. Brahmakamal is one of the most ravaged species. Almost every visitor plucks handfuls either as an offering or as souvenir. Some plant it in the earth to keep it fresh but sadly enough by the end of the trek they wilt away and are discarded by the nature lovers. "Now you have to hunt on the hillside, earlier they bloomed in abundance by the pathway."

Declaration of National Parks is not enough what has to be saved and how has to be decided first. Disuse has its own destructive effects. Overuses has to be avoided. Publicity is important because damages and dangers to the valley can never be culled. Information on valley either by way of photographic exhibition or slide-cum-lectures at Ghangharia, besides signboards in the valley and guards would do a great deal of good. Information on the valley is necessary since it has been kept open for people as a window of the High Altitude Vegetational life. Visiting it should become a learning process—enlightenment about nature's ways, the need is to conserve it with people's cooperation and necessary justification.

The Bhyundar hydel project and the Vishnu Prayag project on the base of the valley are a most serious threat to the valley. The sudden change in the river velocity and course will enhance the erosive capacity of the upstreams. Rapid side erosion due to corrosion of debris by the river causes bank slides, resulting in headward extension of erosion zones. This is inviting heavy attack by the end moraines of the Tipra bank glacier, which proceed towards the valley through the course of the Pushpavati.

Strong conservation measures have to be taken to project the environment of the valley. These measures should be traced out from the traditional beliefs and superstitions of the local people.

Sheep grazing should be permitted to local people and cooperative sheep farms developed in the Bhyundar Valley.

The government has stopped sheep loans in the whole alpine Himalayan region on the grounds that the rapid increase in the sheep population has caused serious damage to the environment by stimulating soil erosion. In fact the number of sheep has fallen considerably in Chamoli district itself as a result of occupational transformation. Moreover, no damage is caused by sheep rearing on the bugyals, as can be observed in the vicinity of Malari village and near Bampa in the adjoining Dhauliganga valley.

The glacial debris should be controlled by stone fencing.

Weeds should be removed. All this work should be done by employing local people.

The plucking of flowers and trampling of plants must be prohibited and at least six months' imprisonment should be the penalty for plucking flowers. Over-ambitious projects, may be fruitful for a short span of time but hazardous for the whole Himalayan environment in the long-term and they should be people planned and exceeding. Finally, the local people must be consulted and all pros and cons of the project must be explained to them, prior to framing and environmental preservation, conservation and regeneration policy.

Exploring nature's garden one comes to grips with the impending crisis in the valley. Frequent human contact seems to be threatening the very existence of the valley which from 1981 was declared the Nanda Devi National Park for conservation.

Enthusiasts scanning the hillsides for flora become disenchanted when they encounter tall and slender lush green leafy plants bearing bluish green and pinkish white flowers—polygonum vaccinifolium and polygonum polystachyum and pink blooms with lips spotted yellow—Impatiens Roylei or balsams in great profusion. Amidst them small colour of flowers struggle to show up. In the absence of printed brochures available at the forest checkpost at Ghangharia or any signboard displaying the names of the species or flowering season of the abounding flora one has no clue as to what one is seeing. Tripping or falling on rocks concealed fully by the polygonum visitors are forced to trample out paths in the jungles of polygonum looking for Smythe's floral store-house, flowers in the colony of thousands and millions, "that wonderful world etc." because the existing scenario seems quite different. Only two plant species balsam and polygonum especially seems to be invading the valipined. In the last five years polygonum has overgrown and the tender flowers are simply suffocated and are being smothered. Some say that the area was opened for grazing in the absence of which the polygonum might have spread a little more.

Polygonum which belongs to the Polygonaceae family grows up to a height of 4-12 ft. and yields white, light pink and rosy and bluish green blooms. Its sub-types in the valley are Delicatulum Meissn, filicayle Wall, Runicifolium Royle, Oxyria Digvna Hill etc. But it is the Polygonum Polystachyum which is on the rampage along with the pale pink or dark crimson balsam of the Geraniaceae family. Investigating high altitude vegetation with specific reference to the valley were across two Himalayan weeds which grow at places whose habitat has been repeatedly disturbed due to reasons natural or biotic caused by men e.g. burning, construction, grazing, digging deposition of new soil to name a few. The sophisticated natural flora is wiped out because their community vegetational structure is upset. Aggressive colonies i.e. the weeds then replace the growth. Smythe's own observation is thus "it was also very noticeable in Garhwal that where extensive grazing is permitted the smaller and tenderer plants soon eliminated in their place spring up a tall knowtweed Polygonum Polystachyum and an even taller Balsam Impatiens Roylei. Once these two plants have got a hold of the ground pasture land is permanently ruined.

Smythe seems to have under-rate the problem. Growing population, cattleheads excessive grazing initially and now tourist traffic in short due to increased human interference the beauty spot of Garhwal is dwindling. The situation seems to be alarming.

Grazing was stopped from 1983 onwards only and before 10-15 years it is premature to assess its harmful effects if any. The valley was closed for conservation and anything responds to conservation, in reciprocation it might change its composition and preponderance thought. The growth and decay of flowers in the valley is a natural phenomenon. Polygonum which is growing today profusely might die out some day totally.

The local residents claim that the cattle grazed on the

weeds helping the growth of flowers and the crisis has arisen due to the declaration of the National Park. The demand of the locals to cross the glacier and move to higher alpine pastures to graze their cattle and not enter the valley was rejected. Their fodder problem remain unsolved because conventionally they cannot move into the neighbouring pastures flanking other villages. The locals were stopped from plucking two species of wild onions and medicinal plants, from the valley, but as labour were engaged in plucking of medicinal plants from July itself when the plants are barely in bloom and the seeds are not set, instead of autumn when the plant is mature and the seeds are set and the continuity of the species is assured. No wonder their double standards have alienated people areas too. Interest in the valley will be lost if Polygonum takes it completely and smothers other plants. Stopping of grazing possibly is the only major change in the area it might have been a mistake and the park may be reopened to restricted grazing and limited cattle. Another reason for the excessive growth of polygonum might be excessive moisture seepage from the high hills.

The question that then arises is, whether there is no way of eradicating the weeds and will the valley be lost gradually? Cutting from the top did not help and chemical sprays cannot be used because they might kill the flowers growing together. The only effective way of eradicating polygonum is to uproot its corns or underground rhizome which spreads very rapidly. Weeding done in this manner has removed 75 per cent polygonum from the affected areas and flowering is in profusion. Done manually considering the area of the valley is 8,750 hectares uprooting, become a very costly operation and in which all and sundry cannot be employed for fear of flowering species also being uprooted. Uprooting also becomes ineffective since it cannot be done prior to the flowering because the weeds and the flowers spring up together.

"Selective grazing is a more feasible method of eradication because it reduces the seed potential". Cattle are selective and they graze on the soft and tender buds of the weeds checking their growth. Trampling much more than grazing is detrimental to the natural floral growth. Yet all methods of eradication can at best be unidirectional, failing to match and balance all components of the ecosystem. There is no way how the natural growth of a plant species can be totally stopped.

The most picturesque valleys of the world, has been overrun by two metre-tall grass, threatening the famed flowers with extinction. It has become imperative that polygonum ploystachyum be razed. As the grass is extremely fast-growing, it is a difficult task, but it is made all the more difficult by the vastness of the area to be covered.

Polygonum has already done irreparable damage to the Valley. The ecology of this area should be studied in detail, and regeneration aspects like seed biology and germination investigated. And—there is no doubt—the weed must be exterminated.

The 1984 decision to declare the Valley a National Park had put an end to cattle grazing. This has led to uncontrolled growth of the Polygonum. Prior to the ban, the cattle used to ensure the weeds did not outgrow the flowering plants. Polygonum ploystachyum is a highly succulent weed, which cattle—and even man—relish: the ban ensured that neither entered the Valley.

Apart from the grazing factor, even cowdung, and the movement of the cattle, used to ensure that the spread of the weeds remained under control. Ironically, it was the very trampling of the cattle which first caused the ban to be imposed—they had not discriminated, and trampled flowers too!

Scientists say the ban has benefited only some species, and might have altered the entire ecosystem. Most varieties of herbaceous flowering plants may be completely eliminated over time, they warn.

The Valley has gone from strength to strength, thousands of tourists visit the place, most of them during the peak season of July-August, when the flowers are in full bloom. But not all plants the Frank Smythe discovered still remain. He had mentioned some 1,500 varieties of flowers and some species of ferns. Today many, like Gentiana Aprica, Capitata, Golerata Wall, Daphne oleoides Schreb etc. have vanished from the Valley.

Nevertheless, some exotic species like the creamy anemone, purple, blue and pink aster, purple iris, blue poppy, white and red potentilla and yellow pansy still grace the place. Rare species of some ferns are also to be found.

Locals be immediately allowed to graze their cattle once again in the Valley, there would be no need for all kinds of external programmes to save the place.

It is high time that the central environment authority, State Forest officials and non-government organizations wake up to save the Valley of Flowers from total extinction.

5

Silk Route Expedition:
Central Asian Cultural Expedition

The Central Asian Cultural Expedition, comprising Indian scholars, journeying 12,000 km. across the ancient Silk Road in Central Asia, China and Tibet, have just traversed a branch of the Silk Road passing through Kazakhastan. The way from Chimnent to Dzambul, now linked by Highway No. 39, has witnessed intensive trading in goods that came from various directions, including India. The pace of trade and the nature of goods may have changed in the last 1,500 years but the buzz and noise of the market remains and you can still feel the dust of the centuries under your feet.

The Great Silk Route was truly a highway of history and culture. Thousands of years ago, it linked the great civilisations of Rome and China, ferrying goods and ideas across several nations and cultures. The first recorded traveller on this 6400 km road was Chi'ien, who was sent by Han Emperor Wu Ti in 138 B.C. to renew ties with distant Chinese allies and to explore possibilities of establishing a forward base for the silk trade with the west. The route, originating at Xian, followed the Great Wall of China and went north-west bypassing the Takla Makan desert and climbed the Pamirs to cross Afghanistan. Silk and jade went westward while wool, gold and silver came east. Other articles of trade included fur, ceramics, cinnamon and bronze mirrors.

As old civilisations fell and new ones were born, the route became not only a channel of commerce but also a thorough-fare for knowledge, art and religion. Missionaries and scholars travelled to the distant corners of the continent with the silk route as their compass. Nestorian Christianity and Buddhism came to China through this route. As early as 100 B.C., there were 12 caravans on this route every year, each with 100 men leaving China for Europe.

The route fell into disuse with the downfall of the Roman empire and remained so till the 13th and 14th century when Mongols revived the traditional trade route. During this time, came Marco Polo, a Venetian trader. At the age of 17, he travelled with his father and uncle, in a camel caravan, to the court of Kublai Khan, where he stayed for many years. Seven hundred-odd years later, a group of Indian travellers have retraced a part of this legend.

In the 13th century, Venice was a prominent trading outpost of Europe. Merchants took their wares to distant centres like Constantinople and the Crimea Niccolo Polo and Maffeo Polo, two brothers, were the leading merchants of Venice and were always on the lookout for a way to reach the Far East.

The Silk Route by then had become unsafe. Europeans had lost control over it after the rise of Arabian empire in the area.

In 1254, Niccolo Polo got a son, Marco. Four years later, the Silk Route opened after the Mongols defeated the Caliphet of Baghdad and established a Pan-Asiatic empire. When Marco Polo was only a toddler of six, his father and uncle left for Peking where they were welcomed by Emperor Kublai Khan, the grandson of Mongol Empire's founder Genghis Khan. After staying in China for nine years, the brothers returned to Venice but not after the Emperor had extracted a promise from them to return with 100 missionaries. Kublai Khan wanted to introduce Christianity in his empire.

In 1271, the Polo brothers went back again but not with

the friars. They took 17-year-old Marco Polo. The caravan took four years to reach the court of Kublai Khan where Marco was appointed as a civil servant. He had a gift for languages which enabled him to rise rapidly in the palace hierarchy and soon reached the Privy Council. Emperor Kublai Khan had so much confidence in him, that young Marco Polo was sent on secret missions and one such mission was to purchase Buddha's tooth in Ceylon!

During his 15-year service, Marco Polo travelled extensively in Tibet and Burma, becoming the first European to study at close hand the life and culture of Mongols and he acquired a great knowledge about India and Japan. In 1290, he requested for a leave from the Emperor to return to his native place. Kublai Khan refused.

Relief came two years later when Marco Polo was asked to accompany Lady Kokachia to Persia where she was to marry Kublai Khan's grand-nephew, Arghun, who was the Viceroy of Persia.

He made the journey by sea and when he reached Persia, he heard of the death of Kublai Khan. He did not return to Peking and continued on his way to Venice and reached his home town in 1295. He was then 41 years old.

There was a war going on in Venice at that time between the Republic of Venice and Republic of Genoa. He found himself drawn into the war when he was imprisoned by Genoese in the eastern Mediterranean Sea. He spent three years in jail where he wrote his famous *Book of Marco Polo*, which inspired, among others, Columbus.

He lived in Venice till 1324 where his townsmen could not believe the tales of his adventure and laughed at him. He was nicknamed "Marco Millions". His grave is in an unknown spot in the Church of San Lorenzo.

Kazakhastan, now the world's fourth largest nuclear power in terms of number of warheads, is a little smaller than India, and the relations between the two have been marked by warmth and affection. In 1920, Kazakhastan maintained trade ties with only four countries—India, Afghanistan, China and Mongolia—selling them in that year 993 tonnes of wool,

10,000 fur coats, 500 heads of cattle, 700 sheep, 300 pairs of felt boots and mittens.

The genuine warmth and love showered in abundant measure on the Indian Expedition by the Kazakh people came straight from their heart. The traditional welcome with bread and salt at the Uzbekhistan border; the sumptuous lunch served with fermented mares' milk on a grassy meadow overlooking the snow-capped Western Tien Shans; the several roadside receptions organised by the village folks; recitation of poems eulogising Mahatma Gandhi, Nehru and Indira Gandhi, visits to local museums that were kept open much beyond normal hours, smiling faces that beckoned strangers to step into their homes, curious onlookers who came up to shake hands and reaffirm *"Hindustan-Kazakhastan Dost"*, the 6-year-old Kazakh girl who danced on the Hindi song. "Zubi Zubi Zubi" could give Sridevi a run for her money; the friendly lady Director of the Cultural Institute who spoke neither Hindi nor English yet broke out into Raj Kapoor songs; the several jovial people who tried to impress the audience with their knowledge of Indian films and stars.

The expedition left the country with an image of the Kazakh people as affirmative and positive, spontaneous and warm, and who have respect and affection for the people of India.

The Great Silk Road is much older than the Kazakh nation. In the 5th century the farms on the Syr Daria were raising crops for sale and barter in the markets along the Silk Road. The Chinese pilgrim, Huen Tsang, who travelled in the A.D. 630s, on the caravan path of the Silk Road mentioned about the Turkis who inhabited the banks of the Syr Daria.

Russian traders on the Silk Road sent the caravan markets of Kazakhastan furs, linen fabric, trained hunting falcon, amber for Buddhist temples, rye barley, Laung and took from here the finest Indian cashmere, Muslim and other veils, rice, tea, semi-precious stones and Persian carpets, Hindu Kush sent it silk; Chinese their porcelain; the Arabs mineral wax. Byzantine brought velvets and silver and gold brocades. For sale Kazakhastan offered processed sheep skins that looked like satin, saddles, bows and arrows, gown, blankets, from tafetta lined with fox and ermine furs and cotton seeds.

Like all nomads and tribals, the Kazakhs value personal freedom and independence. When under Stalin's 5-year Plans, an attempt was made to collectivise the livestock of the Kazakhs, the nomads refused and instead slaughtered 24 million sheep and goats, 5 million cattle and 3 million horses in 1933 alone.

The ancient silk route has had such illustrious persons as Faxian, Xuan Zang, Marco Polo, the Pandit brothers Kishan Singh and Nain Singh traversing it—the silk route".

Spirit of Adventure

It took 8 years for Everester H.P.S. Ahluwalia and his associates to put together a team of mountaineers, scholars, film-makers and adventures and to chart out a route through a landscape which changed seasons with every stop-over. The route linked fabled places like Samarkand, Bukhara, Yarkand, Kashgar, Lhasa ... places imprisoned in the minds and words of other travellers, existing only in the imagination of the expedition members. No one knew what these places looked like and they all had different things to look for. Different things to dream.

The first Indian goodwill caravan led by the intrepid conqueror of the Everest, Major H.P.S. Ahluwalia entered China in June 1994. It consisted of 20 men and three women including H.C.S. Rawat, another Everest climber, scholars, film producers, photographers (including Soli Sorabji's son Harmazd) and an automobile engineer (because the caravan consists of five jeeps).

The convoy took off from Tashkent and wended its way through inhospitable, treeless mountain ranges of Kazakhastan, Uzbekistan and Kurgistan before entering China. It is permitted to drive through China into Tibet to Nepal and back home to Delhi on 21st July in time for lunch.

It was no means the first expedition through Central Asia across the Karakoram, Pamir and Himalayas: traders in skills, spices, fur coats, gold, silver and precious stones have been known to have used these routes over the centuries taking their merchandise to and fro from Europe to the Pacific coast of China. Buddhist monks trod the same pilgrim paths into India. So did the explorer Marco Polo.

It is called the Silk Route. Actually it is not one but dozens of routes, and Chinese silks were only one of the many products to be taken to markets thousands of miles away from where they were produced. It got its name only a hundred years ago when a German explorer, Barm Von Ferdinand Richtofen, wrote of it as *die Siedeustrasse*—the Silk Route.

However, the Indian expedition carried no silks, spices or precious stones. Its only merchandise is goodwill which though weightless, is also priceless.

It took Major Ahluwalia six years to set up this expedition and get clearance from the Chinese government. What do we gain by sending climbers to the Everest? What concrete benefits do our annual expeditions to the frozen crests of Antarctica yield? What is the point of risking lives rafting down the turbulent waters of the Teesta?

Materially, nothing. Spiritually, a lot. They keep the spirit of adventure alive. It may be borne in mind that Major Ahluwalia received bullet injury in his spine which crippled him from his waist downwards. And seated in a wheel chair he led this expedition.

There were 18 persons, including two women, in the expedition when it set off in jeeps from Tashkent, the Capital city of Uzbekistan, on May 18, 1974. Waving them off, the Hakim Bukhara said: *Mahan Resham Marg/Yeh Rishte Nate Jorta Hai/Pyar Mohabbat Bannt-ta hai.* (This Great Silk Route/creates bonds among people/and spreads love and affection. The first 293 kilometres took the expedition through Nurantnag hills and the Turkestan ranges to reach Samarkand, once the capital of Tamerlane the Great. It was then known as Afrasiabe. Bukhara was the next stop.

Both places are famous for aesthetically constructed buildings. Painted minarets and blue domes are part of the skyline here. In Bukhara, there are 360 mosques and 80 madarsas. The onion-domes of Samarkand can be traced to Moghul buildings in India, one such instance is Safdarjung's Tomb in Delhi.

In a dispatch from the Silk Road, Major Ahluwalia said he found the cities of Samarkand and Bukhara quite similar to that of north Indian cities where tiny shops on street corners sell *chhole-bhature*. "Both at Bukhara and Samarkand, *seekh kabab* and other meat delicacies beckon the hungry traveller at every street corner. The mixture of the aroma of freshly baked nan, blood red cherries and plums and delicious *kababs* makes this a gourmet's delight".

Leaving these ancient cities behind, the expedition drove through the beautiful Kazakhastan where the members were welcomed with open hands. The expedition leader recollected, "The genuine warmth and love came straight from the heart." The traditional welcome with bread and salt at the Uzbekhistan border; the sumptuous lunch serves with fermented mares' milk on a grassy meadow overlooking the snow-capped Western Tien Shans.

Bishkek is the Capital city at Kazakhastan. The area is so green and has so many trees that as if you are in a sort of Paradise.

Andhizhan is the home city of Babur, founder of Mughal empire in India. The warmth and goodwill with which they were received at Andhizhan truly make one believe that the real conquest is not of a land or a nation but of the hearts of the people.

Andhizhan is quite like Kashmir before the bullets started flying around all there. The birthplace of Babur is probably even more beautiful than what Kashmir was and, everywhere you go around the city you are greeted with love and affection—'Oh! from Hindustan!', the locals exclaim cheerfully.

Every bazaar has people selling cherries, plums and the choicest dry fruits out of baskets heaped with these exotic wares, and lined all along the streets.

Kirghizthan is like Kashmir, a mountain paradise. It lies

3,000 m. above sea level and has green and fertile fields. Much like our North Indian cities where one finds corner shops selling *Chhole-Bhature* here, both at Bhukara and Samarkand, *seekh kababs* and other meat stalls beck on the hungry traveller at every street corner. The mixture of the aroma of freshly baked *nans,* blood red cherries and plums and delicious *kababs* makes this a Gourmet's paradise. The route goes around Lake Issykkul, the second deepest lake in the world. It is a paradise on earth. Ancient caravans camped here on their way to Central Asia.

It is one of the most scenic places in the world. Incidentally, it was here that Rajiv Gandhi, while on a visit in 1986, had said that it was probably like paradise on earth.

Before entering China, the expedition stopped for a night halt at Tash Rabat Caravan Sarai, a massive stone shelter which is one of the oldest surviving landmarks of the ancient silk route.

Then crossed over into China at Turtgart. Preparations are to be made well in advance, and customs and police on both sides of the Chinese and Kazakhastan borders really work overtime to facilitate necessary clearances.

The expedition crossed over into China on June 3 where the Chinese team joined the Indians. The jeeps drove on to Kashgar, an important trade post on the silk route. Kashgar has always been a meeting point for five main spokes of the silk route. One such route led to Yarkand and across the Laddakh ranges into India. The Karakoram Pass, which fall on the way, was the route taken by Indian spice traders going to Yarkand and Kashgar to meet the silk traders.

On the 23rd Day, the team reached Hotan, the most important Buddhist centre on the southern limb of the silk road. Explorers have found Gandhar, Kushan and pre-Buddhist relics including a painting of Lord Shiva at Dandan-Oilik.

As the days on the expedition calendar flew by, the jeeps raced past Aksu, Kucha, Karashahar to reach Turfan, 950 ft. below sea level. It is the lowest point on earth. Nearby lies the ruins of Gaochang, a city founded in 1st Century B.C.

Chinese, Nestorian, Manichean and Buddhist remains have been discovered here along with ancient texts in 24 scripts and 17 different languages.

Heat began to take its toll here. "The heat would melt the tyres and small sand pebbles would get embedded in them only to shoot out as little bullets hitting at the wind screens and destroying and shattering them. Try and imagine driving through heat and sun without the wind screens, 90 kms. of hot desert roads and no air conditioning. No easy task", said Major Ahluwalia.

After Turfan, the expedition went past the great Takla Makan desert. Takla Makan means "those who enter will not come out". The desert is 1,000 miles wide and has proved to be a place of doom for the ancient caravans. Despite the awesome terrain and the troubles of seasons, the expedition members said it was a marvellous experience. Film-maker Gautam Ghosh was surprised by the sudden turn of weather and the ever-changing landscape. Mesmerised by the beauty of the rugged countryside, he shot several miles of film for his Doordarshan serial on the journey.

Dunhuang was a famous stopover. It is another oasis in the desert and a caravan sarai. Here lies the thousand Buddha Caves famous for their extensive Buddhist wall paintings and the oldest library. The first printed book of the world—*The Diamond Sutra*—and the largest statues of Buddha were also discovered here. After visiting these historic sites, the expedition left for Golmud, the least explored and the most beautiful region of China.

Now from the sandy terrain, the expedition entered the cold plateau of Tibet. The scenery changed dramatically. The altitude levelled at 12,000 to 14,000 ft. above sea level. The temperatures ranged from 50°C in the day to two degrees at night. They remember watching with wide eyes a sand storm turning into a snow storm.

Major Ahluwalia has some other fascinating memories of the expedition. He said there is a place called Kriya at the end of the silk route in China. Here no one has heard of India. "The remarkable feature of life in this part of the world is the daily 'night bazar'. Pavements are swept, tables appear, refrigerators and lights materialise out of nowhere and whole families dress up and come out. People enjoy drinking, dating and dancing at the roadside discos. There is, however, no crime here".

Fifty days after they left Tashkent, the expedition members reached the Forbidden City of Lhasa. "The drive to Lhasa was something special", said Major Ahluwalia, "Seven days and more at altitudes of over 15,000 ft. Most of the members suffered altitude and mountain sickness". The expedition reached Lhasa in time for the 60th birthday celebrations of the Dalai Lama.

After two days in Lhasa, the expedition left for Kathmandu where they crossed the border at Kodari. "It's like coming back to civilization", said young Hormozd Sorabjee, a professional photographer and journalist. He said throughout the Tibetan stretch, the food was awful, the living conditions primaeval and the weather torturous.

The expedition traced its way back to India through Lumbini, and reached Delhi. "It has been exhausting, difficult yet fantastic. The last two months have been wonderful", said Major Ahluwalia. "Throughout the five countries we travelled the feeling was that they were meeting along lost friends ... lost in the sands of time".

The expedition received a tremendous welcome everywhere, and even as they go for shopping they are recognised. "Shop-keepers have refused payment for our purchases. We have been treated like long lost brothers and sisters whose bonds have been rediscovered after centuries. We have been toasted everywhere and showered literally with champagne."

They move along the Silk Route weaving their association into a fabric of warmth and friendship, and even excited by the prospects of continuous and ongoing relationship between the people of these wonderful countries and their own.

The Historic 'Silk Route'

Seven hundred years after Marco Polo travelled the fabulous

route between Europe and China, Iran and the former Soviet republics in Central Asia are hoping to revive what brought prosperity and power to the region's countries up to the 17th century. Around 11 heads of states attended inauguration ceremonies in north-eastern Iran for the rail link between Mashhad and Sarakhs, a small border town with Turkmenistan.

The construction of a 165 km. rail link in north-eastern Iran completes the new "Silk Route" nearly one century after the visionary project was launched to connect China to Turkey.

Their presence illustrates the importance of the project which provides the missing link in the route allowing Central Asia and China access to the Gulf through Iran and to the Mediterranean through Turkey. Chinese Premier Li Peng has labelled the pan-continental rail link as the "Silk Road of the 21st century".

The new railway originates in Mashhad, Iran's second largest city after Tehran, and runs across rough terrain in north-eastern Khorasan province to Sarakhs, where it links with Turkmenistan's network. The Iranian network further connects Tehran through a 850 km. railway to the ancient Silk Route between the Alborz mountain range in northern Iran and the parched deserts of Dasht-e-Kavir in the centre.

From the capital, the network continues west toward Turkey and the Mediterranean.

The construction of a rail link has already connected northern regions of the country to Bandar Abbas port, Iran's main outlet to the Gulf and Oman Sea. The Mashhad-Sarakhs railway will shorten for a week the time needed to transport goods between Central Asia and the Middle East, according to experts.

The transport capacity of the network is presently estimated by officials at 15 million metric tons per year because it is a single rail for almost the entire route. Furthermore, the rugged terrain and often mediocre state of the route limit speedy passage. The layout of the rails also poses a problem as there is a mismatch between the distance between the rails in Iran, which is in line with international standards the former Soviet republics.

"The line is far from being commercially exploitable and its immediate economic impact will be weak as commerce between Central Asia and the West Asia is limited and will take years to develop", a European expert commented. "But in the medium term, if the needed investments are made, the benefits could be enormous for Iran and the region", the expert added.

The World Tourism Organisation (WTO) has taken the initiative in opening up the fabled Silk Road to tourists. Ancient monuments are glittering again under the Asian skies, old caravan serais are once again opening their doors to weary travellers and hotels and airports in exotic locations like Xi'an and Isfahan are getting the much-needed facelifts as the bold and the curious are once again following this enticing trade.

Stretching across more than 12,000 kms. from the Mediterranean Sea to the Pacific Ocean, the Silk Road was once the world's main trade artery linking the great civilisations of China, India, Persia, Mesopotamia, Byzantium, Greece, Rome and Egypt.

Along the fabled highway, cities and towns grew prosperous from the exchange of exotic, luxury goods. Their rulers built spectacular palaces, mosques, temples, caravanseris, mausoleums and other structures.

But it wasn't just silks, jewels, glass, porcelain, and spices that moved east and west but philosophies, ideas, cultures and even religions traversed this fabled thoroughfare.

With the collapse of the Soviet Union some Central Asian countries approached the World Tourism Organisation (WTO) for help. "Their economies were in shambles and with weak manufacturing bases, promoting tourism by providing a common binding factor seemed the only way of providing quick returns to shore up the national exchequers", says Dr. Harsh Varma, WTO's coordinator for the Silk Road Project.

In 1994, the WTO started giving help to the Central Asian republics such as Uzbekistan, Kazakhastan, Turkmenistan and Kirgizstan to market their exotic monuments and culture.

But soon they realised that the major tourist generating markets such as the US and Germany were not aware of the tourism product of these countries.

"Then came the idea of launching a project to promote the fabled Silk Road as a destination by binding all the Silk Road countries into one tourism product", says Dr. Harsh Varma, WTO's Regional Representative for Asia. Over the years, several countries with a Silk Road connection such as China, Japan, Iran, Turkey, Pakistan and North Korea have joined the project which is fast catching the imagination of those jaded with the "done" destinations.

Since it is difficult to cover the whole 12,000 kms. long route in a single visit, tour operators have developed shorter circuits to cover sections of the Silk Road depending on the proclivities of the tourists.

Though there are no precise figures to show how many tourists have so far set their foot on the fabled road, president of Iran's Tourism and Recreation Centres Organisation, Ali Ghamkhar, says that "we expect a big boost to the tourism industry in the entire region because of the Silk Road project.

"A new tourism product such as this will take time to really take off but already there is a considerable increase in the number of tourists coming to Iran to travel to Uzbekistan and other central Asian countries by road".

According to Dr. Varma, "one sure sign of the success of the project is that several airlines such as Lufthansa, Turkish Airline and Iran Air have now started flying to destinations on the Silk Road".

The WTO is promoting the Silk Road by organising travel bazaars at international trade fairs and helping out TV channels of various countries to produce films. One of New Zealand's private TV channel is going to start shooting a 26-part TV serial on the Silk Road soon.

WTO has also produced and released a Silk Road brochure profiling details about the Silk Road countries.

One of the key problems in packaging and promoting the Silk Road has been the travel restrictions as many governments still do not issue visas on arrival at a border post or airport.

Silk Road Project: Samarkand Declaration

With majestic blue-tiled domes and minarets as a backdrop, representatives from 19 countries met at Registan Square in Samarkand, Uzbekistan, on 5 October 1994 to adopt the "Samarkand Declaration" aimed at boosting tourism and economic prosperity along the ancient Silk Roads of Central Asia.

The "Samarkand Declaration on Silk Road Tourism" called on governments along the Silk Roads to reduce travel barriers, such as strict visa requirements, and to develop a joint strategy to promote travel.

Tourism shows great potential along the Silk Road. There are few places left on this planet with such a little-known, yet fascinating human history and wealth of monuments.

The Silk Road meeting was jointly organized by the WTO, the United Nations and UNESCO. It was hosted by the Uzbekistan National Tourism Company, "Uzbektourism".

Among the 120 delegates were tourism officials from Silk Road countries reaching from China to Europe and representatives of other international organizations such as the World Bank and the European Union.

The meeting approved a Silk Road logo to be used in joint promotions, adopted the Samarkand Declaration and came up with a series of recommendations that will form the basis for a Silk Road action plan.

The purpose of the Silk Road meeting was to begin developing a joint promotional strategy to increase tourism along the historic thoroughfares linking China and Europe.

The meeting was very successful in that all the countries involved were able to present ideas for cooperating in the joint Silk Road promotion—ideas that WTO will convert into a specific plan of action.

Pending adoption of the action plan, WTO will take the following preliminary steps to initiate the Silk Road promotion.

1. Maintenance and distribution of a list of contact people

designated by each country involved in the Silk Road project.

2. Distribution, in cooperation with the government of Turkey, of a by-monthly liaison bulletin on Silk Road tourism.

3. Organization of special Silk Road promotional events at the World Travel Market and ITB tourism fairs.

4. Distribution of the Silk Road logo, as a means of identifying affiliated tourism products.

Participants in the meeting listened to presentations from several Silk Road countries, including Turkey, Iran, Jordan, Malaysia and Italy, on their tourism resources relating to the Silk Road.

A presentation was also made on the Mundo Maya project—the world's first multi-national tourism product, which was launched three years ago by the countries of Mexico, Guatemala, Belize, Hobduras and El Salvador.

A full-scale marketing strategy was outlined by WTO Regional Representative for Asia, Harsh Varma. He suggested contracting an advertising agency to develop a Silk Road theme that will help create a clear and easily identified image for the project.

He urged marketing officials in the Silk Road countries to increase their knowledge of tourism generating markets through visits with tour operators, and advertising and public relations agencies.

He also advised Silk Road countries to expand their overseas representation and to publish a core of good-quality promotional materials focusing on the Silk Road theme, such as information manuals, brochures, posters and postcards.

For the Silk Road promotional project to move forward, Mr. Varma suggested that a high-level steering committee be formed, with representatives of national tourism administrations, the private sector and national airlines. The committee would meet twice a year to coordinate marketing efforts and could administer a joint promotional fund, to come from contributions of member countries or from third party donors, such as the European Union, which has been a primary funding source for the Mundo Maya project.

Participants also heard about joint UN/UNESCO/WTO projects at the heart of the Silk Road in Uzbekistan. The projects, which total about US $1 million, include restoration of cultural monuments and tourism development.

The restoration projects are aimed at preserving historic buildings and upgrading surrounding areas, so that they once again become lively, lived-in neighbourhoods with thriving businesses such as handicrafts.

Tourism development projects include training in statistics collection and processing; training in tourism facilitation, to streamline procedures for issuing visas, for customs control, and for improving reception at the airport; and assistance in drafting basic tourism legislation.

A unique feature of the Silk Road meeting was the participation of 18 European and Asian travel journalists selected by WTO. As guests of Uzbektourism, they were able to report on the WTO meeting as well as touring parts of the country, experiencing first-hand the joys and frustrations of visiting an emerging tourism destination.

WTO is to draft the Silk Road action plan, which will be distributed to participating countries for adoption at the second meeting of the Silk Road project to be held in Iran.

The Samarkand Declaration

We the modern travellers along the ancient Silk Roads of Central Asia meeting at the crossroads of these historic highways in the magical city of Samarkand to revitalize this avenue of contacts between East and West through tourism.

Fully aware of the cultural interactions between the peoples of Central Asia, highlighted by the UNESCO project "Integral Study of the Silk Roads: Roads of Dialogue".

Launch our appeal to all concerned for a peaceful and fruitful re-birth of these legendary routes as one of the world's richest cultural tourism destinations, and in particular we appeal.

To governments so that they create and implement joint strategies and programmes to promote both international and domestic tourism, calling on the professional assistance and expertise of the World Tourism Organisation, where appropriate; they consider, as soon as possible, the adoption of facilitation measures that would reduce travel barriers and stimulate tourist flows along the Silk Roads.

To the travel trade so that travel and tourism along the Silk Roads be developed respecting the established political, social, moral, and religious order; priority be given to developing sustainable and environmentally-friendly tourism; local populations always be the net beneficiaries of all tourism development.

To travellers and tourists so that when travelling, they show the greatest understanding for the customs, beliefs, and behaviour of the host communities and the highest respect for the natural and cultural environments.

To the host populations so that they increase their awareness and appreciation of the immense heritage of their countries and enjoy it by participating in tourism activities.

To other international organizations so that they take note of how effective results can be obtained and common goals can be achieved through practical and unimpeded cooperation, such as that undertaken between the WTO, United Nations and UNESCO.

6

Mountaineering and Mountain Climbing

The adventure of mountaineering may be defined as "the sport of attaining or attempt to attain, high points in mountainous region, difficult to access, primarily for the pleasure of the climbs". In mild term it may be known as walking up low mountains which offer only moderate difficulties. However, on the modern sense of the term it is the climbing in localities where the terrain and local conditions present much hazards. Therefore, from safety point of view, experience is very essential. For those contained this sport is going to be very dangerous. Some activities associated with mountaineering sport may be classified as:

- Rock climbing
- Ice or snow climbing
- Skiing in high mountains.

Mountaineering is slightly different from these sports. Firstly, its participants rely almost entirely on their own powers of physical endurance and judgement to reach their goal. Secondly, they require no artificial field of action, and thirdly, the whole environment is just about all of the opposition for the mountaineers.

Man has an urge to climb mountains and conquer nature. He has a desire to achieve what appears him impossible. He has a great spirit of adventure for this type of sport. He has a curiosity to explore unknown region. This all provided him a real driving force to take the adventure of mountaineering.

"Something hidden—go and find it, go and look behind the Ranges. Something lost behind the Ranges, lost and waiting for you; Go!"

The term 'mountain' refers to the most difficult type of land for man to occupy and utilise successfully. For agricultural activities it is most inconvenient. The temperature in these mountainous regions is too low to pursue agricultural and cultured crops. It becomes difficult and in some regions impossible to inhabit during the cold winter seasons. Not only in India, but all over the world, the worldwide practice is the migration of livestock between mountain pastures in summer and lower altitudes the rest of the year. This may be called as trans-humane practice.

Another most important problem is the obstacle to transportation in the mountains. In the interior areas it is difficult to interchange the goods and people between low lands on opposite sides. We find that on all over the northern borders of India the passes and routes are in prominence. The military campaigned to assert control of mountain passes. Moreover the wealth of cities that controlled trade of these passes, and the historical importance of trade routes using these passes always emphasise their importance.

While Indians have discovered the Great Outdoors late, growth has been brisk. More and more Indians are pulling on their hunters, strapping on rucksacks, and wearing faded denims, to explore the hills near their cities. School outings are giving way to hikes, and college camps and picnics are becoming minor expeditions. Posters of Four Square kings with hunks of guys doing rock climbing, and the Campa Cola river-rafting advertisements with all the macho ingredients thrown in, have made mountaineering a glamour sport.

But, alarmingly, awareness of dangers and risks remains minimal. The young, new enthusiasts suffer from over-confidence, ignorance of basic safety rules, and are often under-prepared, ill-equipped, and worse, careless. In 1983, for example, youngsters went to Rudugaira wearing hunter shoes—four returned with frost-bite. These boys just don't listen to you. They are arrogant; they feel they ha *r*e read a book and that's enough.

Commercial interests have worsened matters. Travel agencies, with little experience of the terrain, have announced treks in the Himalaya. Moreover, new climbers are often ignorant about nutrition. Use of inadequate equipment also makes for disasters. Indian mountaineers are known to use helmets sparingly, though it is considered necessary for rock climbing. A 15-year-old boy slipped and died in Kashmir because the rope he was attaching himself to was frayed, and no one had bothered to check.

What is happening is that new mountaineers have reduced mountaineering to only a competitive peak-scaling sport. Older affectionates are appalled by this. The Soviets even wanted to include mountaineering in the Olympic movement, but top international mountaineers vetoed the proposal. Mountaineering is not about conquests: you cannot conquer nature, you conquer your own weaknesses.

Besides competitiveness, high costs are also forcing mountaineers to develop a ruthless spirit of do or die. Expeditions are getting expensive and since mountaineers are dependent on corporations for funds, they do not want to return with failure and the prospect of no future sponsors.

Bringing in an attitudinal change is the prime need. Mountaineers feel discipline and humility can bring about this change. Clubs are debating ways in which injuries can be prevented and slip-shod management by institutions be made more accountable. Also, insurance for mountaineers is a must. A policy of Rs.1 lakh costs only Rs.500 for a four-week expedition, and the high cost of post-accident care is sufficient reason for members of expeditions to insure themselves.

Medical Guide to Climbers and Trekkers, is for more efficient evacuation methods and the elementary knowledge of physiology among mountaineers, since few doctors can spare two months every year to accompany expeditions. The I.M.F.

can organise evacuations, including the use of helicopters, but has no medical facilities at its disposal.

Senior climbers advise parents to check the antecedents of leaders and organisations before packing their kids off on expeditions. The setting up of a centralised permit-issuing authority is essential. At present, the home and defence ministries, district magistrates, state governments, I.M.F., and, in some cases, even tehsildars have the authority to issue permits, allowing inexperienced teams to take to the mountains.

Ultimately, what really matters is that you go with people you know: that establishes trust, reduces competitiveness, and targets like height become less relevant.

Infrastructural improvement, streamlined permissions, responsible leadership, awareness of one's limitations, and especially attitudinal changes, can make mountaineering the rewarding experience it is meant to be—of breath-taking panorama, shimering lakes, sky-high peaks and camp fires on starlit nights. Mountaineering is not so dangerous, as awry altitudes are.

Snow/Ice Climbing

Ice climbing is another adventure and challenging sports on high mountains covered with snow. Winter climbing became popular after 1920 along with the increasing interest in skiing. Some great peaks, either snow or rock, have been climbed in summer and winter. But winter climbing is generally restricted to snow climbs. There may also be possibility of cross-country skiing. In most of these areas a crevasses of a glacier are largely filled up with snow in winter. Therefore, certain ascents may be easier and convenient at that time.

Rock climbing in winter will be difficult. You will find that in mountaineering there are many dangers and risks specially for those who are inexperienced and those who do not take the assistance of guides who are well acquainted with local conditions. Objective dangers are usually due to:

- Weather condition

- Falling rocks
- Avalanches of snow or ice
- Concealed crevasses or cornices.

Before you plan to undertake any ice climbing adventure it is essential to study the weather conditions. You will find that there are sudden weather changes in the mountainous regions.... In Himalayas, the days are extremely hot, they freeze during the night and is very much affected by monsoon seasons. This all presents a great risk and grave danger for climbing.

In most of the mountains sleet on rocks transform easy condition into difficult one. The problems of rock falls are always localised on certain part of the face of a peak, in gallies or couloirs which provide natural funnels for storms that may be loosened higher upon the face of the mountain. Therefore, any climber who takes a route up such gallies are thus exposed to the dangers of other falling rocks. A route which clings to a ridge is practically immune from such risk.

Loose rocks are most likely to fall when the ice of the previous night in which they have been held begins to melt in the morning sun light. Similarly avalanches are restricted to a identifiable part of a peak. The experienced climbers/explorers must identify such places before planning to ascent on the mountains. The condition of a mountain snow also increases the danger of avalanches. Dry flakes when first fallen do not cohere. With an angle of response of around 25° any slope of fresh snow steeper than 25° must be considered with caution.

Snow Climbing Equipment

Indispensable Items

Clothing:
- Woollen or thermal underwear
- Wind proof outer garment preferably parka type
- Head gear and mittens of suitable warmth
- Cleated boots
- Heavy socks

Equipment:
- Snow glasses
- Sunburn preparation
- Compass
- Map
- Water proof
- Match Box/lighters
- Scout knife
- Ice ax
- Climbing rope
- Crampous
- Rusk sack
- Folding lantern/flash light

Occasionally Required:
- Extra rope of lighter weight
- Pitous
- Snap rings
- Hammer (for difficult rock climbs)
- Tents
- Sleeping bags
- Clothing equipment (for major snow climbs)
- Aneroid barometer
- Oxygen tanks (for high altitudes such a Himalayas)
- Camera—suitable according to mountain conditions

Improved Equipment

The training of alpine troops and the improvement of equipment that resulted from research and much to aid the mountaineers. Some items which have appeared are:

- Warmer clothing for freezing weather
- Collapsible stores
- Light oxygen tanks
- Masks
- Feather weight boots
- Other articles of clothing to combat sub-zero conditions
- Lighter portable radio

- Walkie-talkie
- Mortar like avalanche gun.

Personnel: Selection of a Team

The selection of the member of the party depends on the individual personal knowledge and experience and records of the climbers. Personalities of individual have a way of becoming more pronounced under the strain of constant close contact at high altitudes all human responses tend to deteriorate—soundness of judgement as well as normal courtesy.

A party of three members is an ideal one for a single day's climb. A small party will have less delay in traversing unusually difficult, where only one of the party is less than three members, there is difficulty of rescue of a member if he falls into a crevasse. A larger party will be required for an expedition into an unexplored region. The help of porter will also be required for such expeditions.

Guidelines for Ice Climbing: Ascending

If you plan a snow climbing adventure, your party should consist of three experienced amateurs of guideless or two amateurs and a guide. You should start from bivouac or camp close to the snow line as above. Start as early as possible in the morning i.e. several hours before the sun rise. The air should be crisp, your clothing must be warm. Use a folding lantern. All members should be roped together at intervals of about 20 to 30 ft., as soon as you slip into the neve (firm) of the glacier. The experienced climber should lead the ascent and the weakest of three member should be in the middle. As soon as you find the sun rises, you will find, that sun glasses are *de rigueur* on snow or ice. If you find soft snow or much step cutting in ice is necessary, each member must spell the others as leader.

The gait should be slow, so that no one in the party gasps for breath. Vertical ascent is a fast climbing. At low altitude a strong party may ascend up to 2,000 ft. The speed depends and may drop if seriously difficulties are encountered such as difficult rocks and step cutting.

A challenging aspect is to find a point where the bergschrund can be crossed. Bergschrund is the large crevasse just beneath the rock at the end of the glacier. Each member of the team should take sufficient care that their feet are securely placed at every step on snow or on rock. While ascending on rocks do not dislodge any loose stones, lest they fall on those of below. Use your hands to balance yourself. To check any accident slip the rope should be kept tout between members of the party.

If you are going to encounter different rocks, it is advisable to use pitons or pierced iron spike. It is driven by the leader into crack above him as high up as he can reach. A snap ring is then slipped through the piton. The leader passes this rope through that ring, which is hauled up with that rope by other members to the level of the piton. He ties himself with a separate spare rope and proceeds to drive yet another piton still higher. He works way up to it the same way. This helps the party to overcome the difficult pitch of rock. The last man of the party on the rope retrieves the snap rings, and pistons if practical.

This will be safe for securing footing only after the fresh powder snow has become packed into settle snow. It is generally seen that settle snow does not avalanche. The wet snow avalanches in case steep water percolates under an accumulation of snow on an ice base, or smooth rocks or on grass slopes of even moderate steepness. Slides of wet snow are dangerous to the entrapped climber. There is also a danger that an avalanche coming to rest the heavy wet snow settles into a solid frozen block of near, ice from which the climber cannot extricate himself. In case of powder snow avalanche, there are chances of being caught up, suffocation and swept over a cliff.

An experienced and competent climber, you should never venture further when snow conditions are in themselves dangerous. You will encounter many instances of concealed crevasses on glaciers and unsuspected snow cornices that give way suddenly, these are very dangerous.

As regards to subjective dangers in snow climbing, these are basically related to inexperience and lack of training of the mountaineers.

If you are an experienced climber you can easily avoid all the subjective risks and at the some time foretell bad weather physical conditions. You require muscular physical training and acclimatisation to the rarefied air of high mountains. This is very essential. If you are not acclimatised you will definitely have mountain sickness on a climb. Any member of a party, having poor physical condition is a source of danger to the expedition.

At low altitudes the halts could be made after every two hours or so. At higher altitudes you may require a more frequent halts. As a leader you must change continuously under the following circumferences:

- Condition of snow
- Danger of avalanches
- Falling rocks
- Concealed crevasses or glaciers
- Unsuspected cornices
- Possible changes in the weather.

When you are crossing wide snow fields, you are advised to set willow wands. On rocks, you may erect stone claims at strategic points.

Descending

Care should be taken on descent. When you are planning to descent, the strong man of the team should be placed at the rear. He will be able to hold any of the others with the rope. In case you have to ascent, the rope is belayed about a projecting piece of rock, or about an ice ax wedged into rocks or driven into snow. Only one man should move at a time under such conditions. On difficult party, it is suggested to descend en rappel. Fatigue or a feeling of relaxation may make the member carelessness. It is seen that a large number of accidents on mountain have happened on descents in snow climbing.

The Himalayas are not just a refuge, for primitive forms of life. Human civilizations and cultures flourish here. The mountains are a meeting pot of plants, animals and human groups. The Himalayas are more than the word's youngest and highest mountains. They are a treasure house of knowledge that is anxiously waiting to be explored.

The Himalayas are like a magnet, drawing to them all those who have the indomitable will to challenge its slopes and glaciers. For centuries sages have crossed their high and hazardous passes is discover places of pilgrimage like Kailash, Badrinath, Kedarnath, Gangotri, Yamunotri and Amarnath. Again traders, hunters, and porters crossed Himalayan passes thousands of feet high to exploit the natural wealth of the mountains. These traders did not have the luxury of modern mountaineering equipment and evolved crude but functional mountaineering aids like lam, an old mountain boot, walking sticks with ferrule to mountain balance on steep slopes, yak hair ropes and jackets of lamb skin.

Mountaineering now long established in the Himalayas, is without doubt 'a natural high'. If you are physically fit, do not suffer from agarophobia (fear of heights) and enjoy the outdoors then mountaineering is the right sport for you. Government-run mountaineering institutes at Uttarkashi, Darjeeling and Manali offer quality instruction in mountain climbing techniques. A number of mountaineering clubs around the country organise mountaineering expeditions for novices. Rock climbing is also gaining popularity in the country. People are normally initiated into rock climbing by 'bouldering', or climbing smaller rock faces to learn about balancing, holds and the basics of the sport. No specialised equipment is required initially till one gains a fair amount of proficiency and decides to go for the higher rock faces. Most towns and cities in India have bouldering areas close by and it is a great way of staying fit and agile. Other than the mountaineering institutes already mentioned rock climbing courses are regularly run by an institute at Mount Abu in

Rajasthan and by a number of adventure clubs around the country.

Man has the urge to conquer the high mountains. In the past he crossed the valleys, peaks and mountains mainly three reasons: trade, pilgrimage and war. Now the motive of scaling and climbing these high mountains is totally different. Gradually a different kind of awakening has emerged and mountains have become a great source of attraction. All over the world, the high, hills and mountains have turned into adventure sports. The objectives of which are:

(i) Sports and recreation
(ii) Health resorts
(iii) Hunting ground for explorers and naturalists
(iv) Tracking
(v) Mountaineering.

Like Alps and other famous mountains all over the globe, Himalayas has become an adventure playground for men from all over the world.

In 1928, the Himalayan club was established with the basic aim to encourage and assist the interested people in Himalayan travels and exploration as well as to extend the knowledge of Himalayas and other adjoining mountain ranges through science, art, literature and sport. The club is totally dedicated for the cause of mountaineering and brings out its annual publication.

The Himalayan Journal: is serving the people by introducing mountains and hills to them.

Himalayan Mountaineering Institutes

With this accumulated fund of experience, it was thought necessary to formalise technical training by starting moun-taineering courses. Thus in November 1954, Pandit Jawaharlal Nehru inaugurated the Himalayan Mountaineering Institute in Darjeeling Tenzing Norgay the director of field training. The Institute's courses proved increasingly popular. Its alumni began participating in growing numbers on the attempt on peak spread across the Indian Himalayas such as Trisul, Kamet and Saser Kangri.

The year 1958 also saw the birth of the Indian Mountaineering Foundation (I.M.F.), the apex body for the sport in the country. It was now natural that Indian mountaineering should have looked towards Everest. The first two attempt in 1960 and 1962, both came within a few hundred feet of summit. Finally, in 1965, the Indian attempt led by Capt. Kohli, succeeded on Everest with a record nine members reading the top.

The level of participation in the sport has been transformed since last few years. Significant changes have taken place in equipment, technique and the degrees of difficulty being attempted. One by one the peaks of Kashmir, Himachal Pradesh, Garhwal, Kumaon and Kanchenjunga has been successfully visited.

On the very edge of the chain, in 1978 the unclimbed summit of Teram Kangri II (24,300 ft.) was reached by an Indian team which traversed the full length of the Siachin Glacier for 80 km.

Other institutes such as the Nehru Institute of Mountaineering and the Western Himalayan Institute of Mountaineering at Manali have similarly been instrumental in training an increasing corpus of qualified mountaineers. More and more emphasis is simultaneously being laid on steps for the protection of the fragile and the altered environment.

Mountaineering became interesting and adventurous, therefore, Himalayan Mountaineering Institutes were established:

(i) Himalayan Mountaineering Institute, Darjeeling in 1954.

(ii) Himalayan Mountaineering Institute, Manali, Himachal Pradesh.

(iii) Himalayan Mountaineering Institute, Uttarkashi.

These institutes are doing an excellent work for imparting training in different facets of mountaineering. It includes training in high altitudes, physiology, history of mountaineering, mountain fauna and flora, geomorphology, geology, map reading and glaciology, wildlife and methodology for mountaineering expeditions. Practical training of climbing up to 500 m. to 600 m. is also given. These institutes also import advance training and expeditions are carried out to well known peaks like Kamet and Trishul. Rock climbing is also a basic requirement of mountaineering as such the mountaineering club. National Mountaineering Federation and other clubs train young hogs and girls in rock climbing courses. Thus, there are number of clubs is promote mountaineering.

Mountaineering is an adventure sports involving lot of risk yet it is an interesting sport very closely associated with nature. It helps in developing the qualities of self-reliance, leadership and discipline in men and women. It also inculcates a sense of satisfaction in the achievement and attainment of the task. With proper training one can achieve all these qualities and a mastery in mountaineering.

Mountaineering has played an important part in bringing people together all over the world. It develops the traits of self-sacrifice, team spirit and endurance and above all a sense of comradeship amongst fellowmen.

History of Mountaineering

Modern mountaineering started in the Alps about 1850, when English sportsmen first began to climb there for pleasure. In those days the climbing was restricted to men. The expedition included professional guides as well as amateur sportsman. However, in the late 19th century women entered into the field of mountaineering. Many women made reputable remarks. Another turning point was the increase in guideless climbing.

Britishers and Himalayas

Before independence mountaineering as a sport was the pleasure and privilege of the European. The British were mostly concentrating largely on the Himalayas, especially the world famous Mount Everest (29,028 ft.). It straddles the Nepal-China border. It was named after Sir George Everest, Surveyor General for India in 1852. Several British expeditions had to turn back when 1000 ft. or less short of the summit.

There were other British groups which ascended Nanda Devi (25,654 ft.) (Joint British-U.S. Party), Kamet (25,447 ft.) as well as many peaks during 1930s. The famous British climbers in these parties were T. Graham, Browne, C.G. Bruce, George Leegh, Mallory, Eric E. Shipton and F.S. Smythe.

French and Polish parties were also scaling high Himalayan peaks about the same time. German ascent in 1936 of Siniol Chu (22,597 ft.) and Polish victory over the east peak of Nanda Devi (24,379 ft.) in 1939 are noteworthy. In addition, Willi Merki, Paul Bauer, Marcel Hurz and Mr. and Mrs. Gunther Dyhrenfurth were some of the leading Himalayan climbers from continental Europe.

The Himalayan Club created in 1927-28 had all European members. The French ascent of Annapurna (26,391 ft.) on June 3, 1950 under trip leader Maurice Harzog, made a deep impression on mountainous and general public and helped spur ascents of the next two years. Harzog and Louis Latheral, reached the top of Annapurna, the highest peak man had then mastered. They were caught in blizzard on the descent. Both of them suffered severe frost bite that afterward cost them part of their fingers and toes.

Mountaineering as a sport is said to have begun in the Himalayan only in 1883 when W.W. Graham, an European came to the Himalayas for the sole purpose of climbing. Graham was not the first foreigner to explore the Himalayas, many preachers and surveyors had been here earlier. As the interest in Himalayan grew, Indian helped as porters, agents and helpers till 1942 when Holdsworth and John Martyn, two school masters, escorted a team of three Indian school boys to the Arwa Valley. In 1951, Gurdial Singh led the first full-fledged Indian mountaineering expedition to Trishul and successfully climbed the peak.

Mountaineering in India

For centuries, the sprawling pyramid-like peak remained unknown to mankind. Surrounded by two thousand miles of enormous mountains, it was as remote and mysterious as the lands it stood guard; lands which concealed Lhasa, the shrine of Buddha, where no outsider had ever set foot.

It remained the demon-haunted refuge of spirits and mysterious beings, as the Central Asian legend went, until it was discovered by the Surveyor General of India in 1849. It was named Peak XV. And in 1852, after an extensive survey of the Himalayan ranges, Peak XV was established as the highest mountain in the world. This 29,002 ft. (later revised to 29,008 ft.) a massif of rock and snow, which became a challenge thereafter, was named Everest, after Sir George Everest, Surveyor General of India.

It was only after the end of the first World War in 1918 that plans for the first reconnaissance expedition were conceived in London. And in the summer of 1921, a full-scale, all British expedition set off for the forbidden 'playgrounds of the Gods'. Under the leadership of Lt. Col. Howard-Bury, who knew Tibet like the back of his right hand, a team of experienced mountaineers returned with a mass of geographical knowledge, a possible route to the summit and the Everest bug which has bitten all mountaineers since then.

In the team was a young school master with a brilliant climbing record—the legendary George Leigh Mallory. He was to play a crucial role in the first ever attempt on the summit.

Next year, in late March a group of 13 Englishmen, 60 Nepalese and north Indian hillmen, and over a hundred Tibetan coolies assembled in Darjeeling. This was the group of pioneers who took the challenge of Everest for the first time. Led by Brigadier General Charles Bruce, the team had George Mallory besides several other keen climbers.

The first camp was established at the tip of Rongbuk glacier at a height of 16,000 ft., about 16 miles from Everest.

General Bruce had planned to approach the mountain by Rongbuk and East Rongbuk glaciers, pitching three camps on the way, each separated by about five kilometres of trekking distance. The idea was to proceed slowly enough to acclimatise to the harsh and taxing environment. Base camp was set up just below the North Col.

The north-west face of Everest is bound by two main ridges which join at the summit. One ran down to the north-west and the other to the north-east and both equally difficult to climb. But half way along the north-east ridge, a subsidiary spur runs down to the north to a high saddle between Everest and a peak known as North Peak. The saddle is called North Col. It provides the only route to the upper part of the mountain.

Mallory and Somervell, a team mate, set out for North Col to set up the first camp. A difficult 3-day climb and a nerve-stretching steep ice-slope later they reached the Col and established the camp at an height.

During the past 72 years, ever since the first attempt on Everest in 1921, Mount Everest has been the ultimate symbol of human endeavour. During the last 40 years the highest peak in the world has been climbed from 13 different routes, and by over 550 climbers including 27 women. There have been triumphs and defeat, heroism and tragedy, in almost equal measure. 110 climbers and Sherpas have lost their lives on Everest. Over 50 people have climbed Everest without oxygen. One Sherpa, Ang Rita, has climbed Everest 8 times. Year after year there have been a record number of ascents. And yet Everest continues to be the crowning target and the ultimate goal for the world's mountaineers.

We recollect the best in adventure of the 1920s, the philosophy of Eric Shipton and Smythe, the heroic efforts of George Leigh Mallory and many others who in subsequent years blazed the trail through new approaches to the summit of Everest.

Over the years psychological barriers have been broken. There have been significant improvements in the quality and weight of several items of equipment, clothing and oxygen apparatus. Climbing Everest today is easier but not easy. For scaling the summit one still requires to stretch oneself to maximum limits of physical and mental endurance. Even on the comparatively easier South Col route it is a long way to climb. The rarified atmosphere and unpredictable weather still make it a great challenging task. A large measure of individual courage and team work are essential to surmount these challenges.

In the success of our women climbers there is a lesson to learn—"If our women can achieve the ultimate symbol of human endeavour, as a nation with determination and team work we can achieve anything".

In 1924, Mallory and Irvine were seen 500 feet short of the summit on the northern slopes of Everest. Noel Odell who was in the last camp, single-handedly and in a gruelling weather condition searched the missing climbers for three days.

Even today the world does not know whether the two perished before reaching the summit or on return after their maiden ascent. In India, the growth and development of mountaineering in the post-Independence era, has been closely linked with the ascent of Everest by Indians.

Today, as many as 100 mountaineering expedition venture into the Himalayas every year. 15,000 foreign trekkers and 5,000 Indian trekkers wake access its fascinating slopes and valleys in search of natural splendours. The Himalayas are no longer inaccessible. Improved road communications, reliable weather forecasting and well organised search and rescue facilities makes them the most challenging as well as among the fastest mountains in the world.

The earliest mountaineers in India were the Garhwalis and Kumaonis, who provided basic ground support to the expeditions and surveyors visiting the Himalayas at the turn of the century. Some of their achievements were remarkable. However, organised mountaineering by Indian began much later in the 1930s when in 1937 the seeds of mountaineering as a sport were planted by two Doon School teachers John Martyn and Jack Gibson, accompanied by Tenzing Norgay, crossed the formidable 19,000 ft. Alaknanda, Bhagirathi crest, the story was just beginning. Then on, groups of school boys were regularly initiated in mountain climbing techniques on the slopes of the Arwa glacier near Badrinath, Reinsara Tal in the Tons Valley and the lofty glaciers of Bunderpunch.

The first Indian ascent of a major Himalayan peak, Trishul (23,360 ft.) was made by Gurdial Singh in 1951. Two years later a number of events provided a strong thrust to the sport. Two years later a number of events provided a strong thrust to the sport. Mount Everest was climbed by the first time by Edmond Hillary with Tenzing. Further west in the Pakistan Karakoram, the killer mountain Nanga Parbat received its first ascent by Hermann Buhl who reached the summit alone. The Americans were beaten back after an epic struggle on the world's second highest peak F-2, in Kashmir, Nun was climbed by French while Nandu Jayal's team climbed Abi Gamin (24,130 ft.).

Invaluable logistic support to these pioneering ventures was extended by the Himalayan club, which was created in 1927-28.

The history of Indian mountaineering is very closely interwoven with the Everest Saga. Tenzing's climbs of Everest in 1953 resulted in the establishment of the Himalayan Mountaineering Institute, Darjeeling with Tenzing as the Director of Field Training. And with this started the systematic growth and development of Indian mountaineering. Four years later, Indian Mountaineering Foundation came into being.

Mount Everest

The 1953 successful expedition of Mount Everest opened up the gates of mountains for the future mountaineers. The Indian Sherpa Tenzing Norgay reached the summit of Mount Everest and mountaineering was accepted as an interesting and adventurous sports.

The keen climbers of Doon School, Dehradoon contributed towards mountaineering in the Himalayas. In 1942, they organised the first mountaineering expedition when students and teachers of the school—R.L. Holdsworth and John Martyn were able to set up a camp at Arwa Valley, glacier above Badrinath at a height of 5793 m. (1.),000 ft.). One of the student of this expedition late Major Narendra Jayal.

In 1951 the first major expedition was led to Trishul 7,122 m. (23,360 ft.) by Shri Gurdayal Singh with the school boys of Doon School, Dehradoon. A few year later, Shri W.D. Jayal joined J.J.M. Gibson on an expedition to Bandar Poonch.

On May 29, 1953 Tenzing Norgay and Edmund Hillary stood on the highest point on the earth. It was British expedition led by an Englishman, Colonel John Hunt. Ironically, neither of the two summiters was British. New Zealander Edmund Hillary and Indian Tenzing Norgay had climbed Everest.

Having become an instant national hero, Tenzing received many honours, and awards. He toured the country and sought to inspire the country's youth to set higher goals for themselves.

Tenzing's historic achievement is a source of inspiration for Indian youth. It was suggested that Tenzing's talents be used to train young Indians in the exciting and healthy sport of mountaineering. It was decided to set up the Himalayan Mountaineering Institute (H.M.I.) in Tenzing's hometown, Darjeeling.

Accompanied by six talented sherpas—Gyalzen Mikchen, Da Namgyal, Ang Temba, Topgay, Pasang Phutar and the youngest of them all, Nawang Gombu—Tenzing went to the Swiss Mountaineering School in Rosenlaui where they were put through an intensive course of training in the latest mountaineering techniques and also in training methods. A young Army officer, N. Jayal was chosen as the principal designate. He had previous experience in mountaineering and also attended the course in the Swiss School. Later, Tenzing and Nandu did a guide's course in Switzerland in which they distinguished themselves and acquired professional standard as mountain guides.

Arnold Glathard, the Principal of the Swiss School, came to India and surveyed in detail a suitable area in Western Sikkim as the H.M.I.'s training ground; he also drew up detailed training programmes. The foundation-stone of the H.M.I.'s campus was laid on November 4, 1954 by Jawaharlal Ne·iru.

In all these expedition-cum-advance courses, there is a tendency to create "gladiators", by including the stronger climbers again and again. This was a pattern which Indian mountaineering was to follow in meeting the challenge of Everest in later years.

The aggressive forays by our young mountaineers could not really be termed as a systematic or progressive method of training in advanced techniques. They, however, succeeded in capturing the imagination of young Indians for "living dangerously", as well as in focusing the attention of the Government, the public and the Press on the exciting sport.

Spurred by early achievements, a young Bombay solicitor, Keki Bunshah, submitted proposal to attempt Cho-Oyu, the sixth highest mountain in the world, in 1958. The expedition was launched in April, 1958. The team succeeded, with Sonam Gyatso and the famous Sherpa Pasang Dawa Lama reaching the summit. This was a big boost to Indian mountaineering. But India paid a heavy price on this very first major expedition.

After handing over charge to Brigadier Gyan Singh as Principal of H.M.I. in March 1958, Nandu Jayal had made a dash from Darjeeling to join the Cho-Oyu team in the mountains. On this rushed journey on foot, he was escorting Tenzing's sister who was carrying with her an infant. Tragically, she died on the journey. Jayal did double marches and reached the Base Camp only after the expedition had already started climbing up. Without giving himself the badly needed rest, or time to acclimatize, Nandu went straight up to Camp 1 at a height of 19,000 ft. He suffered pulmonary.

H.M.I. converted the advance course from the expedition bias to a systematic training course. The training included instruction in organizing high-altitude expeditions.

With his impatient pace, the irrepressible Nandu had set

the trend for young Indian mountaineers to live up to H.M.I.'s motto, "Climb from Peak to Peak". Since then, the appetite of our intrepid young climbers for mountain summits has been insatiable. Unfortunately, the stress on the peaks rather than on excellence in climbing techniques continued.

In the mean time, the Sponsoring Committee of the Cho-Oyu expedition were so elated by the first big success that they set their sights straightaway on Everest. Everest was booked for 1960 and the search for members, leader and equipment was on.

Gurdial Singh, a house-master of the Doon School who had scaled Trishul and had otherwise been quite active as a mountaineer, was chosen as the leader of the expedition. But for some personal reasons he chose to withdraw his name. The leadership of our first Everest venture, therefore, fell willy-nilly on Brigadier Gyan Singh.

With full support from the Government, Tenzing, individual officials, ordnance factories, industrial enterprises, and our green but keen mountaineers, a near-miracle was achieved. The Everest team was given intensive training on all faces of climbing Everest by Tenzing and his band of dedicated instructors. Newly made photo types of technical equipment and clothing were trial-evaluated and produced in India in record time. It was a matter of some pride for us that, but for the oxygen equipment and limited quantities of clothing and equipment for the summit attempts, most of the gear was manufactured in India. And in only three and a half months from the word go.

In spite of the devastating weather which this Expedition encountered, the peak was missed by only 700 ft.

The fuss and pampering resulted in a craze for "heights and headlines" among immature young mountaineers. Sadly, publicity and not the spirit of the challenge became the main allurement of climbing in the Himalayas.

Having made Everest virtually a matter of national prestige, he booked Everest for 1962 and started preparing for the second attempt by training the "gladiators" of the first expedition and new hopefuls by organizing smaller expeditions. It was a stronger and better equipped team in 1962, but it also missed the summit, this time by only 450 ft.

Undeterred, the Sponsoring Committee lined up the peak for 1965. The three intervening years saw a lot of expedition activity to select the third team. A well-trained, much better equipped and led team under Commander M.S. Kohli finally placed nine men on the summit in 1965. Thus remained a record for 17 years.

Earlier attempts on Everest and other Himalayan giants succeeded only by adoption of "siege tactics" by large expeditions launched on the lines of a military operation. Although there were some strong protagonists, like Eric Shipton, of smaller expeditions for Everest, finally it was a military officer, Colonel John Hunt, who succeeded in breaking the defences of the loftiest mountain.

There has, however, been a radical change in the trend for some years, particularly after the phenomenal rise of the super-star of mountaineering, Reinhold Messner. He has climbed all 14 peaks of 8,000 metres and above without artificial oxygen and, most of them, solo. But that should not make the young think that the new approach, the so-called "alpine style" climbing has become the in thing in the Himalayas. Nor have the Himalayas suddenly become the "Alpine play-ground". The real dangers of high Himalayan climbing are still there. In fact, due to the growing need for economy in the size of expeditions, the dangers loom even larger. The ill-fated Satopanth expedition of 1986, in which all three seasoned members and a high-altitude porter perished, is an example.

In the last four decades, over 1,150 Indian expeditions have been organized. The Indian Mountaineering Foundation, the apex body of the sport has sent a number of Indo-foreign expeditions which have climbed a few challenging peaks. All this has made India a leading mountaineering nation.

Despite this enviable record, Indian mountaineering has yet to evolve its own mountaineering culture. We still have extravaganzas bent upon achievement in the name of national, regimental or other parochial pride or prestige. Happily, we also have a small but excellent new crop of climbers who are highly motivated and sincere to the sport.

The main climbing areas such as Kishtwar, the upper Bhagirathi and Alaknanda Valleys, Lahaul and Pir Panjal divide above the Tosh Nala are all frequented by expedition from diverse part of India and abroad. Beyond the Inner Line, in the Nubra-Shyok triangle across the Karakoram, noteworthy Indian ascents have been made of Saser Kangri, Rind Mamostang Kangri and the peaks of the Chongkumdan basin.

Thus, you find the name of such well-known summits as Nan and Kun, Menthora, Mulkila, Dharmasura, Bandarpuch, Shivling, Kedarnath, Kamet, Trishul and others mentioned repeatedly in accounts of animal ascents. But while it is true that the number of expedition visiting the Indian Himalayas has grown phenomenally, there will always remain very special possibilities for adventure in the timeless dimensions of this spectacular wonderland.

Mt. Everest (29,028) is known as in Tibet as Chomolungma 'Mother Goddess of the Snows' or 'Goddess Mother of the Earth/Air'. It is a mountain to be described in superlatives— the highest and perhaps the most photographed and most written about mountain on earth. The Nepalese call it 'Sagarmatha', which means 'Head in the Sky' or euphemistically 'Sky is the Limit'. The Chinese call it 'Qomolungma'.

However, the most, elucidative name is said to be found in Tibetan secret writing as 'mi-ti-guti-chapu-lung-nga' which means you cannot see the summit from near it, but you can see the summit from nine directions, and a bird which flies as high as the summit goes blind.

Mt. Everest is rising 5½ miles into the air. The first attack on Everest was made in 1921. The first leader of the expedition to Everest was Col. C.K. Haward Burrey.

The Everest success gave a great momentum to the growth of mountaineering in India. The number of Indian expeditions to the Himalayas suddenly increased from 5 to 15 in one year, and kept on growing. Today there are over 150 Indian teams attempting various peaks in the Himalayas.

Chomolungma to Tibetans, and Sagarmatha to the

Nepalese, Everest was discovered in 1952 as the highest peak in the world. The saga of Everest makes one of the most thrilling and exciting accounts of human endeavour. Nepalese Sherpa Ang Rita reached the roof-top of the world, without oxygen, for the ninth time! Seven Indian girls, along with 10 others, reached the summit from the South Col.

The ascent of Everest in 1953 marked the real beginning of mountaineering in India. It was 10.30 a.m. on May 29, 1953 two members of a British expedition attained the summit of Mt. Everest for the first time. They were Edmund Hillary from Auckland, New Zealander and Tenzing Norgay, Sherpa guide and veteran Indian mountaineers. The news of ascent on Mt. Everest reached London on June 2, 1953 the day of Queen Elizabeth II's coronation. The thrilling news was announced on the morning of June 2, over the public announcement system, to the crowds in London who had assembled to witness the Coronation of Her Majesty, the Queen. The British success on Everest, which came after several years of efforts, was a gift to Her Majesty on her Coronation.

The maiden Everest climb was hailed all over the world. In India, Pt. Jawaharlal Nehru, Dr. B.C. Roy and the people of India rejoiced. The team was given a civic reception on arrival at Delhi. Jawaharlal Nehru presented his overcoat to Tenzing who was on his way to London with the British team.

Knighthood and Col. John Hunt was conferred on Hillary and Tenzing was awarded Col. John Hunt. Col. Hunt climbed the Himalayas in 1933, 1937 and 1940. He received recognition for his outstanding leadership and organisation of the expedition, without injury to any of its members. This happened to be the eighth team in 30 years to have attempted to Everest and there had been three reconnaissance expeditions. George L. Mallory and Andrew Irvine disappeared in a cloud high on Everest's northeast in 1924 and a Russian party also disappeared on the same ridge late in 1952.

In 1956, the British launched their final attack on Mt. Everest from South Col. Swiss also sent out two parties under the leadership of Albert Eggler, which reached the top on

May 23 and May 25, 1956. From the south Col. again on May 18, 1956, Frits Luchsinger and Ernest Russ made the first ascent of Lhotse (27,923 ft.), the world's fourth highest mountain. The triple victory was a major mountaineering feet. It has completed the conquest of nine of the word's ten highest mountains.

The sixth highest mountain Dhaulagiri (26,790 ft.) was finally completed in 1960 by six men Swiss team led by Max Eisetin. Team member Norman Dyhrenfurth, photographer for the 1952 Swiss attempt on Mt. Everest and sum of the Gunther Dyhrenfurths, was leader of the successful U.S. double assault of Everest with the first conquest of the west ridge in 1963.

Everest (8,848 m.), being the highest peak in the world, is the ultimate goal of mountaineers all over the world.

India first took up the challenge of Everest in 1960. Three members of this expedition—the late Sonam Gyatso, Colonel N. Kumar, and Nawang Gumbu—led by Brigadier Gyan Singh, missed the summit by 200 m. due to bad weather.

The second Indian expedition to Everest in 1962 was led by Major John Dias with Mohan Singh Kohli as the deputy leader. Three members of this expedition—Kohli, Sonam and Hari Dang—when sheer one hundred metres below the summit, were caught in a blizzard and had a miraculous escape; the trio spent three nights at 28,000 feet, two of them without oxygen, a record which till date has not been matched.

The third Indian expedition to Everest in 1965 was led by Mohan Kohli with Colonel N. Kumar as the deputy leader. This expedition was destined to set up a world record by putting nine people on the summit.

The late Colonel Avtar Cheema and Nawang Gombu reached the summit on May 20. Two days later the late Sonam Gyatso and Sonam Wangyal got to the top. Two days later on May 24, C.P. Vohra and the late Ang Kami reached the summit, and then a huge avalanche from the Lhotse face swept across and buried camp IV and with it all remaining oxygen bottles.

Instead of calling off the expedition the team dug out the avalanche debris and recovered all the bottles. On May 29,

1965 for the first time in history of Everest, three climbers—Major H.P.S. Ahluwalia, Harish Rawat and the late Phu Dorji, reached the summit setting up a world record by a single nation team.

The achievement was acclaimed all over the world. The people in India danced with joy in streets. The team was honoured in an unprecedented manner by the awards of Padma Bhushan for the leader (Sonam Gyatso and Nawang Gombu), and Padmashri to the deputy leader and other members who reached the summit.

Another notable honour was the conferring of Arjuna Award to the team as a whole which has been the only exception during the past 30 years. On their return to India, at Palam the team was honoured by the gracious presence of the acting Prime Minister, Shri Gulzari Lal Nanda along with several Cabinet colleagues. Smt. Indira Gandhi described it as one of the six major achievements of India in the post-Independence era.

Indians have reached the summit of Everest including Nawang Gombu, Director of Field Training H.M.I., Darjeeling who was the first man in the world to have climbed Everest twice—a large number by any standard and perhaps more than from any other nation.

The first Indian to climb Everest was Tenzing Norgay in the company of Sir Edmund Hillary on May 29, 1953. A year earlier, as a member of the Swiss expedition, Tenzing had missed the summit of Everest by a little over 200 m.

The first ever Indian expedition to Everest was sponsored by the Indian Mountaineering Foundation in 1960, led by Brig. Gyan Singh. Three members of the team—Col. Narender Kumar, Nawang Gombu and the late Sonam Gyatso, missed the summit by 200 m. and had to retreat under terrible weather conditions.

Earlier India had made attempts to scale Mt. Everest since 1960 out of which only two succeeded, one under Captain M.S. Kohli and another under Col. D.K. Khullar which included the first Indian woman summiteer Ms. Bachendri Pal and Mr. Sonam Palzor of I.T.B.P.

Two years later in 1962, India made a second bid on Everest, led by Major John Dias. Cap. Kohli was deputy leader of this expedition. They were once again deprived of the success when barely 100 m. short of the summit. Three of them—the late Sonam Gyatso, Hari Dang and Kohli were caught in raging blizzards and had a narrow escape, missing the summit. They spent three nights at 28,000 ft., two of which were without oxygen, an effort which has not been repeated so far.

After 1962, India could obtain the booking of the peak only for 1965. In those days, the Nepal Government allowed only one expedition at a time on Everest. In between an American team climbed Everest in which an Indian—Nawang Gombu reached the summit.

The 1965 expedition by putting nine climbers on the summit, in four parties, a set a world record for a single nation team which was held by India for 17 long years. India was then the fifth nation in the world to climb Everest. Nawang Gombu, who had climbed Everest with the Americans, became the first man in the world to climb Everest twice. Soman Gyatso at 42 became the oldest man to climb Everest; and Sonam Wangyal at 23 the youngest. They had climbed together.

Kohli was selected to lead the third Indian expedition to Everest with Col. Kumar as deputy leader. The team scaled Everest four times in succession within 10 days with nine people reaching the summit. In retrospect, the only single major contributory factor to this glittering record of success may well be the unfounded respect and faith with which they approached the eternally sacred Sagarmatha as if on a pilgrimage.

After a gap of 19 years the Indian Mountaineering Foundation decided to send a mixed expedition of men and women to Everest specially with the objective of putting Indian women on the summit. This expedition was led by Col. D.K. Khullar. It succeeded in putting five members on the summit including the first Indian woman, Bachendri Pal.

In 1984, a mixed team of men and women climbed Everest once again under the leadership of Brig D.K. Khullar.

The five summiteers including the first Indian woman Ms. Bachendri Pal.

In 1992 an I.T.B. Police team led by Hukam Singh reached the summit. In 1993 the Indian Mountaineering Foundation sent an All Women Team to Mount Everest. Two ladies from Nepal also joined in. Seven Indian girls and ten others reached the summit.

During the last decade teams from various countries blazed new trials on Everest. The peaks has been climbed through a dozen different routes. Messner climbed the peak solo and without oxygen. In all over 500 climbers have reached the summit of Everest.

Everest was attempted once again during the autumn of 1985. This time by an Indian Army team sponsored by the Army Adventure Foundation. The team was led by Lt. Col. Prem Chand, but at the last minute because of an arm injury sustained by him in a vehicle accident just prior to his departure, Brig. Jagjit Singh was appointed the leader in his place. This expedition was most unfortunate as five members of the expedition were killed on the mountain. It was, perhaps, one of the most tragic expeditions in the annals of Indian mountaineering.

After the abortive Army attempt and before the I.T.B.P. expedition, there have been two other Indian attempts in between. The Boruka Mountaineering Trust sent an expedition from the Chinese side from the North route, and a Pune team led by Dr. D.T. Kulkarni from the South-East Ridge.

By putting three of its men atop Everest, the Indo-Tibetan Border Police became the first police force in the world to successfully scale the summit of the highest peak on the earth. For the third time Indians have reached the summit of Everest, after a gap of eight years.

They included Assistant Commandant S.D. Sharma, Subedar Major Kanhaya Lal and Company Commander Prem Singh who have also been the summiteers of the third highest peak in the world Kanchenjunga.

The great achievement of the summiteers was that they

were able to make the last leg without oxygen that he is proud of their achievement.

A 15-member Indo Tibetan Border Police Expedition team to Mt. Everest led by Additional D.I.G. Hukam Singh was flagged off by the then Union Home Minister S.B. Chavan from Delhi.

In the annals of Indian Mountaineering this is the first ever endeavour by a Central Police Organisation to plan and launch an expedition exclusively within its own resources.

The team established its base camp at the height of 5,400 m. followed by Camp I at 6,150 m. on April 2, Camp II at 6,700 m. on April 11, Camp III at 7,600 m. on April 15, Camp IV at 7,981 m. (South Col) on April 20.

Thereafter the team made three summit attempts on April 28, 30 and May 2 which were thwarted by bad weather

On may 10, 1992 six-member team consisting of Assistant Commandant P.S. Papta, Sub Inspector Sunder Singh Martolia, S.I. Tajwar Singh, Assistant Commander S.D. Sharma, Company Commander Prem Singh, Subedar Major Kanhaya Lal left South Col. at 4.30 a.m. to make an attempt on the summit.

However, three members Mr. Papta, Mr. Martolia and Mr. Tajwar Singh returned from the midway because of indisposition.

The remaining three members reached the South summit at 11.45 a.m. but when they reached Hillary Steps at 2.30 p.m., they ran out of oxygen.

The team continued their struggle and finally reached the summit at 4 p.m. and returned to South Col at 9 p.m.

The team included deputy leader Dr. C.R. Pattanayak, second in command Vinod Kumar, assistant commandant Harbhajan Singh, assistant commandant S.D. Sharma, assistant commandant P.S. Papta, company commander, Prem Singh, Major Kanhaya Lal, (Miss) Santosh Yadav, S.I. Tajwar Singh, S.I. Prahlad Singh, S.I. Sunder Singh Martolia, S.I. Mohan Singh, S.I. Khem Raj Thakur and head constable Jodh Singh.

In the post-monsoon climbing season of 1985, the Indian

Army team ran into one of the worst kinds of weather that Everest can have and five officers died on the mountain and the expedition was abandoned.

The fluttering of the Indian tricolour on top of the world once again by the I.T.B.P. climbers has electrified the nation's pride. The Indo-Tibetan Border Police expedition, led by Shri Hukum Singh, Addl. D.I.G. of the Force and Hony. Secretary of the Indian Mountaineering Foundation, has put as many as eight climbers on the summit in two parties.

Of great significance is the ascent of Everest by the second Indian woman Santosh Yadav, the only female member of the team. Bachendri Pal had earlier climbed Everest in 1984.

By way of lending added value, reports of the Indo-Tibetan Border Police (I.T.B.P.) team's feat of climbing Mount Everest have repeatedly pointed out that the summiteers included a woman. No doubt, it gave a special thrill to a gender-conscious Indian public.

The quiet, unabrasive self-confidence, so evident in Santosh's manner is what seems to have helped her in developing and maintaining her interest in mountaineering right from her college days till now. She is not only a mountaineer of the highest eminence, but an active duty inspector with the I.T.B.P.

In retrospect, it may sound simple but behind the Indo-Tibetan Border Police successes lies an excellent team work, good organisation, competent leadership, great courage and high skill. With this spectacular success India has again emerged as one of the major mountaineering nations in the world and the I.T.B.P. as the leading mountaineering force in the country.

The first summit team consisting of Assistant Commandant S.D. Sharma, Company Commander Prem Singh and Subedar Major Kanhaiya Lal took eleven and a half hours to reach the summit at 4.00 p.m. on May 10, the last 90 minutes of climb and descent without oxygen.

The Indo-Tibetan Border Police expedition led by Hukum Singh was the seventh Indian attempt on Everest. After accomplishing a hat-trick in 1991—climbing the Kanchenjunga

and Nun and successful maiden rafting of Brahmaputra—
the success on Everest took the I.T.B.P. to its zenith. The
Force, which has climbed over 70 Himalayan peaks including
39 first ascents. Interestingly the I.T.B.P. is associated with
all the three successful Indian attempts on Everest. In 1965,
when led the successful attempt on Everest, he was on
deputation to the I.T.B.P. from the Indian Navy. During the
second successful attempt in 1984, Sonam Palijor, an I.T.B.P.
officer, was one of the five summiters. The third successful
Indian venture is a purely I.T.B.P. affair.

Such major expeditions are an expensive proposition
costing over Rs.50 lakh each but considering their impact
on the youth of the country they play an important role.
Each of such major ventures stirs million of our youths and
puts them on the path of adventure, individual climbers, funds
and foreign exchange required to equip the teams with oxygen
bottles and other essential personal equipment. Both were
advised by the IMF against attempting Everest. However,
considering their tremendous zeal and determination and
realising that on meeting certain basic requirements the I.M.F.
should not really come in their way, the teams were cleared.

The I.M.F. insisted that each member of the team be a
potential summiteer, with adequate experience of major
Himalayan summits. Besides, the organisers should hold
proper pre-Everest climbing camp and select the final team
based on their performance. The organisers should also give
proof of source of their funding and assure the Foundation
of procuring suitable equipment including oxygen. Both the
teams promised to meet these requirements.

There have been nearly 175 Indian mountaineering
expeditions. There is an increasing adventure activity along
our coast line and in the deserts. Apart from the ordnance
factories, several private firms are manufacturing all types
of equipment to make the country self-sufficient. Indian
tourism too has a strong adventure component. With the
deteriorating quality of life on the one hand there is the
welcome upsurge of adventure in the country. As the summer
heat has started there is already an exodus to the hills. Busy

old hill stations are giving way to tented villages. The Indian adventure scene is looking promising.

Women and Mountains

After 1960 Everest attempt, there was a persistent demand for mountaineering opportunities by the girls. In the first four years, the HMI, had already lost six strong and determined young male trainees as a result of a mysterious malady which was later discovered to be pulmonary oedema. The Institute was diffident about exposing young women to the physiological rigours of climbing high.

Young women had to be given a chance to prove that they could face the hazards of the heights, they said. The first basic mountaineering course for girls was, therefore, scheduled for April 1961.

Tenzing was used to see sherpanis climbing high with heavy loads on mountaineering expeditions. He was not one bit worried.

The 270-odd world mountaineers who had climbed Everest till 1984, included only four women. The girls had to be given a chance to show their mettle. Thus it was the main aim of our "Everest '84" expedition to see at least one and, if possible, up to four Indian girls on the Everest summit. Bachendri Pal, with barely three years of mountaineering experience and no other expedition behind her, was the only woman to reach Everest. She became the first woman to scale Everest.

First Indian Women to Assault Everest

Seven women were picked up by the Indian Mountaineering Foundation for the country's first ever bid to put Indian women atop the world's highest peak, Mount Everest, in early spring of 1984.

The seven women included in the team were Chandra Prabha Aitwal, Harshwanti Bisht, Bachendri Pal (all from Uttarkashi), Rekha Sharma (Delhi), Shiaravati Prabhu and Magan Bissa (Bombay) and Rita Gombu, daughter of veteran mountaineer Nawang Gombu, one of the few men in the world to hire the services of 40 to 50 famed Nepalese high altitude sherpas and 700 to 800 porters to ferry leads to base camp and the advance base camp.

The basic aim of the expedition was to create a world record by putting as many women as possible on top of the peak. They have picked up a team with a blend of toughness, experience and youth and are very hopeful that they would succeed.

The team imported equipment including the famous snow down equipment for warmth and clothing.

This was India's fourth expedition to Everest. The first being in 1960, under Brig. Gyan Singh and two years later under John Dias, both of which were abortive. However, a third attempt under Capt. Kohli put a record number of nine summiters atop the peak—a record that remained unbeaten for 17 long years till the Soviets put 11 people on the summit.

The expedition attempt and the peak from the traditional South Col route which was first followed by Sir Edmund Hillary and Tenzing Norgay.

Bachendri Pal

Beyond the South Summit the breeze increased. At that height eddies of strong winds whipped up the powder snow, reducing visibility to nil. On many occasions, they had to get into a crouching position with their back to the onslaught of the icy wind saturated with fine particles of bone-dry powder snow.

It was terrifying to stand erect on a knife-edge ridge, with a sheer drop on either side. They had to dig their ice-axe deep and secure themselves by attaching the waist-strap to the ice-axe head. There was some tricky climbing between the south summit and what is popularly known as Hillary Step. The goal was near. With renewed vigour Bachendri was on top of the step in seconds. The sun had made the snow soft and climbing was easier here than it had been earlier.

They trudged in the heavy powder snow for some time. Then the gradient started easing off noticeably. A few steps later they saw that after only a couple of metres there was no upward climb. The slope plunged steeply down.

"My heart stood still. It dawned on me that success was within reach. And at 1.07 p.m. on 23 May 1984, I stood on the top of Everest, the first Indian woman to have done so", said Bachendri.

There were climaxing moments. There was tremendous excitement in Dominic's tent in anticipation of the call from the summit. At 1.10 p.m. it was Lhatoo:

"Attention all stations. This is Lhatoo. This is Lhatoo speaking from the summit of Everest. As I stand on the highest point on this earth...."

"It took 5 minutes before I could interrupt and speak to him and say "very well done indeed" and to Bachendri, "You have done the team and the nation proud" and her heartwarming "Thank you, Sir".

"The walkie-talkie was back with Lhatoo, and he told us that they would like to be left alone for the next half an hour, for they had a lot to do, digging up souvenirs, carrying out photography and other chores of the religious. Paljore joined them after fifteen minutes, carrying one of his heavy oxygen cylinders.

"Magan had risen to the occasion and carried oxygen and juice for Paljore who was exhausted and resting at the Summit Camp.

"Triumph and tremendous relief. The news was now passed on to Kathmandu. Things would never be the same for anybody on his Everest Expedition."

Bachendri became the first Indian woman and the fifth in the world to go to the top, and Ang Dorji the second man in the world to climb Everest twice without oxygen. Clearly, it was Bachendri's inspired perseverance that had made the success possible. She was, in fact, the very inspiration. The credit was entirely hers. But she would not have achieved this feat without Ang Dorji. Let there be no doub¹ that the Indian Everest 1984 success story came to its cul nination solely because there was a Bachendri and an Ang Dorji on the expedition.

Expedition 1992

Three Indians belonging to the Indo-Tibetan Border Police scaled the 8,848 m. Mt. Everest on 12th May 1992.

Earlier in the day, 9 mountaineers of the Nepal expedition team and their five sherpas and two climbers of the national Dutch team along with their two sherpas had climbed the world's highest peak.

The successful Indians were Mr. Dipak Lokjung, Ms. Santosh Yadav, inspector and Mr. Mohan Singh, sub-inspector along with two Nepali helpers—Sange Muduk and Wangchuk Sherpa also scaled the world's highest peak along with them.

A report from I.T.B.P. base camp said the summit team had set out from the South Col at 3.30 a.m. and Dipak Lokjung reached the top of the world at 11.15 a.m.

He was followed by Ms. Yadav and Mr. Mohan Singh and the two helpers. They were at the top for 20 minutes and returned to the South Pole at 1 p.m.

The first batch of the Indian Mt. Everest expedition team of the I.T.B.P.—Assistant Commandant S.D. Sharma, Company Commander Prem Singh and S.M. Kanhaya Lal—had reached the summit of Mt. Everest at 4 p.m. on May 10.

With today's achievement, six members of the Indian Mt. Everest expedition team of the I.T.B.P. out of 15 members have conquered the world's highest peak.

A record 18 people reached the top of Mount Everest on 12 May 1992 and more were on the way.

Nepal's Tourism Ministry said the number of climbers reaching the top of the world's highest mountain was a record for a single day.

With development of high altitude clothing and oxygen, no doubt, it has become somewhat easier to climb Everest today than in the 50s and 60s. It must, however, be realised that to reach the summit of Everest one still needs to reach one's limit of human endurance—both physical and mental.

Objective hazards owing to blizzards, avalanches, and accidents still remain as in the past. Without exceptional courage one still can't venture into the critical death zone above 8,000 m. To reach the top of Everest one still needs the mercy of weather Gods. Even today no one, even the exceptionally tough, can reach the summit of Everest at will. Conquest of the high Himalayas is still unthinkable.

It will, therefore, be wrong to say that Everest has been tamed. It is of course true that human spirit continues to soar and with advances in technology and self-confidence more and more nations are attempting Everest.

Being the ultimate goal of mountaineers all over the world, Everest will continue to attract more and more climbers in the years to come. However, those privileged to reach its top will always be men and women of exceptional courage and mental endurance.

Everest, towering above the giant peaks of the Himalayan ranges at a mind-boggling height of 8,848 m., has always been a climber's dream. For centuries, it remained a virgin with puny humans trying in vain to struggle across its face to the summit from where the heavens seemed just a hand's length away. After Sir Edmund Hillary and Tenzing Norgay reached the summit for the first time on May 29, 1953, Everest became an attainable dream.

There have been 493 successful ascents of the 8,848 m. high Mount Everest, starting with Sir Edmund Hillary and Tenzing Norgay in 1953.

As Edmund Hillary and Tenzing Norgay prepared for their climb that morning, the legacy of the past 30-odd years of human failure on Everest weighed heavily on them. No one had done this before. It was an awesome thought in itself.

The dawn had broken clear, crisp and windless across the high ranges and by 6.30 a.m. both of them were ready to start climbing. They climbed higher, hard snow-yielding to their kicks and ice axes, ropes leading them safely across gullies and corniced ridges, till a great rock face, 40 ft. in height, barred their way.

It was the most difficult part of the climb. Hillary was to write later: "Taking advantage of every little rock hold, and all the force of knee, shoulders and arms I could muster, I literally cramponed backwards up the crack, praying that the cornice would hold". It held.

· The climbers were now on an endless ridge. The summit was hidden from them, and what they could see was not comforting—giant cornices and steep rock. They continued their struggle which had now become desperate. Body was tired, but not the spirit.

Then, they saw a narrow snow ledge which stopped somewhere in the middle of the azure sky. It was the summit of Everest, the place which till then had remained untouched by any human.

It was a momentous occasion; a triumph of human spirit.

The success on Everest launched a avalanche of interest in mountaineering as a sport both in India and elsewhere. Many began discovering the joys of mountaineering and the Himalayas became their playground. Now that it had been climbed, Everest became the favourite target of mountaineers all over the world.

Indo-Nepalese Everest Expedition

The Indo-Nepalese Women's Everest Expedition 1993, sponsored by the Indian Mountaineering Foundation, made a spectacular success by putting 18 climbers on the summit which included 7 women, 3 Technical Advisors and 8 Sherpas. Women climbers have brought glory to India. They have proved their mettle beyond any doubt. The team, under the competent leadership of Bachendri Pal, has established seven new records.

Three members of the team—Santosh Yadav, Kunga Bhutia and Dicky Dolma—reached the summit at 1215 hours (Nepal time) on May 10, 1993, accompanied by Technical Advisor Baldev Kanwar and four Sherpas. They had left the 26,000 ft. high South Col (Camp III) at 0100 hours, and after spending half an hour on the summit, returned to South Col at 1830 hours. They have been on their toes for seventeen and half hours.

Earlier on May 5, 1993, three members—Anita Devi, Deepu Sharma and Nimi Sherpa (Nepalese member)—under raging blizzards, were beaten back when 250 ft. short of the summit, and were forced to return to South Col (26,000 ft.) past 10 p.m. Moonlit night must have helped in their safe return to the South Col after twenty and half hours of high drama and gruelling climb.

On May 16, 1993, four more girls, Deepu Sharma, Radha Devi, Suman Kutiyal, Savita Martolia, two Technical Advisers, Shri Rajiv Sharma, Nima Norbu, and four Sherpas reached summit at 1045 hours. They returned to South Col at 1830 hours. The first All Women's Indo-Nepalese expedition has set seven world records:

(a) The largest number of women (eight) from a single country to climb Everest.

(b) The largest number of persons (eighteen) from a single nation team to climb Everest.

(c) The only woman in the world to climb Everest twice (Ms. Santosh Yadav).

(d) The youngest woman in the world to climb Everest (Ms. Dicky Dolma—age 19 years).

(e) Largest number of women from a single team to climb Everest (seven).

(f) Deepu Sharma, after having missed the summit by sheer 72 m. (South Summit) on May 5, returned to attain the peak on May 16—a feat unheard of before.

(g) Nimi Sherpa and her husband became the first Nepalese husband-wife team to reach South Summit.

This spectacular success has established Indian women climbers amongst the foremost in the world. The achievement has electrified the entire nation and is likely to usher in a new era in which adventure and mountaineering will receive big boost.

The nation salutes the spirit of adventure displayed by the three Indian women when they climbed the highest mountain peak in May 1993. That they accomplished it against heavy odds and after an unsuccessful attempt by their batch-mates earlier makes it all the more inspiring. The fact that they were part of the first all-women expedition team makes their achievement unique. The Indo-Tibetan Border Police (I.T.B.P.) officer, Ms. Santosh Yadav, has become the cynosure of all eyes because she is the first woman to make it to the Everest-top a second time, the first being in 1992 when she was part of an I.T.B.P. expedition team. Equally creditworthy are the performances of Ms. Dicky Dolma, who, at 19, has emerged as the youngest climber to set her foot on Mount Everest, and Ms. Bachendri Pal, the first Indian woman to climb Everest and who led the expedition. Notwithstanding all this, there is no denying that conquest of Everest is no more what it was 40 years ago when Sir Edmund Hillary of New Zealand and Mr. Tensing Norgay of Nepal created history by ascending the peak. That on Monday there was no standing space at the zenith with 38 climbers having made it to the spot is a commentary on the present state of affairs. As reports have it, the number is an improvement on the previous record of 32 set on May 12 last year. The availability of better communication equipment, insulated boots and clothing and logistical support have·over the years made the expedition easier though cases of failed missions are not few and far between.

There was not even standing room atop the world's highest peak on May 10, 1993.

A total of 38 people climbed Mount Everest, the record for a single day.

The summiteers included the first woman to climb Everest twice, Santosh Yadav, and the youngest woman to scale the peak, 19-year-old Dicky Dolma, the Ministry said. Both are Indians.

The 3 Indian women climbers, who unfurled the Indian

tri-colour on the world's highest summit, Everest, returned to their South Col camp happy, proud and obviously tired after a gruelling 17-hour trek back from the peak.

The three climbers, Santosh Yadav, Kunga Bhutia and Dicky Dolma left their last camp with four Sherpas for the 8,848 m. high summit at about 1 a.m. hours of climbing and a good weather helped them scale the peak in the noon when they unfurled Indian and Nepalese flags and made personal offerings to Sagarmatha, as the Everest is lovingly and reverently called by the Nepalese.

They returned to their camp at South Col at 4.30 p.m., said Capt. M.S. Kohli, president of the Indian Mountaineering Foundation which sponsored the all-women Indian expedition to Everest.

He said the first attempt was made by a three-member team of Anita Devi, Nimi Sherpa and Deepu Sharma on May 5. They had left their camp at 2 a.m. for the summit but bad weather and high winds stopped them just 250 ft. short of their aim.

The successful summiteers, had taken the traditional route from South Col after pitching four high altitude camps at Black Rock, two on the Khumbu Ice Fall and the fourth at Lhotse Face. He said the climbers had opted for the alpine style of climbing which was more strenuous.

The expedition was led by Bachendri Pal, the first Indian woman to climb Mount Everest in 1985. Ms. Santosh Yadav, an I.T.B.P. officer, has also climbed the highest peak last year as part of an I.T.B.P. mixed expedition. With yesterday's climb, she became the only Indian woman to climb Everest twice.

This was the fifth Indian expedition to Everest. He said the first two expeditions were unsuccessful. The third expedition led by him in 1965 put a record nine men on the highest peak. The fourth expedition in 1984 put Bachendri Pal, along with others on Everest.

It was significant and proud moment for India when four women of the Indo-Nepalese expedition conquered Mount Everest at about 10.45 a.m. on 16th May 1993. Two

Americans, along with three sherpas also climbed the highest peak in the world.

The four women who scaled Mt. Everest today are Radha Devi (20), Dipoo Sharma (21), Suman Katiyal (25) and Savita Matoliya (24). While Ms. Radha Devi and Ms. Dipoo Sharma hail from Manali in Himachal Pradesh, Ms. Suman Katiyal and Ms. Savita Matoliya belong to Uttarkashi in U.P.

Mr. Rajiv Sharma, an instructor from Manali, and Ms. Nima Norba, another instructor from Darjeeling, along with five sherpas, also got the honour of conquering the highest peak.

Interestingly, for one of the sherpas, Mr. Nima Dorjee, this was the third climb to the top while Mr. Lapsang Sherpa has been to the top without oxygen.

According to Mr. D.S. Thapa, coordinator of the expedition from the Indian Army, who established contact with the base camp in the afternoon, 11 members of Indian team, including four women climbers, made their final assault to the peak at about 1.30 a.m., and reached the top at about 10.45 a.m.

Ms. Bachendri Pal, leader of the Indo-Nepalese team, had selected four women to make final attempt to climb Mt. Everest from South Col (7,985 m.) and luckily the weather favoured them.

Mr. Rajiv Sharma and Mr. Baldev Kanwar, both instructors from Manali, got the opportunity to conquer the highest peak along with seven women. All members of the group have started descending to South Col after staying at the top for half-an-hour. They hoisted the Indian and Nepalese flags at the summit.

None of the women from Nepal of the Indo-Nepalese team could make to the top, which could be contributed to bad weather and lack of physical fitness. One of the women returned to Kathmandu in the first week of this month because her health did not permit to continue with the expedition. Two other Nepalese women were among those unfortunate climbers who had to return from Hillary Step, just 48 m. short of the top, on May 5.

With the successful completion of the final assault by the

last group of climbers, seven world records were created by the women expedition team from India, which included conquering of Mt. Everest for second time by Ms. Santosh Yadav, Ms. Dicky Dolma from Himachal Pradesh became the youngest woman climber in the world to achieve this honour.

That more and more people are coming forward to climb Everest shows that the adventure has not lost its appeal. But this has in its wake created environmental problems as highlighted by the graphic picture shot by French photographer Pierre Royer at 26,000 ft. on South Col of Everest which shows the mountain littered with debris left behind by the climbers. Among them are human bodies, cans and bottles which in the absence of oxygen and other decaying agents will remain intact for centuries. Efforts to have Everest cleared of such waste material have not so far been successful. The Nepalese Government had in the mid-sixties closed the route to Everest denying the adventurous an opportunity to achieve the ambition of surmounting Everest. As an alternative step the Government has imposed a hefty fee of per person wanting to climb the Himalayan peak. It will make mountaineering the sport of the rich. A way out is to make expeditions environment-friendly, which is, of course, easier said than done.

Being the ultimate goal of mountaineers all over the world, Everest will continue to attract more and more climbers in the years to come. However, those privileged to reach its top will always be men and women of exceptional courage and mental endurance.

K-2

This is the second highest mountain in the world. On July 31, 1954, an Italian party led by Archille Compagnoni and Leno Lacedelle and under the leadership of Ardito Desio, topped the mountain. The party had to overcome early discourage- ment of weather and death of Mario Puchoz, a member of their party. They owned much to the attempt by a U.S. team the previous year under Charles S. Houston.

This party was marooned for nine days at camp 8,25,500 ft., up the mountain, on the enforced descent. Arthur K. Gilkey, geologist, was lost and two other members of the expedition were seriously injured.

Cho Oyu (8,153 m./28,750 ft.)

It is the seventh highest mountain of the world 32 km of the north-west of Everest. Translated, its Tibetan name means Goddess of the Turquoise.

This peak slightly higher than Dhaulagiri, was reached on Oct. 19, 1954 by an Australian Party including Herbert, Tichy, Sepp Jochler and the Sherpa Pasang Dawa Lama. The Sherpa proceeded in three days from an altitude of 13,000 ft. of the summit.

The first Indian expedition to an 8,000 m. peak in the Nepal Himalaya was led by Keki Bunshah, a Bombay lawyer, Nandu Jayal, John Dias, Sonam Gyatso, Sherpas Passang Dawa Lama, Da Norbu, Phu Dorji and Thondup. The climber followed the west route pioneered by the Austrian Expedition, led by Herbert Tichy in 1954. Two members—Sonam Gyatso and Passang Dawa Lama—reached the summit on 15th May. Passang had been on the top of Cho Oyu before with Herbert Tichy. This was the second ascent of Cho Oyu which allowed no more successful ascents in spite of attempts by the best of mountaineers of the world, till 1983. The expedition led to the birth of IMF and had encouraged Indian mountaineers to take on bigger challenges.

Cho Oyu, however, exacted a sacrifice. Nandu Jayal, the best of Indian mountaineers, died on the mountain of pulmonary oedema.

Makalu (27,790 ft.)

A French party plus a Sherpa succeeded in getting all its members to the summit of Makalu on May 15, 16 and 17, 1955. A neighbour of Everest, Makalu had visited a number of previous attempts, including a U.S. party that had been turned back the year before after reaching 23,200 ft. The first summit pair consisted of Jean Conzy and Lionel Terray.

Naga Prabhat (26,600 ft.)

This mountain has the highest toll of climbers. Therefore, it was regarded as the most treacherous mountain in the Himalayas. It was finally climbed on July 4, 1953, when Hermann Buhl, member of friscken-ridden German-Australian expedition, was made a solo climb from high camp to the summit. Reaching the top late in the day, he was forced to bivouac in the open all night a short distance below the summit, and next day regarded a high camp. Naga Prabhat has previously claimed 31 lives over a period of 60 years, 16 being lost at once when an avalanche trapped numbers of the 1937 German expedition.

Kanchenjunga (28,168 ft.)

This mountain has been considered the world's toughest mountaineering problem. The actual summit remained untrodden indifference to a request of the government of Sikkim, which form the eastern side of the mountain, the Sikkimese regard the summit as sacred to their gods. Under the leadership of Charles Evans, who had been deputy leader of the 1953 British ascent of Everest and had reached that mountain's south peak, a British party succeeded in overcoming Kanchenjunga on May 25, 1955. George Band and Joe Brown competing the first ascent. From the same high camp on next day, Norman Hardie and Tony Streather repeated the climb, using the slight variation of the route at its upper extremity.

Mansalu (26,658 ft.)

This peak is the world's north highest mountain situated in Nepal. On May 9 and 11, 1956, two separate Japanese parties climbed Mansalu. This was the successful conclusion to a series of setback the Japanese had encountered in attempting to climb Mansalu in previous years. Later in 1956, on July 6 and 7, British climbing teams led by John Hortog ascended the Karakoram's Muztagh Tower (24,388 ft.) an enormous spore like peak. This was regarded as unaccessible peak. A French party led by Guido Magnone reached the top on July 12, 1956, from south, the British having used the west ridge.

Garhwal Himalayas

The Garhwal Himalayas stretch just over 290 km and are separated from the Punjab Himalayas by the river Sutlej. It is flanked by Tibet on the north. Kumaon in the east, Bijnor in the South and Tehri and Dehra Doon in the west.

Garhwal was the first part of the Himalayas to be explored and surveyed, and the highest peak in these mountain is less than 8,000 m.

Nanda Devi, also called the 'Pearl of the Himalayas' is the highest peak in the Garhwal mountains. Nanda Devi has twin peaks, the main peak and the east peak. The main peak was climbed in 1936 by H.W. Tilman and N.E. Odell while the east peak was scaled in 1939 by a Polish team. Nanda Devi is revered since ancient times and worshipped as the Goddess Nanda. T.G. Longstaft, one of the earliest explorer of the Garhwal region has discovered the holy mountain as: No mountain in the world is more beautiful than Nanda Devi".

Another popular peak in the Garhwal region is Kamet. Ten expeditions attempted this peak before it was finally scaled in 1931 by a team led by Frank S-Smythe.

At the traditional source of the Ganges you can find the best mountaineering area probably in the world. A few kilometre above the ice cave from which the river takes birth are the meadows of Tapovan are Nandanvan, spread at the base of the most magnificent panorama of peak you will ever see. The peaks are mainly over the 20,000 ft. mark and still have unclimbed faces offering alpine style ascents. Mt. Shivaling has often been compared to the Matterhorn. All along the 30 km. length of the Gangotri glacier are side glaciers, some not yet fully explored. One can also traverse to the southern face of the crest which provides steeper ice faces.

In the far west of Garhwal, Har-ki-Dun provides a spectacularly beautiful base for attempts on the Bandan Poonch group and the approach along the Tons valley is one of the last unspoiled areas of the Himalayas. Eastwards, now that the Nanda Devi sanctuary cirque has been closed, climbers have to approach Trishul by the more formidable south face. This involves a ten day trek up the Mandakini valley through impenetrable birch and bamboo jungle to reach base.

Further eastwards, Kumaon provides the fairly easy access to the Sunderdhunga glacier, but the outer certain of Nanda Devi's cirque beetles over the proceedings defying so far, any attempt to climb into her sanctuary from the south. The jagged five Punch Chuli peaks still require special permission for scaling.

Important Peaks in Garhwal Himalayas

Name of the Peaks	*Height (m.)*
Abi Gamine	7,355
Badrinath	7,138
Changabang	6,864
Dunagiri	7,066
Kamet	7,756
Manapeak	7,273
Nanda Devi	7,817
Nilgiri Parwat	6,474
Nilkantha	6,504
Panchchuli	6,904
Shivaling	6,543
Trishul	7,120

The Garhwal hills are an inexhaustible source of wonder for trekkers.

The hills are a vast reservoir of unexpected surprises and

delightful pleasures. The best of the best in this picturesque state are the hills of the Uttaranchal.

The Garhwali Himalayas are exceptionally rich and diverse in their varied offerings. Almost every hill town leads off into some interesting walking paths and trails worth exploring. Because of the sheer vastness of the terrain, not to mention the varying heights of the peaks, trekking trips in the Garhwal hills can be undertaken practically all year round.

Comprising the districts of Uttarkashi, Tehri-Garhwal, Pauri-Garhwal, Dehra Dun and Chamoli, the Garhwal hills and Kumaon hills are an inexhaustible source of wonder for trekkers.

The sheer beauty of this area can transport walkers with its stunning views. The trekking trails especially offer different kinds of terrain with a profusion of flora and fauna. Most of the trekking routes are open from April through October, though the best period is considered to extend from April to June, and from mid-September to November.

There are various trekking bases, starting with Dehra Dun and including Mussoorie, Uttarkashi, Pauri, Lansdawne, Chamoli, and Joshimath. All the essential personal gear and other necessary equipment are easily available on rent at all these individual bases.

Mussoorie is located in the Garhwal hills, its proximity to many important trekking centres as well as other places of tourist interest make it an important hill station in this region.

Also, major Hindu pilgrimages like Kedarnath, Badrinath, Gangotri, Yamunotri, Haridwar, Rishikesh are not far from this place. There is a direct rail link to Mussoorie and the Dehra Dun railway station is the closest one can come by train. However, Mussoorie is well connected by roads to other major cities.

Located at the foothills of Shivalik, on the banks of river Yamuna, Dakpathar is a beautiful and quiet retreat. A perfect getaway, Dakpathar has a well-developed tourism complex. Approximately 11 km from Dakpathar is the Asan Barrage which offers a variety of water sport facilities including water skiing, sailing, boating, kayaking, canoeing and hover craft rides.

Anyone who visits Dakpathar, should definitely go on to Kalsi which is around 6 km. from Dakpathar. After spending the night at the tourist lodge at Kalsi, the next stop can be Lakha Manda, where, according to legend, the Kauravas had made a lac house in which to burn the Pandavas alive.

Another stopover, not too far from Dakpathar and across the Yamuna river, is Ponta Saheb. This is the home of the famous Gurdwara of Guru Gobind Singhji.

Some 25 km. from Mussoorie is Dhanaulti, which is located amidst thick forests of many varieties of trees including deodar, rhododendron and oak. Here, one can enjoy leisurely walks over the thickly forested slopes with a fabulous view of snow covered mountains in just about every direction. Tourism offers fairly good accommodation but it would be a good idea to make bookings in advance.

Another memorable retreat tucked away in these hills is Lansdowne. The *piece de resistance* however, is the Valley of Flowers, situated in the Chamoli Janpad of the Garhwal area.

Though located at a high altitude, it is surprisingly easy to reach this breathtakingly beautiful place. The Valley of Flowers is one of the most famous places on the Indian tourist map, surrounded by an almost mystical aura of legend and mystery.

The valley is surrounded on three sides by high mountains and is spread over an area with an altitude ranging from 3,500 ft. to 6,500 ft. Besides the unimaginable variety of flowers, the valley is also home to many different varieties of birds and animals and a simply marvellous collection of butterflies.

The nearest railway head from the valley of Flowers is that of Rishikesh which is connected to all the major places in India. Just before one reaches the valley, the last night halt is at Ghangria which is 3 km. from the valley. From Ghangria, one trek goes to the Valley of Flowers and another trek of 6 kms. takes one to the Hem Kund Lake, which is a holy place for the Sikhs. The normal route followed by the trekkers is to Valley of Flowers. Then, they return to Ghangria before proceeding to Hem Kund, all the way trekking in trance.

Indian mountaineering had its origins in schools, with some adventurous and far-sighted schoolmasters aking out parties of boys on climbing vacations in Garhwal and Kumaon. Though the early explorations and pioneering ascents, as also the most sensational climbs, were undertaken either by geologists, surveyors or missionaries, generally foreigners, the foundations of the Himalayan tradition by these school-masters led to Indian mountaineers like Nandu Jayal, Gurdial Singh and Tenzing taking to the sport seriously.

Expeditions from the Doon School to Nanda Devi, and the successful training expeditions of large numbers of boys to Jaonli, 21,760 feet, in Garhwal, and the final ascent of Jaonli by schoolboys, were the natural sequel to J.T.M. Gibson and John Martyn's expeditions to the Bandarpunch area.

Perhaps it was the influence of the mountains and the pristine environment, but the entire expedition was a successful example of national and socio-economic integration effectively at work.

Some 100 miles beyond Chakrata lies the upper Tons watershed, with two rivers, the Jamdar and the Ruishar, meeting to form the Tons at the confluence; this Tons then meets the Yamuna, below Kalsi.

You may trip with a night bath in the river, and a quick rock-climb up the buttressed pillars of the old bridge, below the rock edict of Ashoka which proclaims the message of the Buddha. The pillars are made of hewn stone set in relief, and the climb, though only a few dozen feet, was rendered exciting by the inexperience of the boys and the darkness all around.

The next morning you leave early for Chakrata, where transport is waiting to convey you to your roadhead at Tiuni, beside the Tons, just below its confluence with the Pabbar river which comes down from Himachal Pradesh. Here the road ends, but a forest track continues to Naitwar and on to Taluka, just below the high mountains of Bandarpunch. This track is not only jeepable, but can also be persuaded to take one tonners and three tonners, if one can find sufficiently daring drivers, which we happily did.

Visit to Har-ki-Dun

Naitwar is a small but growing hill-town beside the rushing Tons, set amidst vast hill ranges of pine forest, where the road from Chakrata via Purola, the sub-divisional headquarters, also joins. Pine rosin-tapping and despatch is the other major activity after lumbering and the hill trade from high villages. Another 15 miles beyond by jeep, or on foot, lies the rest house of Taluka, where you halt, and where your porters from the villages of Datmir, Gangar, Panwari and Osla may join you, of course after much persuasion and at very high wages for carrying the 100 odd loads of the expedition in 60-pound packs. All members carry their own rucksacks, not only for the sake of economy, but also as part of the training programme.

One should undertake a fairly long approach march trek to ensure gradually increasing fitness, instead of racing into the high hills, and attempting high mountain climbs without an adequate acclimatisation period at lower elevations. The body attunes itself to strenuous days of long marches, and once so adjusted, can take great strains and high-altitude climbs without untoward consequences. To prolong our days at moderate elevations, it may decide first to visit the Har-ki-Dun, which is only two days out of our route to the Black Peak, circa 21,000 feet, our primary objective. Two days march from Taluka, the jeep-point, lay the lovely, undulating and grassy valleys of the Har-ki-Dun, with a picturesque rest house set atop an old, grass-grown moraine, with huge boulders perched on it. These boulders are the introduction to rock-climbing. The party may reunite here to undertake small daytime trips to the Jamdar glacier and the Morinda Gad which leads up to the Borasu Pass over which lies Chitkul in the Bhaspa valley in Himachal Pradesh.

Here the training programme begins in right earnest, with the grown-ups, taking over all the administrative details and the hard work of messing, planning, packing, re-packing and porterage.

Those of you have the fittest and have the maximum promise and technique, you may cross the pass which leads over the brilosing ridge from the Har-ki-Dun into the Tons-Rui-Shar valley, where lay your Base Camp for the attempt on Black Peak. You may spent a memorable night camped below the pass, climbing a 16,500 ft. peak, and glissading down 3,000 feet back to the bivouac camp. The next day this party reunites with the rest at the Base Camp over the pass, the main body having come around the ridge through the forest along the river on the goat track.

Lake Base Camp

An unbelievable profusion of flowers greets you at the Lake Base Camp, with a whole field of the delicately perfumed Primula involucrata, the modest Primula denticulata, anemones and buttercups, iris and potentilla, androsace and fritillaria.

Growing boys are generally very strong and tough, but lung development and stamina, resistance and durability in the face of long exposure to cold, lack of fresh, hot food and the rarified air of high altitudes, are qualities that develop around the twenties to their maximum.

It is, thus, imprudent to allow or to encourage such adolescent frames, however athletic or tough-looking, to very high elevations for long periods. They also require longer periods of acclimatisation at moderately high elevations before they are allowed to go above, say, 17,000 ft. above sea level.

Though you are well-trained by the time you reach Camps I and II, in rock and snow climbing and rescue techniques, and in trekking, camping, hill-walking, packing, ice-axe technique, you are not all nutritionally the same background and there are a distinct difference in stamina, endurance and constitutional resistance, which variation had to be kept in mind.

You may decide to select the most durable and technically

effective team, to accompany the first party to attempt to establish Camp III ridge of Black Peak. The party may move up and along the glacier, training as you go, and others may make the ascent of Black Peak.

Black Peak is frequently climbed, but remains a strenuous and fairly challenging 21,000 ft. mountain. The weather, always unpredictable in the high mountains which generate their own local storms, has been harsh. There is snow almost every day above Camp II.

The first group attempted the long, soft-snow and hard-ice summit-ridge of Black Peak from Camp III at 18,000 ft., Some others, may stay behind at Camp II, below the cliffs over which lies the route to the Dhuandhar Kandi Pass leading to Harsil. When the first party returns from Camp III, the other may complete all other parts of the Basic Course mountaineering, but for the ice and crampon routine. In those verdant and flower-festooned high valleys it is easy to forget aims and objects, and to lose oneself in contemplation, in plant-collection, bird-watching and wildlife photography, so it is natural for everyone to think of descending.

On the morning you may set off from Camp III and struggle up the ridge to the summit, encountering deep crevasses in the hard ice of the summit ridge. You photographed them from a neighbouring 18,000 ft. peak through telephoto lenses, as they, one after another, set foot on the Black Peak crest.

The return is uneventual, but instructive. The long days on the way back from the great heights are the most tranquil and the most memorable. Terrain previously difficult and dangerous seems easy. The flowers and the streams are profuse and gentle. The alpine grasslands a blessing, and the Himalaya in a friendly mood.

It is this face of the mountains which you may recall, though the training and the exposure to the thrill of this great sport will abide you all us much longer as you all grow older.

A Trek to Nag Tibba

When free go to Garhwal for a five-day trek· is rather little known area Nag-Tibba. The mountains always draw you the company would be interesting. If the arrangements were being handled by a reputed travel agency, it appears to be a trek on a silver platter with little worries about making tedious arrangements. You leave on a weekend for Mussoorie and after a brief halt at the Hotel go straight to the Happy Valley settlement of the Tibetan refugees which is almost a township in itself. You may entertained to a typical Tibetan lunch of noodles and momos after which the inmates clad in their fantastic dresses gives you very colourful display of Tibetan dances and dramas.

After a day's stay at Mussoorie, leave by a van for Dhanolti, about 38 kms. away. On the way, from Banaskanda village had a magnificent view of the panorama of almost all the famous mountain peaks of Garhwal glistening in the early morning sun. There is Nanda Devi, Trishul, Kedarnath, Dunagiri, Kamet, Chowkhamba in all their majesty.

The day's trek lay mostly on the ridge with sleepy villages deep down in the valleys. The terrain is mostly rugged but here and there did pass through thick groves of pine and fir and on the barren sloped blooming primulas did add a dash of colour. There is no water on the way and you do not see any springs which is otherwise a feature of Garhwal hills.

However you have a really sumptuous candlelight dinner in our mess tent followed by coffee. Tired as you sleep off soon. The rest day dawn bright and sunny, ideal for trekking. After a good breakfast move on through a thick jungle of blue pines and then the terraced fields. Once again you had a magnificent view of the snow ranges shimmering in the morning light. By lunch you had reached the open field of Moriana Dhar where you had a long rest.

In the evening, passing through some mustard fields, you reach Bhagi village where you think of camping for the night. There is an abandoned cattle-shed where you set up your kitchen and tents that had come so far. You lit fire in the open to keep warm.

But all the while you are listening for the jingle of the mule bells for your kit to arrive.

Next morning you adopt the camping tactics and decide to leave early with one cook and some utensils to set up next camp at Ghariap Dhara and be ready with a cup of tea and some snacks when the rest of party arrived.

The 13 kms. walk from Bhagi is a very pleasant trek through thick forests. Most of the trees were laden with moss and there were patches of snow all over. Here and there the trees looked like grown in avenues more by human devise. It is enjoyable cool to pass through these and our packed lunch in a pleasant open patch. You reach the camping site soon after. It is a big open green space with the forest on both sides. Down below was the village from where you get fresh water and had the tea prepared. One seems in good spirits and started collecting wood for the camp fire.

After a sumptuous dinner you assemble around the camp fire and every one may gave us snatches of old songs. It is the social evening and there is lot of bonhomie.

Next day, the trek from Ghariap Dhara to Nag-Tibba is a steep climb of over 600 m. in about ten kilometre walk. The way lay through a thick forest full of snow on the ground till you reach Tekta which is on a ridge. One half of this open field is under thick snow while the other side is grassy. The young among the party has the thrill of sliding down the snow covered slopes and you may get wet under their bottoms. From Tekta to Nag-Tibba is a huge field of snow, knee-deep at places. By the time you reach Nag-Tibba your toes are benumbed.

Nag-Tibba is a place of pilgrimage. The place is marked with a pole surrounded by piled up stones. You see lot of small coins thrown around by the simple villagers to propitiate their Nag-Devata. No one dare collect these coins lest a curse may befall him. The story goes that the Maharaja of Garhwal is under obligation to come to Nag-Tibba for annual sacrifice to avoid a curse which may befall the royal family otherwise.

Proceeding from Nag-Tibba, go around in circles for good part of an hour till from an opening we can see the Pantwari rest-house about a kilometre down the slope. Keeping the direction reach the camp all wet and cold. You had the luxury of hot tea and fresh pakoras.

For the night you camp in the tumbled down rest house. It is a well designed place but deserted and in bad need of repairs. Its situation is lovely but no one seemed to be using it. One may camp in the open by the side of the rest house. There is lot of snow at the back side. On the side of the hill lot of primulas are blooming in their faint blue.

Next morning, after breakfast you move on to Pantwari village about eight kilometres downhill. You almost had to roll down the boulder strewn path. It is extremely tiring. You find it difficult to keep the pace. From almost two kilometres above you see the lovely spectacle of the three adjacent villages nestling at the base patterned amidst the riping corn fields with the plum, peach and apricot trees all blooming mauve and pink. It is spring time. The slate roofs of the houses shimmered in the sun. You take a number of colour pictures and for once your tiredness had gone.

Reaching the village you see beautiful women, plum children in all their gay attires, and handsome men-folk. The village is really enchanting.

Kumaon Himalayas

Swaying and vibrating to the lively *Nainitalo* you take to the Kumaon trail, or at least a part of it. Kumaon remains as mystic as it was during the days of Jim Corbett, when he spoored the man-eating cats. The trails remain but the cats are gone.

This particular trail is going to take you through Ranikhet, Dwarahat, Someshwar, Almora, Binsar, Kausani and Baijnath. This is a land of gods and goddesses, mountains and valleys, pristine beauty and sylvan surroundings, deep woods and stately deodars.

About 350 km. from Delhi via Haldwani, you hit Ranikhet. A legacy of the British, Ranikhet still remains the charming and unpolluted hill station it was, unlike a lot of others which have become concrete jungles. The Westview hotel is still there and still serves roast mutton and mint sauce! There is a singular ambience about Ranikhet—legend has it that once a certain queen encamped here, somewhere close to where the Ranikhet club stands. Hence the name Ranikhet.

The famous Kumaon Regimental Centre stands here and you must have a look at their museum which houses the sword of Rani Laxmibai.

Five kilometres from Ranikhet is Chillianaula, where stands a magnificent Shiva temple. The main deity is Hairakhan Wale Baba. The temple is managed by a band of foreigners and offers a breathtaking view of the Himalayas.

On the way to Chaubatia, the famous government orchards a short distance away, is the old temple of Jhuladevi. You would be fascinated by the hundreds of bells hung there by folks whose wishes have been fulfilled. There is a fabulous nine-hole golf course maintained by the Kumaon Regimental Centre. May be you could invoke the blessings of goddess Kali from the nearby Kalika temple for a hole-in-one! The place is also ideal for a spot of quiet meditation. And attention shoppers! You could pick up excellent tweeds and exotic shawls at affordable prices. And don't forget to pick up a packet of the delicious *bal mithai*, a speciality of the region.

Time to move on to the temple town of Dwarahat, about 35 km. away. It has a cluster of old temples built by the Chand rajas, dating back to the eighth century. Dwarahat has some fabulous old houses with beautiful carved wooden doors and windows.

You could walk through its quaint, narrow lanes which may remind you of some old Italian village.

You are now on your way to fabulous Kausani (at 1,890 m.), about 37 km. away. Mahatma Gandhi had stayed here and this is also the birthplace of the famous poet Sumitranandan Pant. Here you will find hotels and an excellent K.M.V.N. guest house.

A mere 18 km. away, at 1,125 m., lies the temple town of Baijnath on the banks of the Gomti river. The kids can have a great time feeding schools of fish. Legend has it that

Lord Shiva married Goddess Parvati at the confluence of Gomti and Garur Ganga and it became the seat of power of their son Kartikya Swami, after whom the valley is called Katyur.

We now move on to Bageshwar at a distance of 22 km. It has the famous temple of Lord Bag Nath (Shiva). This is also an important station en route to the famous Pindari glacier.

Almora, the district headquarters, is about 70 km. away, and here you will find good hotels and a K.M.V.N. guest house. Most of the hill stations in India are British legacies but Almora was the erstwhile capital of the Chand *rajas* of Kumaon. You can still feel the old traditional ambience of the place and have a glimpse of the tiled roof houses and paved streets apart from the panoramic view of the Himalayas. You could also have a look at the exquisite copper handicrafts.

You must now prepare yourself for a real steep climb to Binsar (at 2,412 m.), a mere 30 km. from Almora. You could visit the Bineshwar temple, built by Raja Kalyan Chand, take a long, rejuvenating walk through the dense deodar forests, listening to the birds or simply laze around in a comfortable chair on the lawns of the K.M.V.N. tourist bungalow.

As all goods things come to an end so must our Kumaon trail ... for the time being that is. For the trail stretches on and on and it would take many more weekends to fully explore this mysterious region.

Pindari

Bageshwar is the last town where one can get in touch with officials in order to make bookings for P.W.D. guest houses, get information regarding the route and stock up on food and medicines. After doing all these, you make your way to Song, the last road head, from where it all begins.

Day One (*Song-Loharkhet-Dhakuri*)

An uphill slog, the first part till Loharkhet is a warm-up for what lies ahead. After the first 5 km. you begin to observe the extent of the hills, tumbling meadows, gigantic Deodhars, frilly ferns, bolting birds and of course the cool biting air. Just when the travel begins to take its toll, a tea shop turns up miraculously behind the bend offering not just sweet tea but also packets of two-minute noodles, biscuits and boiled eggs.

One kilometre before reaching Dhakuri, the trail decides to ease out and then just as suddenly drops sharply, so that instead of blankly trudging upwards, you have to concentrate with the legs. This is the most strenuous kilometre of the trip.

Hardly half-an-acre in area, Dhakuri has one tourist rest house and a PWD guest house along with three small *dhabas*. Day one ends supping on *dal-chawal* out of smoky *thalis* and watching the very far away Pindari glacier.

Day Two (*Dhakuri-Khati*)

The initial 4 km. from Dhakuri to Khati meanders through the hillsides, playing host to the occasional shack, sudden streams and flowering meadows. Since it is mostly downhill, it takes two hours, leaving the entire day free for relaxing in the village—the last stop for indulging in biscuits, omelettes and orange sweets. Sipping endless cups of *chai*, you let our minds go blank but it isn't until an entire truckload of boisterous men descend on their return journey from the glacier, that you realise how lucky you are to have the place mostly to ourselves. It's like sitting in the middle of a public park.

Day Three (*Khati-Dwali-Purkhiya*)

This turns out to be the easiest stretch of the trek. The trail is more or less even, although at certain points it becomes very narrow. A couple of kilometres from Khati you discover a clear and frothy river.

After six kilometres comes a *chai* stall and one has to cross a temporary wooden bridge to get on the other side. The bridge is notorious for snapping under stress, so crossing it is a high risk proposition considering the river on the rise. Since you arrive well in time, you are advised by the caretaker at Dhakuri to carry on the same day to Purkhiya. Now you begin to spot patches of snow breaking the monotony of the hills. The P.W.D. guest house suddenly appears through the dense mist. Behind it is the tourist rest house which fortunately has sleeping bags, and blankets.

Day Four (*Purkhiya Pindari Glacier-Purkhiya-Dwali*)

The first real glacier appears after a kilometre from Purkhiya, followed by four others which seem to grow in proportion. A sturdy stick always comes in handy, and better still is to do what you do—attach yourself like a leech to any passing porter!

The terrain changes once again and bursts into an endless expanse of bright yellow (wild-flowers) set against the dark green of ground cover, with towering snow peaks cutting jagged triangles into the blue sky. Just below the glacier you find a stone hut of Babaji. An extremely hospitable man, Babaji's tea is the best. Clutching onto your tumblers, you hear stories about the glacier on moonlit nights and then walk the last stretch to zero-point.

Reluctantly, you tear yourselves away from this beautiful place where mountains like Nanda Khat and Nanda Devi look down on mere mortals. Towards the end of a trip the mountains always seem depressing, perhaps because the return journey no longer holds the suspense for what lies ahead. Or then may be it's the thought of going back to city life. Whatever be the case, your constant aspiration in all these years has been to live for just these moments and to take back enough memories to last a lifetime.

Route

Haldwani and Kathgodam are the nearest rail-heads. The busiest road head is again Haldwani but direct buses also ply between Delhi and Bageshwar. The best time for this trek is from April to June and August to October. P.W.D. houses need prior booking and permits. Rooms are available for Rs.150 and meals all along are the same at Rs.40.

Don't forget to take mosquito repellents (non-electric), incense stick for files and a water bottle. A waterproof windcheater also comes in handy since the weather is unpredictable.

Porters and guides can be fixed along the way or even in Bageshwar.

Himachal Himalayas

The state of Himachal Pradesh is made up of ten districts with a total area of 50,019 sq. km. The border of Himachal Pradesh is bounded by Tibet, in the north-western side, it borders Kashmir, in the south lie the plain of Punjab and the eastern border is common with the hills of Uttaranchal. The state is ragged and mountainous, and the Valleys of Lahaul and Spiti are the dream of mountaineers.

Lahaul and Spiti is a desolate region in comparison to the lush Beas Valley of Kullu, also a popular mountain area of the state of Spiti, which overlooks Tibet across the Sutlaj river, in Tibetan in landscape and in the character of its few inhabitants.

Kullu and Lahaul are good areas for mountaineers practising both alpine style ascents and the mountaineering. The jagged ice peaks of Kullu offer good routes for the tiger as well as the less ambitious mountaineer.

A popular peak in the area is Deo Tibba (6,001 m.) which is visible from Shimla, the capital of Himachal Pradesh, and Indrasan (6,221 m.), a challenging peak of steep red granite which can be climbed from four different rent routes.

The Menthosa snow peak in Chamba at 6,445 m. has never been totally conquered, nor has Dharamshala (6,446 m.) in the Bara Shigri glacier region, though they provide opportunity for some excellent mountaineering.

A close cluster of the M&KR series in the Milang river basin has more than a dozen peaks over 600 m. high worthy of the hardiest ridge runners. Himachal may well hold the track record for peaks that have defied a first time ascent. For example, the Chandra Bhaga watershed and the Parvati Valley have several over 6,000 m. peaks, most still unclimbed.

Important Peaks in Himachal Himalayas

Name of Peak	*Height (m.)*
Deo Tibba	6,221
Indrasan	6,221
Kullu Pumori	6,553
Leo Pargial	6,770
Menthosa	6,443
Mulkila	6,517
Papsura	6,451
White sail	6,446

Mountains are challenging the desire to conquer and explore them is irrepressible once you move into the winds of Himachal. Expedition to various peaks are organised every year by the Mountaineering Institute, Manali. Centre Peak, Deo Tibba, Hanuman Tibba, Moulkila and Indrasan are some of the popular peaks in Himachal where rock climbing is an exciting challenge. Among the easier ones are Sitidhar and Patalsu in the Manali region. Besides Manali, adventure courses are conducted at Dharamshala, Bharmaur and Jispa by the regional centre of the Mountaineering Institute. Patalsu is particularly, popular with rock-climbing enthusiasts. In fact Himachal offers a perfect terrain for rock climbing. Manali and Bharmaur are two most popular areas for rock climbing.

The trends are changing. The new breed of vacationers have freed themselves from jaded gateways. For them, a stay at a five-star hotel or a walk down the Simla Mall in designer wear is passed. Adventure is their mantra.

It's – 5° in Rohtang Pass. Fortunately so for the tourists sometimes, the snowfall is comparatively less and visitors may go right up to the Pass. Otherwise the Pass remains under four to five metres of snow till the middle of June. There is joy all around. Dressed like Eskimos, many try their luck with skiis, some on a snow-scooter and the rest are content to slide down snow slopes without any gear!

This is a great moment—to be on snow and slide down these glaciers. Take a ride on the snow-scooter. Finally have a ride amidst laughter and applause at an altitude of 13,500 ft.! It is like a scene from a bygone era. Men, women and children on horseback, trying frantically to protect themselves from the chilly wind. Any one could go in a vehicle. But how many would venture out on horseback, braving these bone-chilling winds.

Nature, Adventure, Clean Environment—these are the buzz words for many out in those wilds. Five years ago many would visit out of curiosity to the tented camps.

There is a problem of overbooking in summer months and guests are least worried about any inconveniences. What was considered to be a typically back-of-beyond valley once, Sangla today is the hottest new destination for adventurists.

Sitting on a rock, behind Banjara Camps, to angling for trouts in the fast flowing Baspa river. You get peace of mind and above all an environment which is equal to none.

Call them whatever generation, today's youngsters are keen to explore.

After a week of inclement weather and heavy snowfall in the upper reaches, the sky clears up over the Solang Valley. Fine weather for para-gliding.

And in a few seconds you are airborne. "Thermals are good". Manali Valley, to the south, comes in to view. You land after 30 minutes of flying. For a moment you are speechless, still relishing the feeling.

The present-day holiday makers are different from those twenty or thirty years ago. The urge to visit new destinations is also coupled with the desire for adventure. And old, established hill stations are no more a big attraction.

Bhrigu Lake

Trekking in Himachal is an enriching experience, and the 10 days that you spent away from the din and claustrophobic routine of city life made me realise how life was too precious and beautiful to be spent scurrying from one engagement to another.

The 10-day long trek to Brighu lake at 14,000 ft. (organised by Adventure Activities Promoters) began with your departure for the base camp. You will draw a sharp breath as you reached Solang Nala, a Himalayan valley a few kilometres from Manali ... bright red and green tents were set among tall pines and surrounded by snow-covered peaks and the gurgling river.

After a day of getting acclimatised to the height and weather, you leave for Kothi where you have your first camp. After lunch, set off to explore the village of Kothi. Kothi is at a height of 9,000 ft. and like most Indian villages, is in a state of transition. Hill women do a lot of work, from farming to household work, besides tending the children.

Next day you involve yourself in various adventure activities—rock-climbing, rappelling and river-crossing. There are experts to teach you the basics and in no time at all you are ready to take on the rugged rocks. You learn about the various footholds and handholds and the equipment used and may scream when you take the first three steps and looked down, but after you get used to the height and angle you are hooked. River crossing, equally delightful and the instructor tell about the different ways in which the river could be crossed—monkey crawling, under the rope, and upon the rope.

Next morning, ready to leave for Gulaba, your second and last camp. The breathless uphill climb is compensated by the beautiful views. When reach Gulaba (at 11,000 ft.), famished but a nutritious meal awaited and soon felt energised enough to go off on a wood-collecting spree. You also up early next morning to begin the final leg of your trek—to Brighu Lake. After a daunting uphill climb (of about 5 kms.) reach a skiing point where learn a bit of skiing. Some take off for Brighu Lake, a 3 km. trek in the snow. It is a steep climb and treading cautiously learn the correct way to walk on the snowpath. Finally rewarded by an awesome sight—the holy lake Brighu, at 14,000 ft., in the middle of the snow-covered mountains. This is the place where Rishi Brighu had meditated and wrote the famous *Brighu Samahita.*

At the base camp the next day everybody disagree the thought of leaving. Time had ceased to exist and no one had noticed how the days had just flown by. The trek has a tremendous learning experience and had gathered enough memories and forged bonds that would last us a lifetime.

Sikkim Himalayas

The Sikkim Himalayas are characterised very strongly with the culture of the region. Prayer flags line several routes to upper Himalayan monasteries, and monks or other resident of these high mountains that you meet on your journey will show you gentle courtesies. Since the Himalayas are considered holy, attempts to scale new peaks are not looked upon favourably.

Only two peaks in Sikkim are open to mountaineering expeditions:

(i) Rathong 22,000 ft. and
(ii) Kokthang 20,176 ft.

Rathong is immediately to the west of Kabra South and appears to merge with the main wall of Kumbhakarna (Jano). The famous Yalung glacier lies between Rathong and Jano. Kokthang has proved easier to scale, and lies along the Sikkim-Nepal border.

Even though permission for climbing other peaks is not available, it is interesting to know that the greatest peaks of Sikkim lie in five areas:

— The Southern approach to Kanchenjunga
— The Zemu region
— The Kanchenjunga massif
— Lhouak in northern Sikkim and
— Lunar landscapes of south-east Sikkim.

The best known peaks are those of:

(i) Rathong	22,000 ft.	open for mountaineering			
(ii) Kokthang	20,167 ft.	"	"		"
(iii) Kanchenjunga	28,146 ft.	"	"		"
(iv) Sinioklu	22,620 ft.	"	"		"
(v) Jonsong	24,304 ft.	"	"		"
(vi) Paulunri	23,380 ft.	"	"		"
(vii) Talung	24,110 ft.	"	"		"
(viii) Pandim	22,100 ft.	"	"		"
(ix) Tent	24,089 ft.	"	"		"

Among the lesser peak are those of—

(i) Kabru Dome 21,650 ft.
(ii) Lame Anden 19,500 ft.

(iii) 20,000 ft. Ting Chew Lalung and forked, Nepal Gap 20,238 ft.

(iv) Zemuha 19,230 ft. and

(v) Keilberg 19,000 ft.

Kashmir and Laddakh Himalayas

The towering mountains of Kashmir—a brown mass ranged solidly against the azure depths of the sky—offer a scintillating challenge to conquer them. And indeed some of the smaller peaks in Sonamarg and Pahalgam can be climbed quickly and easily by making Alpine style ascents.

There are both Alpine and Himalayan mountain ranges in the four regional subdivisions in Kashmir—Kashmir, Kishtwar, Zanskar and Laddakh.

The best known peaks are Kolahoi (5,425 m.)—considered the Matterhorn of Kashmir; Harmukh (5,148 m.)—whose north face resembles Eiger; Tattakuti (4,742 m.); Sunset (4,745 m.)—the highest peak in the Pir Panjal range, and several small peaks in Sonamarg and Pahalgam.

The Kishtwar region has several small Himalayan peaks which even put the technique and skill of an experienced climber to test. More often than not, mountaineers have to make week-long treks to the base region, provide a wondrous variety of flora and fauna.

To trek in the Alpine style, one generally starts from either Srinagar, Pahalgam or Sonamarg. Laddakh's high mountains, lofty peaks and endless glaciers offer tougher treks, camps, before they can even start the perilous climb, up the granite face of the mountains.

The popular peaks in this region are Sickle Moon (6,575 m.); Eiger (6,001 m.); Brammah-I (6,416 m.); Brammah's wife 5,297 m.); Crooked Finger (5,630 m.); Flat Top (6,100 m.); Cathedral (5,630 m.); Barnaj-I (6,100 m.); Barnaj-II (6,290 m.); Arjuna (6,200 m.); Aghyasol (6,200 m.) and Shivaling (6,000 m.).

The Zanskar Range comprises the famous Nun-Kun. Nun at 7,135 m. and Kun at 7,077 m. is the only climbing group which can be reached after a day's trekking from the road head. Also, Nun's base camp can be reached from the Srinagar airport in just two days.

Some of the other significant peaks in this range are the White Needle (6,500 m.), Pinnacle 6,930 m.); Bien Guapa (6,006 m.) and Bobang (5,971 m.). Zanskar also abounds in peaks unnamed and unclaimed, overlooking—the Durung Drung glacier which mutely offers a bold challenge to climbers to conquer them.

Many are the expeditions organised to the Laddakh range, which comprises the peaks of Stok area. And it is only recently that the Karakorams have also been thrown open to selected joint expeditions.

The optimum climbing period is from mid-May to mid October. The monsoons do not however affect the Laddakh peaks, and so the main climbing season here is July/August

With her easy charm and eager ability to please Kashmir is a trekker's delight. The incessantly changing Alpine pastures clothing the rugged face of the mountains the rainbow coloured patches of flowers, the ringing choir of birds and the host of animals which roam.

On Summit Kun (7,135 m.): Multi-Disciplinary Expedition

A multi-disciplinary expedition involving mountaineering skiing and river rafting during September could be conducted in Suru river valley and on the Nun-Kun massit in Kargil district of Laddakh, division of Jammu and Kashmir. The object is to scale the Kun peak.

This beautiful valley at a height of 13,000 ft. is located approximately 130 km south of Kargil, and has lush meadows. It is visited by tourists on their way to Padam in the Zanskar valley and has a certain timeless quality about it.

This expedition is an unique in the annals of Indian adventure sports, with three disciplines incorporated in it. namely mountaineering, skiing, and river rafting. The sporting activities in these remote areas like the Suru or Zanksar river valley helps being these potential sites of adventure tourism on the national and international maps.

On reaching the road head camp at Gelmathangos in the Suru valley on the first day you encounter the first period of bad weather. Bad weather, thereafter continues to dog you for the entire duration of the climb. You have to find the weather good enough for miles to move to base camp. A reconnaissance of the camp as well as an acclimatisation ferry had to be completed earlier.

The base camp may be situated at a height of approximately 15,000 ft. and is ordinarily the home of hundreds of Marmots. This quaint animal soon gets accustomed to you and is thereafter often seen sitting on rocks in the camp whenever the sun comes out.

On the second day you have to look for a point approximately four hours walk away from the base camp. After crossing a rocky ridge, you enter in a heavily crevassed snow field. As you reach the steeper slopes in the snow field, the weather begins to get bad.

You push on and establish base Camp I close to a rabbit shaped rock—Rabbit Rock. The route to Camp II involves negotiating a steep stretch of snow and ice to the right of Rabbit Rock, crossing a crevassed snow field of about a kilometre length and then negotiating an ice wall (short of White Needle Peak) approximately a thousand feet high to reach Camp II at 21,400 ft.

Camp II is located on the Nun-Kun massif. The massif is approximately four kilometres long by two kms. wide and is ringed by eight peaks, internationally famous amongst which are Nun-Kun, Lingsarmo and White Needle. The massif contains a thick coat of soft snow which makes walking extremely difficult. Winds here are extremely high in September and even a blue sky is little consolation as the high winds make any movement an arduous task.

Finding a clear sky you reach Camp II. Usually, movement from Camp II to Camp III takes no more than two hours. The weather after Camp III becomes foul. White out and blizzard condition again set in. Kun proves to be a most difficult mountain. You must carry enough stocks for three four days. The foul weather may freeze all movements of your expedition. You have to brave winds as high as a 100 km.p.h. on the ice wall, from Camp III you have to attempt Kun. After a mere two and a half hours of climbing, and moving rope up, you summit the White Needle at a height of approximately 23,000 ft. You move up beyond the first step and reach Kun summit. By then you are entirely engulfed by clouds.

Now you make its descent from the mountain on *skis* and on foot. You rush back to road head to commence rafting. The water from Pensila to Gelmethangos is placid with small rapids. Therefore the stretch to Tongol is not raftable due to very little water in the river. At Tongol the river disappears under the rocks and hence it is not possible to raft down. This, and stretches of Grade VI rapids, are omitted by your expedition.

Rock Climbing

Rock climbing is risky, but exciting sports. Only those people who have the persistence and patience to master the skill with strenuous practice can finally climb the steep rock structure with perfect ease. Rock climbing is usually to be found only on the upper most slopes of high peaks. It may also be after surmounting its lower reaches of snow and ice. On the eastern Alps (dolomite) are devoid of snow or ice in summer.

Rock climbing on typical climbs may involve.

- Climbing steep slabs or ridges.
- Climbing crack—small for more than a hand or foot to enter.
- Climbing chimneys—Crack large enough for the entire body to enter.
- Couloir or gullies—too wide for the climbers' limbs to touch both walls at once.

The party is roped at intervals of 30-40 ft. The back and knee technique is very popular in chimney climbing. The climber with his back to one wall wedges his knees and arms against the other and works himself up, using alternatively his arms and his knees. For climbing down an extra rope is used which is pass through a rope sling.

The possibility of rock climbing were first called to general attention by A.F. Mummory on the occasion of the first ascent of the supposedly unclimbable Grepon (Alps) in 1881. Among climbers, there is a considerable interest in specialised rock climbing in which special techniques and unusual items of equipment are required. This sport has restricted limits. Only the early hours of summer mornings are ideal for rock-climbing and is totally banned in monsoons.

In our country, this sport is generally carried out on the following places:

- Around Delhi
- Beyond Pune
- On the Western Ghats
- Along Bombay-Nasik highway at place like Membra and Dudha
- In Manali valley of H.P.
- Chamundi Hills in Karnataka
- Sonemarg in Kashmir
- Gangotri in Garhwal Himalayas
- Mount Abu and Sariska in Rajasthan
- A part of wild, gigantic Aravali range of mountains.

India have certain outstanding rock structure extended over great lengths and enjoy championship status. In some other areas it is down right risky, tough and tiring. The most interesting part of rock climbing is the breath-taking beauty of the surrounding landscape keeps up the spirits of rock climber. Like other adventure sports, beginners of rock climbing should get guidance of professionals and do full practice in different techniques.

J.R.D. Tata Rockwall

India's first international standard 'climbing wall' was thrown open for adventure sports lovers and rock climbers at the Indian Mountaineering Foundations premises near South Campus of Delhi University.

It is known as the J.R.D. Tata Rockwall. The sport climbing

wall constructed at a cost of Rs.15 lakh is sponsored by Tata Steel. It's placed amid a landscape of an amphitheatre.

The Rock Art Climbing Systems, which has designed the sport climbing wall. Artificial climbing surfaces have become popular for training and competition in the U.K., the U.S.A., Japan, Singapore and other countries because real rocks get spoilt if used for competition and many climbers know their routes fairly well.

Beginning with using warehouses and even walls of cathedrals as climbing wall by placing huge wooden boards with bolt-on holds of plastic, and resin, sand composite textured surface to give the right feel, they were being used in gymnasiums and were given a steel supporting structure.

The J.R.D. Tata Rockwall is 12 m. high and 4.8 m. wide which is sufficiently wide to allow separate routes to be taken by two climbers on the wall.

The surface of the wall is made of fibre glass and wood, textured with resin, quartz and sand. It has a steel supporting structure.

There are modular bolt-on holds in the surface which can be interchanged to change the route, besides fibre glass bumps on the way, cracks, vertical faces, overhangs.

One of the major advantages of the climbing wall is that the "flexibility which it offers is unprecedented". Because of telescopic tubes on which it is fixed, the configuration of the separate panels which form the wall can be changed giving a over hang of 30° or more or whatever angle one requires, it could be made into a roof or any other shape.

The spacing of the hand and foot holds can be changed so that a climber has to take different routes.

The flexibility of the sport climbing wall would thus allow different levels of difficulty to be introduced into the climb.

In future one can develop a sport wall working on hydraulic system where variations in the mechanism can be programmed through computer so that we can see it on screen and adjust the kind of wall, you want.

The whole system is modular with telescopic tubes with mechanical jacks connecting the mainframe to the climbing surface allowing people to change the configuration of the surface.

Specialising in "space frame" systems the whole system based on mechano-type could be pulled down in a single day.

The artificial rock wall of international standards could be used for competitions at school, college and zonal levels leading to national championships by youth all over the country.

Tughlakabad Area

It is just about a kilometre away from Qutab Minar in New Delhi. This is a prime area for rock climbing. For beginners and learners these 25 ft. high rock are ideal and most suitable for practice. The polo ground in the President's Estate surrounded by thorny bushes and shrubs suit the experienced rock climbers better. The Aravali Hills, skirt Delhi and there are some sturdy rock faces here which can test the efficiency of even seasonal rock climbers.

At Dumdarna, 25 km. away from Delhi the climbing experience becomes a matter of great joy because of the presence of wild birds and beautiful lakes.

Nub 70 km. from Delhi and Dhauj 55 km. from Delhi are also popular climbing sports, surrounded by lakes.

Adventure Academy

In 1992 the foundation stone of the Delhi Adventure Park-cum-Academy was laid near Qutab Minar. The function was attended by Sir Edmund Hillary, the first man to climb Mount Everest.

If such projects are developed in an organised manner then it "won't antagonise" the ecological balance. In fact adventure tourism would be a friendly help to the environment. It helps educating young children in preserving the environment.

The academy would provide ample opportunity to the

school students in the vicinity for training programmes in adventure activities.

This kind of projects should not be taken up by the Government alone but "it is the responsibility of all organisations throughout the country".

By encouraging this kind of adventures one helps the children to meet the challenges of the society. The children are better equipped to face the challenges. It is nice to see the young children meeting challenges.

The D.D.A. has given 2 acres of land for the academy in the vicinity of Qutab an Indian Mountaineering Foundation (I.M.F.) is providing all technical help. The academy will provide not only training programmes in various adventure activities, but will also provide with a library and equipments for the members.

A camping site has also been located and those who are interested in trekking and mountaineering would be provided with tent accommodations. It plans to hold courses for training the youth for national training programmes.

The academy is an ideal institute for adventure tourism and it should be extended all possible help because in a way it helps educating children preparing for a great future.

I.M.F. has an integrated plan for aero and aqua sports, besides trekking and mountaineering. This kind of projects help in the character building of the nation.

Western Ghats

The gentle hills and picturesque rock structure near western Ghat's of Pune, Membra and Dudha on the Bombay-Nasik highway and other places near Pune are also popular rock climbing centres. Here, the hill, some of them as high as 1,000 ft., offer a challenge to the climbers.

Manali

The Manali valley rock in Himachal Pradesh are fun to climb.

These are across the river which is 100-200 ft. in length. The Manikaran peaks are with 12,000-14,000 ft. high rock needle. They are really a challenge to climbers. The Rohtang Pass mountain ranges also offer excellent rock peaks to climbers.

Chamundi Hills

Along the Bangalore-Mysore highway, these hills of Karnataka offer good rock climbing slopes.

Sonmarg

Sonmarg in Kashmir is also quite popular with the climbers.

Gangotri

For High altitude rock climbing is, Gangotri Hills in the Garhwal Himalayas are an excellent rock for this adventure sport.

Chakrata

Drive down the Dehra Dun-Chakrata picturesque place, it is thickly forested with rhododendrons, conifers, oak and other higher altitude trees. The rocky terrain is difficult but even a novice could pick up some of the finer details with help from the local guides and freely available coaches. On the way to Chakrata one can stop for quick bite and rest at Dak bungalow—a beautiful spot developed under the Yamuna Hydel Scheme that boasts of green lawns and blooming gardens. Accommodation is available at the government tourist bungalow there.

8

Automobile Racing: Motoring

Automobile racing is the broad term for an amateur and professional sport of many categories:

- Grand Prix Racing
- Sports Car Racing
- Production Car Racing (Stock Car Racing)
- Endurance Events
- Maximum Speed or Maximum Acceleration Events (Drag Racing)
- Hill Climbs
- Rallies
- Trails etc.

Automobiles have been used for sport from the dawn of the history. The self-propelled vehicles were made for a utilitarian service was also tested in competition of one style or another for the purpose of providing not only its speed and its safety and reliability. By 1885, racing in a formal sense had begun. It has flourished in all the major western nations of the world, drawing huge spectator crowds and stimulating large investment of money by some manufacturers—who may have all dual motivations, to use racing as a testing laboratory in which new and advance designs are evaluated, and to earn popularity and good reputation as sales promotion aids.

The cars used in early races were either those which were already in production or prototypes for future production, both submitted publicity to the most strenuous test possible. The races had, therefore value as experiments leading to the publicity of better cars.

Motoring history began during the last decade of the 19th century. By 1895 automobiles were a booming industry in France and Germany. Races easily became a means of publicising the new automobile. The straight thoroughfare of France and Germany were ideal for this purpose. By 1906, the large French automobile industry was no longer willing to be restricted to only three automobiles in the Gordon Bennett races and so organised the Grand Prix race with no limitations on the number of cars that might be entered from any nation. The first of the races was run in 1906 and it marked the end of the Gordon Bennett series, the French Grand Prix continued as a major automobile event. An annual 'pleasure' motoring event in the U.S. known as 'Glidden tours' attracted nationwide attention. The increasing comfort and reliability of the motor car stimulated its use for popular training.

While automobile events grow in numbers and popularity in Europe, interest in automobile kept pace in the U.S. Driving or touring by automobile for pleasure has emerged as one of the most socially significant development of the 20th century, an influential factor is the leisure hours of an even-more affluent society and an integral part of the world's economy. Related subjects such as the history and development of roads, and highways, and the law's governing the operation of motor vehicle, are getting due attention.

From the heavy ascent on pleasure motoring at the beginning of the century, the emphasis has switched to the competitive aspect. The over-riding aim of proving reliability has remained constant. International rallies were now 'big business' and are supported extensively by automobile manufacturers who sponsored their own 'work' team, and also give help to private entrants using their make of vehicle.

Europe remains the rallying centre of world where most of the famous rallies are held but the sport enjoys popularity in U.S.A., and Canada and even in Africa where the unique East African Safari event offers additional hazards in jungle and wild beasts.

The best rally in the Monte Carlo, first held in 1911. Other leading rallies include the Alpine, the Aeropolis, the Tulip Rally in the Netherland, the RAC British International, the Swedish Midnight Sun, the Norwegian Rally, the Finish Thousand Lakes, the Sun Remo 'Rally of the Flowers', the German Polish and Geneva.

From the Monte Carlo Rally, there are usually several starting point in a near widely separated towns. From each of these, the competition are sent off at one minute intervals to drivers over routes of approximately equal length to a common rallying point and from there a single route is taken to the finish. A fixed distance is covered by each competitor either continuously day and night or in four or five daily runs with overnight halts. The basis of this and several event is regularity by means of an average speed which has to be maintained, but merely over the route as a whole but on every section of the route between control points. Legal speed limits has to be observed high speeds being achieved on special sections (private land) and race circuits. Special tests of driving skill are held in different terrain route at finishing point are made against the stop watch, and results are used, in combination with the penalty marking system for general time keeping, in assessing the winners in the different classes.

Hill Driving

The summer sets in and seen on the roads are vehicles with dark black tinted glasses. Many private cars are noticed even fitted with curtains in the interior preventing total transparency.

You are tempted to increase cooling efficiency. Using these measures though may slightly increase cabin cooling of your car, don't forget that the safety of your vehicle in close proximity with other vehicles will be jeopardised. The motor vehicles rules make it abundantly clear that every motor vehicle shall be maintained to ensure minimum 70 per cent visual transmission of light.

The glasses used and fitted to the vehicle shall be maintained in a manner to provide visual transmission of light not less than 50 per cent conforming to ISO standards.

These rules have been framed to permit clear vision from outside to inside and inside to outside. We have therefore to be extra cautious not to fit to our vehicles tinted glasses or sun control films that are so dark as to obscure clear vision.

Plan a holiday to nearby hill stations and other cooler climbs, warrants special driving skills and techniques to drive through hilly terrain, sometime in adverse weather conditions as well. So you must take the following precautions:

- Test the brakes before setting off.
- Shift to the correct gear while climbing and descending.
- Avoid changing mid-way on a gradient.
- Give way to heavy vehicles and the traffic that is upcoming.
- It is risky to switch off the engine or shift to neutral gear for saving fuel. If we do so, we may lose total control on our vehicles.
- Religiously follow traffic signals and use caution by blowing horn reaching blind comers and sharp turnings. At night use dipper instead to forewarn the oncoming traffic.
- Avoid always overtaking near the bends and at the crest of a hill.
- While passing the traffic coming from the opposite side use dim lights only.
- Use the same gear for descending a gradient which would have been used by you to ascend it.
- Allow the brakes to cool if found fading which happens due to excessive heating.
- Care for parking rules when stopping on a steep gradient.
- Use hand-brakes and place stones or bricks under the wheels but remember to remove these while resuming your journey.

- It is highly important to position your vehicle while negotiating sharp curves. The vehicle should be pulled towards right to bring it as close to the road centre as possible. More gently to the left inner side of the corner to reduce sharpness of the curve. Put your vehicle straight.
- On leaving the corner, move to the left.
- Before arriving at corners, the vehicles should be pulled to the extreme left. Then move towards right close to the centre of the road. Move well thereafter to the left and leaving the corner steer your vehicle straight.

Fitment of T.V. in a vehicle seems to be yet another craze though it also jeopardises vehicles safely. Must you find this irresistible take precaution not to use the unit while driving on hills. As far as possible, refrain from switching on your stereo while you drive on hills. Hill driving is somewhat different and, therefore, needs special skills to be safe.

Hill Climbing

This is the earliest method of testing an automobile's power and performance characteristics. Every country has its special hills to which a car financier would drive to see if his vehicle 'take it in high'.

In modern hill climbing events each driver is alone on the course, racing only against the clock. Winding curves and rough road surfaces are perhaps more of a challenge than the overall steepness of the hills.

Competitions are organised in all parts of the world and event attracts top drivers and huge crowds. All types of motor cars—sports antiques, classics and stock cars under strict safety rules and regulations. This competition is especially rough or on the low gears of the car's transmission and on the tires.

The annual Pikes Peak club in the famous hill climbing in the U.S.A. It is held since 1916 at the Colorado mountain. The outstanding events are:

- Colorado Mountain
- Giant's Despair (Pa)
- Mt. Washington (NH)
- Mt. Equinox (Vt).

Hill climbing is very popular in the British Isles, where an annual British Championship is awarded to the driver who wins the most of about a dozen such event, competition is well organised and driver must have Royal Automobile club competition licences.

Midget Car Racing

The sport of racing undersized cars emerged in the 1940s and quickly gained popularity. The cars must comply with rigid specifications, wheel bases, are 66-76 in. and tread width 42-46 in. Racing at specially built tracks usually is conducted on a circuit plan providing series of races. The sport is supervised by the Midget Driver of U.S.A.

Grand Prix Racing

In the whole firmament of racing G.P. events are the most elite. G.P. (i.e. international formula) automobiles are commonly the ultimate in design, speed, horsepower and romance. There are true racing cars in laymen's language. In Europe they are painted in national colours:

- British   —   Green
- Italian   —   Red
- French   —   Blue
- Germany   —   White
- U.S.   —   Blue and White.

The painting is done by their manufacturer in events as team (usually two or three cars) and driven by the best professional drivers. Races are held on closed circuits, 3 or 4 miles to the lap, the total distance varying from 150 to 400 mile. All modern G.P. cars confirm to one of the various formulas or sets of specifications which are laid down by F.I.A. and which govern the size, weight and type of vehicle permitted.

Based upon points earned in major Formula I events each year, admirer is designated world champion. The qualifying event called *grandes epreures* are customarily the G.P. of Monaco, Belgium, Netherland, France, Great Britain, Germany, Italy, Mexico, South Africa, Canada and U.S.

In 1966, F.I.A. announced new rules under which beginning in 1967, driver's performance would count in 9 out of 11 championships events. Points would be scored in first placing in the first six races of the season and on the four best plains in the remaining five events. Competition for title of World Champion began in 1950.

Sports Car Racing

The G.P. cars are normally single seat design with spartan cockpit furnishings and utterly functional equipment throughout, the sports, or Gran Tourism. (G.T.), car in usually a two seater sometimes four, and is characterised by it nimble abilities (if not speed and power) together with general stability for high special touring on ordinary roads. Unlike G.P. car, it is intended to be privately owned vehicles also unlike its more exotic cousin, it is usually series produced, seldom handmade. Although not usually designed exclusively for racing. Sports car are nevertheless also racing machines and are often entered in competitions with their own kind. Some of the world famous races are sports car events and may even be designated as G.P. The development of sports cars for racing, specially in such important events as the 24–hours endurance race at Le Mans (where the reputation of manufacturers are very much at stake) has brought about some sports cars that are in reality, little different in their power and speed potential for full Formula I machines. Based upon results each in a select list of sports car races, a sports car championship is awarded. It should be noted that whereas the world championship in

Formula I is awarded to a driver, the same title in sports car competition is awarded to a make of automobile.

Stock Car Racing

All automobiles that are not racing models and not sports models usually are termed stock cars or production models. Production cars are the bases of some of the most widely attended and most commercially important events in the whole of motor sports. The origin of stock car racing are said to stem in past from the prohibition period to the U.S. when bootlegger needing private cars of more than ordering speed capacities, turned and altered ordinary passenger automobiles to suit their needs. Subsequently these 'hopped up' cars were often raced for pleasure. Among these beginnings, an important branch of motor sports, has grown. In the U.S., stock car racing flourished after 1949. Racing, is conducted in several classes, grand national modified sportsmen etc. depending upon the type of automobile raced and the degree of modification allowed. Because results in three events are widely believed to have a powerful influence on brand preferences among buyers of cars, competition among manufacturers in the sponsorship of teams, engineers, drivers etc. is often intense.

Hot Rod Racing

Hot rod racing is an exciting motor sport which is largely confined to acceleration contests between privately designed and privately built automobile which have been constructed along individual lives to provide maximum performances. Hot rods in various classes may also compete against time distance in speed and endurance attempts.

Hot rodding as a hobby sport suffered and survived an early period of bad public and press relation because of its association with illegal street racing, but under the National Hot Rod Association (N.H.R.A.) became self policing and widely accepted by youth organisations, police officials, services clubs, and automobile manufacturers.

No definition of a hot rod is universally accepted. These cars may be constructed of components. From many makers of old and new automobiles, certain basic types are well-defined and well organised, however, such as roadsters, coupes, and sedans, pickups, streamlines etc. depending upon style of body and intended use. Thus a street roadster would be high performance automobiles, yet suitable for general use, a streamliner, by contrast, is designed for top speed performance at dry-lake or salt bed courses and would be unsuitable for other purposes. All are usually constructed with strict regards for safety.

Drag Dancing

Conducted at specially constructed and often elaborately equipped strips all over this is one of the most widely auto parts in U.S.A. A drag, or acceleration test measures the time required to cover a quarter mile from a standing start. The most specialised hot rods—so called sling shots (in which the driver sits on an extension behind the rear wheel) compete in this category. Standard production cars and sports cars may also compete in drag races.

G.P., sports stock hot rods etc. participate in race or contests with their own kind. They also make solo attempts against established time distance records. Records are established in both standing—start and flying start categories and in distance. They may also be expressed in terms distance achieved within a given period of time, the record for one hour. Engine size in cubic centimetres of cylinder volume is used as the basis for determining ten competition classes, designated A through J by F.I.A.

Motor racing is a dangerous undertaking in all its form. Manufacturers and race promoters are usually reluctant to acknowledge the danger. Spectacular and death-dealing accidents have marked the history of the sports from its earliest days. At various times following fatal accidents involving their participants or spectators, the very continuance of motor racing has seemed to be in doubt because of public or official protest. For example, in 1903 during a race held on the roads between Paris and Madrid several drivers and an uncounted number of persons were killed and maimed along the route. As a result the event was stopped short of its destination. This marked the end of the area of so called point to point racing on open roads.

Automobile events grow in number and popularity in Europe. Interest in the automobile kept pace in the U.S. Following World War I the development of motor sport continued at a rapid rate. Almost every nation of Europe boasted it own Grand Prix event in addition to scores of lesser contests. As the automobile became man's useful tool, so too, it became one of his most popular instrument of sports.

Himalayan Car Rallies

Motor car rally is an ideal sports full of adventure if, you enjoy zooming cars and vehicles as the epitome of excitement. The major events associated with car rally in India has been:

- The Vintage Car Rally—a periodic event in most of the metros.
- The Monsoon Rally—Starting from Calcutta the Charminar Challenge Rally.
- The Himalayan Car Rally—Most exciting and full of interest.

The topographical distribution of India makes it an ideal centre for motor car rallies. Here we have desert roads to beach, hill mountain and forest tracks, which offer an exciting terrain that can be tamped by competition cars in a rash of dust as radical tyres of these participating cars speed across the macadam.

The Vintage Car Rally

A rally can take many terms. The picturesque vintage car rally is a periodic and recurring event in most of the metros of India. During the rally, participants are colourfully dressed, cheerful with period costumes. You will find some very rare collector cars displayed and ran the rally '35 Jaguar convertible or a '54 Austin Saloon Deluxe or 1898 Humberette are also included in the rally. These rallies have become regular.

The Federation of Indian Rally Drivers Championship (F.I.R.D.C.) organises fine championship rallies of national and international status:

1. The Scissors Action Rally (national) sponsored by the Karnataka Motor Sports Club.
2. The Rally D'Endurance (national) organised by Indian Automotive Sports Club Bangalore and 9th Charminar Sports club.
3. The Para Observed Trials—August.
4. MRF Nylogrip Talent Search Rally—August.
5. Night Rally—August.
6. The Kinetic Para Ladies 50 cc Rally organised by associations at Pune, Jaipur, Bangalore—August.
7. Pagal Gymkhana, Chikmanglur—September.
8. Great Deserts, Himalayan Cross Country Rally, Bombay—September.
9. Popular Rally, Cochin—September.
10. MRF Manipur Rally, Imphal—September.
11. Good year Women's Car Rally, Bombay—October.
12. Memorial Rally, Chikmanglur—October.
13. Drag Meet and Hill Climb, Chikmanglur—November.
14. Habitat Motor Cross Event, Bombay.
15. Miny Rally, Chikmanglur.

Himalayan car rally has a cut above all other rallies in India. It attracts international attention and is now vying for championship status. Participants from all over the world gather for this premier event. New Delhi is the beginning and conducting point of this rally.

Like all other rallies, Himalayan car rally is the test of the skill and endurance of a car and its driver. The rally ignores the heavy traffic roads and takes to lesser known and traversed routes. In addition, this rally has some peculiarity such as detailed charting of rates, using dirt roads, forest roads dry river beds, mountain roads. Approximately 65 to 70 of its routes are in the highly competition, parfume zones, with about 30 per cent being diverted to the transport section.

The rally is open to any one who is in possession of a valid driving licence. The rally routes or begs usually permit regrouping halts of 2 to 5 hours duration *en route*. The event is run in compliance with the national and international sports code, rallies and regulation as laid down by the following associations:

(i) Federation International de I' Automobile.
(ii) Federation International due sports Automobile.
(iii) Federation of Motor Sports Clubs of India.

The Himalayan Car Rally is divided into four legs totalling over 3,200 km. It mostly concentrates on the mountain terrain of Himalayas i.e. hills of Himachal and Uttar Pradesh. The cars you intend to race needs to be homologated according to specifications. Several prizes and trophies are offered for the event suchas. Air India Trophy, the Coupe des Dames Trophy, class prizes, Charminar Challenge Awards several team and other prizes.

The Himalayan ran changes every year. The important towns *en route* are: ex-New Delhi, Mussoorie, Dehradun, Haridwar, Dharamshala, Shimla, Narkanda, Mandi, Nainital, Ranikhet, Corbett National Park and Garh Muktesvar. Since the route of the rally is not fixed, therefore, each year need tracks are marked. More undiscovered routes are discovered. This helps in retaining the surprise element for old rallyists, and a challenge for the new and old one.

The Himalayan Rally is India's only international motoring event. The first Rally was held in October 1980, starting from Bombay with the planned route taking the competitors through Central India, the Himalayas and finishing at Delhi. Much of the event was to run off the main roads and it had generated a tremendous response from competitors and media personnel both Indian and foreign. Unfortunately the political undertones which lead to stone-throwing and violence marred what would have been an excellent event and resulted in much of the Himalayan sections being cancelled. The second Himalayan Rally ran in November 1981.

As could be expected, most foreign competitors adopted a wait, watch and see attitude as far as the second event went.

The third Himalayan Rally is to start from Delhi on October 30, 1982 and the level of foreign enquiries was most encouraging.

The Himalayan Rally Association

The Association is a non profit organisation formed under the Societies Act and registered with the Charities Commissioner in Bombay as a Trust.

The Management Committee of this Association, which is the policy making body.

National Income

A working paper for the 1980 event shows that conservative figures of the foreign exchange earned in India by holding the first Himalayan Rally exceeds Rs.42 lakhs. The outgoing foreign exchange, assuming the crude oil for the fuel utilised to be imported at the then spot prices, works out to Rs.70,000 and the prize money remitted to Rs.52,000 giving a total outgo of approximately Rs.1,25,000.

From 1981 onwards the Organisers appointed Messrs Thomas Cook as the official travel agents for the Himalayan Rally and it is expected that special purpose tours will begin to visit India at the time of the Rally.

Exposure and Income Potential

It may be mentioned that special purpose tours form an integral part of the Tourism earning of many countries whose rallies have reached very high standards.

For example the Safari Rally of Kenya which enjoys a

'Championship of Makes' status—which we hope to achieve over the next few years—(the Safari incidentally is 30 years old) boasts of an annual income to the country of Kenya in liquid currency of over 5 million pounds sterling. The annual exposure value exceeds 250 million pound sterlings—it is therefore not surprising that the Government of Kenya treats the Safari as one of its major tourism promotional activities.

Even communist countries have rallies on the international calendar and the latest addition (which will in time become our greatest rival) is China. Plans have been announced for China's first Rally from Hong Kong to Peking to be held in 1983. One of the main reasons given is the exposure, tourist potential and foreign exchange earnings!

The 1980 Himalayan Rally was televised in prime time by German Television II and Austrian Television. The German programme had a viewership of 15 million people and has been valued at Rs.28 lakhs, while the Austrian programme has a viewership of 10 million and has been valued at approximately Rs.20 lakhs. Furthermore with Air India as one of the main sponsors every competing car compulsorily carried Air India stickers and with it the consequential exposure. With the Department of Tourism on our committee and with their assistance, the tourism aspect was also covered in the television presentation.

Foreign television is not used by our country for tourism promotion as it proves too expensive under normal circumstances. The sport of rallying provides this opportunity as part of its inherent character by not being a stadium event.

Apart from television, a number of motoring correspondents and journalists covered the event and reports appeared in motoring journals and newspapers all over the world.

Rallying the World

Throughout the world, all motor sports is controlled by the world body called the Federation Internationale de

L'Automobile (F.I.A.) headquartered in Paris. The sporting arm is known as the Federation Internationale du Sport Automobile (F.I.S.A.) as the F.I.A. is also involved in the touring aspect.

Each year the F.I.S.A. nominates ten events as qualifying towards the Championship of Makes status. This year's events are in the following countries: Monte Carlo, Portugal, Kenya, Greece, Argentina, Finland, Italy; Britain, France, New Zealand.

As a matter of policy the F.I.S.A. has expressed a desire to run a Championship event in Asia. However, as no country runs a suitable event, this slot at present remains unoccupied, and our objective is to fill it.

Manufacturers the world over aspire to winning this championship and participate in most of these events in order to generate championship points. There is a tangible link between car sales and its rally performance. A manufacturer's rallying programme normally forms part of its marketing operations and their budgets are commensurate with this objective. As examples Porsche were reputed to have spent Rs.50 lakhs for a two car entry in the Safari in 1978 and Daimler Benz Rs.4 crores for a four car entry in 1980. Forty to fifty percent of this figure can be considered as the income to the country holding the event.

The fuel crisis has caused a major rethinking and redesign of the automobile all over the world. This is especially true of the American motor car and the days of the large and heavy American cars are over. Consequently the world market today centres around vehicles of the size manufactured by Japan, Europe, Great Britain and this is the market the American manufacturers now try to enter. The competition for sales is expected to become fierce and our Rally can have a direct benefit as a result of this activity as it establishes itself as being one of the finest proving grounds for their product.

Motoring reports of our first event confirm that India has the finest set of Rally roads of any country in the world and the changes in terrain, altitude climate and the endurance aspect that we can offer cannot be equalled. In time, a win in our Rally will be considered as the ultimate in determining a motor car's ruggedness and reliability.

The permanent paid members of the Association number seven people. The entire administration is carried out by enthusiasts on a voluntary basic and involves totally approximately 2,000 people.

The Route

Himalayan Rally promises to be the toughest ever. Even though the total distance has now been reduced to approximately 3,600 kms., the start from Delhi on October 30th has resulted in more challenging sections being included. The event has been planned in a way that the back-up for the competitors is now much easier and at the same time filming the event poses less problems.

Commencing from Delhi the cars will travel to Ramnagar and from there into the Corbett Park and on to Haridwar. Followed by more forest sections the cars will reach Dehradun after a short run in the foothills of Himachal Pradesh. Dehradun is the first Regrouping Control after which a circular run through Barkot and Pauri brings the cars back into Corbett Park for the final forest run and Nainital where Leg 1 ends.

Leg 2 takes the cars to Lohaghat (near Pithoragarh) up a very challenging run towards Almora and on to Berinag, Bageshwar, Kausani and Ranikhet (Regrouping Control). A night start from Ranikhet takes the cars towards Badrinath crossing over a high forest road (10,600 ft.) to Tilwara, Tehri and Mussoorie for the overnight halt.

Mussoorie starts Leg 3 which takes the cars towards Nahan, a treacherous dirt road towards Solon, Khandeghat, Dhalli and Narkhanda (9,000 ft. and a Regroup Control). Once again the difficulties of the Jalori Pass have to be encountered (where snow causes a major disruption before entering Kulu and Manali, for an overnight halt.

Manali commences Leg 4 taking the cars through the

Rohtang Pass (14,000 ft.) to beautiful Lahaul Valley from which the cars return by the same route to Mandi. A final dirt section near Bilaspur brings the cars back to Delhi for the finish.

Suggestions for the Rally

General Considerations

(a) The basic purpose of such a device is to protect the driver if the car over-turns or is involved in a serious accident. This purpose should always be borne in mind.

(b) One continues length of good quality tubing should be used for all the main hoops with smooth continues bends and no evidence of crimping or wall failure.

(c) The main hoops should be placed as close as possible (or touching) to the roof and coach-work in order to limit crushing in the event of an accident or somersault.

(d) All welding should be of the finest quality with full penetration. Welding may be electric arc or oxy-acetylene.

(e) The safety cage must be conceived in such a way as not to obstruct the access to the seats and not to encroach on the space provided for the driver or the passengers.

(f) All bolts and nuts used for attachment should be good quality hexagonal headed bolts and nuts. Square head bolts and nuts should not be used.

Main Structure

(a) The safety cage must be made of three main hoops viz.: front hoop ABCD, central hoop EFGH and rear hoop IJKL.

(b) The front hoop shall run along the roof close to the wind screen following the wind screen pillars.

(c) The central hoop shall run along the door pillars and curve (as close to the roof as possible) rearwards at the roof so as to provide a clearance of min. 10 cms. and max. 15 cms. between drivers helmet and top of roll bar, with seat in full back position and driver in normal driving position.

(d) The Rear hoop shall run along the roof close to the rear windshield and proceed at an angle through the rear shelf behind the seat to the luggage boot floor.

(e) To the rear hoop shall be attached any one diagonal KI or LJ. This diagonal shall also pass through the rear shelf to the luggage boot floor.

(f) All holes provided in the shelf be just large enough so as to accommodate the tube only.

(g) These three main hoops will be further supported by longitudinal members, viz.: BF, CG, FJ, GK.

(h) These longitudinal members shall be attached as close as possible to the roof.

(i) All tubes should be mild steel seamless tubes and should be of at least 33.7 mm. OD and 3.25. mm wall thickness OR 42.4 mm. OD and 2.65 mm. wall thickness. The minimum specification of the seamless tube is IS 1161. The tubes will be back and not galvanised.

Attachment of Main Hoops to the Body

It is specified that all roll bars must make use of two plates for attachment.

(a) A tube of min. 30 mm. long having its internal diameter such that it is a "good-fit" over that roll bar tube and a wall thickness of min. 14 swg (2.6 mm.) is welded on to a plate having a min. thickness of 14 swg (2.6 mm.) and whose area should be at least 50 cm². This plate and tube should be welded to the end of the roll bar hoop.

(b) The part of the floor of body where the hoop is to be attached is reinforced either by welding or riveting of a plate of min. 10 swg (3.25 mm.) thickness and having a min. area of 50 cm².

(c) The plate attached to the end of the hoop shall be

joined to this plate by at least four hexagonal headed
bolts and nuts of min. 8 mm. diameter.

(d) In no way shall the roll cage be welded or riveted
directly on to the body shell or chassis.

Attachment of Longitudinal Members to the Main Structure

(a) A tubing of suitable length, having a wall thickness
same as that of the main hoops and its internal
diameter be such that it is a "good-fit" over the tube
of the longitudinal member, shall be welded on to
the main hoop.

(b) The longitudinal pipe shall be bolted to the main hoop
by two hexagonal headed bolts of at least 6 mm.
diameter and bolted at 90° to each other.

The drawings referred to will be sent to those competitors
who have sent their entries and may be collected by others
on payment of Rs.4.

All 82 Himalayan Rally Cars Flag-Off

All 82 cars slated to run in the Himalayan Rally was technically
cleared after scrutiny from the starting line at the Jaipur Polo
Grounds.

The Acting President waved off the cars and the first driver
to mount the ramp and collect his card was Jayant Shah in a
Datsun Violet. Being the only participant with an international
ranking he, to use the golfing term, "has the honour".

Being waved off first is not merely a ceremonial privilege
and Shah strive to maintain that place for as long as possible.
On dirt roads, the surface was least disturbed for the first
car—and there was no dust which can make things uncomfortable
for those running behind.

While it is true that a rally is more than a race and the
man who finishes first need not be the winner, most seasoned

rally drivers like to stay as close to the front as possible to benefit from less disturbed road conditions.

People in Delhi had the opportunity of looking at the rally in the city itself. From the Polo Grounds the cars took Aurangzeb Road, go past the Taj Hotel towards India Gate, use the Hexagon Road to reach Purana Qila Road, go past Pragati Maidan and use the underpass in Bhairon Road to get to the Ring Road. They will use the Nizamuddin Bridge to take the highway to Mohun Nagar—and on to Ramnagar.

As "zero hour" approached the activity increased. The cars were given a final tuning, the service teams were setting out to predetermined points. A number of film and television units were also getting ready to move on Friday evening.

Cars and drivers are what the public sees in a rally—to keep them running requires a great deal of organization and the volunteers of the Himalayan Rally Association were working themselves at fever pitch. Their task is an order as tall as the mountains after which the event is named; with the dedication of genuine sportsmen they will strive to reach their summit.

A Tough Going for Car Rally

Having succeeded in running through a fusillade of brickbats and extricating itself from the slush in a snowfield, India's prestigious motor sport event to drop into top gear autumned. The third Himalayan Rally of 1982 ran from October 30 to November 5.

It was no "Ocean to Sky" exercise this time; unlike the initial two ventures the rally started and ended in Delhi. The organizers have done away with the Bombay-Delhi section. Thus the major part of the 3,600 km. route, was in the hills— on rugged, unpaved, stretches which the knowledgeable had dubbed the "best rally roads in the world".

The scrapping of the Bombay-Delhi leg, which was really an armchair ride for the more seasoned competitors, reduces some of logistic and technical support needed by both organizer and competitor to keep the event going. A number of foreign teams had expressed their dissatisfaction with that section.

Four Stages

Bombay was the starting point of the first two events mainly because the majority of the organizers are based in that western metropolis. And they had banked on receiving much financial support from there—which did not quite materialize.

The rally was run in four legs. The flag-off was at the Jaipur Polo Grounds, and the cars set off for Ramnagar, through the Corbett National Park, and on to Haridwar; along some more forest roads to Dehradun for the first Regrouping Control.

A Regrouping Control was unique to this event necessitated by the fact that Indian vehicles are unable to match the better foreign entrants in terms of speed. To avoid the rally getting spread out, cars were bunched together at Regrouping Controls, and then restarted with man with the best points-position setting off first. The others, in order of points, followed after very brief intervals.

From Dehradun the Rally took a circular run through Barkot and Pauri, back to Corbett Park, and on to Nainital where the first leg ends. As is evident, the main traffic arteries were carefully avoided, driving skill and the technological status of a vehicle best tested "in the rough".

In the second leg, Rally moved to Lohaghat (near Pithoragarh), on a stiff run towards Almora and then on to Berinag, Bageshwar, Kausani and Ranikhet where the second Regrouping Control functioned.

A night start at Ranikhet, and off towards Badrinath, the Rally went crossing a forest road 10,600 ft. high to reach Tilwara, Tehri and Mussoorie where the second leg ends—and there was the first overnight halt.

The going gets even more difficult as the third leg gets underway, a treacherous dirt road takes the cars towards Solan, Kandaghat, Dhalli and Narkhanda—where the Regrouping Control was done at a point 9,000 ft. above the sea level. The next port of call was Manali, but before that the Jalori Pass.

In 1981 early snow gave the rally a spicy test on the Pass with only the better cars getting through. It is hoped the Indian participants have learnt their lesson and will remember to carry snow chains.

The fourth leg starts out with a high objective—Rohtang. The stretch through that famous Pass and a brief stint in the Lahaul Valley could be the zenith of the event's challenge. Unfortunately, it has never been fully savoured, for on both the previous occasions the Pass was closed to traffic on account of snow.

The Rally turned around and return to Manali. The final dirt section near Bilaspur takes the route to Mandi, and back to New Delhi via Rai. A long run indeed, with 75 per cent of the route on roads with no paved surfaces.

August is the month in which the entries really come in according to the Chairman of the Himalayan Rally Association and one of this country's best rally drivers, Mr. Nazir Hoosein.

Foreign entries have been received, including that of Rudi Sthol of Austria, and a works-entry from British Leyland in the shape of one of the Rover line. The organizers expected 80 to 100 cars to start off, about 25 of them from abroad.

Overlapping

With over 350 rallies listed on the international calendar, there is bound to be some overlapping. A rally team cannot flit about from one section of the globe to another, each event requires weeks of preparation.

The Himalayan Rally Association has been preparing from almost immediately after the prize distribution ceremony of the last rally. Route surveys, road books, and a host of other arrangements are necessary. Communications provided by amateur radio operators are vital.

The planning of the rally route has shown an improvement in that now it runs in a sort of loop formation. This enables the service vehicles to tend to a competitor, take a direct route and reach the next service point before the rally car arrives.

Although still in its infancy, the rally has already started generating response from the domestic motor car industry. A number of technological improvements, although minor ones, have been made on the basis of experiences gleaned during the event.

The Sponsors

While Air-India remains the main sponsor of the event—flying in cars free of cost and contributing handsomely to the prize-money—other agencies also do their bit. The Shipping Corporation of India transports cars from places where Air-India's Boeings do not operate, and the Department of Tourism helps ship away plenty of procedural red tape. The tourism potential of the rally are tremendous.

The Indian Oil Corporation made extensive arrangements for fuelling the cars. Existing stations are geared up and a couple of temporary ones set up so that no car has to travel more than 300 km. for fuel.

What, however, really fuels the rally is the spirit of the volunteers. The entire organization is a voluntary effort and having seen the manner in which the people staging the event have sweated on previous occasions one can safely say that their efforts have been commendable. Nobody claims the organization is perfect, but it has amply displayed its capacity to improve. And that is saying a lot.

Perhaps the happiest surprise are the showing of Indian cars and drivers. The equipment cannot be described as first-rate (by rallying standards at least) and our drivers lack competitive experience. Yet what they have been able to do has made many a foreign observer sit up and open his eyes. Some have even described such performances as "miraculous".

London-Sydney Marathon

The London-Sydney marathon which passed through India in 1993 had many lady participants who bravely undertook the gruelling journey in situations that would have daunted many males. While sports activities of various kinds have over the years shown that women are not lagging behind, long distance marathons are such a test of endurance, that the participation of as many as 11 ladies in the marathon is no mean feat.

Three lady participants travelled with their husbands and one was travelling with her father. The all ladies team—car no. 60, a Volvo 120—had two tall strapping ladies from New South Wales in Australia. However, the most amazing lady on the trip was undoubtedly 66-year-old Pamela Durham, who was travelling with co-driver Barry Summer in a 1953 Morgan Plus convertible, the oldest car in the rally.

Pamela had a few years ago (in 1990) participated in the London-Peking marathon with her daughter, driving the same Morgan. At this rally there were 65 participants and the journey took the mother and daughter team through many countries that have since totally changed such as southern Europe and U.S.S.R.

During the Indian leg of the London-Sydney marathon, Pamela and Barry had a major problem with the canavas roof of their car. On the Delhi-Jodhpur leg, the heat was so intense (43°C) they decided to remove the hood of the car completely and travel with wet towels on their heads, worn Bedouin style.

Their luggage was strapped on the tyre at the back of the car, since there was no space inside. From Jodhpur when they left for their next stop, they had added a colourful blanket on top of the canvas roof of their car, to make the heat bearable.

Virginia Bevan and Georgina Chaseling were the two ladies who braved the journey in a Volvo 120. Virginia says that she decided to join the rally when she discovered that her husband was planning to participate with a friend. She and Georgina had earlier been on a rally in Australia in 1989 in the same car. This rally in Tasmania known as 'Targa' was one of the most prestigious rallies in the world in which cars worth over 30 million dollars took part. Virginia and Georgina in their old Volvo made all the other participants smile.

This marathon has also been very exciting for this "all ladies team" as they have had to cope with many difficult problems on the way. While leaving Istanbul their car engine decided to pack up and since they were the last to leave, they suddenly found that everyone had left.

Hunting around for a mechanic was not easy and no one was prepared to help. After much ranting and raving they finally located someone who grudgingly agreed to fix the engine when they explained that unless they could reach Ankara by 7.30 a.m. next morning, they would be disqualified from the race. The car was fixed at 2 a.m. in the morning and these brave ladies managed to reach Ankara five minutes before the deadline. Needless to say, they were running last in the marathon at that time. At the time of reaching Jodhpur, they had managed to move up by eight places.

At the gala banquet hosted on the lawns of Umaid Bhavan Palace by H.H. Gaj Singh II at the end of the Delhi-Jodhpur leg, Virginia was seen anxiously enquiring if it would be possible to have 400 bottles of iced mineral water for the rallyists—to beat the desert heat on the Jodhpur-Udaipur run. Next morning all the participants were seen carrying their precious bottles of water to the cars. At the flag-off by H.H. Gaj Singh II all were unanimous in saying that the night halt at Umaid Bhavan Palace was the "Jewel in the Crown" of the London-Sydney rally.

Jill Diamond in car no. 93, a Triumph 2000, was travelling with her father Barry Gardner. Jill, who is a trained nurse, gave up nursing to sell tours in U.S.A. This she found more lucrative and was very successful in this field, according to her proud father. Barry Gardner who is a radio engineer supplies radios for special occasions such as those used by teams crossing the South Pole, mountain climbers etc. He has supplied the radios being used for this rally.

According to Barry, he chose Jill as his co-driver because she was very tough and has proved to be an excellent navigator. Her skills in navigation were recognised by her other team-mates, who would enquire for directions over the radio.

Peter and Mary Hall in a green Ford Escort (car no. 25) were using the rally to raise money for "The Great Ormond Street Children's Hospital Fund". In this marathon their aim is to somehow reach Sydney. Twenty-five years ago their car (the same car) had a clutch problem 200 miles before Sydney, and they had to drop out of the race.

There are others also raising money for worthwhile causes such as Roger and Margret Ealand in car no. 91, who are raising money for the "Royal Marsden Cancer Fund". Their car has signatures and good wishes from all their friends and relatives on the bonnet and the roof.

Of the 110 cars that were participating in the rally, only 97 were able to complete the Indian leg of the marathon. The cars came gayly painted with the most interesting slogans such as car no. 56 sponsored by "Kellogs Coco Pops", car no. 108 sponsored by "The Ink Group" with a visual of a large ink pot spilling over on the bonnet. There was one bonnet dedicated to "Genuine Draft Beer", and another to "Surgicraft Medical Products" but possibly the most eye catching ones were the bonnets that promoted "Queen Anne Silver Plated Tableware", and "Good as New Recycled Clothing, Epping".

To sum "its hard being a woman in a man's world and trying to keep up with them in a gruelling marathon like this one. What makes it worse is that when calamity strikes, it is to men that we have to turn".

9

Jeep Safari to the Top of the World

It's Himalayas' best kept secrets where nature has jealously
guarded its pristine beauty. And here, all you need is a streak
of adventure and a stout heart to endure the jeep safari from
Shimla to Kalpa, a distance of 238 kms. You skirt through
river Sutlej through Narkanda, Rampur Bushair and Rekong
Peo and onto Kalpa and Chitkul ... two of the most stunning
habitation on the old Hindustan-Tibet Road.

Forget Switzerland. There cannot be a more picturesque
sight than this. Even as your jeep passes through snaky
mountain roads, take an eyeful of the scenic surroundings.
Kinnaur is God's own country. So dramatic is the land that
on the one side there are dense forests, fruit orchards, lush
green valleys, while on the other, rugged mountains and miles
and miles of high altitude desert.

Sutlej enters India from this region and cuts the great
Himalayan belt of Kinnaur in the centre carving spectacular
gorges. Looming ahead of us is the Kinnaur Kailash range—
the abode of Lord Shiva—rising up to a height of 6,050 m.
which changes colour several times a day. This is one of
Himalayas' best kept secrets where nature has jealously
guarded its pristine beauty.

We are on a jeep safari to Chitkul at a heady height of
3,450 m.—the last village on the Indo-Tibetan border. Closed
to tourists till 1993, it has now opened its magical beauty to

the world. It is a verdant village surrounded by lush green fields and high mountain peaks. Here, quaint little houses, temples and gompas conjure up a perfect image of a Shangri La.

The journey to Chitkul is best begun from Shimla. All you need is a streak of adventure and a stout heart to endure the jeep safari from Shimla to Kalpa. A distance of 238 kilometres and eight hours skirting river Sutlej through Narkanda, Rampur Bushair and Rekong Peo and on to Kalpa—the first stop en route.

Once the favourite haunt of Lord Dalhousie, Kalpa is the place where the Dalai Lama delivered the Kalachakra Sermon in 1992. Legend has it that the people who earlier inhabited the region were half birds and half human beings because you need to have wings to reach Kinnaur. But now, thanks mainly to border roads, it has become accessible though the journey may be hazard-prone at times and, bone-rattling in parts. But once Kalpa is reached, the long haul appears quite worth the trouble.

Looming in front of Kalpa is the magnificent Kinner Kailash range of the Greater Himalayas raising to the height of 6,050 m. on top of which rises a natural six-metre tall Shivalingam. The ancient villages of Chini, Pangi, Rogi, Telangi, Kothi, Poari and Peo offer an excellent opportunity to observe the traditional and tribal lifestyles of its inhabitants.

Here in the midst of stunning wilderness, an enterprising young man, Sanjay Verman, had set up camp sites offering exotic activities like star gazing, mountain biking, river crossing, trout fishing and rock climbing. Unlike your usual tour operators, Verman has a thing about nature preservation. "Save and enjoy the environment", is a sentence you will hear him repeat even in his sleep. He recycles all waste material and has brought bio-degradable chemical toilets all the way from Italy. Lanterns and hot water are solar-provided and sun cookers used to rustle up meals which range from simple Kinnauri food to a three course western repast.

A remarkable feature of Buddhism in Kinnaur is the almost indistinguishable border-line between this and the Hinduism practised here. Some of the important monasteries of this region are in Nako, where the second Buddha is said to have stayed, the monastery village of Kanum, the three Nyigmapa temples of Lippa, Lhanan monastery at Moorang, Thakurdwara temple in Tashigang which has a sandal-wood image of Lord Buddha, a 12th century Ge-lug-pa monastery at Chini and the Kalchakra monastery of Peo.

The tell-tale signs of an era long gone by are all around. On the old Hindustan-Tibet Road, washed by giant waterfalls, you are transported back to the days of the Silk Route. And it is here that some of the ageless secrets of the Himalayas are unveiled.

In Moorang, a little distance away from Kalpa, is the Bhim Fort perched precariously on a hilltop. The Pandavas are believed to have spent some of their time in the last year of their exile here. The small fort which still has the remains of Abhimanyu's clothes and some weapons and cooking utensils, has now been declared a national monument. A little distance away from the Bhim Fort is the Moorang Monastery dotted with caves. The Lamas who wish to become monks have to spend 39 months in meditation in these caves called 'Monk Cells'. Meals given to these Lamas are said to be so spartan that many perish in the process and some take to eating raw mud.

For miles on end there are neither tourists nor buses nor cars nor any other rashes of the Shimla-Kasauli-Chail circuit. Just rugged barren mountains, a desolate stillness and the sounds of silence broken only by the gushing rivulets, high passes and breath-taking gorges.

You are now on the road to Nako. For a newcomer the ill effects of high altitude start being felt on the final climb itself. The nights are worse because the air is more rarefied. It is not for nothing that the locals call this the land of the moon with fairy castle-like monasteries perched precariously on rocky crags. They are, in fact, the main point of interest in Nako where people follow the Tibetan form of Buddhism.

It is an innocent life they lead. The school here is the focal point of Nako. Girls in blue dresses and maroon pullovers with bags slung around their necks could pass off as school children anywhere. Here the summer days are for farming for the food which will not just meet their daily needs but will also be stored away from the cruel winter months. Early morning and evenings are spent in the monasteries revolving the prayer wheel and singing hymns in praise of Padmasambhava, popularly known as the second Buddha, a Bengali saint who imparted the teachings of the Enlightened One of the people.

According to one legend, Padmasambhava in a demonstration of his tantric powers is said to have landed on a rock in the village of Nako. The rock on which his footprints are believed to be embossed is worshipped even today. In the past, Nako had been a hub in the caravan routes on the old Hindustan-Tibet route. The little village is said to have played host to traders from Yarkhand, Kashgar, Lhasa, Amritsar, Khotan and Persia.

The descent from Nako is steep as the Kuchcha road hugs the Spiti Valley. Both geologically and archaeologically, Spiti is a living museum. It is bereft of any vegetation as erosion by sun, wind and snow over thousands of years has laid bare the rocks.

Spiti is an inhospitable land, a cold desert, located on the Tibetan border and flanked on the south-east by Kinnaur, on the north-east by Tibet, north by Laddakh and to the south by the Kullu ranges. A nature's marvel of rugged crages and slopes that change colour from pale pink to bright scarlet alternating with soft blues to bring greens of the glaciers.

You are now on our jeep safari's final leg—the road to Chitkul, the last village on the Indo-Tibetan border. This is a fairyland surrounded by green fields and high mountain peaks. Slopes wooded with Bhoj Patra, miles of alpine meadows, Lammergeiers, golden eagles all greet the eye in a wondrous splendour.

This is the most memorable part of our road journey. The Sangla Valley is full of wooded slopes as far as Chitkul (3,435 m.) where our Base Camp is situated. The last inhabited village in this valley surrounded by green fields and high mountain peaks, Chitkul is like fairyland. The quaint little houses are built on a slope with one rising one above the other.

10

Hot Roads in the Himalayas
Joy Ride: Long Distance Biking

There are two routes to Leh. The shorter and comparatively easier one is through **Kashmir Valley** (420 kms. from Srinagar) to go up. For the return, the 475 km. and more punishing Leh-Manali road after riding astride the 140 km. Pangong Tso lake on the **Changthang plains** bordering China.

The most difficult part of the journey is the first 25 kms. through the 11,575 ft. high Zoji La. Traffic on this stretch moved in one-way convoys controlled by the Army. Barely wide enough for a truck to pass, it was a dirt track blasted into the mountain side. Past the high watershed mark, rivers and brooks babbled along. And the dense pine-clad slopes of Kashmir valley gave way to bare, multi-coloured mountains of stark beauty with just a trace of Alpine grass.

Next is Drass, the second coldest inhabited place on earth after Siberia. Temperatures here drops to minus 60°C in winters. From here one had to cross Kargil, under fire from Pakistan, and tame two more passes before one could be in Leh. From here the run to Leh is a downhill affair through a landscape of astounding colours. At first glance, it shows a bland oneness where only texture seemed to differ. But a closer look reveals the existence of dozens of hues in perfect harmony—purples, tender greens, improbable tangerine. Situated 11,000 ft. above the sea on the banks of Indus, Leh proved to be a voyage of discovery with its bustling bazaar and quaint historical comers. After a few days of rest and stocking up on food and fuel for onward journey to Chushul, one is ready to roll.

Snaking up a beautiful chocolate-brown landscape of rounded hills and snow-sculpted rocks, the road is well surfaced. From Karu, 40 kms. from Leh, one leaves the Leh-Manali 'highway' for a jeepable track that formed intricate serpentine loops to the 18,000 ft. high Chang La. The pass affords one first view of the Tangtse valley lined with razor-sharp peaks of the Karakoram range towering into the sky.

For the next 60 kms. to Chushul, bikes rocked and rolled along the lake's southern shore on a surface of scree and boulders. But these are nothing compared to what lay ahead. A little way from the memorial at Chushul, erected in memory of the valiant troops who laid down their lives to save the country during the 1962 Chinese invasion, hit upon a vast sea of sand. This is the Changthang plains, a high-altitude desert that is home to the Changpa tribe. With the tyres sinking into tractionless motion, the bikes had to be pushed for several kilometres through the howling wind. And all the while one had to keep a close watch on the tyre marks left by Army trucks. One miss, and even a vulture would find it difficult to trace you in the windswept expanse of the Tibetan plateau.

One is caught up with the Indus as it entered India, a little ahead of Nyoma, around 100 kms from Chushul. For the first time in two days, one may encourage a non-military human presence. A dusty jeepable track now ambled along the river to join the road to Manali 60 kms. ahead of the 17,558 ft. high Tanglang La. Temperature at the pass drops considerably. The cold sliced through our woollens, the wind is a whiplash. From here, one descends to the More plains, a windswept dusty barren plateau that could accommodate hundreds of football fields.

Swaying in tune with the rocking bikes as these toiled over the craggy surface to ascend the incredibly desiccated Lachalung La (16,800 ft.), and Nakee La (14,000 ft.), one comes down to Sarchu, a plateau at 14,000 ft. that is roughly halfway to Manali.

Manali, with its promise of the spoils of civilisation, is only 13,500 ft. high Rohtang pass away. After so many days of gruelling austerity. One deserves it.

Joy Ride: Long Distance Biking

Fun, adventure, excitement and romance is the thrill of long distance biking. Cool wind in your hair, and the heaven above you; joy in your heart and the road before you. Not to forget, of course, that powerful piece of throbbing metal below you, scorching the earth with a triumphant roar and a glint of the sun as it eats up the miles and races with time.

It's biking we're talking about. Not bicycling, which is for the poets, but motorcycling which is for the powerful. Even as you read this, many a biker is on a thrill and a high, traversing the length and breadth of the country, and bridging continents as well. For the avid biker, biking is as addictive as anything else, whether he goes solitary or with a companion or in a group.

There are motorcycling clubs in most major cities. In Delhi there are 'Bullet Clubs', sponsored by Royal Enfield where people, mostly foreign embassy personnel, go out on weekend jaunts on 350 cc Enfield Bullets, which in India is the most favoured mode of transport.

The embassy crowd, says Mr. Carlos of the Brazilian Embassy, even have their own personal clubs; one such is 'Rolling Thunder' with members from different embassies. While there are a few Indian aficionados, it is mostly foreigners who are into biking in India in a big way.

In the U.S., there are Harley Davidson clubs, whose members zoom across the country from coast to coast, with some gangs even spreading a trial of terror. One such infamous gang was the Hell's Angels, who were associated with shoot-outs at rock concerts, including a Rolling Stones one, and people often fled at the sight of approaching bikers, all dressed up in black leather boots, pants and jackets with chains dangling.

In India, fortunately, things are somewhat tamer. Some bikers bring their own bikes from as far away as Europe, overland. Others come to India and buy a second-hand Enfield, which they sell back on completing their expedition, or even ship back if their final destination is elsewhere. Others simply rent out a bike for the duration of their tour.

A biker from France called Eric, in Manikaran, had come there all the way overland from France on his 1200 cc BMW, traversing through Spain, Libya, Tunisia, Egypt, the Middle East, Iran, Pakistan and into India at the Wagah border, then Amritsar, and straight up the Beas Valley to Manikaran, because he had heard about it way back in France. From Manikaran he planned to go to Manali, and then down to Delhi and all the way south. Must have been some trip that.

The Australian couple, Miles Carpenter and Teresa Richards, hires out bikes to enthusiasts. They were there to sell their Bullet, or alternately arrange to ship it back to Australia.

They had bought it second-hand from a dealer in Paharganj for just Rs.27,000 and then gone on a 7,000 km. odyssey for six months.

Amitabh Ghosh, claims to have visited every district in every State of India on his Enfield! He works as a location hunter for Merchant-Ivory productions and shoots stills of exotic locations.

Anil Agnihotri who, hold your breath, took his scooter right from Delhi to Leh.

Then there are those who hire out bikes on a day to day basis.

The most favoured routes, and the only ones he takes, are to Himachal Pradesh and Rajasthan. Especially popular are the Kullu and Kangra valleys in Himachal, and Ajmer, Pushkar, Bikaner, Jaipur, Jaisalmer and Jodhpur in Rajasthan. If required and paid for, he also takes a mechanic along.

Most bikers, come from either West Europe, the U.S. or Australia, and India is a much favoured destination because of the ease and freedom of movement and a lovely countryside that varies from the mountainous to the desert, forested and coastal. Goa is a popular destination and in fact many foreigners hire their bikes in Goa itself for local sightseeing. While bikers like to go to Himachal during September-October, in November-December they prefer Rajasthan and Goa. Some even take along tents.

There are the most popular Indian bikes with foreigners. For one, they are sturdy and rugged and the most powerful bikes available in India, secondly they have a good maintenance value and even if they break down, any mechanic anywhere in India can repair them easily.

Then there are certain people who own their Enfields, writer Bill Aitken being one of them. Bill has traversed the entire Himalayan range on his bike, and even, aged 60-plus, travelled the coastal route up from Kanyakumari along the Western Ghats.

He had to abandon the trip after he fell down a slope and dislocated his shoulder. "Youth is a great thing, you must do all the travelling you have to while you are still young".

Having done the Delhi-Kanyakumari route is an incredible, memorable, awesome experience.

What is it about biking that makes it so addictive? Simply, because you are out there in communion with nature, with the sun, the wind and the rain, it's you and the elements, in short, and it's an experience that changes your whole life.

Unlike public transport, which is even cheaper, it gives you the freedom to stop where you want, when you want, or even go off on a tangent, with detours into remote and inaccessible areas. In short, you indulge your wanderlust wantonly, spontaneously, impulsively.

It's like falling in love and the world seems to be made anew. And you learn so much about life, about adventure, about hardship, about camaraderie, about the world. And as the saying goes, it is truly the wise man who travels. The fool just wanders.

What You Need?

- A will-serviced, reliable sturdy bike (preferably an

Enfield, but any well-maintained bike will do. Some even go out on scooters and jeeps).

- Money: Cash for immediate need, but mostly travellers cheques, as they are safer in the long run.
- A spirit of adventure.
- A change or two clothes: jeans, boots, a windproof jacket, a raincoat (keep the luggage minimal as it has to be carried on a special carrier attached behind the bike for that purpose).
- A light-weight tent and a sleeping bag in case of emergencies or if you do not wish to spend the nights in hotels *en route*.
- A rudimentary knowledge of motorcycle maintenance and repairs, including a basic tool kit. In any case you will find mobike mechanics in every nook and corner of India in case your bike breaks down and you can fetch them rather easily.
- Licence and motorcycle papers.

11

Camel Safaris

Camels are exotic, picturesque beats whose antics and personalities add a special dimension to any trip. On these camel safaris, all arrangements are much like a trek. Each group is a self-contained unit travelling alone in the desert with all gear and water carried by pack camels. There is a staff by camel handlers and camp assistants to do the cooking and camp chores. Depending upon the trip, you may ride part of the time and walk part of the time. You don't have to carry anything.

The mystique of Rajasthan is largely built on its valorous forts, ornate palaces and the intrigues their walls were fabled to contain.

Lesser known is perhaps the culture of the money-spinning Marwari community which has its roots not just in Marwar but in the Shekhawati region of north-eastern Rajasthan. It was here that this enterprising community built its country houses or *havelis* during the 18th and 19th centuries.

The region comprising the present day districts of Sikar and Jhunjhunu was also the major trading point for incoming foreign traders.

Now, not much remains of either. The expanding British Raj pushed out the local traders towards the ports. Later the remaining Marwaris also moved out to in search of better trade opportunities, leaving their *havelis* derelict and run-down. However, most Marwaris still regard Shekhawati as their home.

To commemorate the community's achievements and to highlight the region's heritage Mumbai-based Murarka Foundation organises the Shekhawati Festival every year. Though a largely inter-village affair the festival draws out the best of rural talent in dance, music and sports. But the region has more to be proud of than the annual fair.

Known as the "open air gallery", "Shekhawati is home to a peculiar genre of frescoes. Pained on the inside walls of the *havelis* by *chiteras*, who were specialised *kumhars*, the frescoes are primarily made from vegetable pigments. *Kajal* for black, lime for white, indigo for blue, *harabhata* (terra verte) for green, *geru* (red stone powder) for red and *kesar* for saffron. The colours have only now begun to show the years of disuse.

Though extremely imposing from the outside the inside reflects the builders' scant regard for light, air and space.

However, the *chiteras* seem to have more than made up for the architectural short-sightedness. The frescoes are remarkable for their ingenuity and intricacy. There is painted in one niche an image of Jesus Christ while the neighbouring ones bear those of Hindu gods.

On another frame is painted Krishna riding a humanly-impossible, elephant-shaped phalanx of *gopis*. Others portray family patriarchs in heroic stances and attire.

While some show every Indian-looking 'mems' and 'sahibs' indulging in supposedly very English pursuits of gramo-phone-listening, hunting and posing for daguerreotypes.

The *havelis* are scattered in and around the two districts.

Some of the havelis are in dire need of restoration, with scarred frescoes telling a story of neglect and vandalism.

Though not exactly a destination for the desert-seeker, Shekhawati has its modest share of sand and sun, if you can wriggle out of the maze of bylanes. But it definitely is a treasure-trove for the research-oriented, scholarly types.

There are Shekhawati Express (daily), or by bus to Sikar (299 km. from Delhi) via Jhunjhunu (251 km. from Delhi). Accommodation is available in:

Hotel Shiv Shekhawati, Jhunjhunu
Desert Resort Mandawa, Jhunjhunu
Mukundgarh Fort, Jhunjhunu.

Safaris—Wildlife and Natural History

These safaris are require professional or amateur natural guides. Wildlife trips are informative adventures which pave the way for a greater understanding of the world's wild places.

The key to getting the most from any safari is to have an experienced leader, one who knows wildlife biology and can plan a game viewing strategy which maximises your chance for observation. A wide variety of safaris fall into this category.

(i) *Lodge Safaris:* These are in classic game lodges, some of which are very deluxe.

(ii) *Camping Safaris:* These are exiting safaris with walk in safaris tents and travel by landrovers. These are the ideal 'wildlife adventure' with the maximum chance of wildlife encounters and most intimate contact with wild.

(iii) *Walking Safaris:* It offers freedom from vehicles and a chance to wonder in the bush and experience India in an intimate way.

The Thar Desert of Rajasthan is a world of its own. It is an unrelieved ocean of sand, dotted with dunes and patchily covered with xerophytic shrubs, date tree and with its own distinctive wildlife. Navigation of the ship of desert i.e. manning of the camel in this nerve ending sea of sand requires special skill and experience. Route navigation in the desert is an acquired art. *Caravans* must be manned by riders who know how to study the stars and sense the direction by studying in the bright sparkly stars, like diamond in the black valvet sky. They should also know the shifting sands of the terrain.

If you have time and sensivity to experience, the camel safari in the Thar desert is an exciting experience. It is a holiday with a difference. It is an adventure sport that calls for little exertion. The mounting popularity bears out that a developing rapport between the desert, man and beast make the safari activity rarely experienced. It is an activity rarely experienced but treasured to memory, forever.

Romantic fantasy of a camel caravan of the 18th century passing through the great desert gets revived as the camel safari beam slowly passes through the sand dunes, cases, small villages and the wayside forts and historic places. Camel safari were in vague right from the time when India and China had developed trade units. Camel caravan loaded with spices, herbs, jewels, used to more along the usual trade routes.

Camel safari could only be organised in the savage and vast Thar desert of Rajasthan in India. As the sun sets you would see the pleasant savage brown desert meadows down into safer and cool shades of red, ochre and mauve. The tide-patterns in the sand are smeared in grey shadows. The nature with the help of wind draws abstract patterns on the huge sand dunes of the desert.

The swinging gait of the camel which often makes the rider very tired in soothened by the hospitality villages in route. A campfire under the stars, the stillness of the night, hides the overriding features of the thar, primeval, savage, lonely. By day its monotonous regularity lies broken only by welcome cases surrounded by villages, and the remnants of historic wayside forts and palaces. Aided by the warmth of the hospitable Rajasthan villagers *en route*. The camel safari will be a once in a lifetime experience for you.

You may organic camel safari ranging between 4-15 days. The optimum time limit for ideal safari is of a week long duration. You must organic the safari in such a way that it does not pass close to any major towns, camping at small villages. You should also avoid any proximity to road with vehicular traffic.

The best safaris are possible in the Thar around the famous city of Jodhpur, Jaisalmer and Bikaner.

Bikaner-Jaisalmer Safari

It takes about seven days and completes about 25-30 km. daily. You may cut across the desert on a route known to no one other than the camel riders. The journey may begin at Bharal, a four hour ride from Bikaner. The first major town your route would be Nokha Mandi, which is a historic trading post that to day retain its commercial focus. From here you may proceed via unknown villages to Mohangarh and finally on to Jaisalmer.

From Jaisalmer, a round trip lasting four days would include some totally undiscovered villages. These villages bear the purity and asceticism of the Thar desert itself. Kava, a deserted village haunted by legends of love and chivalry, anger and intrigue will be a landmark in your route.

It is advisable not to adopt a fixed route. Each days journey could be decided at will. Therefore, in addition to the desert heartland the most exciting option for you as a camel safari would be in Shekhawati region. Here you will find towns such as Ramgarh, Nawalgarh, Dundlod, Mandawa and Churic.

As an organiser you should attempt to create an atmosphere of old caravan journeys. Picture a camel caravan quietly, winding its way through these desert dunes, the soft golden sand breaking to the passage of lonely riders accompanied by a pair of musicians playing a haunting, stringed instrument, which is a fantasy of a 16th century camel caravan on its trading route. Musicians must accompany the caravan. Halts of safaris should be called outside villages where you may invite the local people to enjoy campfire hospitality and make it an exciting experience.

Remember that cooking equipment and materials, and twin bedded tents form a regular part of the safari. Staff should be made available for all assistance including the pitching of tents.

One/Two Day Trips

(1) Bikaner to Gajner and Kodamdesar or to Deshnoke.
(2) Jodhpur to the neighbouring Bishnoi village or to Khimsar.

Another interested route is Jaisalmer to the Rann of Kutch (in Gujarat) via Barmer.

A tattered cloth banner will proclaim 'Apple Pie' as the fare on offer in a bazaar overflowing with antiques. A camel safari of tourists will settle into camp at a deserted village on the edge of the Great Thar Desert as the frost of winter nights begins to chill you to the bone. The head of the descendants of the Lunar race will perhaps pause on the balcony of a palace built in the shape of a Muslim *Tazia*, as a gift from grateful subjects of his forefathers, to watch the sun descend behind the cenotaphs of his departed ancestors on a distant rocky ridge. The sounds of the night will arise. You will have a special feeling. You will be in Jaisalmer, Rajasthan.

Imagine yourself on a bus hurtling along with a deep rumble through a vast sandy plain, flat as a *chapati*, with ancient stunted trees dotting the landscape to the distant horizon. Suddenly you are at a town whose name is associated with a single nuclear blast almost two decades ago, where cenotaphs of dead kings of yore sit upon a barren slope wearing ostentatious domes in far better state of repair than the fort which crowns the ridge directly opposite. Race on, and a railway line appears, slicing through the wasteland in a straight line due south of west, as watch-towers placed perhaps a kilometre apart shimmer in a line on the horizon marking the position of something beyond them that you must not see.

Camel carts bob along the road carrying loads of women dressed in red and black with chunky silver jewellery on every appendage including their noses and toes. Fences fabricated from slim lengths of rock flash by. Up ahead, the vision wavering in dry scalding air, a large hump arises 250 ft. above the surrounding desert edge. Details emerge as you approach, and the crest of the hump rises to battlements, ramparts, turrets and half-towers of an imposing fortress ruled by kings styled as heads of the Lunar race, yet descended from Lord Krishna under whose personal umbrella they still sit. Kings upon whose shield it is written that they be "guardian of the northern gate of India". The wonders begin....

Visualise three concentric walls to this fort, and four massive gates, over one of which porches and windows of fine stone lattice-work mark the chambers of the palace. Recall the tragedy that twice the womenfolk of this fort were immolated to prevent capture by invaders. And that once, a king in a hurry killed his women with his own hands, unnecessarily it transpired, as he went on to defeat the invaders and blew the leader to bits over the end of a cannon. Drink from a well dug by Lord Krishna's *Sudarshana Chakra* to slake the thirst of the Pandav prince Arjun. Sit, if you will, upon the battlements, high above the surrounding plain that was ruled from these walls. Is it any wonder that eight Jain and four Hindu temples are nestled in these walls, where one idol is of pearl-coated clay, another is the size of a grain of rice, and a third is sculpted from emerald?

Yet can anyone count the idols of these temples that number in hundreds and even thousands? Could it be possible that the people who lived among these symbols of God drove away an entire community from the surrounding lands allowing substantial villages to crumble and verdant farmlands to turn barren and desolate? There is a strange air around the place. Nomads roam the street hawking primitive bowed musical instruments. Tales are told of a man with the largest moustache in the world abandoning a life of dacoity and murder to become a professional musician, only to lose his head to old enmity.

Havelis, the houses of nobility and the rich, dot the township with exquisite stone trellises and ornate balconies and windows. The house of one prime minister had the facade duplicated on both sides of the door by two master craftsmen, who competed only in the intricacy of detail. The house of another *Diwan,* a tyrant we're told, was so magnificent that the two top stories were removed on orders from the King when the prime minister dared to conceive of a bridge over the bazaar from his house to the palace.

Then there were those that had their way against the wishes of their King, for a nearby lake with temples on its banks is entered only through a gate named after a prostitute. It is said that the lady was eminent in her profession in a neighbouring land, but returned during the rains every year, using her accumulated wealth to construct the ornate gate. When advised that there would be certain ignominy in passing under the gate, the King sought to demolish it, but his hand was stayed when the lady of the night crowned the edifice with an idol of the God of Truth.

A bard may sing of the lady to you some day as you sit on the roof of some royal apartment turned hotel in the fort. Perhaps he will play a flute, or a jew's-harp, or a *Kamayacha* or *Khartal* or *Satara*. If you are lucky a large, turbaned man with a flowing red beard will rise on his knees to provide percussion with blasts of his breath into a clay pot tossed about in time to the music. To the west a drunken camel shadowed by desert nomads will perhaps be carrying a load of heroin into the country.

Festival Time in Jaisalmer

Was Jaisalmer in a festive mood or had a magical spell been cast on it? For three days from 18th-20th February, Jaisalmer resembled a fairyland where all fantasies seem to come to reality. The occasion is the Annual Desert Festival. Craftsmen, singers, musicians and visitors both from home and abroad rubbed shoulders with each other in a sea of myriad colours. Bejewelled rustic faces smiled behind heavy veils as their 'pajebs' tinkled.

Introduced seven years ago, the 'yatra' has become a major attraction for the local people. Led by folk artistes, the 'yatra also saw the participation of Bankia players, school children and the B.S.F. band.

Some other major attractions are the 'rain dance' performed by the school children, 'gair' dance performed with sticks by a troupe from Barmer, camel polo about the legend of Moomal-Mahendra which was performed with the help of tableaus.

Everywhere one could hear the sounds of *bankia, shehnai* and *khartal.* Among the lances, the 'Terah Tali' was quite fascinating. Hollow metallic discs tied on hands and legs are struck together to produce 13 different sounds. The fire dance, started by Sidh-Jasnathji of Bikaner 500 years ago, is performed on a long pit covered with burning coal. The performers sit on them, and even eat them with no harmful effects. The *sapera* dance is also a major attraction.

Folk songs like 'Hitchki', where the loved one is remembered by the beloved and gets hiccups, Ghoomar and Gair dance were some other attractions.

The events that are most popular are the dance.

The festival site is dotted with tiny shops selling handicrafts, colourful tie and dye cotton and silk fabrics in striking hues, camel hair blankets and other knick-knacks depicting the rich heritage of Rajasthan. With exquisite and cheap items it turned out to be a shoppers' paradise.

12

Horsemanship:
Horse Racing and Horse Riding

The horse is an important and valuable member of the mammalia. The term horse is used to designate a mule, either stallion, or gelding as well as whole species. A normal sexed male horse is a stallion, and an unsexed male is a gelding. A female is a mare and her young is a foal. A male foal is a colt, a female foal is a filly. Ordinarily the horse is ranked fourth in intelligence among the lower animals, following the elephant, the ape, and the dog but it is sometimes dropped to tenth or eleven lower on the scale.

The art of training, riding and handling horses is full of adventure and glamour is called as horsemanship and riding. Throughout history the man on horse back has been awarded respect and clothed in an area of glamour and adventure from king to cow boy, from cavalry man to jockey, from polo player to trail rider. Through the ages horses have been ridden of necessity, as a means of transport for hunting and to carry warriors into combat and by the leisure classes as a form of diversion, for exercise sports and pleasure. The owner of the riding horses have been, in large part, relatively wealthy members of the upper classes, and the ownership of riding horses demoted and provided status.

Exchange of breeding horses has always been an international scale. Racing tended to offer more and more competition between leading horses of different countries after World War II. Contests between different horses from different continents became feasible with the development of long-range transport by air, especially after the use of jet powered planes became common. On a continental and regional basis, there are many international races notably in South America, Eastern Europe, and Western Europe. Of all the international events, the 2,400 m. Prix de I'Arc de Triomphe, at Long Champ (Paris) confers the highest prestige and monetary reward upon the winner.

Great Britain and Ireland remain the leading exporters of blood stock, and the volume of racing in the U.S. far exceed, that of any other nation. But racing is a part of culture in nearly all major countries. In continental Europe, racing has been long established. Its most important centre is France, where it was developed in the 1st century until destroyed by French Revolution. It recovered afterwards and in 1830s began to develop the organisational format which, under governmental authority, continued to the present time. European racing tends generally to follow the French pattern. Wherever the British Empire or commonwealth extended, horse racing often followed. There were race meetings in India as early as 1795 and important races has been maintained since 1857.

Wagering

Commercialised racing is supported mainly by commission drawn from betting pools. Proceeds from the pools are divided in proportion set by law, between the race track and the governmental entities, national, state or local authority to grant racing privileges and collect taxes. In most countries legal wagering on races is restricted to the pari-mutual system and totalizators are used to issue tickets, summarise the betting and report its progress. The totalizator's speed, efficiency and safeguard against error and unethical practice account for much of the growth and expansion of racing.

Horse racing, the most nearly universal of the great

spectacular sports of modern times, is also among the oldest diversion of man. The first historical record of races for mounted horses is given in connection with the XXXIII olympiad about 644 B.C., but the horse had been used for riding more than a thousand years earlier. The Greek made less use of horses, and were perhaps less skilled in handling them, then the earlier peoples of Asia on the later Roman. In Rome each of the various racing function had its own colours and spent enormous scenes in anticipation of competitive honours. Wherever the Romans went in conquest, they took with then the fleet runners derived from the stock of Arabia, Asia miner, and North Africa. When Caesar invaded Britain in 55 B.C. he was opposed by skilled charioteers, and it was in the British Isles that modern organised racing had its beginning, together with the sovereign breed that came to be known as the Thorough breed.

India offers all fun and frolic to a person interested in horse riding. One can trout down or gallop to high level of excitement. Horse riding can stretch four to five days with camping facilities *en route*. Horse back travel through never ending lanes by the countryside in the stillness of the night, the romantic campfires under the blue stars revive the charm of the gone by days.

Chariot Racing and Equestrian

The Olympic games were initiated about 776 B.C. These games included a number of equestrian events and featured chariot racing. So popular were these events that a separate arena, the hippodrame, was built specially for them. The modern Olympic games have included equestrian events since 1912. The team and individual events included in the Olympic games are:

(1) Three-day event (all around competition) in three phases.
    Phase I: A Test of Racing (dessage).
    Phase II: An Endurance Test (consisting of a read test and cross-country and steeple chase performance).

Phase III: Stadium Jumping.
(2) Grand Prix de Dressage: Individual dressage.
(3) Prix des Nations: Stadium Jumping Competition.

In addition, the modern pentathton includes riding cross country on unfamiliar horses as one of the requirements. The others are swimming, running, fencing and pistol shooting.

Race Courses

The race course in Bangalore is so entwined with the history of the erstwhile Mysore State, that one can't imagine the city without it. On the other hand, few people in Delhi have even heard of its race course, let alone visited it. The racing season in the two cities is a study in contrast.

For the last 75 years despite the groans, snarls and fleeting curses, the Bangalore Race Course has grown with the city. The Race Course sits pretty over 83 acres of super prime land worth over a hundred crore rupees virtually overlooking the stately Vidhana Soudha housing the Karnataka Legislature. A valuable lung space, the Race Course is so entwined with the history of old Mysore state and Bangalore that one cannot imagine the city without the racing track situated where it is now. Since 1920 when the Race Course was built, racing in Bangalore had been essentially a local affair with moderate stakes and not much of outside participation.

But for the three months, racing is on in Bangalore through the year thanks to the salubrious climate which is ideal for horse-rearing and racing. The prestigious season in Bangalore is in summer when races are not held in other cities. During the hot season, leading horses from all over the country including Bombay, Hyderabad, Madras and Ooty are brought to Bangalore.

In sum, the Bangalore racing circuit is "fairly clean" and compared to some other cities, "doctoring" of horses' performance is more an exception than a rule.

And, with a view to making transparent the procedures by which horses are given weightage, the Bangalore Turf Club has for the first time in the country made it known how the horses are rated. Much before the race begins, the information is given over to punters, trainers and the jockey so that assessments are easily possible.

In the racing world, the open rating system is considered near-revolutionary when one takes into account the extreme secrecy that conventionally surrounds the weightage given to the horses which is revealed just seconds before the race begins.

The racing track in Bangalore is undulated. So much so, horses that do well here are said to perform exceedingly well elsewhere. A "challenging" track, it is oval-shaped and curves sharply at least in four places with steep gradients. Probably due to this, Bangalore-based horses have time and again won several major races all over the country.

Most of the days, the brown turf lies forlorn. Only crows and mynahs hop about searching for morsels in the sand. The sunlight creeps slowly across the silent race track, untouched by the auto fumes covering the city just outside the racing ground's boundary walls.

Then on some days, everything changes. The turf comes alive. The stands are full. There are people milling about. Crows and mynahs escape to the nearby trees in the neighbouring polo ground.

Look there; right at the end of the racing track in the Delhi Race Course (D.R.C.). There are a row of gates behind which stand horses, brown, tan, dark, pale muscles flexing, tense, alert, eyes bulging with anticipation. On the horses, jockeys in their bold coloured shirts and tight breeches and helmets sit, equally tense, bent with anticipation, head down but eyes on the gates and to turf stretched around the circuit. The afternoon light picks up the rim of the flaring nostrils and twitching muscles on the oiled hind legs of animals ready to shoot off.

The race track is buzzing with energy. Bets have been placed. Favourites have been chosen. Bookies are counting the hard cash. Punters are peering into their books, furiously reading the form books. All eyes are on the row of gates where their destiny awaits the starter's signal.

The gates open. A roar goes up. The horses pound their way out into the open, hoofs kicking up dust, and hopes of punters who have betted heavy sums. Bent on these flesh and bone locomotives, jockeys hang on to their reins, their feet firmly in the stirrups. They are driving the animals as passions rise to a feverish pitch around the circuit, in the stands.

At the end of the day, there are more losers than winners, afterall only one horse wins the race. Those who regularly bet on racing horses at the D.R.C. say it is an addiction, like that of gambling. Some have spent fortunes, others have lost fortunes, on that tiny speck of a hope that their horse will see them through.

For the moment, the fortunes of the D.R.C. are equally dismal, punters and trainers bemoan its mediocre standards. The turf is average and the prize money, compared to other centres in Bangalore and Bombay, is a pittance. Even the officials admit that the D.R.C. is way behind the racing clubs of Maharashtra, Bangalore and Calcutta where prize money in the range of Rs.50 to Rs.70 lakhs and the standard of races is on part with international racing events.

Racing in Delhi has hardly any following among the sporting public. In fact, few people have heard of it and fewer take interest in the racing notes hidden in the obscure corners of sports pages in newspapers. To put, it simply, the racing in Delhi suffers from lack of patronage.

Racing thrives on cigarettes and liquor: Since the cigarette companies and liquor barons find it difficult to advertise their products easily, they prefer to invest in racing, an easy avenue for a wide publicity since horse racing is now being covered by television networks and newspapers more exhaustively.

These companies get their favourite image: the macho rider and a brute animal, as the bonus. Most of these conglomerates have now begun to involve themselves greatly into the racing circuit since the returns, they have found, might be long in coming but is substantial.

Horse racing, in the Capital is nothing but gambling on horses and there is hardly any popular support.

13

Polo: A Spectacular Sport

Polo is a spectacular sport and though no longer the rich man's preserve it has got to possess quality.

"We need total dedication, because polo is a highly specialised sport".

It is apparent that polo has been labelled as a game purely for the elite to indulge in, which has created a mental barrier to it. India has such a far-reaching historical connection to the game and it constitutes one of the many colourful facets of the nation's rich heritage.

Interestingly, India has one of the oldest and most renowned polo clubs in the world at Calcutta, established in 1862. In India, polo was initially played at Gilgit, Chitral and Manipur and was very popular amongst the Mughal emperors, who referred to it as *chaugan*.

During 1869, India introduced polo to England via the 10th Hussars. The Indian Polo Association dates right back to 1892. At that time Jodhpur, Alwar, Bhopal, Bikaner, Jaipur, Patiala, Hyderabad, Kishengarh and Kashmir entailed some of the leading teams.

The polo circuit covers a range of cities in India, the season commencing in September at Jaipur, then moving to Madras in October, Delhi in November, Bombay in December, back to Delhi in February and Jaipur in March.

What do you immediately associate the game of polo with—horses, grandeur, flamboyance...? It seems that a considerable number of people parallel polo to aristocracy and the old days of British rule in India. Certainly, the game does have an image of pretension and decadence attached to it, but is it really confined to the wealthier stratum of society here in India?

According to those involved in the game, it is not, since access to playing polo is not restricted in any way. Determined effort made to generate a greater public interest in polo, by bringing on new styles of play and encouraging youngsters to participate.

The impressionistic attachment many people have of polo and the elite, may have culminated over time, beginning at the earlier stages of the game. For instance, perhaps the fact that it was popular amongst the Mughals may account for it to a degree. Similarly, during the British occupation of India earlier this century, polo was a favourite pastime of the English, developing as a highly social and prestigious game, reflecting an aura of elitism and pomp. English ladies with their milky complexion, fashionable hats and elegant attire, would attend polo matches, adding to the creation of a grandiose ambience. In addition, the association of polo to Indian Royalty has also contributed to some extent in giving it an image of elitism.

It also appears that the general public have overlooked the fact that most polo players come from an army background. Rather, there has been a tendency to focus on the nobler ranking polo players such as maharajas and the like.

Furthermore, in India the bulk of polo ponies are halfbreds, since thoroughbreds are exorbitantly priced.

Another reason as to why polo has been connected with the elite is due to its wide coverage on the occasions when a famous person plays the game.

Because of the general economic situation of this country, elitism tends to get attached to anything that is not practised by the masses. That seems to be problem with polo's image, too.

Admission to a polo match in most cases is free and during the season there is nothing quite as delightful as spending a leisurely afternoon watching a match.

There are about two-hundred active polo players in India today, and twenty-two polo clubs are affiliated to the Indian Polo Association. The most active of these is the Delhi Polo Club. We are no longer Big League in world polo and bring up the rear with Pakistan. Following Argentina is America, who is catching up fast, followed by Australia, the United Kingdom, Spain, India and Pakistan. Argentina also has the world's Number One player—Von Carlos Harriet, who plays at No. 3 with '10' handicap ("when playing badly"). Argentina has another five players who are '10's'. And yet, there was a time, when India was in the top-bracket. How can India get back into the Big League? First of all, we need total dedication, because this is a highly specialised sport. The first World War was a setback for Indian polo. Between the two wars, India retrieved her position somewhat. World War II really made a casualty of Indian polo—when 'mechanisation' depleted the stables: It was like a tap being turned off.

We need a plan which must help produce inexpensive horses and plenty of them. We must start at the grassroots level with tent-pegging at cattle-shows! From this wide base, we can expand into the sort of pattern prevalent in the U.K.—a profusion of pony clubs. The army will remain the base, with its polo-tent-pegging and teams for the Olympics but you can't change things with one Horse-show a year in Delhi! We need more co-operation between the race clubs and the polo clubs, and went on, "Remember, a 4-chukker game requires four horses per player and these have to be trained from a base of Ten Horse! One needs a large number of horses from which to breed". The army had a very important part to play in any scheme aimed at improving the game in India. "The army can give the stallions", "Mate your tonga-horses with a strong sire—second and third generation army horses, sporting horses and horses from the B.S.F. We have to upgrade the Indian horse. Make

stallions available at all veterinary centres and let them cover
the mares from the defence services, B.S.F. and police. The
army produces the horses. Issue them"! When the horses
are there, interest in the game can be generated. Raising
funds can follow.

There is a great demand for Indian horses in the Middle-
East and Far-East countries—particularly Singapore, Brunei
and Malaysia. At present, these countries are importing horses
from Argentina and Oman and paying out more than 2,000
dollars in freight alone! An Indian horse travelling by sea
from Madras to the Far-East would cost about a thousand
rupees in freight! "Why don't we swop horse-power for oil-
power".

Today the accent is on the thorough-bred-the big pony—
going flat out from start to finish. "There is a 12 goal difference
between polo today and yesterday due to this terrific pace in
today's game', and that's something else Indian polo players
have to catch up with."

"Polo is a way of life! Horse-breeding is a means to an
end. Indian horses are the best-trained in the world. The
Indian syce is a gem of a person. We tend to blinker
ourselves and look at our own little cabbage patch. We have
to study what's going on in the rest on the polo world. We
must not vegetate. We must look outwards. We also need
to indulge in more competitive polo. If 50,000 people can
turn out to watch polo in Jaipur, why not in other polo
centres? The reason is simple? If we give quality, the people
will show up.

We also need new faces, and a high standard of polo,
because this is a spectacular sport and though no longer
the rich man's preserve it has got to possess quality! The
army has certain restraints but what is really needed is
dynamic guidance. Let's get back to the drawing-board and
start all over again. Let's take polo to the colleges and
schools of India. It's easier to cross over and play in Lahore
than stage a tournament in Calcutta! And yet, we seldom
play Pakistan. This time its 'politics' not 'red-tape'. When
the personalities are famous and the competition is keen,

huge crowds will turn up to witness the game. The army can channel its activities through 'civilian' clubs which do not suffer from constraints. Until we do something about raising the standard of Indian polo we cannot expect the top teams of the world to play in India. The future of Indian polo depends on young men who can either restore the reputation of India as a polo playing country or let it slide downhill towards the last 'chukker'.

14

Horse Breeding: As a Sport

Horse breeding provides tremendous support to the Racing Sector. Right from facilities like land, employing specialists like vets and pathologists to building private turf tracks with crash proof polyvinyl rails and actual betting, horse breeding has flourished into a profitable industry. It is no longer restricted within the confines of a sport.

An ancillary of the agriculture industry, an estimated 3,000 brood mares in the country at the minimum value of Rs.1 lakh each, the value of the horses is phenomenal. The propagation of thoroughbreds, from mating to training to eventually running the race, has become highly specialised. It also provides tremendous support to the horse racing sector.

There are an approximate 167 stud farms in the country of which 80-100 can be recognised as big breeding establishments. The rest are small outfits with a handful of brood mares and no resident stallions. There are 3,000 mares on these farms and producing 1,300 progeny, annually auctioned at the age of 2 years. Auction prices may range from Rs.15,000 to a lakh but the best of the lot is sold directly from the farm to the buyer for which the prices are left unmentioned.

Ten years ago, the number of stud farms was less than 50. The new figures reflect the growth in the breeding industry, particularly in the last 3 years. There is a constant upgrading of stock. Breeders are ploughing back profits by importing stallions from Iran, Canada, Ireland and France, as well as, improving the infrastructure.

There exists 3 kinds of breeders:

(i) *The Poonawala-type*, who have been in the business for over 40 years, progressive, modern and with a passion for horses, they give personal attention to every aspect essential to breeding better and stronger Indian race horses.

(ii) *The Farmer-type in the North*, who discovered that if they could keep buffaloes and cows, a few horses could be added as well. However, they are becoming a force to reckon with at the race course. They enjoy the advantages of, ancestral land, fodder produced at home and time, motivation and proximity for personal attention, over other stud farm owners.

(iii) *The Investor-types* who leave everything in the hands of professional managers.

Licence up to Rs.10 lakh per annum is given to each farm for the import of stallions. This is nominal compared to international standards. A good Ireland stud costs 30,000 Pounds.

Land ceilings are the bane of Indian stud farms. Here, 20-acre farms are considered small, and 200 acres farms, big. In the west 200 acres farms are considered small while the big ones can cover over 2,000 acres.

The future of the thoroughbred industry has a lot in the offing. We have come to a stage where the indigenous production of horses is more than enough to meet our requirements, given the number of race tracks in the country. We are on a threshold where we could export horses, and if the government can see that, they will view the industry from a different angle altogether. Today, at an auction abroad, a horse is sold for something like 3.5-5 million dollars. We may not be anywhere near that standard, but horse racing is a global phenomenon. Even poor countries have racing tracks. Countries like Singapore and Hong Kong have no breeding farms. They import from England. Buying horse from India would be much cheaper for them. The industry can grow with the right government support.

"For the government this industry is insignificant as far as support is concerned, but enormously rich when it comes to the question of taxation".

The spin-off from horse breeding/racing has its impact on the sectors of travel, tourism and transport, hotels or restaurants, entertainment, Press and printing sectors, as also real estate.

Thoroughbreds are high spirited, sensitive horses. They have powerful lungs and strong legs which makes them especially suited for racing. Thoroughbreds weigh from 1,000-2,000 pounds (450-544 kg). They stand from 62-65 in. (157-165 cm.) tall.

Thoroughbreds are not allowed to race until they are 2 years old. The age of thoroughbreds born during the same year is automatically calculated from January 1 for all. This method of determining age simplifies the basic age-grouping of race horses. Most thoroughbreds that race are 2, 3, 4, or 5 years old.

Under domestication, the horse has diversified into 3 major types based on size and build.

- Draft horses
- Ponies
- Light horses.

The 300 crore horse racing industry in India is primarily dependent on the breeders. There are about 3,000 race horses in India today—Bombay, Calcutta, Bangalore, Pune, Hyderabad, Ooty and Delhi being the major racing centres. Considering the millions wagered on them, horses are a pampered lot. The horse breeding business is no longer a royal pastime but a 100 crore industry.

As long as man's gambling and sporting instincts are intact, the future of the thoroughbred is safe. With their eyes on 'the magic millions' the breeders carry on their business hoping that the conditions of the industry will soon improve.

15

Eyeing the Target: Archery

Archery is one of the oldest Olympic sports. But gone are the days of wooden bows and arrows. Not only is the modern archery gear highly sophisticated with bows made of composite material and lightweight aluminium arrows, scoring is also registered electronically.

Originally introduced at the 1900 Games in Paris and continued in various forms in 1904, 1908 and 1920, it was eliminated from the Olympic programme for more than 50 years. It was brought back at Munich in 1972 under a standardized set of rules.

Technology has transformed the sport. Yet, its object remains the same—put an arrow in the centre of a 10-ring, 4.8 in. diameter target standing 70 m. away.

Arrows which fly at 150 miles per hour to a target, which is hardly the size of a thumb tack held at arm's length. Korea has emerged as the sport's international power. It has won both the men's and women's team titles at the 1995 World Target Championships in Indonesia. India pins its hopes on Limba Ram. A total of 64 men and 64 women will compete in Atlanta—no more than three men and women per country, based on results at the 1995 World Target Championships.

The Archers of Meghalaya

The traditional art of archery has evolved into a novel betting system in Meghalaya's Khasi Hills. As a result of the government's failure to curb it, it is now being considered as a potential source of revenue for the State's coffers.

Archery is a way of life, handed down through generations in Meghalaya's Khasi Hills.

But for thousands of fans who know it as *teer* across India's north-east, the traditional Khasi sport represents the pot of gold at the end of the rainbow. In its quest, they stake lakhs of rupees daily on the results of an archery meet at Mawiong, a small village on the outskirts of the Meghalaya capital.

Seven days a week, the archers of Mawiong lose hundreds of arrows at a butt of trussed straw. The hits they score from the basis of a unique 'numbers' game, which the Meghalaya government—having failed to suppress—now intends to legalise.

Saitkhnam ("arrow shooting") was the traditional highlight of festivals and celebrations. In the post-harvest season, *Iasiathong*—competitions between neighbouring villages—helped to pass time all the next planting season. Shooting arrows painted red or black, the customary 'team colours', the village bowmen played either *Namhali*, using 8 arrows each, or *Namspah*, using 10 arrows.

The object was to score the most hits on a target 8 in. long and 2 in. in diameter from about a hundred feet. The prize—usually a bull or a pig—ended up being slaughtered for a community feast in the victorious village. Ritual matches also featured in funeral ceremonies, according to Woodward Sohliya, a vice-president of the Archery Association of India and honorary secretary of the Meghalaya Sports Council.

Organised on a league basis by the Khasi Hills Archery Sports Institute (K.H.A.S.I.), two of 12 clubs—Mawprem, Kynthuplang, Senglang, Laitumkrah, Pynthor, Jaiaw, Laitkor, Malki, Mawlal, Rangbiria, Laban and Wahingdoh—field bowmen every weekday to shoot with stewards nominated by the Khasi.

Squatting in an angular are around the target, the archers—sit at a range of 80 ft., ten respectively at 75 and 70 ft., and the stewards at 60 ft.—shoot two times rounds controlled by a foreman. In the first, each bowman is required to shoot 32 arrows—his 'holding'—in 3 minutes. In the second, holdings of 22 arrows are loosed at a smaller target.

Three 'Counting Masters' take charge of the riddled target after a round is shot and as punters and archers watch, the arrows are pulled out, counted and stacked on a board. Each score is declared immediately on the field, and as soon as both are known, they are relayed to Shillong's Barabazar, headquarters of the far-flung gambling network.

The betting system is simple. Punters back numbers in the range 00, 01, 02 ... 99 hoping to pick the last two digits of either or both scores. Bets on individual two-digit numbers are in multiples of 25 paise, with a standard stake-to-payoff ratio of 1 : 80. Thus, a lucky punter collects Rs.20 on a winning 25 paise bet, or Rs.80 on a Re.1 wager.

Bets can be laid on more than one number under any of three conventional systems: Line, Ending and Forecast. In the first, the gambler stakes an equal amount on every number in a continuous series. Playing 25 paise a number on the line 31 to 60, therefore, he wagers a total of Rs.7.50 to make a Rs.12.50 profit if he wins.

In Endings, the betting is on all numbers in the 00-99 range ending with a particular numeral, say 5 (hence, "all 5 or ending 5"). The 1 : 80 ratio holds for bets below a rupee, but for a minimum stake of Rs.10—a rupee a number the payoff is Rs.95, though some bookmakers may offer up to Rs.100.

Forecast involves predicting the last two digits of both scores in sequence. Though less common than in Lines or Endings, Forecast winnings are the largest: Rs.303 for a 10 paise bet; Rs.501 for 25 paise and Rs.2,001 for 50 paise. Bets of a rupee are rarely accepted, though the few bookmakers who do may offer up to as much as Rs.5,555 in payoffs.

Who gambles? In Shillong, almost anybody: the low stakes required to play and the ease with which bets can be placed—every locality has several well-known bookies— have given *teer* a following that covers the entire social spectrum and cuts across divisions of age, class and occupation.

Attempts to rig the shooting are not infrequent, though Khasi officials insist these are getting rarer, 'Making' (or "making pass, making fail"), as rigging is called in *teer* jargon, occurs when two clubs shooting together restrict the number of hits to within a certain range of values, or, less commonly, to a specific number. This is done by deliberately shooting a predetermined number of arrows wide. The clubs involved are bribed heavily for successful Making by the parties behind the attempt, who stake large sums on the designated numbers.

The stewards shoot with the club archers expressly to frustrate. If too many club arrows seem to be missing the target, the stewards 'push'—shoot into the target to increase the score, if no making is apparent they may 'drop'—shoot wide. Also, clubs may be fined for every arrow left unshot by their archers at the three-minute whistle.

The size of the target is also changed daily to introduce greater randomness in to the scores. Depending on the 'form' of the clubs scheduled to shoot on any day, the dimensions of the target generally vary between the limits of 50" × 30" and 28" × 34".

Teer gambling, first began in the early 1960s, becoming widely popular by the end of that decade. Over the last 20 years, the 'industry' has spread through the north east: by 1967, bookmakers were doing business in Guwahati, 103 km. away from Shillong. By 1974, as far as can be ascertained. Teer had reached Calcutta. Today courtesy, the trunk telephone, gamblers play the numbers in every capital and district town in the north-eastern region, the sources said.

Exactly how many bookmakers operate in Shillong is anybody's guess. I counted 123 betting shops on the Barabazar Police bazar areas of the city alone, but this apparently is only a small proportion of the total figure. In addition, an army of 'flying'—itinerant—bookies work fixed beats at Government and private offices, public thoroughfares and residential colonies.

Unlike the predominantly Khasi gathering at Mawiong,

the business end of *teer* is controlled by a more cosmopolitan set. Refugees from the erstwhile East Pakistan are thought to control more than half the business but at least a dozen bookies who are household names are from as far failed as Uttar Pradesh, Bihar, Rajasthan and Nepal; these last having carved out lucrative "territories" comprising the sprawling Assam Rifles and the Army and Air Force bases ranging Shillong.

The Meghalaya government had prohibited wagering on teer in 1970, but recently acknowledged the failure of the ban by legislating to "control and regulate betting on arrow shooting". The Meghalaya Amusements and Betting Tax (Amendment) Bill, 1982, passed without discussion in the budget session of the State Assembly, aims to 'licence both bookmakers as well as those "seeking to organise arrow shooting for the purpose of betting".

The financially-strapped State expects to collect lakhs of rupees annually in revenues from licence fees and a 5 per cent 'betting tax' on stake monies received by bookmakers. That estimate, however, is considered much too low, and according to some sources, is apparently based on seizures made during police raids. Khasi members, like punters and bookies, welcome the legitimisation of *teer*, but feel the government should help develop the standard of archery in the State. Moniyal Pde wants modern fibreglass equipment to replace the indigenous bamboo bows and hand-fletched arrows currently used by the clubs. He also wants a proper venue for the shooting, preferably Shillong's Polo ground, where it was held before the 1970 ban forced it to Mawiong.

Despite these drawbacks, Meghalaya archers to manage to shine on occasion.

Introducing 'bare bow tournaments' in the country, patterned on the World Field Archery competitions, could help Khasi and other tribal archers to emerge as a force on the national scene. Under W.F.A. rules, archers cannot use sights, and more instructive shooting is called for as competitors are required to estimate ranges, which are not disclosed. As these conditions are closer to those under which tribal archers shoot, bare bow tournaments are expected to bring about a levelling of performances.

As long as men like them are around, the saga of *teer—* would carry on, and fortunes would continue to be made and lost on the arrows.

16

Cycling as a Recreation

Cycling is very popular as a recreation. It is also very popular with the racing and touring clubs. It is not only an exercise but a sport as well. Moreover, it is the most economical means of personal mechanical transport. It is widespread sport all over the world and has been represented by several events in Olympic games since 1896.

It is recognised as a beneficial and enjoyable experience. As a past time cycling is most popular because of its cheapness and it is easily mastered by children and adults and is relatively safe. Bicycle is simple, and a popular vehicle without noise. At national level there are cycling clubs for touring purposes. There are separate tracks for cycling in most of the countries. Many types of cycling and cycles have been developed such as light weight and fully equipped touring roadster.

In Britain there are small cycling clubs which hold social events. Most of these clubs affiliated to are or more bodies, which organise and control cycling for touring or sport cycling could be used to teach road safety through the cooperation of public and schools in organising campaigns and competition to educate children.

Mopeds i.e. motorcycles were made after World War II in Europe. There are made from standard cycle parts and need pedal assistance to start. Some countries require no licence for small mopeds which makes it popular. Slowly these mopeds are substituting the bicycles.

Touring Clubs

There is very bright future for forming cycle touring club. These may be of social characters. They may promote cycle touring, public road books, maps and journals. They may appoint representative to and their members when touring may succeed in enduring most governments to allow members to travel across frontiers without duty on their machines. They may also help in erecting warming signs and dangerous places. The introduction of cycle led to improvement of roads. They towed road, a cycle tax was introduced and devoted at first to the construction of paths on which cyclists have equal rights with pedestrians.

There are many touring cyclists who are not interested in speed but concentrate upon piling up mileage. These enthusiasts are associated with colleges, clubs and youth hostels. These are the remnant of the area before the automobiles arrived before the scene, when mixed groups pedalled along leisurely and enjoyed the beauty of the countryside. These members of the touring groups write and tell their experiences. Some of them are camera enthusiasts who deliver with the aid of colour slides and motion pictures on their rides.

Muscle and Machine: Cycling

This unique combination of man and machine has been a staple since its inclusion in the first modern olympics. Competitors race around a banked track, called a velodrome, at high speeds on bicycles without brakes. Some are strategy affairs in which competitors jockey for position as individuals and teams; others are flat-out sprints. And when mountain biking joins road and track cycling at Atlanta, it marks one more step in the evolution of one of the world's top participant sports.

Cycling as sport had begun in France in 1868. The cycles then were cumbersome and uneasy to ride. Often they were double-seated and double-paddled. Modern race bikes are aerodynamically designed and light-weight. The cycles can reach a speed up to 60 kilometres an hour.

The first Olympics included a 12-hour endurance race. Women were belatedly added to the Olympic programme in 1984. And to make room for mountain biking, the team trial road event has now been eliminated. Mountain biking will be a single six-lap men's race and a five-lap women's race over a specially-constructed 12-km. cross-country course at the Georgia International Horse Park in Conyers. France, U.S.A., Australia, Germany and Italy have dominated the sport in the Olympics. France alone has won 64 medals in the event. That Americans are coming to Atlanta with specially-designed hi-tech cycles. In fact, cycle design has been a major factor in chipping off seconds from the earlier world records.

Competition cyclists are the fittest athletes in the world. Takes a few gentle rides of about five miles, ridden at a moderate pace, and you will soon be strong enough to tackle ten mile jaunts with ease, or even long distance fun rides.

All forms of regular exercise are of benefit to the body but cycling is especially good because the bicycle acts as a supportive platform, reducing the risk of impact, injuries such as 'Shin splints', common in sports such as running.

When a runner is out of puff they have to stop, the muscles cannot stand the constant pounding. But when a cyclist runs out of puff, the bicycle as a supportive platform means the rider can still ride, albeit slower. The cyclist also has the advantage of being able to stop pedalling when tired, and free-wheeling instead, resting the muscles in the process. And, of course, when going downhill, the forward motion is totally free!

Riding a bike helps to improve muscular fitness and blood circulation and can be a valuable part of a weight loss programme. According to the British Heart Foundation, cycling at least 20 miles per week reduces the risk of coronary heart disease to less than half that for non-cyclists. Cycling also makes you feel younger and reduces stress. According to Sharp the National Forum for Coronary Heart Disease Prevention—regular cyclists typically enjoy a fitness level equivalent to being 10 years younger (that's why, everybody in this bike shop looks so young, we practice what we preach)!

Cycling is chiefly an aerobic activity, one that uses great gulps of oxygen. This is beneficial to the heart and lungs work together to bring oxygen and nutrients to the muscles: The lungs expand to bring as much oxygen into the body as possible. The heart beats faster to transport this oxygen around the body. A strong heart and powerful lungs are the building blocks of general fitness.

Even if you only cycle a few miles per day your muscles will feel and look stronger. The main muscle groups used when cycling are the upper thigh muscles (quadriceps), the back side muscles (gluteus maximus), and, to a lesser extent, the calf muscles (gastrocnemius and soleus). Contrary to popular belief, cycling does not necessarily lead to bulging leg muscles. What most people find is that their legs become trimmer and more toned, in other words, shapelier.

Cycling increases energy levels. This helps the body to burn fat when you are exercising but will also help your body burn lots of calories even when sedentary! A period of 20 minutes cycling at moderate speed, five days per week, will also significantly increase your energy levels.

Exercising releases endorphines into the blood stream-substances produced in the brain which create a feeling of contentment and happiness. Aerobic exercise therefore can help to reduce stress.

Cycling at a moderate intensity of 12 m.p.h. on a flat road uses approximately 450 kcal. an hour. That's burning off a large cream cake every sixty minute!

If you start to exercise very gently and work up to a fitter you over a period of a few months there should be no need to get a medical check-up before starting a cycling fitness programme. Nevertheless if you have any doubts in this matter at all it is wise to seek advice from your doctor.

It is certainly wise to discuss the best exercise for you if:

- You've had chest pains, high blood pressure or heart disease.

- You have chest trouble like asthma or bronchitis.
- You get arthritis of joint pains.
- You are recovering from an illness or operation.
- You are worried about exercising.

Stop exercising if you start to feel pain, dizzines if you become unusually fatigued. Choose low impact exercising such as cycling on the flat slowly before you attempt speed or big hills.

It is best not to exercise hard every day. In fact too much exercise can lead to a decline in fitness. Rest days are essential if your body is to benefit from exercise. Muscles need time to repair themselves and you need time to replenish your glycogen reserves—glycogen being the form in which the liver stores carbohydrate. After every training session eat a piece of fruit within ten minutes of stopping, it will help your body recover naturally.

Changing your life-style is not easy. The key is to make small changes which you know you can stick to, whether it is in the way to exercise or what you eat.

If you want to reduce your weight, aim to do it over a period of 6 months, not one week.

And if you can not do it the first time, do not be disappointed or give up. Most smokers try to give up 6-7 times before it actually works. Reset your goal, write down a starting date and have another go. Your health is worth the effort!

Tips for keeping healthy on a long charity ride.

- If it is cold put some tin-foil under your helmet.
- Apply 'warm-up' cream to the knees (or wear loose trousers, or cycle tights).
- Eat well in the morning. A good breakfast is essential and take food with you. Fig rolls, dried fruit or muesli bars are excellent.

Cycle Racing

The man who made the first ridable bicycle, Kirkpatrick

Macmillan, under took the first race. On 3rd May 1868, Napoleon III offered a gold medal for cycle race. Championship races on the high bicycles were established and the universities of Cambridge and Oxford recognised the new sports. In response to growing interest in racing in 1830s and 90s, organisations for the government of the sports were established in many countries.

The road race has been divided into two major styles. In Britain the main class of racing is the time trial where in the riders start individually and are timed again, so that the rider with the shortest elapsed time is the winner. Parimutual betting on bicycle racing is permitted in Japan, Denmark and Central America and the races attract great crowds as a result of the wagering that million attended the sports in Europe, Asia, South America and Acomedia every year.

> *To the lure of the mountains,*
> *the beckoning of the wild,*
> *the indomitable spirit that seeks adventure,*
> *of man's greatest passion.*

Cycling is inherently satisfying. To travel under your own power is a joy. You could indeed conquer the world with just a bike under you. Mountains, rough roads, shallow canals, deserts, forests—virtually any place.

While cycling you produce no smoke or noise—no pollution of any kind—without the burden of excessive mechanism and, best of all, with a freedom unknown to those travelling by any other vehicle. The cyclist's freedom is of spirit and direction. Perhaps only at the helm of a sailboat can you enjoy the same sort of liberating contact, with your environment and direct control of course.

That freedom is only enhanced when a bicycle can be built to go anywhere at the rider's will. The all-terrain-bike (ATB) opens up the world to cycling. Previously limited to paved roads or reasonably smooth dirt tracks, cyclists can now choose almost any direction and change it at will. If a paved route calls, so be it; but should a woodland trail beckon, the ATB rider is not deterred by the limits of his machine.

Kirkpatrick Macmillan was the one who adapted the basic design of the velocipede, invented in Germany in 1817. The velocipede had two wheels and a steering mechanism, but it was powered with riders' feet. Macmillan added to this a system of cranks which powered the machine when attached to the rear wheel.

This type of cycle is a far cry from the cycles of today and the one-inch steel tyres that Macmillan used to grip gravel roads are totally impractical for the road surfaces of today. It is known that Macmillan rode his machine to Glasgow on at least one occasion, but despite the apparent success of the machine, he appears to have made no effort to realise any commercial gain from his invention.

All-Terrain Bikes

ATBs or mountain bikes first began in the late, 1970's, when a bunch of cyclists in California tested each others' nerve by riding down the fire trails of Mount Tamalpias. The bikes were heavy, very stable and tough but difficult to handle. Soon the riders were making their bikes lighter and easier to handle. The ATB was born. The addition of 15 gears and new cantilever brakes meant that the bikes could be ridden fast uphill too and were just as good to ride across rough terrain. The craze soon caught on and now the bikes have been even further refined so the ATB's are lighter, more comfortable, very stable and tough but they are still as much fun to ride as when they were first invented.

Recently more people are discovering that the design characteristics of ATBs made them excellent for use in town too and of course ideal for casual trips into the country. The wide cushion tyres will cope with all of the pothole problems as well as bumpy gravel paths. The head-up position gives superb all-round visibility and the wide flat-bar makes handling at slow speeds easy.

Braking, traction, range of gear ratios, controllability and overall durability give these newcomers to the cycle market a hands-down advantage in an off-road environment, but those same features, combined with the comfort offered by the wide tyres and upright riding position make the ATB an outstanding city bike as well. Urban environment offers nearly as many wheel-crunching obstacles as the high mountains and countryside.

Much is made of the "ruggedness" of ATBs, or of the tremendous "stopping power" of their brakes, "incredible traction" of their tyres and "comfortable riding position".

These attributes, and many more, can be cited but the fundamental feature which the ATB offers is versatility. Simply, there is no other style of bicycle which a rider can reliably take as many places with as much comfort and care as an ATB".

Adventure Biking

Adventure enthusiasts all over the world have taken to mountain biking.

Hallam Murray of South America gave up his well-paid and secure job to embark upon a cycle tour through Peru, Bolivia, Argentina and Chile, riding no fewer than 10,000 kms. on his trusty 'Mancha'. The story of his epic ride is full of amazing adventures that befell him on the way. Bridget Middleton a graphic designer, Sophie Cox, a typesetter and Graham Cliff, an engineer, all from London, went on a great cycle adventure covering 37,000 kms. They travelled through France, Italy, Yugoslavia, Greece, Turkey, Pakistan, India, Nepal, The Himalayas, Burma, Thailand, Java, Hong Kong, China, Korea, Japan, Alaska, North and Central America, Mexico and back to London via Ireland.

Jeremy Ashcrofts' adventures on bicycles over high mountains have ended up in his writing a guide of routes to the peak of the highest and most popular mountains in Wales—Snowdon.

In India "Mountain Rovers" an organisation, founded by adventurous young men of Jamshedpur went on an expedition right up to the origin of Ganga in Gaumukh to its confluence with the sea at Gangasagar islands, on Atlas cycle. They covered a distance of over 2,500 kms.

An Indian Air Force high altitude expedition was accomplished on Atlas bicycles in which ten men travelled from Faridabad to Leh and back, thus covering a total distance of 2,500 kms.

As far back as 1981 two Indians Srikantha Acharya and Honnavaily Gurufatta traversed the vast stretches of African deserts through Tanzania, Malawi and Zimbabwe on Atlas bicycles. They also went to Himalayas Nepal, Ceylon etc.

Mr. Jagdishan recently made a record of sorts when he drove his Atlas bicycle to Khardungla Pass (Height 18,383 ft. above sea level). This is the highest motorable road in the world.

Adventure biking has, and will continue to, put the fun back into aspects of cycling which have, for too long, been in the doldrums.

There are barriers to overcome but, in the long run we will all benefit from the massive boost that the mountain bike has given to cycle sport.

So pack up your troubles in your kit bag, hop on your bike and head off on a cycle holiday.

Adventure Cycling Competitions

1. *Tour de France:* The course covers over 3,400 kms. with 22 teams of nine men each competing. The tour charts through some of the most rugged terrains in the world, including the Alps. With an overall budget of over 10 million francs, the winner get over 2 million francs.

2. *Milk Race:* The longest and toughest adventure cycling races of Great Britain. Its 1,150 mile begins at Land's End and finishes at Liverpool.

3. *Bicycle Hard Ride:* A short but tough mountain bike competition in Britain.

4. *Falcon's Nations Cup Cycle Cross:* It is a four race European challenge.

5. *World Mountain Biking Championship:* The American version of world championship in mountain biking.

6. *MBC National Championships* held in Dalley Forests, North Yorkshire in June every year.

7. *European World MTB Championship* at SPA Belgium.

8. *Cleveland Mountain Bike Championship:* A 30-mile test of stamina and courage.

9. *Grundig World Cup Final* at Cannes, France a major MTB race in the world series.

10. *NORBA Mountain Bike World:* Mammoth Cross Country.

Biking Accessories

1. *Shoulder Strap with Tool Bag:* For carrying necessary tools to meet any contingency. The shoulder strap provides comfort in carrying the bike through those passages where cycling is not possible—marshes, cliffs, etc.

2. *Drinking Bottle:* For carrying water or juice. Very convenient to drink even while cycling.

3. *Air Pump:* For maintaining correct tyre pressure and in case of punctures.

4. *Safety Accessories:* Reflectors (front, rear, wheel, pedal, seat, etc.) normally provided as OE as in case of Atlas ATB Helmets.

5. *First Aid Kit:* With all the necessary first aid equipment.

6. *Goggles:* Curved vision lens with "ram air" ventilation. Soft foam face surrounded with headstrap.

7. *Elbow Sliders:* Though plastic protectors with padded backing. Adjustable elastic straps and velcro fastenings.

8. *Knee Sliders:* As elbow but larger size.

9. *Gloves:* Cushioned back and PVC reinforced palm.

10. *Track Bag:* Made of tough proofed nylon with nylon zips.

11. *Helmets:* As essential safety accessory guarding

against head injuries. Very vital. Outer reinforced
plastic shell with foam padding inside.
12. Night light/Road lights/Panniers (Front and Rear).

Cycle touring in India has not yet become as popular as
it is in the West. The main reason for this is probably the
lack of the right kind of equipment, like geared cycles and
panniers at the right price. For the adventurous cycle tourist
there is a large network of roads in the Himalayas which
offer adventure in all forms coupled with vistas of astounding
beauty. For the professional cyclist who wants to train there
are routes which will take him through forests and across
high passes.

In fact, the Indian Cycling Associations and cycle
companies would be doing yeoman service to Indian cycling
if they organise a cycle rally/race in the Himalayas on lines
of the 'Tour de France'. This would not only act as a training
ground for Indian cyclist but would also bring a large cross
section of young people from all over India in close contact
with the mighty Himalayas, suggest the boys. "As for the
physical requirements, we are individuals and with a little
effort and some determination, we successfully tackled a very
difficult route. So our message to the Indians is, anybody
with a little determination can pick up a cycle and go a long,
long distance".

The Himalayan Odyssey Cyclo-Crossing

The Mother Nature had already blown up the pass better
than any terrorist could. Torrential rains had just washed
away the approach road so badly that it was dangerous to
attempt the pass even on foot, let alone with loaded bikes.
So be sensible, he advised, and take a better road.

Recross the Sutlej and pedal back some 150 km. to Shimla.
From there you would have to go to Bilaspur and Mandi
along a horribly plain road. Unthinkable. Also there is the
time factor. It is almost mid-September. Unless you reach

the Kashmir valley by the end of the month, you may be too late for Laddakh. It's Jalori or bust.

You wave cheerfully to the curious crowd and pedalled ahead fast.

The 15-speed gears on your bikes are proving their worth, enabling you to pedal up the rough slope at a steady 7 kmph.

It seems to get steeper at every hairpin bend. Loose soil gradually gave way to small boulders, forcing you to get down and push.

Families troop out of their little slate roofed wooden houses to watch the four lunatics from Delhi. Children stare at you hypnotised, obviously seeing bicycles for the first time. Laughing teenagers pitched in to push your bikes up, so energetically that you had to break into dignified trots to keep up. Though slender and famished looking, these boys are amazingly tough.

Often people of one village would accompany you to the next one giving you plenty of chance to exchange views. Naturally much of your conversation may centre on the life in the mountains.

Like the other parts of the Himalayas you had passed through, the heavy monsoon toll. The Himalayas are extremely vulnerable to the vagaries of weather, being the youngest mountain ranges in the world. The force that created them in the first place—the tectonic movement—is still at work. In spite of the millions of tonnes of rock and earth tumbling down from their unstable slopes, the Himalayas are getting taller each year, levered up by none other than the Indian peninsula, which keeps wedging itself deeper and deeper underneath the Tibetan plateau. This natural instability is worsened by human interference. Deforestation was an ongoing process.

Soon you come to the first landslide spot. Leaving the bikes you go to inspect it. Some of the road had slid right off, leaving a neat 60° slope. After considering various options, you cut crude footholds and carry the bikes and the luggage separately across. It is tiring and hazardous—one slip and the next halt would be two hundred feet below.

Next comes a broken bridge spanning a rough-and-tumble stream. More obstacles followed, making increasingly skilled in landslide management.

The blockade of the road had depressed the morale of the local people too. The higher we went, the sadder the people looked.

In view of the special nature of your visit, the local *chaiwallah* agree to make dinner for you. You are ecstatic. The *dal-roti* had in the little tea-shop with plenty of stimulating conversation with the assembled assorted Khanagites is one of the gastronomic milestones of your expedition. The dinner is on the house, despite your protests.

From Khanag it is only 1,500 ft. climb to Jalori top. The scenery became increasingly extensive and lovely. A dense growth of pine and deodar gave shade throughout, chilling you whenever you stopped for a breather. It is noon by the time you ambled up the last hairpin bend and reached the top of Jalori pass.

The place is a bit of an anti-climax. The first thing you notice about it is a couple of boards. One reminds the traveller that it is indeed Jalori pass. The other sternly warns against catching butterflies there. There is no butterfly worth catching around there. For the topography gave little indication that were at 10,300 ft. What could be seen is a grassy mound, slopping gently to the north and the south. Two green hills flank the east and the west. But for the conifers and the nip in the air, the place could have been in central Kerala.

The place is surprisingly inhabited. There is a temple there. Nearby two busy *dhabas* serve frugal fare to travellers walking their way between the valleys of the Beas and the Sutlej. From April to July the pass is motorable. Once the rains start the road falls off in chunks. And by the time repairs are complete, it would be winter, and everything gets buried under deep snow.

The natives recall with pride how Jalori pass had risen to prominence a few years back as the most exciting stretch in the route of the Himalayan car rally. Lately, however, the rally has been taking a different route, pushing Jalori once again into oblivion.

The northern slope of the pass is reasonably intact. The view is spectacular, the distant snowcaps of Lahaul-Spiti partly framing the northern horizon. As you freewheeled gingerly down, a heavy downpour catches you unexpectedly, drenching you before you get a chance to don your raincoats.

In spite of the chill, you feel good, knowing you had *made it*.

The Jalori Pass Crossing

In March 1989 three young men set out on cycles over the Himalayan car rally route. Adventure alone was not their motive, they wanted to spread the message of wildlife conservation to people along the route.

Crossing the Jalori Pass, at a height of 10,300 ft. was the high point of the 3,200 km., which takes one over the route of the Sixth Himalayan car rally (1985)—on bicycles.

On March 20, 1986, they set out on a mission. They wanted to know Himalayas. How did the idea of cycling over the Himalayan Car rally route occur to him? They read a magazine interview of a foreigner who had participated in the Himalayan rally. He described in vivid detail the natural beauty of the route. The accompanying photograph showed a dirt road meandering through a beautiful fir forest.

Their only regret was that he had to go through this route at rally pace, while the true essence of its beauty could only be absorbed if one went over it slowly. Well, one could wonder what could be slower than a cycle! And so the idea as born. Embarking on the enterprise, however, was easier thought of than done. For six months they broke our backs over the project, approaching companies to get a sponsorship, poring over maps and road books, drafting endless letters, and to top it all, having to deal with that enlightened species who believed that a cycle expedition was nothing more than picking up a cycle and finding a road to roll on.

The expedition did not start on a hopeful note. An hour

after it was flagged off, they had their first breakdown. Being new to gears, they overlooked the seriousness of the problem initially but the reality soon dawned upon us. They removed the wheel and after three hours of hard work managed to amend the fault.

The next 64 days were bizarre—they seemed to have left their civilized habits behind ... the first thing they did on waking up was to check the air in our tyres. Brushing teeth and baths became taboo, because water was too precious to waste on these trivialities. Each day they faced a new stretch of road and ate our meals in three different villages. And all along not knowing what the 'unknown' had in store for them.

Their route took them from Delhi to Panipat, Haridwar, Dakpathar, Mussoorie, Paonta Sahib, Nahan, Solan and on to Simla. From Simla they went to the Jalori pass, Mandi, then back to Simla and via Dehradun to Mussoorie. From Mussoorie they cycled to Tehri, Chopta, Karnaprayag, Ranikhet, Almora and then to Nainital. From there, they peddled to Kaladhongi, Corbett National Park, Kotdwar, Ghaziabad and back to Delhi. A total distance of 3,200 kms.

On March 28, 1986, they encountered their first major climb, en route to Mussoorie. The climb began from Yamuna bridge and it went on and on and on or so it seemed. After every few kilometres they stopped to regain their strength and wonder whether the next turn would bring them to the top. By the time they reached Mussoorie they were totally exhausted but it was an extremely satisfying day in terms of cycling.

At Mussoorie they decided to stay in dormitory accommodation. Some young men staying with them in the dormitory enquired about our expedition and wondered aloud as to why they were travelling on cycles when buses could take us across much faster.

They have been asked this question so many times that they felt they must clarify cross commercial tourism of the kind which takes you on a whirlwind tour of major hill stations has become popular now-a-days. These kind of tourists seem to take pride in the fact that they have seen so many places in so little a time. What is the main difference between such tourists and travellers like them? While the normal tourist just scratches the surface of a new culture, they seem to delve appear and really get to know its people. For the normal tourist plies well beaten paths and reaches places which have been prepared to receive them, while they burst in unannounced in unprepared scenarios and extract the best that it has to offer".

Travelling in the hills, convinced them that 'a whole load of values like' kindness, love and hospitality' had not disappeared. On April 12, they were cycling towards Narkanda in Himachal Pradesh. The road conditions were terrible-lots of stones mingled with sand. To top it all the road was climbing towards the 8,500 ft. mark. Soon our struggle ended, but by then it had become dark.

Just as they were wondering what to do, a villager comes to them and enquires about our expedition. He was very happy to hear that three young men from Maharashtra had come thousands of kilometres to see his countryside. He immediately offered to be their host of the night. They stayed in his small hut that night and relished the simple food that he offered.

Adventure alone was not the driving force behind their venture—they had a serious project in mind. They decided that they would spread the message of wildlife conservation to the people along their route. They had been sponsored by the World Wildlife Fund (India), which provided them with audio-visuals which they showed at some places on our route. The National Museum of Natural History provided them with a large amount of printed literature on various aspects of nature conservation, posters, and nature education kits.

They concentrated on children in the age group of nine to fifteen. They found children in both the rural as well as urban areas to be very receptive to the idea of wildlife conservation. They explained to them why tree felling was harmful and how even apparently exotic creatures like the tiger must be preserved in order to maintain the ecological balance. At Woodstock school in Mussoorie they gave a one-hour audio-visual entitled 'Vanishing Forests'. People often mentioned to them that the message of nature conservation could be spread much more extensively if they had a motor vehicle. Well, they feel that although a cycle is slower and can cover less distance, it has the advantage of attracting a lot of attention. Whenever they reached a village or town they were immediately besieged by hordes of children. They kept all our printed literature and posters handy and they would immediately start distributing these and telling the children about the need for conservation.

They began the ascent to Jalori pass from Luri. The dirt road ran parallel to the Sutlej covered with thick layers of sand, it made the ascent difficult. Often the cycle tyres would get embedded into the sand, throwing them off balance. At times the cycle would skid and turn through a 90 degree angle and they would stand sweating in the sun trying to figure out what went wrong. They reached Ani on that hot afternoon of 15th April, 1986. After lunch they started towards Khanag, 18 kms. away.

After two or three kilometres the road became very steep. Soon the cycles stood still and refused to budge despite their efforts. The road had suddenly become unbelievably rough and steep and they were forced to get off their bikes. Walking with the heavily loaded bicycles in the scorching heat on the steep rough roads required considerable effort. The only compensation was the magnificent Fir, Pine forest through which the road made its ascent.

They reached Khanag just as the sun dipped below the horizon. After having toiled for the day, nature had its own way of rewarding them. They were treated to the awe-inspiring spectacle of that fiery ball of red bidding them adieu and leaving splashes of pink in that all encompassing sky. At Khanag they were told that the Jalori pass was under snow for 3-3½ kms. and crossing the pass on bicycles would be a foolish thing to do, for there had been a accident that very day when one horse had slipped and had fallen in the valley!

Well, after having done so much nobody was going to stop them from crossing the 'Jalori Pass' which was both literally and figuratively the acme of our expedition. They brushed aside all suggestions to hire porters to carry the bikes through the snow and went to sleep. They began the next day with renewed pep and vim and our morales soared higher as they gained height, for they were about to scale the summit which had, for so long, been their idea of high adventure. They took the final bend and there they were, staring smack in the face, majestic but aloof, the Himalayas.

They looked up and saw that the road which they had to take was also covered with snow. The snow, though sublime to behold, was a scary proposition, especially when one had to walk across it with a loaded bicycle. The road was very narrow and as a matter of fact it had become a part of the snow slope that began from the top of the mountain and ran down to the bottom of the valley.

One false step on the slippery surface spelt death— headlong fall into the valley below. The snow was six to eight feet deep and the walking space so narrow that there was not an inch left to manoeuvre. Dragging heavily loaded (35- 40 kg.) bicycles on this surface posed a unique problem. And there was the ever-present danger of glaciers moving under our feet.

They were scared to death-and that would be the under- statement of the year. The bicycles were covered with snow very soon and that did not make matters any easier. Another thing they realised very soon was that the torn canvas shoes which they were wearing were not at all manufactured with snow in mind. Against all odds, lifting and dragging the bike along, taking careful steps, they crossed the snow-bound section.

Adventure of Cycling

In December 1974, Jay Mandal, a young man from West Bengal, set off on his bicycle to explore several far-flung areas in the world. He has covered more than 1,95,000 kms. in 102 countries in Asia, Africa, Europe and U.S.A., on his "Little Queen" (as he called his bicycle). He left for South America to resume the last leg of his cycling odyssey through 45 countries.

There was much tension at his home. The fact was, he was going away leaving everything behind, shedding all 'responsibilities'. His father was clear about not contributing a penny for his world tour. He even warned him that he wouldn't be allowed at home when he came back. He said: "Baba I don't need money from you. I will earn on the road".

His mother, a simple, soft-natured woman didn't say much but kept weeping. That certainly upset him; but he was determined to go. Things improved in a few weeks, although it was an ordeal convincing his parents that he would return pretty soon, visiting only a few neighbouring countries!

He started his planning and preparation. Fortunately, many organisations came forward to help him. National Cadet Corps took the initiative to sponsor him, as he was its active cadet. T.I. Cycle Company of Madras donated him a new Phillips cycle. Lions International also came forward. Eastman Kodak Co. agreed to supply film rolls and get them processed free anywhere in the world. Help from several other international business firms was indeed heart-warming.

And so he set off, with the blessings and good wishes of his parents, seven brothers and sisters and many friends on Christmas Eve in 1974. Since then up to December 1974 covered 102 countries, and the wheels of his "Little Queen" have taken him over 1,95,000 kms.

His travel programme is long, extensive and strenuous. But at the end of each successful day, Mother Nature would remove all pains and revive him for the next day. Often, the sky proved to be his roof and the bare earth his solitary bed. Many times people from distant hamlets as well as urban homes helped him and inspired him. He recollect, with gratitude the affection of these people from different walks of life.

Even so, this pleasant trip was at times marred by the hostile attitude of unkind people. For instance, his life was in danger while crossing the deep forests in Africa. That's the continent where he spent more than 3 years and travelled extensively. His travel through Africa was most exciting and eventful.

It was on 29th of November, 1976, that he flew into Nairobi (Kenya) with his "Little Queen". Africa has been portrayed as the Dark Continent, an area replete with wildlife and dark, savage people—a continent where night holds sway. On the contrary, he learnt over my 3 years there that it's in Africa that civilisation exists in unadulterated form. The urban African still prefers to identify himself with his tribe and follows the tribal customs which are fascinating and peculiar.

The major problem was language. The guide could speak only his own tribal dialect. They were walking through equatorial forest and within a mile, they started climbing the mountain. It was quite an adventure to go through the tropical mountainous forest. Many times the guide had to cut the bush and creepers to make out a path. He was carrying a strong and sharp *Panga* (a sword like thing), a common companion of every tribal—especially in the bush. At times, they had to crawl through certain areas. Meanwhile, it started raining. They had no umbrella. The articles he was carrying with him, including his cameras got soaked. The deep forest and heavy clouds with rain in the afternoon made the whole area dark.

"The spirit of adventure" is perhaps dormant in all of us especially the young. He has been on this long trip, which will take 5 or more years to complete, to understand human nature in its myriad manifestations. People in various countries encouraged and helped him with shelter and food. But for their help his journey would have been unpleasant and perhaps fatal too.

At the same time he noted with much pain that some people did not receive him cordially—some treating him with suspicion, even refusing to give him shelter. Some humiliated him on many occasions on the belief, perhaps, that he was a poor Indian on two wheels. This does not dishearten him; on the contrary he realised their ignorance of the spirit of adventure. The totality of his experience enriched him so much that it will remain ever bright in his mind. And, he is addicted to travelling as he felt the road calls him again.

17

Game-Hunting: As a Sport

Hunting may be defined as a sport of taking animals by the end of hounds that haunt by nose. It is seeking, pescuing and taking of game and wild animals for subsistence profit or sport. It also includes the field sport of shooting small and large game.

Hunting was necessary for primitive man. He used to get necessities of life such as food, clothing and tools outfit. However, in the later stages he domesticated some of the animals for serving his daily needs and requirements. In much later period hunting became a privilege sport. The increase in population resulted an increase in hunting activities and resulted a considerable reduction in the population of wild animals.

In this stage man did not felt the need of hunting for necessity and hunting turned into a sports activity. Excessive hunting led to extinction of many species such as quagga in Africa, beson in America etc. Some of these now exist because survivors were breeded and carefully preserved. The indiscriminate slaughtering of game by market hunters and sportsmen, led to an awakening all around and laws were passed in every country to protect wild animals and game. Limits were put on the number of animals that each hunter was entitled to kill. Licences were also used for the purpose as a part of game management. Highly developed programmes and trained staffs to enforce regulations are regarding hunting seasons, game in season and possession limits.

In spite of these measures, the game again became plentiful in many areas. Game conservation schemes were introduced and implemented in India in 1860, in Africa in the year after World War II. However, the right of hunting is still attached to the ownership of land and the preservation of wildlife is a function practised and delegated to landowners.

From the sporting point of view old *shikaris* have always felt that a lion shoot does not provide the challenge, excitement and thrill of a tiger shoot. Tigers are more elusive, cunning and calculating, and it called for greater *bandobast* in organising a *shikar*. Even then no one can be certain of a successful shoot. You could have a hundred drummers and have even spotted the animal but there is every chance of it sneaking away or being missed by the shot. Lion, in comparison hardly ever take cover and would generally face the hunter without fear.

Gangs of poachers have been defying security arrangements made by the Forest Department and authorities of Project Tiger and quietly killing tigers in this park over the years. They are not doing it for excitement or thrills, but rather for the skin and other parts of a tiger which fetch enormous sums in the international market.

Traditional hunters belonging to the Mogia tribe living in sixty villages in the periphery of the forest are used by the people engaged in the smuggling of tiger skins. In fact the Mogias have been executing their game plan with perfection.

Hunting Sports in Himalayas

In climate and physical features Asia contain great variation. It offers unique attraction to the game hunter although it does not have much species or number of game. South of the Kunkun mountains lies the Tibetan plateau. This is the highest and most extensive in the world. The 'bharal' or wild blue sheep of the Himalayas, is the only one animal which seems to be almost ubiquitous throughout Tibet. This is regarded as the connecting link between sheep and goat. Tibetan antelope roam the Chang Thang, a desert in north Tibet which has an average attitude of 15,000 ft. Herds of wild yak are also found there. Tibet gazelle is also obtained there. In the lower districts to the east of Lhasa, there are forests, which hold Thorold's deer, a larger deer very few specimen of which have been obtained by European sportsmen. Small bluish bears and wolves are also found here. In the west bordering Himalayas, the snow leopard (ounce) and Tibetan lynx exit but very rarely observed.

The Himalayas provide magnificent stalking. The quarry of Himalayan wildlife includes other animals such as ibex, tahr, markhor, urial, goval, two species of bear (blue and brown). The brown bear exists only in the higher ranges near the snow-line and is variety of brown bear of Europe.

In the Western Himalayas are to be found specimens of the Kashmir star and in the East in the isolated pocket of territory in the Chumbi valley, is the home of a larger star, the shoe.

India contains the oldest and best known hunting ground of all sportsmen. It was accustomed to shooting tigers long before any big game hunter had set foot in Africa. The principal game fields were:

- *Tarai*—A narrow belt of tropical jungle which runs along the foot of the Himalayas from Yamuna river to Assam and which holds tigers, elephants, rhinoceros, sloth (honey) bear, black Himalayan bear, sambar ceylone, elk, cheetah, swamp deer etc.
- *The jungle of the Central India*—Tigers, gaur (bison), sambar, sloth bear (most important big game).
- *The damp and intensively thick jungle of South India and the Mysore plateau*—Elephant, gaur, big tiger.
- *The Nilgiri Hills*—Species of wild goats (ibex), a variety of tahr.
- *Assam and Sundarbans*—The semi flooded delta of the Ganges—buffaloes.

In India there are some firms and government agencies

that make the business of conducting visiting sportsmen or hunting tours.

Shooting Small Game

It is a field sport of small game and game birds and is practice all over the world. Game may be defined as a product of the wild that is killed for meat or an animal or bird that is hunted for sport or that state or other law specific as legitimate quarry.

Stalking Method

The method of sport hunting will depend on the size of the region in which the game is found and the size of the creatures. In open regions, free from trees, game can easily be viewed from afar. A slow and steady approach will be most appropriation in these regions. The sportsmen should make use of every tuft of grass, rock or hollow for concealment. Attention should always be paid to the direction of wind. This action is called as 'stalking'.

Still Walking Method

In dense bush or scrub it is impossible to see more than a few yards. The game could be visible suddenly. The best chance of getting a shot is walk slowly and cautiously even on the alert.

Tracking Method

Big beasts, elephants and herds together cannot be stalked or still-hunted. They leave well defined tracks, or spoon in soft ground and as a skilful hunter–sportsman you can follow their trail even on hard ground.

Driving and Beating

There is yet another category of animals which inhabit or

retire to patches of dense jungle, which may be thick. It is impossible for you to advance silently within a shooting distance. The first two methods could not be practised. The best method is to divide the animals out into open or along some path where the sportsman is awaiting. This you do with the help of men or dogs or with a line of elephants.

The big game hunting has always exercised great fascination for mankind. As a sportsman you should ascertain the best time of year for hunting. This is important from the point of view of health as well as chances of sports. This will depend upon the local condition of the area. High rise grass plenty of water etc. are some of the factors which may prevent you from seeing. The following information should be collected from the concerned region:

1. Sports and equipments locally available.
2. Means of transportation between the proposed base and the active shooting ground.
3. Availability of transport.
4. Availability of takers.
5. Map of the region and other information.

Another question of selection is the suitable firearms which basically depends on personal experience and preference. The best weapon for stalking is a rifle of the 'magnum' small calibre type which develops a high mizzle velocity and gives a flat trajectory, this eliminating the difficulties of judging distance. For dangerous game shot at close quarters the inexperienced hunter should use a heavy double-barrelled rifle of calibre of about .470.

Sitting Up/Sitting

If no help is forth coming, the best course for sportsmen is to wait in hiding over some spot where the animal will probably pass or return. Such a place could be a water source, game tail, crossing point or a salt lick or in case of boast of prey it could be half eaten kill. This method of setting over water or salt lick is not considered a sportsman like procedure and it is impossible by law in some regions.

Calling

This is mostly used for 'deer' hunting. In this method the sportsman waits in and makes noises in imitation of the call of a female during the rutting season or else of the challenge of a male. The male deer answers and advances gradually right up to sportsman believing him to be possible mate or probable antagonist. Calling deer is an oldest hunting technique dating back long before the introduction of firearms.

18

Caving and Speleology

Cave Diving

Cave is a cavity in rock large enough for human entrance and traverse. Cavern is nearly a synonymous. It means a large cave or a large connected group of caves. A rock-shelter is a cave whose entrance (mouth) is the largest cross section of the cavity and whose roof has adequate projection out over the floor. Collapse of part of the cave roof to make hole completely through to the surface constitution are common type of suite hole, a cave without a roof.

Since last few years, cave are in prominence and has gained ground as an adventure activity. Cave may originate with the making of the rock which encloses them. They may also be secondary to rock-making. To the first group belong caves in congealed lava flows. These are made generally by freezing of the surface of the lava stream while the deeper portions remain liquid and continuous to flow. Failure of supply under these conditions may allow the fluid lava to drain out and leave a linear hollow tube perhaps tens of feet in diameter.

Most of the cave belong to the second group having been made by removal of material after the enclosing rock was made. Some of these occur along exposed coasts where mechanical erosion occurs under vigorous wave attack. These seas caves are not limited to any particular kind of rock and they lack marked linearity and subterranean extent. Rock shelters commonly are the result of crumbling and falling away of weak rock on a hillside beneath stronger rock which form the roof.

Ancient Shelter in Caves

Looking back at the primitive man, we find that in all lands he utilised the natural shelter provided by caves, the rock shelter type caves have been the favourite of the primitive man. The tools, weapons, ornaments, hearths, the bones of kills, wall paintings and photographs of primitive man have provided archaeologist a lot of information. The 'cave man' has become a popular term for our early ancestors.

Ice age (Pleistocene) extinct carnivores—cave bear, cave lion, cave hyena also used caves as refuge and dens. Their remains being preserved in early floor deposits and beneath secondary floors of tavertine.

Important Caves of the World

The most famous cave area in the world lies in the calcareous Alps of central and southern Europe stretching from France through Switzerland and Austria to Yugoslavia. You will find deepest cave of the world which are yet to be described by man. The greatest size and depth of the Alpine caves is due to the highly faulted lime stones and the solution caused by the rainy and snowy climate.

Himalayan Caves

Well known caves exist in the Himalayas. There are numerous caves in the lime stone areas of the humid tropics. They usually contain much traventine stalagmite. This is a consequence of the high rainfall and evaporation in these areas. Tropical caves are also renowned for the large numbers of bats which inhabit them. Many of the caves are opened up and commercialised and are accessible to the general public.

The modern man is enthusiastic to study the caves. A scientific study of caves from all point of view is known as speleology. It includes the following:

(i) discovery of caves.
(ii) the techniques of exploration in caves.
(iii) cave surveying.
(iv) cave photography.
(v) study of the geological and chemical problem connected with their origin and development.
(vi) the physical and metrological condition in caves.
(vii) the study of cave fauna and flora.
(viii) the study of cave deposits, both calcareous and non-calcareous except where these form a series of layers important from a archaeological stand point.

Thus, you will notice that speleology is a complex science, involving the knowledge of many disciplines. In most of the countries of the world, there are societies for the promotion of speleology. Since 1930, there are great advances in the study of caves. The first international congress of speleology was held in Paris in 1953.

The exploration of deepest caves necessitates the use of many different types of ladders and of complex engineering techniques; camping for long periods underground is frequently essential. Submerged passages at the level of the water table can only be explored by the trained members of cave diving groups.

For sportsmen, it is a sporting science, involving certain risks. It attracts many amateurs, who are known as 'spelunkers' in the U.S.A.

The study of caves have many interesting everyday applications. This is particularly true in the field of hydrology where a knowledge of caves and springs and the movements of underground water are often needed to prevent water pollution. The best known applications are those connected with the tracing of underground water flow, for this purpose fluorescent, a chemical compound which colours water a vivid green, and coloured spores are frequently used. Countries which possess large areas of lime stone terrain, such as France, and Yugoslavia, engage trained speleologists to help solve many of their distinctive hydrological problems. Speleology has been of use in settlement of at least international hydrological dispute.

Cave Shrines

The Himalayas have been the abode of Gods and people from every nook and corner of India pay a visit to the holy shrines of Jammu and Kashmir situated on the Shivalik range of the Himalayas. Many of these are cave shrines and barring the cave shrine of Mata Vaishno Devi near Katra, most of the shrines are dedicated to Lord Shiva.

Among such shrines is the 'Shivkhouri' cave. Situated on a hillock about 140 km. nor.h of Jammu in Tehsil Reasi near Katra Vaishno Devi, this cave is the longest of the cave shrines in the State. Buses and other traffic go up to Ransoo, the base camp. People have to trek about four kilometres to reach the entrance of the holy cave. This trek is along a small natural water channel and is most fascinating, charming and enjoyable.

About 200 m. long, 9 m. wide and 2-3 m. high, this natural cave contains a self-made Shiva Lingam. According to some people the cave is unending. Inside the cave, the double chamber is quite spacious and can accommodate a large number of people.

At one spot, the cave divides into two—one of which is believed to lead to the Kashmir Valley. It now stands closed as some sadhus who ventured in, never returned.

To reach the sanctum sanctorum inside the cave, one has to bend, crawl or adjust his body sidewards where about a one metre high naturally created image of Shiva is visible. In addition one finds a number of other natural objects resembling the Goddess Parvati, Ganesha and Nandigan etc.

310 Adventure Tourism and Sports

The cave roof is etched with snake-like formations. Water drips constantly through these on the 'Shiva Lingam' in the cave.

A number of legends have grown around the discovery of this holy cave. According to one, the cave was discovered by a Muslim shepherd who, while in search of his missing goat, went inside to find to his surprise a number of 'sadhus' engaged in meditation and 'Shivapooja'.

Deeply impressed by the divine power he started pooja there. However, later he disclosed this to other people despite his promise to the sadhus who had advised him not to disclose about them or this cave.

People believe that for spiritual attainment and meditation this is the ideal place. A number of famous saints who have spent decades inside have been associated with this cave.

Shivkhouri has gained popularity during the past few decades. An annual three-day fair takes place here on the occasion of Maha Shivaratri and thousands of pilgrims from different parts of the country visit the cave shrine during this time and other festivals.

Rockshelters in Hoshangabad

Most of the shelters are high on the mountains. The view from there extends for miles over the top of the forests which have trees a hundred feet in height. While some shelters are on the fringe of high cliffs (difficult to approach) others are covered by a dense growth of trees and thorns. There are signs of habitation there of a period gone by. They must have shielded man from the sun, rains and wild animals.

Rockshelters in the forests of Hoshangabad district are located around Churna, Pattan, Keria, Kukra, Bori and Dhain. Churna is about 60 kms. from Hoshangabad off Bhonra on the Hoshangabad-Nagpur highway. Churna has a beautiful rest-house owned by the Forest Development Corporation. The rockshelters discovered by Nasir Beg are at Churangundi, a picturesque place near Churna, Jhalai (close to Churna) also has two rockshelters at Chitrakatri. One good forest road from Churna leads to Kukra, and another to Bori. Churna-Kukra

road runs along Tawa reservoir and passes via Pattan and
Keria, each of which has a small inspection hut with night
halt facilities.

Pattan is surrounded by five rockshelters—Kanbhar,
Bidni, Kharadhar, Khumbajhiri and Pinkapadha, discovered
by Takhat Singh Parihar, the game supervisor of Pattan. Ahead
on the same road lies Keria, around which the rockshelters
of Gajpathar, Lambijhot, Bidarya Amwall Khap Havalen.
Kukra lies beyond, at the foot of upper Satpuras; and across
Dhoda saddle is the rockshelter of Bhurbhundi glen (2,500
ft. high) discovered by Ravishankar Meena, game guard of
Kukra.

On Churna-Bori road, Dhain has an old but good forest
rest house; close by flows the Sonbhadra river with its beautiful
forest-clad banks. Several rockshelters have been discovered
near Dhain at Malolmattha, Karborianala, Deokhala and
Jhunkarnala by Gurdayal Choubey, game guard of Dhain.
He also discovered Belkhandar and Garhakoti rockshelters
near Bori. Bori has one of the oldest rest houses of Madhya
Pradesh, with an inviting landscape.

Cave Paintings

The horizontal paintings on the walls sometimes tell a story,
but usually show groups of human and animal figures.
Superimposition on earlier creations, which is common,
makes it all a confusing mass of human and animal figures.
The battle scenes suggest that the cave dwellers belonged to
the historic period.

Most of the human figures bear a bow and arrow or a
shield and sword. At one place a group of small figures, below
a pair of peacocks, is engaged in a fierce battle. The painter
brings out effectively the force of the action. In the same
panel a human figure holding a sword and shield is charging
at a person surrendering. Another painting shows a warrior
pursuing tortoises with a bow and arrow, with a stack of arrows
on his shoulders and a sword tied to the loin. Elsewhere a
man, hands up, is followed by a horseman and an armed

soldier. At one place, a severed animal head lies near the feet of a soldier with a strange sword; another painting shows a soldier shooting an arrow at a strange figure, probably some spirit. In a hunting scene, a tiger is encircled by people (hand-to-hand)—probably a scene of *Hanka*: Some scenes depict children at play.

In an another painting, an elephant carries three warriors armed with spears and swords and the driver has an *ankush* and a spear. A ladder hangs from the elephants back. Another elephant, with elaborate decorative motifs, has only one rider blowing a long trumpet; nearby, a warrior on horseback, reins in hand.

A striking black figure of a huge bison is shown—facing a man with sword—in yet another painting. This probably belongs to the mesolithic period of pre-historic times. Other animals are tiger, chetah, panther, barasingha, cheetal, porcupine, pangolin, tortoise, goat and dogs. Amongst birds, peacock, figures frequently.

Human figures wear different dresses, ornaments and headgears and human activities were the artists' priority. These figures are stylised, dynamic and forceful. Barring the figure of the great bison (in black), all the figures are in dark brown, pale white or greenish colours. The outlines of figures are in dark brown and the inner space is filled with pale white or greenish colours. The outlines of figures are in dark brown and the inner space is filled with pale white or greenish colours.

Fortunately, these rock paintings have remained quite undisturbed so far. The area should be further explored. There may be many more rockshelters.

Bhimbetkar

A visit to Bhimbetkar in Madhya Pradesh, the largest gallery of primitive rock art, takes you on a journey far into the past.

Man has always had this urge to reach out, to capture and influence the world around him. Even if it's only wishful thinking.

Nowhere is this basic urge more evident than in the rock shelters of a place in Madhya Pradesh called Bhimbetkar.

If you drive 40 kms. south of Bhopal, and then turn right, you will come to a level crossing. Bump over it and follow the often-rugged road winding up a hill where, in season, palas flowers bloom like clotted blood. At the end of the road is a rough car park. In front of it is a fenced-off area protecting huge, mansion-sized, outcrops of rock in a dry, deciduous forest. This is Bhimbetkar. And you are about to step far into the past.

An estimated one lakh years ago, our Stone Age ancestors first came here. Some lived in caves, but they seemed to prefer the convenient rock shelters: large overhangs of sandstone. These protected them from rain and sum and yet did not hem them in if their enemies, including wild animals, tried to attack them. But though they were armed with primitive stone weapons, they still wanted to control their environment. So they set about developing a new form of expression, beyond song and dance and conversation. They created painting, ten thousand years ago.

Bhimbetkar is our country's largest gallery of primitive rock art.

You may have visited this amazing place many time but, the next time you plan a trip there, you decide to give yourselves the greater part of a day to wander around unescorted. Even so, you are only able to see a small fraction of the 130 shelters which had paintings on them. But what you see is stunning.

The paintings of animals and humans range all the way from, at least 100 centuries ago to the medieval era. Amateurs like us can learn a great deal from them. Particularly about the fears, hopes and joys of these ancient people and the land in which they lived.

For one thing, it must have been a wetter, greener, land. Elephants, bison and wild boar roamed freely. Clearly, during the years that intervened, there was a major climatic change, reducing the rainfall, drying the rivers and marshes, driving away the animals. But, when our ancestors made the first pictures, they faced fearsome beasts. High on a rock; you see a painting of a monstrous bison goring a tiny hunter.

Humans, however, struck back. In other rocks, there are hunting scenes of men attacking animals with stone-tipped spears and bows and arrows. They went even better than that. They frightened herds of animals into stampeding over a cliff, tumbling to their deaths. In the, so-called zoo rock, there is a picture of such a stampede. There is also, it is believed, a drawing of a device still used by some forest people to imitate the roar of a tiger. The man with a spear sitting in the foreground of the picture seems to be using such an instrument to scare the animals.

On other rocks, you see pictures of community dances: probably to celebrate a successful hunt.

To make these paintings, the artists had to prepare the rock surface with animal fat; grind the coloured rocks to make the right, powdery, pigment; shred twigs to make brushes; clean out hollow bones to blow the pigment into the outlines of the drawings; and then crouch awkwardly to reach their standstone 'canvas'. It is painstaking work.

'Why', you ask ourselves, 'did our artists make these paintings'?

They weren't merely decorative. If they wanted to paint pretty pictures, they would have painted flowers and birds, the sun, the moon and abstract designs. They didn't do so. Most of the earliest paintings concentrate on animals or hunting for animals, with only a few depicting dancing. They were the action movies of those distant days.

By depicting a successful hunt the stone age ancestors hoped to capture the living essence of the animals and make their own wishes of hunting come true. And when you see political cartoons depicting the downfall of opponents it is clear that you, 10,000 years later, are still painting your wishes on the walls.

Khandgiri-Udaigiri Caves

The Dhauli hill lies 8 km. south of Bhubaneshwar on

Bhubaneshwar-Puri road at the bank of the river Daya. The Kalinga battle was fought here in 216 B.C.

The conquest of Kalinga involved a great carnage, captivity and misery of the people, proving to be a turning-point in the career of Ashoka. The earliest records of India—a set of edicts of the great emperor Ashoka (circa 272-36 B.C.) of the Maurya dynasty are inscribed on the rocks of this hill.

Incised on a rock with the sculptured forepart of an elephant at the top, it contains 11 out of the well-known set of 14 rock-edicts found on the confines of his empire. Of late, a Japanese Buddhist monk has constructed Shanti Stupa (Peace Pagoda or White Pagoda) atop the Dhauli hill.

The twin hills of Khandgiri and Udaigiri lie 6 km. west of the Bhubaneshwar railway station on Bhubaneshwar-Chandka road. A narrow defile passes through this road. It separates the two hills rising amid a wide expanse of arid lateritic soil.

The Khandgiri (broken hill) has 15 (caves) and a Jain Temple dedicated to Rishabhanath—the first of the 24 Jain Tirathankaras. Here in cave 8 Barabhuji Gumpha there are 25 figures of all the 24 Tirathankaras with the 23rd Tirthankara-Parsvanatha being repeated twice.

Similarly, all the 8 caves of the Udaigiri (hill of the sunrise) of which cave 1 (Rani Gumpha) and cave 14 (Hathi Gumpha) are the most famous.

The Rani Gumpha is double-storeyed, the largest and the most beautiful of all the Khandgiri-Udaigiri caves.

These caves were meant for Jain recluses, who are unparalleled for the rigour of their asceticism and extreme self-mortification. So, these caves were equipped with little amenities. Even in exceptionally large Rani Gumpha a man can not stand erect and stretch himself.

Bhubaneshwar is connected with Mumbai, Calcutta, Delhi, Hyderabad, Nagpur, Rajpur and Varanasi by Indian Airlines.

From Bhubaneshwar to the Dhauli hill and the twin hills

of Khandgiri and Udaigiri autorickshaws and taxis are available.

Bhubaneshwar is also connected with Mumbai, Calcutta, Delhi, Guwahati, Hyderabad, Chennai and Thiruvanantha-puram by superfast and express trains.

At the foot of the hills, there is a small inspection bungalow with limited accommodation. For the occupation, permission of the sub-divisional officer, Khurda (district Puri) is needed. At Bhubaneshwar accommodation suiting to all budgets is available.

Uttaranchal: Patal Bhubneshwar Cave

The Patal Bhubaneshwar cave temples have not been exposed so much yet but inside them lies a fascinating world of achievements, history, mythology, legend and sheer wonder.

Firstly, the approach to the cave temple is unique, with one having to literally crawl to get inside, and climb down some 82 steps. Dan Singh Bhandari, the Pujari at the temple, proudly and knowledgeably tells us the story behind the temple and the wealth that it contains. It is virtually a who's who of Hindu mythology.

The Patal Bhubaneshwar finds a mention in the Skanda Purana, which are one of the 18 Puranas, repository of the best of Indian culture and philosophy. Incidentally, Patal Bhubaneshwar, said to be over 6,000 years old, has non-Brahmin priests.

Till some years back, there was no electricity inside the caves, and one had to go inside with oil torches. This explains the sooth deposit on the rocks.

Sheshnag and the 1,000-leg Eravath (elephant) are the imposing and lasting impressions in rocks at the first layer of the caves.

Incidentally, the temple from outside seems to be a normal, small one, but once inside, it is vast with many floors, as it were. As one would expect, many a legends and stories are attached to the caves.

The scene of Kaurav-Pandava playing *chaupar* in the cave,

as also of the natural *abhishek* of the deities one by one is to be seen to be believed.

Towards the end of the *kalyug*, two formations—stalactites and stalagmites—would meet, and there would be *pralay*—end of the world.

Patal Bhubaneshwar is about 100 km. from Pithoragarh via Gangolohat, Patal is 14 km. from Gangolohat, where there is a Kali Temple.

There are PWD and Inspection Bungalows and dharmashalas, and the Rhythm Camp at Chandak.

At other times in summer, one can visit and enjoy the peace and natural beauty, even as you marvel at the whole creation and the rich stories inside.

Himachal: Dhung Caves

How do you feel about visiting caves and that too very near to your own city? Well it's not just thrilling but a real adventure you can plan with your friends. All you have to be ready for is a 7-km. trek which stars from Chamba Ghat near Solan (Himachal Pradesh). If you are still lacking in motivation note it down that these caves are not just an opening in the mountain but more than 15 km. long.

Solan is on National Highway-22 connecting Chandigarh to Shimla. Chadigarh is the nearest airport and Solan has a narrow gauge rail connection. Just when you are at Solan's entrance a left turn takes you on to the bypass. A few kilometres later you reach Chamba Ghat. It is at this place you park your vehicle and get ready for the trek.

If you can manage it fast you need a minimum of two hours for the up trek and another half and one for the down trek.

Before you start your trek, book your room for the night stay in any one of the many hotels in and around Solan. Barog Heights a multi-storeyed hotel on the highest peak of the region is the best option. Now starting with the trek, nothing will trouble you for the first hour, not even your thirst as you will find many spring water outlets.

The mid-way stop is Dhung, a small village and from here onwards you will not find anyone except wild animals. But nothing to worry about as you will find only the herbivorous animals here. After reaching the top, you have to trek down a height and then climb again to reach the cave.

This part of your adventure is through thick forest and if it is winter you will definitely find snow. A climb of a few metres will take you to the caves. Whether the caves are natural or artificial it still remains unanswered but the villagers say that the Pandavas used this cave to escape from Lakshagrah.

It is better not to enter the caves if you are not fully prepared. The things you must have before entering the cave are torches, safety belt, gloves, leather jackets, full face helmet (important), heel boots and heavy stockings. Mind it that no part of your body should be exposed. Your first likely encounter is with bats which are hiding right at the mouth of caves. You may be lucky not to find even one but safety saves.

You have to descend over a 100 m. before finding way to a large number of sister caves. If you are not leaving a trail behind you with the help of rope or marking your way with a piece of chalk you are likely to loose your way and be trapped inside. The passage through one of the caves will lead you to a lake. This discovery puts all big question mark regarding the origin of the caves.

The stalagmites and stalactites are common inside the cave but the nature of rock does not appear to be that of limestone. Don't show enthusiasm in crossing the lake as it is a serious risk to your life.

Pacify your high spirits here and move back. More reasons for you to retreat are that you need oxygen cylinder, extra battery for your torches and the most important that you have to complete the back trek before it gets dark. But don't forget to take a few snaps of your team which has completed an adventure to be admired.

Historical Tabo Caves

In Himachal Pradesh a large number of centuries-old caves on the high mountains surrounding the village where the 1,000 years old Tabo Monastery is located remained largely overlooked.

These caves, which are visible even from a distance in the remote Spiti Valley, were pushed to the background as the monastery hogged all the limelight during the millennium celebrations.

Still partially inhabited in the summer months, these caves are actually the winter abode of the monks and other people living in this barren valley. With winter temperature dropping to a freezing –30° the caves serve a dual purpose for the monks of the monastery. They not only provide an escape against the cold spell in this valley but also the opportunity to the monks to meditate. Local people say that as in the past many of the monks who shift to the caves continue to meditate for months together during the winter season which is quite a prolonged one in these areas.

Perched on the sunny side of the sky-high sandy mountains of the area, the caves serve as a winter habitat for the monks. Locals believe that these are as old or perhaps even older than the Tabo Monastery, which is celebrating its one thousand years in 1996. There are quite a few caves on the hill side. Their sizes do vary. While some can accommodate up to four persons, other caves are bigger and can have 10-20 persons.

One of the larger caves even has murals and paintings inside it which are said to be ages old. The paintings inside are now a dim reminder of their erstwhile glory. This main cave has an assembly hall for the monks, who make the caves their dwelling units. The paintings have been done on the rock faces of the mountain inside the hall.

19

Golf

Golf is also unique in that it is probably the only popular sport where the participants compete against themselves instead of each other. This lends golf to versions like the increasingly popular professional-amateur tournaments. Golf can be a great leveller and in pro-am tournaments, company Chief Executive Officers (C.E.Os.) and captains of industry with, say, an 18-handicap, could have a perfectly enjoyable round of golf with top rung professionals.

Golf courses are developed on vast expanses of land. The smallest golf courses measure about a hundred acres. A regular 18-hole course would be about 200 acres or more. It might sound incredible but Japan has a 126-hole course measuring over 1,000 acres!

In spite of the geographical diversity and terrain variability in India, each stretch of land has some kind of uniformity within its fold. Normally, no natural landscape provides all the different golf course features. Hence, developing a golf course involves a lot of landscaping efforts. Fair ways, wooded roughs, sand bunkers, water hazards, putting greens and a host of other features have to be carved out of the land earmarked for the golf course.

It is not without reason that golf courses are viewed as environmental hazards. Landscaping operations on golf courses include clearing shrubbery, uprooting trees, levelling the ground, digging up ditches etc. Bulldozers are often used for developing a golf course. This kind of landscaping not only plays havoc with the top soil but also puts the local wildlife on the run as their habitats and food sources are destroyed.

Use of chemical fertilizers and pesticides for the upkeep of fairways and greens take a toll of the insect population. This creates gaping holes in the food chain and disturbs the ecological balance of the area. Insects form prey for several species of birds. Hence, the bird population of the area is automatically affected. Chemical fertilisers and pesticides also seep down and pollute the underground water table. During monsoons, these fertilisers and pesticides are washed away by rain water. Flowing through drains, they end up at the water works, polluting water all the way.

Golf courses need gallons and gallons of water to keep the grass green through the year. Most of the water comes in tankers. During summers and in warmer regions, the requirement of water is even more as the fairways and greens have to be frequently watered to keep them green. This strains the already scarce resources of water which would otherwise be available for domestic, agricultural and industrial use.

Some golf clubs claim to meet their water requirements from tubewells within their golf courses. But, this is nothing to be proud of. Regular pumping of water from tubewells in water scarce areas could bring down the level of the underground water table.

Golf courses deprive the general public of open spaces available for recreation. They also destroy natural heritage by superimposing artificial landscapes on the original landscapes of the area. When new residential areas are starved of playgrounds and parks, there is little justification for stashing away vast tracts of land in prime locations for golf courses. Since golf is patronised by ultra-rich and influential people, they always manage to get the land they fancy. It is no secret that golf is essentially a game for a minority of the elite group. To play golf, you need a leather golf bag stuffed with an assortment of golf clubs (or, that is what the beginners are led to believe!). A full bag of golf clubs may contain half a-dozen 'woods', and an equal number (if not more) of 'irons'—not to mention the 'wedge' and the 'putter'. Even as a game golf is of not much interest to the general public. Thus masses rightly feel deprived of the large patches of green which after being turned into golf courses become inaccessible to them. There certainly is no reason why the general public should be alienated from their due share of open spaces to serve the interest of an elitist group.

No new golf course must be allowed to come up on any green or livable land. Discerning members of the public and non-government organisations must take up this issue in a big way. The existing golf courses must undergo a change of character so that the place is not an elitists club but a green space where any one can walk in to enjoy its rich biodiversity, which a golf course—if managed on new lines, can offer. Because of a growing consciousness of the damage golf courses can cause to the environment, a global movement to oppose development of new golf courses is gathering momentum. Environmentalists have successfully persuaded quite a few existing golf courses to develop their potential as sanctuaries for local flora and fauna.

A Sanctuary Programme should aims at improving and enhancing the environmental and ecological value of golf courses through ecologically sound management. Among other things, the programme enlists the participation of the golf community in conservation efforts and promotion of environmental awareness amongst the general public.

The golf course managers submit a map of the course, details of golf course features, land features, flora and fauna, irrigation and public involvement. The Committee's recommendations on environmental planning, wildlife, cover enhancement, wildlife food planning, water conservation etc. are passed on to the golf course managers for implementation. They should not only trying to improve and enhance the environment of golf courses but also recreate, as far as possible, a setting which existed before the golf courses were developed.

It is time the managers of golf courses in India took a

cue from this and developed golf courses as sanctuaries in a similar way. A good way to begin is to plant a lot of different species of native tress in the wooded rough and on the periphery of golf courses to make up for trees uprooted during landscaping operations. Use of organic manures and bio pesticides in golf courses will reduce water pollution. Water harvesting, which simply means collecting and storing rain water for future use, can reduce their water requirements from external sources and make them self-sufficient to an extent. Identifying and planning vegetation that originally existed in the area, may encourage and support the original wildlife of the area, once again.

This is the least the golf community should do to show that it is serious about making golf courses environmentally responsible projects. Indian golfers have been putting golf balls for several decades now. It is time they started putting the green ball.

The eighteen-hole golf course at Gulmarg, high above the world, is rated as one of the highest anywhere. You can tree off on the rolling green downs of the golf course at Gulmarg under the guidance of seasoned golfers who can swing their clubs with graceful, enviable ease. So, tree off in the green coolness of Gulmarg. Instruction for beginners can be arranged by becoming temporary members of the exclusive golf club. The golfing season lasts from mid-May to end of October.

Golf courses with their lush grass fairways dotted with tree clusters and smooth velvety putting greens, bear a relaxing spectacle. For the hard-pressed urbanites trapped in congestion and daily hassles, the open vistas and quiet of the golf courses provide a haven of respite. The rise of industrial activity and urbanisation have sparked off a corresponding boom in golf which has by itself become an industry. The highly developed countries choked with buildings, human settlements and industries have put little space left to meet the increasing call for golf courses.

Their demand for the sport is, therefore, spilling over

into the underdeveloped world where the professional golf architectural companies are seeking natural scenic land to lay golf courses for the recreation of the rich communities in the developed nations. The endeavours of the golf companies to build golf courses is reinforced by the tourism development organisations who sponsor golf as an added attraction to draw foreign tourists.

The construction of golf courses leads to a number of adverse effects. The golf course developers normally have their eyes set on islands or wooded land or undulating hilly land or headland. Such a choice robs the people of their natural beauty spots. Furthermore, the construction involves cutting down of trees, clearing of vegetation and the drawing up of landscapes and the creation of artificial roughs and rugged features to test and stimulate the skill of golf players.

For such architecture, bulldozers and other mechanical means are brought into use which not only cause soil erosion but also drive out the animals and birds and kill plant life. In short, golf course building operations deface the fragile natural environment and deprive the ordinary people of their open spaces that provide them with re-life and rest from the humdrum of city life.

Golf courses are great guzzlers of water for they have to be constantly sprayed and this particularly in the hot countries. The heavy investment of water on golf courses proportionately reduces the availability of this vital resources for the people's personal or agricultural needs. The argument that golf courses fend water for themselves through tubewells etc. does not hold water, because the water table below the surface is a common limited pool. Malaysian scientist, Dr. En Maketab Mohamed, has assessed that the water required to maintain a medium-sized course for one year is equal to the water ration of 20,000 people. And not only this, golf courses are also responsible for a good deal of water pollution in their neighbourhood. Water pollution is caused in two principal ways: first, due to the use of pesticides of which two tons are needed per annum per golf course and second, by certain toxic chemicals which are used to lend a glow and smooth texture to the grass on the fairways and putting greens.

These poisonous chemicals are emitted into the water and air which the local inhabitants, including the golfers, inhale into their systems. The Ministry of Health in Japan which is seized with the problem, has estimated that "850 running water systems, or one-fifth of the country's total" are adversely affected either by pollution or reduction in the water supply by golf courses.

Golf has developed into a veritable mania in Japan which has about 2,000 golf courses that are increasing at 100 per year causing in their wake, a mosaic of environmental destruction such as of fish and trees, in addition to water pollution. Nevertheless, these courses are not adequate to meet the mounting needs of the swarming Japanese golfers. Within Japan, the golfing fees are so high that it is cheaper to fly into Malaysia for a week's golf. Malaysia is one of Japan's golfing colonies abroad. Mr. Kuji Tsutoma, author of a white paper on golf courses says that there are 150 Japanese-owned golf courses abroad.

In certain countries—both developed and developing—a confrontation has emerged between the ecologists and the tourist-cum-golf developer organisations. The ecology activists view golf courses as invasions on the natural and unspoilt beauty of their land. Notably, Jean Hulmann of the World Wide Fund for Nature in Geneva is engaged in a seething battle against the authorities in Switzerland who have proposed three golf courses including one in the valley of Sion that harbours wild life. In Japan and Thailand, too, people's protests are becoming increasingly more vocal and have succeeded in arresting the work on some golf course projects. In Malaysia, the consumer associations, which are even more aggressive, have raised this question in their Parliament.

Understandably, they are bulking the construction of golf courses in the Penang Hill which is well-known for its natural scenic charm. The Penang Consumers' Association is also deeply exercised against the plan for a golf course in Fraser's Park which is a bird-watching venue and a popular picnic and camping spot for the ordinary people. In disgust, a spokesman of the Association observes: "Slowly, but surely, our natural heritage is becoming the property of an elite group of foreigners and locals". He also boldly opines that a bulk of the profits from the golf course activities go to the foreigners or are enjoyed by the select few locals.

Golf course activities are, no doubt, on the increase. The club houses are becoming larger with added accommodation for bars, restaurants, card rooms and even apartments for stay as also additional games such as swimming and equestrian sports which collectively help to raise small urban niches at the cost of open spaces.

Driven by the urge of gigantism, in certain countries like Japan, large golf courses spanning as many as 126 holes have been laid out covering 1,000 acres or more. The current trend for more and bigger golf courses is obviously detrimental to the environment. It is evident that a balanced view in the use of golf as a sport is essential lest it should further aggravate our already depleting environment. The apprehension that golf is promoting "green deserts" and is catering only to the few rich elite is certainly gathering momentum.

Sports historians agree that it was the Scots who taught the world to play golf. But who actually invented it is open to debate. The Scots certainly have strong claims to the title, but so do the Dutch, the French and the Belgians. One way or the other, there's no disputing the fact that golf has been around for over five hundred years ago, any club and ball game meant just that: one club and one ball. The club would have been fashioned out of a branch of a tree—thornwood or beech or ash—and the head carved out of holly, dogwood or blackthorn, spliced and then attached with glue. The ball would have been made from leather, stuffed with either feathers or cork.

According to golf historian John Pinner, the first authentic record of a recognised clubmaker appears in 1603 when William Mayne, a maker of bows and arrows, was appointed to the court of James I of England to make, among other things, clubs for the golf-loving king and his courtiers.

Three hundred years later, wood had given way to steel. But now, thanks to state-of-the-art technology, including computer-assisted designing, the shafts of golf clubs are made of graphite and carbon-fibre and used by professionals and amateurs alike. And their manufacture, like other sports equipment, is a billion-dollar business with millions of clubs mass-produced each year. India has been manufacturing golf clubs for quite some time, but most golfers prefer foreign-made clubs!

The ball too has kept pace with technology. In the 16th century it used to be called a feathery. Piner, in his book *The History of Golf*, writes: "Making the ball called for much patience. The leather was of untanned bull's hide that was cut into two round pieces for the ends and a narrow strip for the middle, then softened and firmly sown together, leaving a small hole through which to stuff the feathers. To give the ball a smooth finish the leather was turned inside out so that the rough seams were hidden inside. The leather casing was then placed in a cup-shaped stand and the boiled feathers—as many as would fill a top hat—were stuffed through the hole with the aid of a metal pusher. Inserting the feathers was a slow and laborious operation and the inhaling of small particles from the feathers often caused respiratory problems. A ballmaker could feel well satisfied if he produced three featheries in a full working day".

Then, in the second half of the 19th century, ballmakers discovered that the reddish brown, horn-like substance of the juice of the Malaysian gutta-percha tree could be moulded into perfectly good golf balls. They were quick to make and cost but a fraction of the feathery.

But the real credit for making this discovery goes to a golf-loving clergyman from St. Andrews, England—the Reverend Robert Adam Paterson who hit upon the idea after receiving a beautiful marble statue of Vishnu from India wrapped in a protective padding of gutta-percha.

In 1953, this ball, christened 'gutty', was superseded by

the Haskell ball. The brainchild of an American dentist Dr. Coburn Haskell, the ball was made of strips of elastic wound around a liquid-filled rubber core, with a casing of gutta-percha. However, most balls now have a covering of the more durable balata or surlyn instead of gutta-percha and have a solid core.

Golf being an elitist game, style rules over everything else. Like tennis players, golfers love to exhibit their equipment. And so you have the golf bag, the trolley to drag the bag across the course or like in India, caddies to do the needful. There are also golf buggies, powered by diesel, petrol or batteries.

That's not all, golfers these days wear shoes with specially moulded or metal-spiked soles, suede gloves, sun-visors and designer clothes. The caddies carry umbrellas to shield the golfers from the harsh rays of the sun or the pitter-patter of the rain.

In the next decade there is going to be a sea change in golf as the Japanese, who love golf with the same passion as they do their *sushi*, set the pace. There being not enough land to meet the Japanese's insatiable appetite for golf, the mega-industrial and business conglomerates of Japan have begun putting up mini indoor golf courses in Tokyo and other cities, for their employees to relax, in between their hectic schedules. This craze is now spreading to the USA and Europe.

With the Japanese slowly making inroads into India, thanks to liberalisation, it will come as no surprise, if indoor courses crop up in this country too.

It was the British who introduced the game in India in the second half of the 18th century and established the Royal Calcutta Golf Club. In 1876, the Bangalore Golf Club (B.G.C.) came into being, with the young Winston Churchill being a regular on weekends.

Golf has come a long way since then. The exciting news is that the B.G.C. will soon figure in the Guinness Book of World Records for continuously hosting the world's oldest

Inter-Club Championship (Madras Golf Club versus B.G.C.). Begun in 1878, it has been held every year since then, except for interruptions during the two World Wars. "Can you believe it? Golfers from Madras used to ride on horseback and carriage to Bangalore and vice-versa for the tournament held twice a year. The journey used to take about a week in the good old days".

20

Mountain Runs

This recent sport could well have had its beginning in rustic Britain where shepherds raced up the nearby mountains with the spectators betting on the results. Today, mountain running is all professional: the runners are equipped with a compass, maps, water bottles, torches, sophisticated shoes, and the running trail is lined with well-stocked aid stations.

Mountain running, began in an organised manner in Germany but the credit to popularising it goes to the Americans who took it to a new high. And this sport has become a fad with the obsessive ultra-runners of the world who are always on the lookout for unique and exciting feats to test their endurance.

Mountain running this unique adventure sport is happening in the Indian mountain-scapes. The Indian Himalayan range is, of late, being invaded by a new kind of adventure freaks called 'ultra-runners' from the world over. What could be more exciting to those seeking ultimate adventure than to run amidst the world's highest peaks under the sapphire skies!

Although a few intrepid individuals had completed solo runs on their own in the Himalayan range, it was only a few years ago that an extended foot-race called 'Himalayan Run and Trek' was organised in the higher reaches of Darjeeling at an altitude varying between 7,000-12,000 ft. With this India became the first Asian country organise this novel sport of mountain running.

There is an immense potential for mountain running sport in India, and the vast hilly terrains in Himachal Pradesh, Garhwal, Kumaon, Kinnaur, Ladakh and Darjeeling are perfectly suited for that purpose. Mountain running, besides offering adventure, gives participants an opportunity to experience the beauty of the geographical, cultural and historical heritage of the hilly areas.

Though picking up gradually, this sport in India is restricted to medium runs. In longer runs, like those in America and Europe, helicopter rescue teams stand by in the case of health emergencies or in case a participant loses its way.

Despite the tough test of endurance and the small health risks involved, this sport is being encouraged the world for its obvious advantage over environmentally-damaging motorcar rallies. Each of the race is an environmental mission. Such races can be a good medium of creating awareness about the preservation of hills and in particular, the Himalayas.

On the personal level, this sport remains what it has been: a race with no one but oneself. The sense of personal achievement is immense. After days of extreme physical effort one certainly ends up feeling on top of the world!

However, in the spectacular Himalayas, this unique adventure sport started eight years ago when, American professional runners organised a 100 mile stage race, Himalayan Run and Trek. The response to this annual race has been tremendous, with the number of participants shooting up from mere 14 in 1991 to over 100 during the last few years.

Recently, the eighth international five-day 100 Mile Stage Race began at dawn in the small, sleepy village of Manebhajang, about an hour bus ride from Darjeeling town. The village is at an altitude of 7,000 ft. and is surrounded by the snow-capped peaks.

The trail traversed by runners is said to be made on the order of the Nizam of Hyderabad, who thought it the best place from where to view the Himalayas.

So impressed are the professional runners by the view, they've called it 'the world's most beautiful running trail'.

On one side was the clear view of Mt. Everest, Lhotse and Makalu, the last two being among the five highest peaks of the world. On the other side was the magnificent Kanchenjunga. The runners ran above the treeline and the cloud base and there was nothing to obstruct the stunning mountain view.

You may be in for a nasty surprise if you consider mountain running to be a mere sightseeing exercise. The participants had to complete the gruelling 100-mile course in five days, fighting altitude sickness, rapid temperature drop and dehydration, a major problem in the hills.

Muscle pulls and sore feet is a common occurrence and that's the reason this sport is also called 'endurance running'. As one of the participants from Britain put it: "Although swollen limbs, headches and nausea are common at high altitude, one of the lessons of running in multi-day race cocerns recovery; you can push your body mercilessly one day and with good food and rest, be back to running the next day."

Multi-day stage races cover from 100 miles to 5,000 miles, spanning a period from one week to a few months. While short runs are meant mainly for amateurs, the longer ones are for professionals and the experienced lot. And it needs more of mental application in longer runs than mere physical endurance to get through.

SECTION III

ADVENTURE ON SNOW
SOFT AND HARD

21

Adventure of Ice Hockey

Although ice hockey, ice skating, sledding and other winter sports have long been popular in many parts of the world that have sufficient ice and snow, they gained national and international stature only, in the 20th century. Figure skating on ice became the first Olympic winter sports event in 1908, followed by ice hockey in 1920 and skiing, bobsledding, and speed skating in 1924, the year the separate cycle of winter Olympic games was inaugurated. The soaring popularity of winter sports in the 1950s and specially the 1960s resulted in a great increase in facilities, for example, ski runs and ski lifts, and the development of new recreational activities, among them touring and racing in snow mobiles.

Canada is regarded as the mother of the modern sport of ice hockey. It was the first country to organise ice hockey game on a national wide bases, with a codified form of playing rates. For long the sport was confined to natural ice. With the advent of artificial ice rinks its popularity spread rapidly.

One school of thought holds that ice hockey is a development of field hockey. Another is of the opinion that it is a development of old Irish game of hurting. There is a group of experts who believe that the game of handy played with a ball and bent sticks by two teams is a forerunner of ice hockey. There is also evidence that the Indians played a similar game in Canada centuries ago.

In 1908, the international Ice Hockey Federation was

formed with Great Britain, France, Belgium, Switzerland and Bohemia as founder member. The international rules are applicable to most attaliated countries and govern the world and European champions. The rules of the same are easy to follow. There is provision of defensive tactic known as body checking whereby the defending player is permitted to hit with his body on attacking player in possession of the pack. This is a complicated situation similarly, confusion also arises from the application of the off side rule (bringing the pack forward illegally) and the penalty rule. A breach of certain rules results in the attending player being sent off the ice for a number of minuts during which his team has to play short handed under circumstances a penalty shot may be awarded.

Under the international rules, the number of players per team permitted on the ice at any one time is six:

- goal keeper (goal tender)
- two defence men and
- three forwards.

In addition, the international rules allow eight others, one of whom must be a goalkeeper, the coach is permitted to change players and when he chooses, provided that not more than six players are on the ice at the same time.

Before the change to six men hockey, teams were made up of seven men and the position were goal tender, point, cover point, rover left wing, centre and rightwing.

Players were permitted to wear protective equipment the specifications of which are covered by the rules. The equipment is essential because of the inherent hazards of the sport.

The 'pack' the term applied to the dislike object which the game is played—is made of valcanished rubber, or other approved materials, is 1" thick and 3" diameter and weighs 5½-6 oz.

The game consists of three periods of 20 minutes each of actual playing time. The playing surface is divided into three areas, known as the defending zone, neutral zone, and attacking zone. The neutral zone is again divided by the centre line. These lines govern the off side.

The Game Procedure: Ice Hockey

Off Side

In this game three zones are established in which the puck could be passed forward. You may pass the puck forward or in any other direction with in the zones. It may also be moved ahead from zone to zone, with certain limitations.

For example, in U.S.A., forward pass is permitted within three zones and forward passing to a team mate from the defensive zone up to the attacking zone blue line i.e, a two zone forward pass is allowed. No attacking player can penetrate the attacking zone ahead of the pack, if he does he is offside and a face off is called.

In case of Canadian ice hockey forward passing is permitted within the three zones and forward passing to a team mate from his defensive zone upto the red line which halves the neutral zone. No attacking player can penetrate the attacking zone ahead of the pack.

Goals

Like hockey, the object of the game of ice hockey is for one team to shoot the puck into its opponent's goal in the face of the opposing team's efforts to prevent such occurrence. Each goal counts one point. The player scoring the goal is credited one point and the players assisting in the scoring of the goal are credited one point for each assist, but no more than two assists are credited with each goal. The last two assists prior to the actual scoring are the ones considered for credit.

Positions

One of the positions on six men ice hockey team are goal tender. The popular term for goal tender in the U.S.A. is goalic and goaler in Canada. In addition there are left defence, right defence, centre, left wing and right wing. The wings and the centre constitute the forward positions and they operate most frequently as an offensive unit or line.

Technique of Ice Hockey

Ice hockey is played in a series of short dashes such as:

- fast starting
- sudden stopping
- turning
- feinting
- dodging
- shifting
- weaoing
- hurding.

All these are the part of the player routine. For fast starting and break away purposes, the short, choppy stride is used to propel a player rapidly away from opponents, the player lengthens out his stride to get maximum benefit speed of every stride. The lengthening outstride is more of a high-striding movement that gives the player smooth, rythemic, powerful speed. The skating stride is confine to as narrow as a path of ice as possible. The professional player rushes a puck in a path as narrow as street feet.

Stick Handling

After you have learned the art of good hockey skating technique, you must learn the art of puck control. This includes the almost distinctive reaction of taking a quick, wide, lateral dribble with the puck as the player nears an opponent. It is known as the protective dribble, whereby the puck current keeps his body between the puck and the opponents, so that the opponent can not poke check the pack from the stick to blade. The protective dribble is very effective when it is made with a quick wide movement—the technique for deception and the width of safety.

Many mediocre skaters have held position on good teams through their clever stick handling and scoring ability. Years of constant practice are necessary to crown the efforts of the expert stick handler. Professional players stick-handle the rubber puck in a manner that is uncanny pushing, dribbling, and flipping the smaller rubber disk about the ice between a maze of sticks and skates with a speed and accuracy too bewildering for the human eye to follow. Methods of rushing or carrying a puck along the ice vary. Some push the disk ahead at stick's length when the play is open; others play the puck from side to side as they approach dangerously close to an opponent. Some flip the rubber against the side boards, depending upon the rebound for recovery of the desire behind the opponent, while other attempt to poke the back between the opponents' feet and skate around the man to regain possession of the disk while the opponents are off balance.

The Art of Checking

Stick checking calls for quick thinking and clever action. The poke, sweep and hook checks are effective means of taking the pack away and stopping opposing forwards in their rush towards the goal. A body check is an effective means of body blocking which, in a sense dicorments the puck and thereby intercepts his dash to the goal. A legal body check is one with hip or upper body from the front or straight from the side and limited to two slips, and only the puck carrier can be body checked.

Playing the Game

While skating and stick handling perfected to a point where they are combined into one mechanical operation, the player can direct his whole attention to playing the game. A good hockey player never look at his feet, stick or puck during the progress of the play. His eyes are focused on his opponents at all times in order to size up the confronting situation and react intelligently. Once he comes into possession of the puck he has the three forwards, two defence men and goal tender to beat before he can register a sure by shooting the desk into the goal net guarded by the opposing team.

Left wing centre and right wing (forward line) practice

passing the buck from one of the other across the ice, while
skating at top of speed, to perfect their combination play to
a point that enables them to beat the opposing forwards,
swoop past the opposing defense, and set up a man in the
best scoring position for a shot at the net. Left and right wing
players play their position in their respective lanes and leave
the centre lane mid-ice section to the centre player. Member
of the forward line try to score goals when the opportunity is
presented and never at the cost of allowing the opposing
forwards to breakaway for a two or three man combination
attack on the home team's net. The good defense player holds,
at all times, a position between his goal tender and opposing
forwards who attempt to carry the puck close enough to the
net for a shot that may mean a score.

A goalkeeper has 5 or 6 feet of open net to protect and
study the shots from all angles and position on the ice. He
must cover as much of his net as possible with his body and
shoft his position between the posts continuously in such a
manner that he will cut down the shooting angle and thereby
eliminate as such vulnerable opposing behind him as possible.
The four most vulnerable sports for scoring are of two upper
corners and the two lower corners of net. Only the most
skilful shooters can hit these four vulnerable sports and only
the most skilful of goalies can block these sports.

The ice hockey is very popular in U.S.A., Czechoslovakia,
Great Britain, Soviet Union and Sweden.

22

Ice Skating

Ice skating is a very popular winter support in America, Canada, Japan and some Central European countries. Every year thousands of skaters are drawn to ice skating in these countries and a much larger number of eager spectators enjoy this interesting but exciting sport. This popular sport is being introduced in other western countries and more and more people are taking to ice skating every year. Ice skating is now considered an important winter sport and has universally been declared to be an Olympic event.

The Ice Rink

This game is played on a surface called rink which should measure as nearly as possible; 20 ft. in length and 85 ft. in width. The rink side boards and end boards should be at least 3 ft. 4 in. high and no higher than 4 ft. The goal case stands out at each end of the rink, at least 10 ft. and not more than 15 ft. from the end boards and equidistance from the side boards. It should be fixed firmly to the ice. The goal is 4 ft. in height with an opening of six feet facing the centre of the playing area. An area 8 ft. wide and 4 ft. deep in front of the goal is called the crease. In this area the goalee has certain privileges and other players do not. The three zones are marked on the playing surface by lines drawn across the ice, 60 ft. from the goal line. The goal lines, blue lines and the centre line all continue vertically up the side boards.

Sticks

Except for the goalee each player is provided a stick with which he plays the game. Each stick terminates in a blade approximately 45° from the shaft. The degree of the stick blade angle to the shaft varies with the lie stide lies range from 3 to 10 and the players preference for lie depends on the position on which they like to "carry the back" infront of them. A player who likes to carry the back in close to which skates prefers a high lie of 7, 8 or 9. A player who likes to carry the back way out in front of his stakes prefers a low lie of 3 to 4. The average or normal lie used by most players is 5 or 6.

Sticks are lefts, rights and neutrals according to the side the player shoots them. The neutral is preferred by shooters who get too much 'rise' in their shot. The sticks are of standard measurements and must be made of wood.

The shaft not more than 52 in. long (55 in. NHL) are 1½ in. wide by ¾ in. thick but the blade, up to 14¾ in. long (12½ NHL), increases in width of 2½ in. and must not exceed 3½ in., except at the heel, where it must not exceed 4½ in. The widened position of the goalees extending up the shaft from the blade must not exceed more than 24 in. from the heel and must not exceed 3½ in. in width.

The Game

The game starts with a face off, the referees dropping the puck between the opposing centres, who face each other in the exact nature of the rink. Each of the centres seeks to gain possession of the puck, and one who does contrive to advance it, either by himself or by passing to team mate, to the region of the opposing team's goal.

Icing the puck, that is passing the puck from the defence zone beyond the opponent's goal line, results in a special face off at the end zone spot of the offending team. The passing between members of same team may be intercepted at any time by the opponent.

The face off is held to start play wherever it is stopped for any reason, such as when an off side is called, a puck is shot of the rink, an intraction of a rule is comitted by both sides, or a puck is held against the boards otherwise can not be played by either team. The three periods of 20 minutes each have 10 minute intermission between them. In case of a tie at the end of that time rules decree that at the end of the third period there shall be a 5 minute intermission, after which ends shall be changed and a 'sudden death' 10 minute over- time period played. In this sudden-death period the team that scores first wing and the game is ended. If no score is made in overtime period, the game is ended and result is a draw.

The Shimla Ice Skating Club:

The Shimla Ice Skating Club is perhaps the only ice skating rink in the East. It was founded by a couple of senior British Army officers, who were attached to the General Headquarters of the British Indian Army in Shimla. These two British officers had witnessed ice skating competitions in some Central European countries and had learnt the exciting sport during their posting there.

On their transfer to India and posting with the General Headquarters at Shimla the two adventurous officers found a spot for the skating rink in the heart of Shimla town, which is perhaps the coldest spot in the town and is never touched by sunshine, not even in hot summer. Even in hot summer one shivers there after the sunset. During the summer this spot was used as tennis courts by some British officers and is popularly known as the Blessington Courts.

In 1921 Mr. Blessington of the Blessington Hotel, who had earlier laid the tennis courts, happened to notice that water freezes on the cold spot fairly regularly. Thereafter, he carried out a few simple experiments and decided that he could build an open air skating rink. Initially the rink was meant for Mr. Blessington and his close friends. The rink rapidly gained popularity and only Westerners were members of the rink in those early days. Mr. Blessington was joined by the two British Army officers and the Shimla skating rink became the first and the only skating rink in the whole of south-east Asia.

Towards the beginning of December when the temperature in Shimla touches freezing point, these two British officers got the Blessington tennis courts area filled with water and with the help of some chemicals, the entire water forze during the night and was turned into a thick and smooth sheet of ice in the morning. The place covers an area of four tennis courts.

They tried their hand on the frozen ice with their skating boots on and thus laid the foundation of ice skating in the East. Since then it has become a popular winter sport in Shimla and in the country and has drawn thousands of skating enthusiasts from Canada, Germany, America, England and some South-East Asian countries besides various parts of India. Various British Viceroys, Governors, Ministers, Army Generals and other dignitaries enjoyed ice skating in Shimla. The club is run and managed by an elected body and provides the cheapest ice skating in the world. The skating books are locally available on daily or seasonal bases. Every day ice skating is held for three hours in the morning and three hours in the evening.

Of late various hill stations including Darjeeling and Kashmir are putting up ice skating rinks to attract tourists during the winter months as well. Even if ice skating rinks are set up in various parts of the country. Shimla will always attract more people. Ice skating has come to stay in Shimla, and it has a very bright future provided the Club is run on scientific and modern lines and the Himachal Pradesh government contributes its bit to make it a real success.

Visiting tourists contribute quite a bit to the economy of Himachal Pradesh particularly after the growth of militancy in Jammu and Kashmir, therefore, it will be in its own interests if the State government helps the Club to attract large number of tourists even in winter.

Though the Shimla Ice Skating Club is affiliated to the Portland Ice Skating Club of America, the Winter Games Federation of India and the International Ice Hockey

Federation of Australia, the Club does not have any coaches to train those having the potential to represent the country in winter sports events abroad.

Ice skating is a means of self-propelled locomotion over ice on steel blades fastened to the bottom of the shoes. The word skates is at least as old as 1573. The word skates is derived from the Dutch word Schaats. Early Dutch prints show the metal skates as having an extremely wide travelling surface. Until the middle of the 19th century the metal portion of the skate was fastened to a wooden base on foot plate and the whole of the skate was fastened to the foot with the leather thongs or straps. There were many development of the balde of the skate specially during the period 1830-80. An average figure, skating blade is 5/32 in. wide and is shaped with a curvature approximately that of a circle having a six foot radius. The blade is hollow ground when sharpened, emphasising the two edges of each skate. The hockey skate is also given a hollow brinding which allows perch are in the ice. The speed skate uses a thinner blade and it is sharpened with a flat surface and every long radius affording the a races a longer stroke. The popular length of the outdoor racing skate is 16-17 in. with the skate caps which hold the blade to the foot piece set low to the ice. For indoor racing the cups are heightened, the blade shortened to about 15 in. and the skates set for over to the left of the shoes to allow for the sharper turns.

Ice Skating Rinks

The ice skating used to be a seasonal sports. However, the invention of mechanical refregeration and the development of refregerated ice rinks started the transformation of ice skating from a seasonal past time to a major sport. It also launched the eminently practical skate on its way to the atrical history. The ice arenas, many with large seating capacities, gave impetus to skating as recreation and participation sports. It also was a major factor in establishing ice-show productions as leaders in spectator entertainment.

Ice Shows

The professional skating spectacles, and outgrowth of the amateur ice cannivals, combined the colourful movement of huge cates of skaters with all the arts of the theatre—brilliant lighting, gorgious costumes, special music and direction. By the half of twentieth century these were established as among the most popular form of entertainment. International shows were arranged—special among them are Ice Follies, Ice Capades, Holiday on Ice Shows.

Figure Skating

Among the most scientific of all sports is the figure skating. It is also the most artistic division of skating. It is most difficult exercise, requiring skill in plan skating, both forward and backward, a high degree of body control and assiduous practice. Modern figure skating was influenced to a profound degree by the revolutionary style of the American, Jackson Hane's (1840-76). Hanes is known as the father of figure skating. He gave skating a freedom of movement which it had not formerly possessed. The figure skating is divided into various divisions—school figures, free skating, dancing, pairs and fours. In competition, the event for individual consists of two sections, the prescribed school of figures and free skating, or optional routine, for specified number of minutes.

School Figures

The elements of school figures are simple motion, which are done in the direction of motion, and the so called forced turns, which are against the direction of motion. There are four direction in which the skate may go, outside edge, both forward and backward. Skated first on the right and then on the left skate to form full circles, those simple curves became the fundamental figures light. Combination of these circles became the change of edge. Following difficulties are threes, double threes, loops, bracket, counter and rockers. Advanced figures are the so called one foot figures in which the full figure eight form is done on the same skate instead of making a transistional change of feet at the point of start, as is done in elementary figure eights. There are many possible combination. Definite rules have been set down concerning the correct tracing of school figure on the ice. There are also definite rules for the body position of the skater while performing the figures.

Free Skating

It is a free adaptation of the various parts of the circles and the turns which make up school figures. It is skated to music. The design of the free skating programme must be varied one and should include spirals, dance steps, connecting mores, jumps, and spins. Jumps are an important element in a programme the salchow, the Paulson, the Boeckl, the Pat Low, the Luta, three jumps, the loop, the counter, the flip.

Dancing

Ice dancing has been known for many years. After 1930, it became the most popular brach of sport. Unlike baloon dancing, in which steps may be improvised, ice dancing is skated in set pattern and with set steps which never vary. The steps are, as in free skating based on parts of circles. The free turn is mostly used with an occasional bracket, rocker or counter.

Competitions

When each skater has completed a particular figure, it is given a mark by each judge independently. Judges represent their numerical opinion as to its value. The correctness of the shape of the figure, the turn, tripple repetition, the largeness of the figure and the form in which the figure is skated are the factors upon which judgement is made.

Figure-skating, speed skating or ice hockey are available at the Shimla Ice Rink. The ice-skating months extend from December to February.

Speed Skating

Speed skating was tremendously popular in northern section of the U.S.A. and Canada. In this adventure sport, the blade, when planted on the ice with weight upon it, describes a nearly straightline.

The Stroke

When stroking, the last few fact only curve slightly outward as the skate leaves the ice. The length of the stroke has tended to diminish since the days of the 12-18 yd. strike attributed to the old champion William Smart on the fen 'runners'. The modern racing stroke rarely exceed 10 yards and is usually 6 or 7.

Courses

The international system of ice racing involves a course with straight sides and curved ends of such as redium that no slackening of speed is necessary. The competition race two at a time on a double track, and the time test is used. Each skater must keep his own course, to prevent either from using the other pacemaker or wind shield. The advantage of linear curve on a continental course is given alternatively and a space left open between the tracks at one point from the skater to cross. The track measures 400 m. The outdoor track is 6 laps of the mile.

Form

Compititive speed skating requires skill, strength, muscular coordination and great stamina. The body should be poised so that the centre of balance is in the hips. At racing space the body should follow an imaginary straight line. The stroke should be kept 'straight as possible for sawaging widely from side to side results in loss of momentum. To obtain the most effective strokes with minimum efforts, the skater must learn forward from the waist and lend the knees. The force of the leg drive is directed forward, not upward, the push should be made forward the side, not balanced, and the push is from the centre of the blade, not from the toe.

Skate Sailing

Skate sailing is the sport of moving over the ice on skates propelled by the wind. Learning how to skate sail on the ice before and against the wind requires only a basic proficiency in skating, for the sail gives added stability and bears much of the sailor's weight. Speed up to 55 m.p.h. has been reported.

The modern skate sail, generally rectangular or triangular in shape, has approximately 50-60 sq.ft. of area. The Skate Sailing Association of U.S.A. recommended that the sail be perfectly flat and stretched to drumhead tightness. The spares and rigging should be moderatily light, yet strong and simple as possible so that they can be handled easily in cold, windy weather. In sailing the skate sail is always carried on the shoulders between the sailor and the wind. The sail material could be a good grade of sheeting or unbleached muslin but for best result it should be a non-porous, lightweight sail cloth, balloon silk or nylon. Long tabular racing skates 16 to 18 in. in length are used.

The skate sailing was originated in the Scandinavian countries and was practised in some form or another almost immediately after the invention of skate. One of the first skate sailing organisation was the 'Ice Skating Sailing Club' formed in Stockhome in 1901. The sport was taken up by members of the London skating club in England in the 1890s and was introduced to North America in the early 1900s. The Skating Sailing Association of America governing today over the sports in U.S.A. was organised in 1922.

23

Snow Skiing

Nothing could be more exiciting and thrilling to you than skiing on the lovely snowy slopes. As a skier you will feel on top of the world. It is a sport of moving over a snow, wearing a pair of long flat runners called skis attached to the shoes or bóuts. This sports you may practise for recreational, competitive or utilitarian purposes. On the level or on slight grades, you as a skier, should use a gliding gait, down hill ice slides effortlessly over the snow, turning to avoid obstacles, in plaken speed, or to change directing special slips are used in climbing steeper slopes. The most exciting part of skiing in the skii jumping. It is usually performed in artificial inclines of varying size which are specially designated for the sports.

Initially, the skis were used for utilitarian purposes, for transportation, hunting and in warfare. Now, we find that recreational skiing is a natural outgrowth of such uses. In most of the skiing resorts, this sport developed chiefly as a downhill skiing, At first only the mountain railways and aerial cable cars, or funiculars were available for the tophill transportation of skiers. However, in early 1930's many new devices were designed and built for the purpose such as chairlifts, bar lifts (T-bar, tramway, gondola lifts, rope tows etc). This greatly promoted the popularity of skiing. The skiing was possible for four or five time in a day, as skiers had climb uphill. They made the sports more enjoyable for all participants.

In most of the Scandinavian countries and Eastern Europe touring and cross country skiing developed as a popular sports. Competition in skiing increased and we find skiing of the various types:

(i) Nordic or classic events—cross country racing and jumping.
(ii) Down hill events—down hill or straight racing.
(iii) (a) Slalom (bigzag down hill racing).
  (b) Giant slalom.

As alpine skiing developed, the nordic manner of skiing was eventually changed to allow the skier to cope with the long, steep runs in the high mountains, and the obstruction filled glaciers and forested hillsides. Outgrowth of these changes were the ski school where the new method was taught. The downhill could slalom competitors tested the relevant skills.

To Hannes Schneider of Austria is attributed the credit for laying the foundation both of the modern ski technique and the throughly systematised ski school. He taught in a methodological profession from snow plow, through snow plow turn, stem turn and stem christianea to parrel swing initiated with only a slight, quick stem. The important factors leading to these development were the introduction of the steed edge in 1930s and the increase in ski left in the 1940s. The former formed the base for parrel, narrow tracked and precise running and turning, the latter-which greatly increased the number of skiers and multiplied the number of runs each one could make downhill, with the consequence that nearly all up to the year 1850 only a toe strap was used as a binding. The skiers used a long pole for braking when skiing downhill. Skiing as a competitive sport began about 1850. Competitive skiing started in California in the 1880's. The skiies had only toe strap bindings. It was impossible for them to make turns. They ran only straight down hill courses. Sondre Nordheim used willow bindings around the heels to fasten the bottle to the skis, these making turns and jumps possible. Nordheim constructed the Telemark skies with incurved slides, which formed the pattern for all modern skiers. With such skies he was the first to evolve the christianea and Telmark turns and was the inventor of slalom.

It was the Norwegians who brought skiing to most countries at the end of 19th century. With the rebirth of slalom in the early 1920, pioneered by Sir Arnold Lunn, who invented Slalom gates in 1922, skiing became increasingly popular and as the sport spread, both proficiency and equipment developed rapidly.

Norwegians have been skiing since the Stone Ages. But it was only in the last century that Sondre Nordheim from Morgedal west of Oslo showed that skis could also be fun. Modern ski sports have spread from Norway to the rest of the world. Winter sports are part of the Norwegian cultural heritage. In the early 1970s, the national authorities extended the concept of culture to include sport. Winter sports are extremely popular among Norwegians, particularly in those parts of the country where snow and ice dominate the winter months. Originally a means of getting about by hunters and soldiers, skis are used by Norwegians today for both recreation and competition.

Famed Norwegian skiers, such as Polar explorers Fridtjof Nansen and Roald Amundsen, have helped to popularise the sport in many countries. The father of modern skiing as a winter sport is generally considered to be Sondre Nordheim (1825-97), who hailed from the little community of Morgedal in Telemark country west of Oslo.

Nordheim revolutionised the ancient art of skiing in several ways. He devised the first binding that attached the foot firmly to the ski. And he narrowed each ski towards the middle. Combined with the spring in the skis and the improved bindings, this made turning easier.

With these enhancements, a new skiing technique developed naturally—in soft snow, Nordheim kept one ski in advance of the other and flexed his knees to absorb impacts with unexpected obstacles.

He turned by twisting his forward foot, creating what

was later called the Telemark turn. On firm or trodden snow, he brought his skis parallel when turning—a method known today as the christie.

Skis have been employed for several thousand years in the far north, and their tracks—left by both soldiers and civilians—can be discerned through the Viking and Middle Ages.

The development of skiing remained in the hands of the military until the mid-19th century, when Nordheim converted it from transport to sport—a sport since enjoyed by virtually all Norwegians.

A varied landscape of mountains and valleys helped to nurture skiing skills among Telemark's people, who learnt to make skis that suited the terrain. Smallholder Nordheim showed how to apply these skills for pleasure, and created his own ski designs in line with old local traditions.

Skiers from Morgedal and its vicinity won all the prizes at the first skiing contests staged in Oslo—then known as Christiania—during the 1860s. They also won the first race held at Holmenkollen outside the capital, today a famed venue for skiing competitions.

"Telemark is the true home of the skier", wrote renowned Norwegian polar explorer and statesman Fridtjof Nansen in 1886, "Its people are indisputably the finest skiers in our country and therefore—I can probably safely say without exaggeration—in the world; they have taught the urban lads a completely new style of skiing and thereby raised this sport to the stature it has attained in recent years". A statue of Nordheim stands today in Morgedal.

The Norwegian Ski Adventure centre has opened in Morgedal alongside an existing skiing museum. This NOK 20 million facility offers visitors a half-hour tour through the history of skiing in Morgedal and Norway, employing video, film and other media. Built in timber, stone and glass, the centre is an architectonic attraction in itself.

Precautions, Safety and Courtesy

The number of skiers is increasing day by day all over the

world. It requires a code of safety and courtesy for the problems both of the skiers and person in the ski resorts. At present the most experienced skiers follow certain rules of the road. The main objective of ski in control is that sking is in such a way that the skier at all time can turn or stop. Some of the rule which you as skier must follow are:

1. All skiers approaching each other on opposite traverse must pass to the right.
2. As an overtaking skier, you should warn the skier, ahead with the cry 'on your right' or 'on your left'. The call 'TRACK!' signifies a warning that a fast skier is skiing down a trail or course, or a loose ski or other object is sliding down hill.
3. As an uphill skier, you would be responsible for avoiding a skier below yourself.
4. A skier entering a trail yields right of way to skiers already on the trail.
5. A moving skier avoids a standing skier, and passes at an ample distance.
6. A skier does not stop at any stop that will obstruct a trail, or impede the passage of following skiers, or where he is not fairly visible from a safe distance above. If you are fallen in such a spot, move to a safer location as soon as possible.

Ski patrols composed of volunteers or professionals who are specially trained for first aid and rescue work. These should be available at all times in most ski areas to assist skiers who are lost, ill or injured or otherwise are in need of help.

Organisation of the Sport

The International Ski Federation (Federation Internationale de Ski, or F.I.S.) was formed, and the first winter Olympic games was held in Chamonix in 1924. This included the Nordic ski events only. In 1926, in Germany at Garmisch—

Partenkirchen, the Alpine event was also included for the first time.

The world's first ski club was the Trysol in Norway. It was formed in 1861. The first in U.S.A. was organised in U.S.A. at Berlin NH, in 1872. The ski club of Great Britain was founded in 1903 as a national administration body. It was superseded by the National Ski Federation of Great Britain (1964). The first intelligiate ski meet, between McGill Dartmouth and Montreal, was held in 1914 in Qubec at Shawbridge.

The basic skiing organisation are the local clubs of individuals. The most clubs are members of regional associations (divisions), which are composed of ski foundation associations. It the U.S.A., the National Association of America was founded in 1904 at Ishpenuing, mich. At the international level we have F.I.S. which sets the rules for and sanction international competitions.

The Ski Equipment

The essential equipment you require for skiing is as follows:

1. *The Ski*

There are three type of skis:

    (i) Down hill
    (ii) Jumping
    (iii) Cross country.

All these have certain common characteristics. They are pointed, turned up and usually slightly wider at the front (the tips or shovel) and are squared at the rear (or heel). They are thickest in the mid section under the foot, thinest just before the ends, and are built with a slight arch or camber. This helps to distribute the skier's weight evenly among the length and thus impress a maximum running surface, with maximum edge-length, on the snow. These skis have been refined over the years in their shape and camber and in precision of stiffness.

Skis may vary in length. The down hill skies for the average man being about 7 ft. (213 cm.) long. Much shorter skis, slower but maneuverable have enjoyed some vogue. They were formerly fashioned from one piece of wood, usually hickony. From 1930's laminated construction were also used. After 1950's plastic running surfaces were introduced to increase speed and durability. Later on, skis of metal, usually with a wood or plastic core, became increasingly popular.

The downhill ski, which is about 3 in. (7.6 cm.) in width typically has a shallow grove running longitudinally along the centre of the bottom (a sole). This imports directorial stability. In addition, you will find skis have sharp edges of steel along the under surface, in order to bite into hard snow or ice.

The jumping skis are longer about 8 ft. (244 cm.), wider, thicker, and heavier and ordinarily have three groves in the bottom. They have no steel edges. Cross country skis are narrower and lighter in weight than downhill skis. These are often laminated. They have one grove but no metal edges.

2. *Leather Boots*

For downhill skiing, you require close fitting, heavy, leather boots with flat and stiff soles in order to exercise precise control over the skis. These boots should be firmly attached to the skin by bindings. After safety or release bindings are used to free the skiers foot in case of falls. For purpose of jumping and cross country, a lighter and more flexible boot is used, with a binding which allows the heel to be raised.

3. *Light Pole or Stick*

For downhill skiing a light pole or stick, of metal or bamboo, about four feet long is required in each hand. For cross country skiing the size of pole varies in length. This will aid you in pushing yourself along on the level, and in climbing. You have to use them in maintaining balance when running down hill and to assist in turning. Each of these sticks have a wrist strap at the top and a ring, or wheel, near the bottom, which prevent the point from sinking to deeply into snow. There are various quality of waxes which could be used on the bottoms of skis to prevent snow from sticking. The quality of wax will depend upon the temperature and snow condition. Sometime plus are strapped to the bottom of the sticks to grip the snow.

It is a great winter sport, with season lasting from end of December to March. The snowy slopes of different gradients are a delight for a skier. These provide the most economical ski holiday World over and this is one reason the number of enthusiasts is compounding. Also *heli-skiing* in which you are lifted to the top of a slope by the chopper and you whiz down the slope, an ultimate in thrill and fun. All good resorts cater for heli-skiing.

The oldest skis were found in bogs in Sweden and Finland, which were of about 4,500 years old. A rock caving of two men on skis were found near the Arctic circle of two men skis from 2000 B.C. In 1200 king of Sverne of Norway sent out men on skis to reconnoitre before battle.

The Norwegian hunters and trappers and the Lapps had been using skiing for centuries in the mountains. In mountaining as a sport they have been used since the 1880s in Norway and since mid 1890, in the Alps. From the beginning of the 20th century, French, Australian, Italian and British Skiers also took part in skiing.

The Basics of Skiing

1. *Stemmed Turns*

These are based on planning one or both skis at an angle to the direction of the movement. The chief turning force is shifting of weight. The snow plow turn is made from a snow plow or double stemp (skis in a 'V' shape) position by shifting the weight to one ski and exerting outward turning pressure with that heel to make a stiered turns. The stern turn is made from the traversing position (with skis parallel) by turning (angling out) the upper ski and turning as in the snow of plow. The stem christiania is similar except for the manner of shifting the weight and mooing the body, while the christiania is a swing from a slight initial stern that continuously across the full time. The pure christiania is a series of sweeping swings back and forth across the full time.

2. Slide Splipping

The manoeuvre became necessary to avoid ruts and bumps as hard packed traits became common. It also indicate the parallel ski position and teaches edge control. These have become basis of modern instructions. The skis are skidded side ways by flattering the skis to disengage the edges and pushing the heels downhill and the skis out from under the body.

3. Traversing

This technique involves running down hill, diagonally across the fall line with the skis parallel and close together for greater control.

4. Straight Running

In the downhill position for running in the fall line the skis are flat, parallel, close together and equally weighted. The goal is graceful, relaxed position, slightly forward learning (vorlage), with smooth movements to adjust the skier's centre of gravity to changing condition of snow slope.

5. Short Swinging and Wedeln

These consists of consequitive short, parellel swings across the fall line, one after the another. In the short swing there is a alternating pole planting. In the Wedeln there is prectically no edging. The legs and hips are used a great deal in the sequence of swing and counter swing.

Ski Adventures

Cross country tour or nordic tours are for all levels of skiing ability, novice to expert. No precious experience is necessary, but most tours are best suited to people in good physical condition. Ski mountaineering tours travel high mountain routes and glacial terrain using special skis modified for alpine ascents and descents. These tours are for experienced downhill skiers.

Most people in India would think it crazy to suggest a holiday in near zero temperatures, your feet covered in snow and surrounded slope upon slope by icy mountainscape. But try to whizz down those slopes at over 60 m.p.h. with the magic of the wind rushing past and the sheer exhilaration of speed and momentum and you would be craving—craving for another skiing holiday.

In a country where mountains stretch across 2,500 miles from the icy wastes of Ladakh to the remote vastness of Arunachal Pradesh, the winter delights of the mountains are little known or exploited. Like well seasoned wines, they are savoured only by the connoisseur and the enthusiast. In summer thousands rush to the mountains seeking solace from the blistereing heat of the plains, when winter is really the season for the mountains: there are discounts for the taking, no jostling with 'madding crowds' and nature decks herself out in virginal colours, filling the gaps and smoothening the contours of the slopes with soft snow.

Icicles, snowflakes, sleighriding, snowmen and logfires are only a few of the winter delights. Far more exciting is the delirious happiness that grips every skier when he goes 'whoooosh' down a slope of soft powder snow, like one of heaven's ethereal creatures. As queues for the ski lifts in Europe grow longer and skiing holiday prices higher, it is more often the foreigner who indulges in our winter delights, searching for untouched snow and unexpected challenges. Not many people in India are aware that skiing facilities are available in this country—and that too at a choice of locations—and are also probably the cheapest in the world.

Skiing started as a sport in India as early as in 1927 when the Ski Club of India was established in the lush green valley of Gulmarg, 50 kms. from Srinagar in Kashmir. Soon after, Kufri, 12 kms. and Narkanda, 40 kms. away from Shimla in Himachal Pradesh, became popular ski resorts, much frequented during the hey days of the Raj. Skiing enthusiasts would wait for the snow to pile up to about three feet height and then set off for Kufri. A mule track led to the top of the slope and without the luxury of ski lifts they would carry their wooden skis and trudge the steep slope for the short though exciting descending flight. Today Kufri receives little or no snow. But when it does, most of Shimla turns out for the celebration.

However, Narkanda at an altitude of 9,000 ft. is more fortunate. Still blessed by the icy manna, Narkanda's nursery slopes, though neither as long, nor as gently undulating as Gulmarg's are adequate for students and greenhorns.

But besides these traditional ski resorts, several new locations have been identified as ideal slopes for skiing. The slopes around Manali in Himachal Pradesh as well as those at Patalsu, Kothi and Rohtang are rated, by international standards, to be superior to Gulmarg and among the finest for alpine skiing. Though not as well developed as Gulmarg, (which has benefited fron the Centre's special attention to Jammu and Kashmir), the natural slopes at Manali run a course of seven to nine kms at heights running from 8,500 ft. at Solang Nala to Patalsu and Rohtang at 13,000-15,000 ft. where one can ski above the tree line for almost 30 kms. in snow leopard territory. Manali also has the added advantage of being easily accessible by road, and of offering the longest skiing season—for six months, from January right upto June or even into July.

For skiing enthusiasts, nearer the eastern ranges of the Himalayas, there is Auli, India's newest ski resorts, 1984 is when it all began in the Chamoli district of Uttar Pradesh. The five Auli slopes ranging from the easy to the more challenging, enjoy a snow cover of between 3-5 m. However, Gulmarg remains by far the best equipped, promoted and frequented of all the ski resorts. Come winter and Kashmir readies itself for nature's munificence. The first snow falls by late November or early December coating Gulmarg in a blanket of white. A few more snowfalls and the valley is well iced over to receive the winter sports lovers who assemble along her slopes and dales, as much in awe of her transformed virginal beauty as the challenges she tosses out to them. At altitudes ranging from 8,700 ft. to 10,500 ft., Gulmarg's ski runs stretch from 2-10 kms. with an average gradient of 35°.

At all the locations there is the Indian Institute of Skiing and Mountaineering or its branches, which conducts short-certificate training courses from seven to 21 days, at rock-bottom prices, inclusive of boarding and lodging for anyone willing to learn. As an added incentive in Himachal Pradesh, for all those residing in the state, the skiing lessons are offered free of cost. A private ski school, opened in Manali. The initiation begins with rudimentary lessons on how to stand and manoeuvre on skis on a gradual slope. Within a week or ten days the trainees work their way up to the dexterity demanded on the more advanced slopes. No previous experience or athletic prowess is required of potential skiiers, though being in a relatively fit physical condition undoubtedly makes skiing less strenuous and more enjoyable. About a 20 minute spot of limbering up and knee-bending exercises for two to three weeks prior to a skiing holiday are sufficient preparation for the grand challenge.

Some of the latest imported ski equipment including sophisticated skis costing Rs. 6 lakhs a pair, safety binding ski boots, goggles and gloves are available at the institutes and also on hire from the various tourist offices on location. Private ski stores, some travel agents and ski tour operators also hire out whatever equipment may be necessary.

Skiing in Kashmir

Kashmir is the best known and most developed region for skiing in India. The valley's premier upland resort, Gulmarg is situated at 2,730 m. and is the country's largest and best equipped winter sport resort. There are good snow conditions from December to April and modern facilities such as T-bars, ski lifts, chair cars, and ropeways are inbuilt. Ski equipment is available for here and is of international quality. Instructors trained at European ski resorts are available to guide, if required. There is also the Indian Institute of Skiing and Mountaineering where 10 and 21 days courses are offered.

For those who enjoy Ski-Mountaineering a nordic skiing, there are other possibilities. A popular ski mountaineering route is to go from Gulmarg to Khilangmarg (3,045 m.), 5 km. away. This place afford some magnificient views of the valley and its surrounding ranges. From Khilanmarg it is another 8 km. to a lake.

For skating enthusiasts there is a skating rink and equipment is available for here. For the more enterprising, heli skiing is also possible with local authorities willing to encourage all form of winter sports activity.

Gulmarg is well provided with chair and ski-lifts, rope-tows and T-bars to propel you to the top of the slopes from where you come whizzing down. There are French ski lifts of 400 m. on three different slopes, a 500 m. chair-lift which gives a run of about 900 m. and a beginners T-bar of 200 m. on the lower slopes. Manali and Auli boast of only one ski lift each of 400 m., while Narkanda has a 200 m. lift, but there are plans to step up more facilities at these locations too. A new chair-lift is already under construction at Auli, while a 4 km. rope-way when ready will dispense with the arduous one hour trudge up from Joshimath to the top of the slopes.

Apart from downhill skiing, the veteran skiier can also enjoy cross-country runs along the gentle undulating slopes and limber up for the annual skiing championship, at which some of the best skiers from within the country and without, test their skills and endurance.

For the less adventurous, besides the occasional gambol in the snow, or the making of snowmen, there is the chance to go tobaggoning or sledging, which though not as enthralling as skiing, is proving to be a fun alternative. You climb to the top of the slope with your sledge, a flat wooden board without a navigator, and then sit astride it and come sailing down, gaining speed as the momentum builds up, shouting out to all (woe-betide them!) who may be in your way. Also gaining popularity in Gulmarg is the snow-scooter which unlike the bob sleigh or the tobaggon, can be manoeuvred with a steering wheel. Children, in particular, can be seen zooming down the slopes on these contraptions, when not staging snowball fights or swinging on the T-bars.

The highlight of the season, the annual skiing championship, held around mid-February at all the locations is an occasion to watch some superb skiing and join in the festivities at the end of the day. In fact, for some holidaymakers, the winter evenings are the best part of the vacation; sitting around a logfire or merry-making at a club or local bar can inspire an infections spirit of bonhomie.

Downhill skiing is the most popular winter sport in Europe and North America. Even small children can be expert skiers. With skiing in Gulmarg having been suspended the other places where it is possible to experience the sheer exuberance of skiing in India are Solang Nala, Kufri and Narkanda in Himachal Pradesh and Auli in Garhwal. Imported equipment is available on hire and courses of fifteen days duration are organised.

Real Skiing

Real skiing, say the connoisseurs, begins beyond the margins of the smooth-shaven pistes, where no caterpiller vehicle has passed to flatten out every natural asperity, where no signals stand to announce the next switchback, where no fanatics come plunging down in deadstraight swoops to catch the next cableway cabin back to the top. Real skiing begins in the deep snow where the big runs end.

Only those who have climbed steadily for hours step by deliberate step, far from the hectic atmosphere of downhill through-fares, occasionally struggling for breath on the step bits, enjoying a brief rest before the last spurt to the summit, can really be classed among mountain-lovers. Every skiing tour is an experience that lives on in memory. And it is not by any means only the glorious descents in clouds of powdery white or in soft spring snow that are remembered for years, it is no less the often laborious climbs, the tracks made in the virgin white expanses. It is on skiing excursions with skins on one's skis and a haversack on one's back that one really discovers the beauties of the mountain world. And discovers oneself too. One realises how small and helpless one is, and the next moment how resilient and tenacious one can be. During the ascent there is time to think, time to look around, to note the perfection of snow crystals, to marvel at mighty cornices and yard-long icicles, at deep cravasses and precipitous walls of ice.

The Thrill

And then the descent. The thrill of being the first to swing down over a field of fresh snow to leave the first tracks, and later to look back with pride at the harmonious pattern of the curves; the adventure of the cautious advance to test whether the top snow crust will bear or break—these things are real skiing! Here the skier is on intimate terms with nature. Here he finds complete relaxation, even if the ascent and sometimes the descent too, should be full of effort.

It must at once be added that any careless sallying-forth into the winter mountains, without experience and possibly without adequate equipment or knowledge of the terrain, is irresponsible and dangerous. It must never be forgotten that once you are off the beaten track there is nobody to look after you, and no officials to check that all is well. When you leave the run, you have only yourself to depend on, and in this sense you are taking a certain risk. A wise cross-country skier consequently never goes out into the wilds alone. An experienced mountaineer ought to be of the party, and when the tour is a difficult one it should be escorted by a mountain guide or a ski instructor.

The dangers that may be encountered on skiing tours are either subjective or objective. The subjective ones are due to inadequate knowledge or skill, insufficient preparation and training. The objective ones are such things as weather, avalanches, equipment. Careful reading of guides and maps before a tour is undertaken is just as important as suitable clothing and correct packing of one's rucksack. The rule of thumb for clothing is a simple one: always go prepared for the worst eventualities. Even if the weather is beautiful when you set out, it may change very quickly in the mountains, sometimes within a quarter of an hour, and warm sunshine is followed by mist, cold and possibly even a blizzard. Careful attention must therefore always be paid to weather developments. To turn back before reaching the summit is not the mark of a coward; but not to turn back may be the mark of a fool, and in the worst of cases can even cost lives.

The Danger

It would also be foolish to go on a skiing tour without previous training and without the necessary fitness. The height alone takes its toll, often seconded by cold; the ascent saps energy, and the downhill run itself is often very different from a long glissade on a prepared piste. A touring skier must be in good shape to make up for the increased danger of accidents.

And very special caution is called for when avalanches threaten. There is no absolute safety measure against avalanches, but there are rules of procedure and behaviour that must be observed without fail if one is not to risk one's life and the lives of others. That is why those who wish to partake of the joys of skiing in the untrodden places should first make sure that they have all the information they may need.

Skiing in Garhwal Hills (Uttaranchal)

Up in the Garhwal Himalayas, Auli is now being developed as a skiing resort. A rope way is under construction to take visitor from the town at 6,000 ft. to the slopes of Auli and Gorsain near the Kauri Pass at 12,000 ft. The panorama of Himalayan snow peaks from Kauri is perhaps the most spellbinding in the world.

The bonus for winter visitors in this region is the weather. For three months from January through March of the skiing season there are no clouds as there are at most times of the year. The clear blue sky and the surrounding snow giants make this the ultimate ski resort in the making.

All to this the fact that Auli and Gorsain are actively looking down the legendry Rishi George which holds the key to entering the mysterious Nanda Devi sanctuary and have the best view of the great goddess as she soars clearly out of the encircling ring of ice. Here is skiing to a background of the most sublime mountain music.

The hills of U.P. offer immense opportunities for adventure sports. The region abounds with a splendid combination of flora and fauna, flowing rivers and snow-capped mountains which are magnificent enough to infuse the spirit of adventure in all. The exhilarating sport of skiing is a big draw. A serious protagonist or a one time prospector of thrills, all find Garhwal a perfect spot for this sport. Thrilling water sports beckon enthusiasts to try out their skills on the gushing white waters.

The panoramic Garhwal and Kumaon hills of Uttaranchal are a combination of mountain peaks and valleys. The large slopes when covered with seasonal snow become ideal for skiing in the winter months.

The thrill of skiing over snow covered terrains remains unparalled. As the elements are defeated and unimaginable distances traversed, exhilaration swells up. In skiing the use of only the simplest forms of implements serve to add to the adventure. Skies consists of long, narrow and flexible runners with curverd fronts ends turned up and pointed. To aid the process of acceleration and balancing, a pair of poles with leather strips on the top and sharp metal tips at the bottom are used to prevent the skier from sinking. With these elementary implements, the skier triumphs over steep gradients and often charts new paths.

Captivating Auli-Garhwal

Auli, 16 kms. from Joshimath is an ideal winter resort run by Garhwal Mandal Vikas Nigam (G.M.V.N.), a U.P. Government Undertaking. The natural advantages of Auli's slopes, couples with state-of-the-art facilities provided by G.M.V.N. have made it comparable to the best in the world.

The snow capped slopes of Auli are flanked by stately coniferous and ock forests which cut wind velocity to the minimum. Auli offers a 180° panoramic view of Himalayan peaks like the Nanda Devi (7,817 mts.), Kamet (7,756 mts.), Mana Parvat (7,273 mts.) and Dunagiri (7,066 mts.), seemingly only a snowballs throw away.

Auli offers perfect skiing conditions. Seasonal skiers have a clean stretch of 10-20 kms. of absolutely virgin slopes to sport on. These slopes provide excellent opportunities for crosscountry, slalom and downhill skiing events.

A 3 kms. long slope ranging from a height of 2,519 mts. to 3,049 mts. is a major attraction.

G.M.V.N. has snow beaters which beat the snow to keep the slopes fit for skiing at all times. A 500 mts. long skilift carries skiers back to the slope top, thus saving them the trouble and time to bridge up wearing long skis.

Apart from skiing festivals, official National Championships are also been held here.

An Excitement of Snow Adventure of Auli (Garhwal)

Situated in Garhwal Himalayas, Auli is a beautiful skiing resort. It over looks the towering Himalayan peaks of famous Nanda Devi, Mana Pravat, Kamet etc. Outlined by wild lush green forest the area is being developed as a major skiing resort.

Auli is 16 km. from Joshimath by road and only 3.8 km. by the ropeway still under construction. State Transport buses ply regularly from Joshimath to Rishikesh (253 km.), Hardwar (277 km.), Dehradun (298 km.) and Delhi (500 km.). Hardwar is also connected by rail with different parts of the country.

The slopes at Auli are of an international standard. Over two and a half kilometers long and with a drop of 500 m. at the peak of winter, they are well-guarded from high-speed winds by the deodars that surround the slopes. A thick forest on all sides and over the ridge and occasional sightings of Black Bear make the environment even more exciting. We were fortunate enough to see a black bear from a distance of half a kilometre on the ski-slope on our very first day.

The ideal time for a visit is during the months of January to March during which time the Nigam conducts 7 and 15-day ski-courses for both beginners and advanced learners. Qualified instructors, from the Indian Institute of Skiing and Mountaineering impart proper training to the participants. Joshimath, which is the base can be reached by State Transport buses which ply from Rishikesh every morning. The G.M.V.N. also has its buses going up. Vehicles can go up most of the way to Auli and only the last three kilometers have to be trekked. Hospital facilities are available. All equipment for skiing is provided by the G.M.V.N. as is the bedding and lodging. But it is advisable to carry along with you a sleeping bag and a ruck sack. Mountain or trekking boots are also required. Bookings need to be made well in advance. For these, write to: Garhwal Mandal Vikas Nigam Ltd., 74/1, Rajpur Road, Dehradun, U.P. You may also write to: The Public Relations Officer, Garhwal Mandal Vikas Nigam Ltd., c/o U.P. Tourism Office, 36, Janpath, New Delhi.

Although skiing is possible only in the winter months, Auli makes for a wonderful destination at any time of the year. In summer, the snow melts away and rolling grasslands and alpine meadows and pastures are left behind. These make for ideal camping grounds. The flights of snow pigeons and the exciting call of the monal pheasant, the clouds of accentors and the parties of buntings and chats will not fail to please.

The thrushes, jays, magpies, bulbuls, ravens, wood-peckers, tits, babblers and fly-catchers will with patient bird watching become conspicuous.

The flights of red-billed choughs that take to the skies as the day warms-up will circle the high peaks and call resonatingly across the valleys in pleasant tinkling notes. The fields of primulas, gentians, marsh marigolds and buttercups will leave the jaded city-dweller enchanted and with an awe for the beauty and closeness of Garhwal's Himalayas, as seen from Auli, a true window on Garhwal!

With the descending treat of summer funs, the Land of Garhwal revitalizes itself to unfurl yet another of it's seasonal chams—to delve you into the delights of winter joys.

Amidst a blend of Coniferous and Oak Forests, at 9,000 ft., Auli slopes offer thrilling excitements of breathtaking experiences to ski enthusiasts. Skiing the slopes, or just watching the flowing movements of skiers, fills you with a sense of bewilderment. And, Auli, just 16 kms. motorable from Joshimath, is accessible by buses plying to Joshimath from Rishikesh, Haridwar, Dehradun and Delhi and through rail and air connection to Haridwar and Dehradun respectively.

Added to the delights of Auli fiesta, soak yourself in the gleaming views of Nanda Devi, Kamet, Mana Parvat, Hathi & Ghori Parvat and Dunagiri. Or stroll in the city of Joshimath where ancient temples beckon you to bask in the aura of religious sanctity. En-route from Rishikesh to Auli visit the Panch Prayags', the five holy confluences on the course of river Alaknanda viz., Devaprayag, Rudraprayag, Karan- prayag, Nandaprayag and Vishnuprayag.

Garhwal Mandal Vikas Nigam offer, as in every season, 7-15 days ski courses at Auli for those who yearn to pick up the skis. Boarding and lodging arrangements are provided for at nominal additional cost. Course fee includes modern ski equipment in total.

Auli—a skier's ideal—a snow-lover's romance—and a mountain-lover's paradise. Yes, that's how I would describe Auli. Away from the humdrum, tensions and monotony of city-life, it is in the lap of the Garhwal Himalayas, in the midst of nature's bounteous beauty in all its snowy splendour.

The breathtakingly beautiful view of the Himalayas as the bus wound its way along the tortuous paths of the mountains, the sound of the gurgling waters and the cool balmy air accentuated by periods of sunshine, was an invigorating and exhilarating experience. The small road side village dhabas, so typical of the Indian mountains, the hubbub of the slow village life and the cheery faces of rosy-cheeked cherubs and women, all add to the scenic beauty of the place.

You trudge-up past rustic houses, green barley fields and bubbling streams for a long while. Shortly go out of the Joshimath village area and entered thick spruce-and-pine forest. As crossed a grassy forest clearing, the clear notes of a flute rent the air. And as you go higher, peaks of enormous dimensions started emerging from behind the bare hills that surround the mountain town of Joshimath. It was surprising—one would never have suspected those tall dark hills of hiding such a breathtaking sweep of Garhwal's Himalaya.

You reach Joshimath a good 253 kms. and a 12-hour drive from Rishikesh. The Garhwal Mandal Vikas Nigam resthouse proved to be a haven. You had made our reservations well in advance. The mercury dipped as low as 10°C or perhaps even more. But the "angithi" is a big boon on the cold night.

You have to trek up and that there were no jeeps that would take up to Auli, you would go up the steep, slippery, snowy slopes in your casual action shoes instead of the hunter or the snowboots.

Anyway, you hire the locally available "sherpas" and start the seemingly endless ascent. Slipping, falling and panting like dogs you reach Auli.

From this point, you could see the small cement cottages and the fibrehut dormitories at Auli—and though they didn't seem too far, they are a good half kilometre or more away. But here the steep climb ends and though you are nearing the top, the snow-covered land lay outstretched before you rising in slow gradation. You stand and breath in the cool mountain air.

On the first day you had bussed-it for a continuous eighteen hours, all the way from Delhi to the back-of-beyond town of Joshimath via Rishikesh. The next day, trekked nine kilometres to the snowed-over alpine pasturelands of Auli where we were to do a seven-day course in snow-skiing organised by the Garhwal Mandal Vikas Nigam (G.M.V.N.).

Further ambling brought us into forests of flowering rhododendrons and then the path opened-out into expansive rock-and-snow covered slopes. Perched higher on that hill lay the fibre huts constructed by the G.M.V.N. for housing participants of the seven and fifteen-day skiing courses that they organise through the winter months, between December and March.

You are allotted neat bunks in two and four-bed dormitories within the fibreglass huts. With a common corridor down the hut and a "bukhari" in the common room, they are neat, clean and comfortable. You issue your skiing equipment and after a modest lunch at the dinning hut, set off with your heavy and awkward ski-boots, six-foot skis and ski-sticks, up a steep one-kilometre path to hut where you deposited them in a lockable room. Although the ski-slopes extend right down to the huts at the peak of winter, you are there rather late in the year and had to pay for the beautiful snow-views and hill-sides of Primulas and Gentians by having to walk two kilometres to the slopes everyday.

The first day you see unsteadily skidding down gentle slopes with the ski bindings loosely-attached so that they would detach the skis from the boots when under tension. The instructors drilled into us the basic lesson—to fall and to fall the right way at that, for the greatest risk while skiing is the possible twisting of an ankle when falling on a slope. All this, under the exhilarating spell the 200 degree sweep of the high mountains of Garhwal that surround Auli cast on us. Nanda Devi in the not-too-far distance loomed over the rest to the north-east, with wisps of cloud blowing over its summit, sometimes forming an umbrella-shaped cap, as synonymous with Nanda Devi as is the famous "plume" of Everest.

After lots of slipping, falling and getting wet, you injure

yourself to walking on skis, progressing next to swishing-down gentle and then not-too-gentle slopes and falling when one wanted to stop. The snow plough comes next and in this one learnt how to control speed while on a slope and also come to a halt within a few seconds. The instructors surprised at our rapid pick-up of the sport and they went on to teach us how to turn while ploughing and also the basics of Slalom. On the exciting slope of monkey top and came swishing-down at breakneck speed under the close supervision of the well-trained instructors who were themselves under the guidance

A temporary spell of bad weather mid-way through the course did nothing to dampen our spirits and even as six inches of snow fell, you are up on the slopes practising out tumbles.

It is your first day in Auli—and instead of going straight for the post-lunch session of skiing you hung around our cottage, getting the trick of walking on snow, meeting the staff and students who already there on the regular skiing courses.

Auli is unique in one respect. It is different from the other two skiing resorts of India viz. Gulmarg (in Jammu and Kashmir) and Narkanda (in Himachal), in that it is in total isolation from the world around. High up in the snow-covered mountains, where there is not even a village dwelling, except for the Indo-Tibetan Border Police (I.T.B.P.) settlement on the far left. They have their own skiing slopes and friendly as they are, it is by no means a hindrance to the calm and peaceful atmosphere of Auli.

Another fact that comes to mind about Auli is its non-commercial nature, at least as of now. Gulmarg being the oldest of India's three skiing resorts, has an international reputation where its skiing standards are concerned and is, therefore, immensely commercialised.

Narkanda, in Himachal Pradesh, is also a beautiful place and though as yet not as heavily commercialised as Gulmarg its slopes are not so varied, and are meant more for the beginners.

All around is stretched a vast expanse of snow and a 180° panoramic view of peaks like the Nanda Devi (7,817 m.), Kamet (7,756 m.), Mana Parvat (7,273 m.) and Dunagiri (7,066 m.). People of all shapes and sizes could be seen on the slopes.

You do some skiing and come back for some more in the post-lunch session.

By the time you reached Joshimath, snow is practically invisible and the snowy Auli slopes seemed a distant far-fetched dream once again.

Back in Joshimath, you get to know more about the 'Auli festival', held in the first week of March every year. It comprises various cultural events organised at Joshimath itself, so that the villagers can see and participate in them. The skiing competitions take place on the Auli slopes. Preparations are in full swing for it. The 4 km. long ropeway from Joshimath to Auli being built by Triveni Structurals Limited (T.S.L.) in collaboration with an Austrian company. Not only is it expected to be the most beautiful in the world, it will also be the longest ropeway in Asia. The tourists need no more trek up to Auli then.

Besides this, an 800 m. chair-lift, a 500 m. ski-lift and 2 snowbeaters have been sanctioned by the State Government. The whole project as well as the masterplan for the resort infrastructure is being managed by the R.I.T.E.S. In the years to come, even the accommodation provided is expected to be centrally heated, thereby shielding the skiers from the spine-chilling cold outdoors.

Last, but certainly not the least in importance, is the new communication system in the offing, consisting of independent wireless sets to be installed at 14 different locations.

General Information

Altitude:	2,915 mts. to 3,049 mts. expendable to Gorson 3,400 mts.
Area:	5 sq. kms.
Temperature:	Summer—Ranges between 13°C and 29°C. Winter—Rangers between 9°C and 2°C.
Rainfall:	180 cms. average yearly.

Clothing: Summer—Light woollens. Winter—Heavy
           woollens.

Infrastructure

- Simple hotel accommodation and tourist bungalows
  with hot and cold running water, cable TV, intercom
  and attached toilet facilities at Joshimath and Auli for
  350 pax.
- A 3.9 kms. long cable car linking Joshimath (1,906.3
  mts.) with the upper slopes of Auli and ending at Gorson
  (3,016.6 mts.)
- 16 kms. motorable road from Joshimath to Auli.
- A 500 mts. long ski-lift and 800 mts. long chair-lift
  linking the lower slopes with upper slopes.
- Two snow beaters imported from Germany.
- Two snow packing machines for maintenance of ski
  slopes.
- Dressed and improved ski slopes.
- Ski equipment available on hire.
- Assistance of ski instructors and skiers from G.M.V.N.
  and Indo-Tibetan Border Police.
- Efficient communication available in Auli.
- Easy accessibility of medical assistance from Army and
  civil hospitals including emergency rescue available by
  helicopter.

Season: End of December to early March.

Equipment: G.M.V.N. provides modern ski equipment.
  Participants are advised to bring heavy woollen clothings
  like caps, socks, gloves, mufflers, pullovers, trousers, long
  johns, wind proof jackets, dark glasses, gum/snow boots
  and a torch for personal use.

Travel Information

Road: Local Transport Union and State Transport buses operate regularly between Joshimath to Rishikesh (253 kms.), Haridwar (277 kms.), Dehradun (298 kms.) and Delhi (500 kms.).

Rail: The nearest railhead is Haridwar (299 kms.) which is 24 kms. from Rishikesh. Connecting trains—Howrah-Dehradun (9 UP), Delhi-Dehradun (41 UP) and Bombay-Dehradun (19 UP).

Air: Jolly Grant Airport (Dehradun) is 273 kms. from Joshimath and 17 kms. from Rishikesh.

Pithoragarh in Kumaon Hills

The easternmost hill district of U.P. bordering Nepal in the east and Tibet in the north, Pithoragarh, is often called 'Miniature Kashmir'. Nestling amidst spectacular Kumaon Himalayas at a height of 5,412 ft., in a small valley, barely 5 kms. long and 2 kms. wide, the town was an important landmark of the Chand Kings of Kumaon. The ancient trade route to eastern Nepal passed through this area. Pithoragarh and its environs are known for their abundant natural beauty and fine temples that are important points of pilgrimages. It has some excellent skiing slopes.

Besides Auli numerous places in Garhwal and Kumaon are full of potentials for skiing where an individual or a group can enjoy this winter sport on their own.

In Garhwal

- Dayara Bugyal and Kush Kalyan in Distt. Uttarkasi.
- Panwali & Matya in Distt. Tehri Garhwal.
- Mundali in Distt. Dehradun.
- Bedni Bugyal in Chamoli.

In Kumaon

- Khalia Top in Munsiyari in Pithoragarh.
- Chiplakot Valley in Pithoragarh.

Skiing in Himachal Hills

You can go ski-crazy in Himachal during the months of winter. From elementary skiing to the slalom, Himachal offers myriad thrills. The mountaineering institute at Manali organises ski courses from January onwards, while the Himachal Pradesh Tourism Development Corporation helds similar courses commencing from January at Narkanda. There is also a winter carnival at Manali, in the middle of February every year. Apart from cultured evenings, the high point at this carnival is the ski competition held at Solang Nallah, 10 km. from Manali.

Himachal Pradesh Tourism Development Corporation organises Snow Ski courses during January to March every year at Narkanda and Near Manali (Solang-Nallah) in collaboration with the Institute for Mountaineering and Allied Sports, Manali. It is commonly believed that only athletes can aspire to be skiers. This is not true, however, good physical conditioning will only ensure quick all round progress. It is, therefore, recommended that 30 minutes exercise for about 25 days prior to joining the courses w7ill help to tone up the required muscles.

The package fee, inclusive of transportation, lodging and boarding and skiing instructions/equipment, at Narkanda, Manali are 2,500 per person and 6,000 per person respectively for 9 days.

For Ice skating lovers you can try your hand at Figure-skating, speed skating or ice hockey which is organised during the Winter Carnival at Manali in the month of February every year. You may contact:

Directorate of Mountaineering and Allied Sports
Manali 175 131 (Himachal Pradesh)

Basic Skiing Training Programme

Duration	Capacity
Jan. to Feb.	20 men and women
	Age: 17-40
Feb. to March	"
March to April	"

Advanced Skiing Training Programme

April to April	15 days
	men and women
	Age: 18-40
June to June	"

Every winter when it snows heavily around Shimla thousand of winter sports enthusiasts flock to the skiing slopes of Kufri and Narkanda near Shimla and the Kulu district of Himachal Pradesh, to enjoy skiing, one of the most thrilling winter sports in the world. However, skiing is less popular as it is a costlier winter sports. Moreover a heavy snowfall is also required for holding various skiing events. Judging from the crowds that throng Kufri and Narkanda near Shimla and Solang Nallah in Manali during the skiing season, it can be safely said that skiing as a popular winter sport has come to stay in the country.

Skiing was introduced in India some 80 years back not as a sport but as an accessory to hunting (shikar). Skiing was first introduced in India by Lieu C. Kirkpatrick of the British Indian Army. The venue was not Kufri near the summer capital of the British Indian Government but Gulmarg in the Kashmir Valley. Nothing was heard about skiing in the country thereafter till 1928, when some British Army officers on Christmas holiday at Gulmarg formed the Ski Club of India, with Maj-General C. Kirkpatric, which by then he had become, as its President.

The first efforts to organise skiing at Kufri near Shimla was made in early thirties but it failed because of various reasons. It was only in 1953 that the Himachal Pradesh Winter Sports Club was formed. Following the formation of the Club, a large number of ski enthusiasts, including members of diplomatic missions in Delhi, came to the Kufri slopes during 1953-54 winter to participate in the skiing festival, which proved to be a grand and colourful show.

But the Club was still in its infancy and the skiers had to face many difficulties and hardships. There was shortage of equipment as well as of accommodation at Kufri. A few diplomats in Delhi came to the aid of the local skiing lovers and supplied equipment free of cost thus putting the Club on a sound footing. During the skiing festival held in 1954-55 winter, for the first time nearly 5,000 skiing enthusiasts from all over the country came to Kufri to participate in various skiing events and an equal number of winter sports lovers throng the slopes to watch this exciting and breath-taking sport.

The Himachal Pradesh Tourism Development Corporation is making all out efforts to develop winter sports with a view to diversify tourist activities during winter which is supposed to be a slack season for tourist trade. The Corporation organises 15 days certificate course and 7 days non-certificate skiing courses at Narkanda and Manali every year from January to the beginning of March in collaboration with the Indian Institute of Skiing and Mountaineering, Gulmarg.

Narkanda lies forty miles north of Shimla on Kipling's famous Hindustan-Tibet road at a height of nearly 9,000 ft. The nearby peak, Hather dominates the great watershed of India for from here you can see both the Satlej and the Giri which flow into the Indus and Ganges systems, respectively.

The skiing season in Narkanda starts in January and lasts into the first weak of April. While you may have six to ten feet of snow, the motor road to Shimla usually remains open and this makes Narkanda a very convenient destination from the cities of North India.

The slopes will appeal to the cross country skier to Narkanda is set amidst fine conifer forests. A short distance to the west of a PWD bungalow are the beginners' slopes in a clearing and a tow-bar (a T-bar) has also been installed. The Hather slopes on the east delight those who want to get away from it all, and it is possible to ski down towards the famous strokes (the apple king of India) country at Kotgarh.

The government-run classes provide their own equipment. The beauty of Narkanda is that being only an over-night journey from Delhi. One can fit in a skiing weekened at rates easily the lowest in the world and against a backdrop of the finest forest and mountain scenery. While Narkanda is quite developed, skiing at Kufri is still taking off, and has the advantage of proximity to the plains.

The Manali region offers scope for both winter as well as summer skiing.

When the snows herald in winter, the area around Solang Nallah attracts skiers to its extensive natural slopes. In the summer months, there are limited skiing possibilities on the slopes of the Rohtang Pass.

The government-run classes provide their own centre with a natural open air ice-skating rink. Under Scandal Point on the north side of the ridge facing the Dhauladhar are Blessington's tennis courts, which become in the months of December and Jauuary, Shimla Ice Rink.

The Shimla Club is privately run and has been instrumental in popularising all three disciplines on ice for more than twenty years—figure skating, ice hockey and speed skating. Boots are made to measure in Shimla itself, seasonal membership. Membership is inexpensive and national championships are held annually.

Manali (Himachal Pradesh)

Manali is a beautiful hill station in Himachal and offers ample opportunities for summer as well as winter sports. The slopes of the hills are natural and beautiful.

In Narkanda, the skiing season is from mid January to mid March. Skiing is open to people. Himachal Pradesh Tourisn Development organises a skiing course for 7-15 days from January to March each year. The fee covers basic lodging boarding and equipment.

Solang (Himachal Pradesh)

Solang offers one of the best skiing in Himachal Pradesh. The skiing season is from mid December to early March.

Exhilarating Slopes

With their wide open spaces above the snowline, Garhwal and Kumaon offer yet another exciting possibility—ski touring amongst the glaciers. For the avid skier, cross-country runs of 10-20 km are now available, with the added advantage of fresh powder snow, away from criss-crossing streams of skiiers that overtake the slopes of the European Alps. Winter skiing in Garhwal is now being professionally run at the Auli slopes. The normal season is January to March, depending on the snow conditions. The runs are upto three km. in length and offer fine views of the peaks of the Nanda Devi Sanctuary.

India now offers attractive winter sports options. In January 1988, Air-India and the Department of tourism invited the famous Sylvan Saudan, the famous Swiss born ski-mountaineer, to introduce the exciting sport of heli-skiing in Kashmir. Heli-skiing is the ultimate in the sport of adventure skiing, the heliskier is dropped to the top of a mountain or ridge by helicopter, saving the skier the arduous task of climbing up. The skier can now negotiate virgin, unchartered, terrain and experience the thrill and the danger of sking on powder snow. A necessary pre-requisite of this dangerous though thrilling sport is the skiing experience and careful prior study of physical features, cornices, crevases, wind-direction and potential avalanche hazard areas.

Along with enthusiasm and zeal, skiers should being the following items with them.

(1) Woollen Cap, (2) Rubber Boots/Hunter Shoes, (3) Woollen Socks, (4) Small Torch with cells, (5) Woollen Trousers, (6) Woollen long johns, (7) Thick Jerry, (8) Woollen Gloves, (9) Anti-sunburn cream, (10) Dark Glasses, and (11) Wind Proof Jacket.

Training

Skiing courses are organised by the Indian Institute of Skiing and Mountaineering at Patnitop and Auli, starting from January to March at extremely reasonable package rates inclusive of board and lodge.

Skiers are invited to correspond with Principal of the Skiing Institute.

For the sheer thrill of skiing, be it for the professional or the beginner, no other place matches Auli, the newest ski resort in the country and the biggest in Asia. Scenically among the best in the world, it provides apart from the 3 km. long slope, as breathtaking 180° view of the Greater Himalayan grandeur.

Majestic peaks like Nandadevi (7,817 m.), Kamet (7,755 m.), Mana Parbat (7,273 m.) and Dunagiri (7,066 m.), seemingly only a stone's throw away, exude an air which is at once awesome and sublime. The slope ranging from 2,514 m. to 3,049 m. is flanked by tall stately deodars which cut wind velocity to the minimum, thereby offering the ideal opportunity for a cross-country or a straight downhill run. In summer the slope trasforms into a lush emerald meadow sprinkled with wild flowers of myriad hues.

Auli hosted the national skiing contest as part of the youth festival organised by the Garhwal Mandal Vikas Nigam Ltd. The various competitive events drew as many as 50 participants, including teams from the Indo-Tibetan Border Police, the Skiing Institute, Manali, and the High Altitude Warfare School, Srinagar, some of the contestants had earlier represented India.

Some of the professionals demonstrated the intricate techniques of skiing and put up a fascinating display of acrobatics and fancy free-skiing, the highlight of the day being the 'country skiing' which had local boys skiing down the slopes on their crude, hand-crafted skis-potential champions one might say.

To popularise the sport, the Garhwal Mandal Vikas Nigam has been conducting ski courses of various durations from January to mid-April every year depending on prevailing snow conditions at Auli. Instructors from the Indian Institute of Skiing and Mountaineering, Gulmarg (J&K), especially trained in Austria, are engaged for the purpose.

How About a Trip Down Adventure Road?

For those who thrive on adventure, who yield to the romance of nature's beauty and its luring mystic, the Himalayas beckon you. Misty mornings, sunny days and snow clad mountains await your presence, to engulf you in their visual delight. Take a feel of steep mountain paths weaving their way across sharp ridges, deep gorges, stretches of alpine meadows and listen to the music of the rushing streams ... your heart would want to break into a song. Imagine skiing or trekking in this virtual paradise or taking a bird's eye view paragliding over such breathtaking locales. It is a feeling we couldn't put in words, so we offer you to experience it.

Our Courses to Match Your Desires

The Institute of Skiing and Mountaineering is offering Snow Ski courses at Patnitop in Jammu province and at Auli in Garhwal (Uttaranchal). Apart from imparting training in skiing and organising treks in different parts of the Himalayas, the Institute has started training programmes in paragliding at Auli and Patnitop from 1993.

Beautiful Locales to Complement Your Spirits

Patnitop, Sanasar

The area between Patnitop and Sanasar has been found to be perfect for skiing. The place offers comfortable accommodation and is just 110 km. from Jammu. Jammu is well connected by Road, Rail and Air. Hourly buses connect Jammu to Patnitop.

Auli, Joshimath

Apart from its excellent Ski-slopes with latest Ski lifts, Auli offers a wonderful view of the Garhwal Peaks such as Nanda Devi, Kamet, Dunagiri, etc. A Mere 16 km. drive from Joshimath, which in turn is connected by regular state transport buses from Rishikesh, Haridwar, Dehradun and Delhi. Garhwal Mandal Vikas Nigam also offers taxi and bus services. For those wishing to fly in, the nearest airport Jolly Grant is only 17 km. from Rishikesh and 26 km. from Dehradun.

Excellent Facilities

There are the best skiing and paragliding instructors having had advance training from abroad. Most of the equipment is imported or the very latest. A recently installed 500 m. State-of-the-art ski lift is available at Auli. Accommodation with proper heating arrangements is provided to all trainees. The Institute makes arrangements with local medical authoritites for medical facilities. However we suggest you bring along a few medicines for general treatment like sprain, headaches, cold etc.

Do You Fit In?

In case you think it is only athlete's and Sportsmen's stuff then you couldn't be more wrong. Anybody with a normal physical condition can handle these sports. All it needs is a strong aspiration and a will to do it.

Anything Else You'd Like to Know?

Show It Off!

And when you go back and narrate your exploits to everyone, we give you certificates to prove them. Students can avail of travel concessions from their respective institutions.

Course fees are inclusive of boarding, lodging, equipments and training but participants have to reach the locations on their own. Fees are applicable for 1994, subject to annual revision therafter.

Skiing—True Skid-n-Slide Excitement!

The search for the beauty, the serenity, the excitement and the ultimate passion in adventure ends here. The unspoilt undulating terrain veiled in snow with the lofty mountains falling against the backdrop of clear blue skies are a joy to behold. Here for a moment even time seems to stand still. Imagine the sheer pleasure of slithering down the snow, with all this scenic delights whizzing past you like pictures in motion. It is a feeling you are bound to cherish for years. If you are already sensing all the excitement and dreaming about it, let's just disturb you for a moment, and request you to go through all those earthly trivialities to experience this eternal bliss.

The Institute provides the Ski Equipment, however it would be convenient if the trainees bring along with them: Woollen Cap, Underwear garments, Rubber/Hunter boots, Woollen Socks Thick—4 Pairs, Torch, Toileteries, Woollen trousers, Woollen Long Johns, Thick Sweaters, Leather Gloves, Woollen Mittens or Gloves, Wind Proof and Padded Jacket, Anti Sun Burn Cream, Reading Material, Stationery, Dark Glasses, Sewing Kit.

Training Programme

Month	Course	Location
January	10 days Basic Course	Auli
to	7 days Introductory Course	Patnitop/Sanasar
March	12 days Intermediate/ Advance Course	Auli
	15 days	Auli

24

Heli Skiing

Heli Skiing is another winter sport full of attraction and adventure. This exciting sport was introduced in Kashmir in January 1988, in collaboration with the famous Swiss born ski mountaineer, Sylvan Sweden. With this India became the first Asian country to offer Heli skiing facilities.

It is an attractive sport on the snow covered mountain tops of the encharting Himalayas. You must be a real dare devil and a daring adventure seeker. A helicopter drops you on the ice top of a mountain or ridge. Yoy will be saved the tiresome and risky task of climbing up. Once at the height and with all your energies at your disposal you can now negotiate virgin, undiscover, the uncharted terrain and experience the thrilling experience and the changer of skiing a powder snow. But, before you want to be a heli skier, it is absolutely must to have prior skiing experience and careful study of physical features, cornices, crevases, wind direction and potential avalanche hazard mountain areas. Thus skiing is the altitude in the sport adventure skiing.

Most of heli skiers of the world prefer Canada for skiing, although there are well reputed skie centres in Switzerland, Austria and Italy. But Kashmir has an edge over Canada. In Canada heli skiers are dropped in remote places, very far away in remote resort areas which are completely cut off from civilization. The skiers are often marooned by bad weather in these isolated areas. In case of Kashmir heli skiing, the beautiful

Himalayan range is always infront of the heli skier. We have about 5,000 first skie descent locations available in Kashmir. Facilities are provided of instructors who are Sweden-trained. They provide help and guidance to the devotees of this exclusive, unique, exciting popular and expensive winter sport.

With the introduction of heli-skiing, the professional skiers are now dropped at the distant peaks which have gradients of 60° and more, allowing them the exhilarating opportunity to face the challenge of negotiating this harsh and difficult terrain as well as some sensational cross country skiing and ski mountaineering.

Putting India squarely on the winter-sports map of the world is the newly introduced sport of heli-skiing—the ultimate in adventure skiing. A helicopter drops the skiier at the top of a mountain or ridge from where he starts skiing down, saving him the effort of climbing up. Suitable for the unexplored heights of the Himalayas, this sport though hazardous, enables the skiier to get the benfit of miles of skiing territory before the helicopter picks him up once again for another exhilarating run. Jammu and Kashmir introduced this sport in 1987 for the first time into India and Asia—in collaboration with a Swiss ski-mountaineer, while Himachal Pradesh hopes to start heli-skiing in Manali in winter season of 1989. But given the nature and expenses of this sport it is unlikely to find many takers in this country.

However, other than heli skiing, the range and variety of winter experiences that India offers can cater to all income groups. Undoubtedly, the facilities in no way compare with those provided in the winter adventure resorts of the west, but the salubrious surroundings and extremely reasonable rates are adequate to whet the appetite of the well-heeled Indian with a yen for adventure. In fact, those willing to try are warned; so capitvating is the novelty of skiing, each ski-run so full of challenges and surprises, so invigorating the cold, and so enchanting the spectacular views of the snowcapped ranges within such close proximity, that once tried, like an addictive will entice you to return each season. And then every year it will be another and yet another winter party in the snow.

25

Tobogganing and Bobsledding

Tobogganing is a sport probably originated on the slopes of Mt. Royal near Montreal, Canada. During the late 1880s it spread to the United States, where it had considerable popularity until the early 1930s then widespread enthusiasm for skiing brought about its decline.

It is a sport of sliding down snow-covered slopes and articifical ice-covered chutes on a runnerless sledge called a toboggan. The toboggan was originally a primitive American Indian sled made of poles tied together with thongs. The 20th century toboggan is usually built of thin, straight-grained boards of hickory, birch or oak fastened together by light crosspieces. Some toboggans are made of metal or laminated wood. The front end is bent up and back to form the 'hood' and is braced by rope or leather thongs. The flat sliding surface is generally about 18 in. (45 cm.) wide and from 4-9 ft. (1.2-2.7 m.) long. The toboggan is light in weight and will support a heavy load on soft snow. It is useful for hailing roads over wilderness trails or cross country as well as for sporting purposes.

During the heyday of tobogganing many artificial chutes were constructed. They were about three feet wide with slides of ice or wood and frequently were built with several parallel tracks to accommodate more than one toboggan at a time. The chutes were quiet steep at the top in order to accelerate the toboggan quietly. Speeds up to 60 m.p.h. were attained from the bottom of the chute the toboggan coasted along an open track which occasionally extended for 1-2 miles.

The totoggan is well adapted to sliding down open slopes where its large surface rides easily on loose, prone or in a sitting position. The toboggan can be steered by lifting and twisting the front or by extending one's leg to the rear and dragging a foot in the snow.

In England and on the continent, the cresta, or skeleton shed, consisting of steel runners fastened to a light frame, is called a toboggan. It is ridden in a head-first prone position like the steel runnered sled that is common in North America. Skeleton tobogging has been practiced on a major scale exclusively on the 1,320 yd. long Crestaran, built in 1884 at St. Moritz, Switzerland with steeply blanked curves including a notably hazardous bend called the horse shoe. Annual grand national championships have been contested on this cause since 1885. This sport, administered by the St. Mortiz Tobogging Club, was included twice in the Winter Olympic Games, in 1928 and 1948 each time at St. Mortiz.

Another form of small sled racing is luge, or lugeing also often called tobogging. The sleds are of wood or wood and iron construction, with the wide runners faced with steel. The luge is ridden in a sitting position and streered with the feet and with a hand rope. Lugeing is traditional winter sport in Austria and is also popular in Germany and Poland. It has been separately governed by the International Luge Federation since 1957. With single and double seater events the first European Luge Championships were held in 1914 at Reichenfeld, Austria and the first world titles were contested at Oslo, Nor, in 1955. Lugeing was included in the Winter Olympic Games for the first time in 1964. Speeds up to 60 m.p.h. have been attained and, on some points of the Krynicatran, Poland, 80 m.p.h. has been recorded.

The sport of sleding down an ice-covered natural or artificial incline on a four-runner sled carrying two or four persons. Bobsledging originated in Switzerland around 1890, and is attributed to two U.S. vacationers who endeavoured to increase the thrills of tobogganing by adding runners to increase the toboggan's speed. The sport grew in popularity and in 1898 the first organised competition was held on the Cresta run at St. Moritz, Switzerland, which has been constructed 13 years earlier for one man-toboggans. The bobsled travelled much faster on the icy run and with improvements in sled construction during the next few years the Cresta, built for lower speeds, became too dangerous for bobsledding.

In 1904 a separate bobrun was built at St. Moritz having a gentler slope and high banked turns. In 1923 bobsledding became an internationally recognized sport, with the organisation of the Federation Internationale de Bobsleigh et Tobogganing and it was included in the first Winter Olympic games at Chamonix, France, in 1924. In 1931, the first bobrun in the United State was built on Mt. Van Hoevenberg near lake Placid, N.Y., for the 1932 Olympics.

Runs

The bobrun used in international competition must be atleast 1,500 m. long and have an average slope between 8 per cent and 15 per cent. There are generally from 15-20 turns ranging in size up to huge hairpins of more than 180°. Most bobruns have permanent foundations of concrete or stone set into the earth. The foundation is covered with several inches of wet snow which is then saturated with water and allowed to freeze. The straight aways have side walls of reinforced ice about 18 in. high. The large turns are banked very steeply and are built up as high as 20 ft. to prevent the fast travelling bobsleds from flying out of the turn.

European bobruns are quite narrow, only 4-5 ft. wide, leaving less than a foot of clearance each side of shed. The American bobrun, at Lake Placid, on the otherhand, is 6-8 ft. wide, and has about a half inch of snow frozen on the ice, giving the runners a better grip for steering. The major turns have an overchanging lip of ice to prevent the sleds from going over the top.

Sleds

Early bobsleds were built mostly of wood. Steel runners were adopted with in a few years and by the second half of twentieth century steel and aluminium were used throughout. The four runners are generally mounted in pairs on the two axles, allowing them to rock freely. Steering is accomplished by turning the front axle either with ropes or by a wheel linked with the axle by cables. The brake is toothed bar which is pressed against the ice between the rear runners. Racing bobsleds have a streamlined cowling infront of the river to reduce wind resistance. The principal manufacturer of bobsleds for many years was the Feierbend family of Engelberg, Switzerland. The Italian Podar bobsled was introduced during the mid-1950s and soon proved its superiority by winning most of the major races. In addition, many sleds are built and raced by individuals.

Two types of bobsled are used:

(i) Two-man bobsleds, as they are called in Europe, and
(ii) Four-man bobsleighs.

Rules limit the maximum weights to 363 lb. and 507 lb., the maximum length to 106 in. and 149 in. and the minimum runner thickness to 320 in. and 400 in. respectively for the two types of sleds. Furthermore, the runner surfaces must be half round and separated by $26^3/8$ in. The crew is limited in weight to an average of 220 lb. per man.

Racing

A racing team originally consisted of 5 persons (4 men and 1 woman). The team of 5, which lay prone on the bobsled, was last used in the 1928 Olympics, after which it was reduced to 4 men. The team must now sit upright. The 2-men event was began in 1929. Since 1931 both 2-men and 4-men international competition has been held each year except for a 7 year interruption during World War II.

A race consists of four descents by each team, the total time for the four heats determining the winner. Electrical timing equipment measures elapsed time to 1/100 of a second. A running start is used from a fixed position of a few feet behind the start line. The heavier four-man sleds attain speeds approaching 100 m.p.h., while the smaller and lighter two man sleds are only a little slower.

The technique which a racing team must master involves pushing the sled at the start to attain maximum starting velocity and balancing their weight to prevent the sled from skidding. Many early teams had a technique of bobbing their bodies back and forth with a sudden snap (hence the name) which was presumed to increase speed of the sled. It is doubtful whether bobbing accomplished this result. In any event it was discontinued as higher speeds were attained through improvements in sled design. The driver, who is the captain and most critical team member, must learn to sense the stability of the sled and to react quickly to prevent skids and to manoeuver properly on the turns.

26

Curling

It is a winter sport similar to bowls or shuffleboard, is played on the ice. The rink is 138 ft wide. There are two contending teams of four players, designated lead, two, three and skip or captain, each of whom delivers two stones alternatively with his opponent. Which lead goes first is determined by the loss of a coin or by one throwing his broom to the other to catch, and their then placing hand overhand till one comes out on top. The stones are slide down the rink towards the tee, a fixed mark in the centre of the circle, which may be marked with a series of concentric circles or bands to aid in scoring and which is called the house when all the sixteen stones have been delivered, a team scores from one to eight points according to the number of its stones that lie nearer to the centre of the house than any of its opponents. If neither side has a stone in the house, or the two opposing stones nearest the centre are equally distant from it, there is no score and a zero is posted. This constitutes an end or inning. Play is then resumed is the opposite direction by the lead of the winning team, or rink, which is the term commonly employed by curlers. The number of ends in a match varies. Once it was as many as 17, even 21 for a final of a bonspiel or tournament. Then 12 and 14 end became usual. With the increasing multitude of curlers, the multiplication of contending teams and the limitation of most curling to enclosed rinks with artificial ice, matches are often reduced to ten ends. In case of a tie extra end is played.

Technical Terms

Beson:	Broom or brush used for sweeping (sooping) the ice.
Bonspiel:	A curling tournament.
Building a House:	Strategy of placing a team's stones to protect each other and block opponents.
Button:	One foot circle around the tee.
Chipping the Winner:	Striking a winning stone of which only a small part can be seen.
Crampet:	A metal plate with spikes to hold on the ice, just infront of the foot score, used as a foot brace, or hack, from which to deliver a stone.
End:	An inning, constituting the delivery of all stones to one end of the rink.
Granite:	Curling stone.
Hack:	A shallow depression in the ice just in front of the score used as a food brace from which to deliver a stone (see Chainpet)
Head:	The stones in the house after all 16 have been played.
Hog:	A stone that fails to cross the hog line. It is removed from the rink, unless it has struck another stone.
House:	The 12 ft. circle around the tee.
Pebbling:	Spraying the rink with drops of hot water from a sprinkler.
Port:	Opening between two stones.
Raise:	Promote a stone toward the tee with another stone.
Rink:	The ice on which the game is played; also a team.
Soop:	Sweep

Tee: Fixed mark on the ice indicating the
               centre of the circle, or house.

Wick: To carom off a stone.

Equipment

The round stones are about a foot in diameter between four
and five inches high and weigh around 40 lb. Opposing team
distinguish their stones by the colour of their handles. Only
a few inches of the rounded bottom of a stone touch the ice,
so that it slides along readily. These are made of bone (fine
whetstone) which has a superior smoothness and texture. It
takes a stone, put down with average speed, about 17 seonds
to traverse the rink.

The curler has a broom or a long-handled brush with
which he may sweep (soop) or scrub before the stone as it
moves down the ice. Outdoors the chief was to keep the ice
clean and remove any obstacle brought by the wind. The
ice is prepared for curling by pebbling. Pebbling forus tiny
specks of the ice which slightly roughen its surface, prevent
the stone from sliding too much and increase its tendency to
curl on bond to the right or left. Sweeping presumably lessons
the pebble and so makes the stone travel straighter and farther.
Some curlers mop the ice instead of pebbling it.

Rink

The rink is composed of a tee, the centre of the house. The
outer circle has a radius of 6 ft., concentric circles with raddi
of 4 ft., 2 ft. and 1 ft., also may be drawn on the ice. The foot
score is often marked by a slab of wood firmly embedded
on the ice. Behind the block score or line, the opposing skip
stands until the stone coming toward him has reached the
sweeping score, drawn through the centre of the house, when
he is at liberty to sweep it through. Otherwise no one may
sweep an opposing stone. Such a stone is out of play after it
passes the back line, and should be pushed away where
another stone may not be stopped on that line by it only

those stones can count in scoring which are in the house or touch its outer circle, but stones are not out of play until they pass the back score/line or touch or cross the side line of the rink, or fails to cross the hog line. But a stone which strikes another lying in play remains itself in play though touching the hog line.

The Play

In delivering a stone, after thoroughly cleaning the bottom to ensure an evencourse, a right handed curler stands with his right foot bracked against the left hack, a shallow depression made first before the foot score, or in a metal crampet laid on the ice. A left handed curler similarly places his left foot on the depression, or the crampet to the right. Holding the handle of the stone, with his eyes fixed on the skip's broom, placed for him to aim at, and his feet pointed toward it, he swing the stone back slowly so that its handle remains on a line directly toward the broom, and then follows through without bending his elbow and so that his hand and arm after releasing the stone point directly toward the broom. Be on the broom' is a fundamental of curling. If the skip has signalled for an 'inturn', the palm of the right-handed curler should turn to the right and be upward at the end of the stroke. For an 'out-turn' the hand should turn over to the left with knuckles uppermost at the conclusions of the delivery. For the right handed curler an intern should curve (curl) to the right toward the end of the stone's course, and an out-turn should curve to the left. The curler balances himself by holding his broom or brush in the other hand. Many slide out from the back before releasing the stone, but they must let go if it before the sweeping score is reached. While a stone is being delivered, the courtesy and etiquette of the game require that the other player remain motionless and slient. Crossing the rink is particularly heinous offence.

The other two members of the team stand on either side of the rink at the nearer hog line, ready to sweep in front of the stone as soon as it crosses that line; if so directed by the skip. In the "running" game where fast knock out shots are played, some sweepers take a running start from behind their hog line and sweep the stone at full speed in order to keep it straight in line against the opponents stone. Sweeping with in the house is the skip's prerogative, and he may sweep one of his own stones through rather than leave it in an easy position for an opponent to rest against. If a stone is 'marred' by touching the groom or person of a curler, it is declared out of play, if one of his own side's stones. If it is that of an opponent, if may be placed where ever the opposing skip directs.

The lead stone should be placed where they are difficult to dislodge or where they will obstruct the opposition's shots. Which policy to pursue may depend upon which side curls first. Normally a stone in the front of the house is preferable to one on the back. Some skips will not leave an opposing stone on the centre of the ice, even though outside of the house, since it is in the way and it is liable to be promoted to count against his side. Unless specially asked to lay a guard out in front, number two should not be short on his shots, or his stone way block this own side. The skip indicates which are the opposition's stones by pointing at them with the handle of his broom; he identifies his own by pointing with the straw end. Then the signals what kind of shot is to be played, and where the stone should go.

Variation of speed and distance are indicated by such expressions as draw weight, tee weight and hack weight. Finally, making allowance for the condition of the ice and the amount which he expects the stone to curl, he places his broom for the player to aim at. After the stone has been delivered, he watches its course and directs the sweeping either in accordance with the original intention, or if the un expected happens, to attain some other advantageous objective. When his own turn to play comes, number three acts as skip for him.

Of common shots, the knockout (bumping an opponent's stone away from scorcing position), guard (placing a stone as to protect a teammate's stone from a knowckout) and promote (bumping another stone so as to move it closer to the tee) have already been mentioned. Others are 'Wicking' off another stone toward the tee, coming to rest first in front of and against an opposing stone so that years cannot be knocked out without dislodging it, drawing around a stone or stones to lie behind them nearer the tee, and drawing through a porl or narrow space between two stones either to lie or to displace opposing stones. The point game, which is good practice and may be played by as few as two curlers, consists in attempting, both by inturns and outturns, such a variety of shots as these.

There is no generally accepted costume for curling. Some clubs have uniform coats or sweatens, but the most distinctive feature of the curler in the 'bonnet', a plaid tam-O'Shanter, balmoral or Glengarry, adorned with medals won at bonspiels and club pins exchanged with the members of opposing rinks. An essential feature in the footgear that will not slip upon the ice.

History

Curling like golf is especially associated with Scotland. But the earliest representation of it is a winter scene by the Flemish painter Pieter Bruegel (C. 1525-69), in which a bond of hunters with their dogs lookdown upon two expanses of ice. On the farther one are skaters, on the nearer are pairs of curlers with brooms and stones with handles. The Grand Caledonian curling club was founded at Edinburgh in 1838 to unite curlers throughout the world in to one Brotherhood of the Rink. In 1842, it became Royal Caledonian curling club under royal patronage. The Canadian branch of this organisation was established in 1852, and in 1956 it affaliated with the Dominion Curling Association. The Royal Montreal Curling Club dates from 1807, however, and celebrated its 150th anniversary by bonspiel in 1957.

In the U.S., the Grand National Curling Club of America was founded in New York on June 26, 1867, and was affaliated to the Royal Caledonian. Of its seven original member clubs the only surviving one is the Caledonian curling club of the New York city. St. Andrew's Golf Club at Hastings—on—Hudson, N.Y., the oldest golf club in U.S.A., has source its foundation and by its original constitution been devoted to curling as well as to golf. But the oldest curling club in the U.S. is the orchard Lake Club in Michigan, founded in 1831. United States organisations are the Mid-West Curling Association at the U.S. Women's Curling Association. The first annual U.S. men's national curling championship was held in Chicago Stadium, March 27-30, 1957. There also is curling in varies contain of continental Europe as in Australia.

27

Himalayan Glaciers

Glaciers are the masses of ice which under the influence of gravity, flow out from the snow fields where they originate. Permanent snow fields occur in every continent except Australia. The height of snow line, i.e. the level upto which the snow melts in summer, varies with latitude from the sea level in the polar regions to 2,000 ft. in Greenland and Chile, 5,000 ft. in Norway and Alaska, 9,000 ft. in the Alps, 14,500 ft. (Assam), 19,000 ft. (Kashmir) in the Himalayas and 17,000-18,000 ft. on the high equatorial peaks of Africa and the Andes.

The Himalayas constitute one of the most important glacier systems in the world ranging approximately in latitude from 27°N to 36°N and longitude 72°E to 96°E and covering a vast area. There are nearly 15,000 glaciers in the Himalayas, extending from Kashmir in the west to Sikkim in the east. Resources of water in the form of ice and snow, cover extensive areas in the Himalayas. The fresh water locked in the Himalayan glaciers, has a very special significance for India as they are an important source of fresh water for North India's perennial rivers and surface water reservoirs. The water reserves contained in Himalayan glaciers, are comparable to the ground water reserves of India.

The glacier releases a very significant portion of the annual melt water during a fairly short summer season i.e. June to September. In the glacier melt streams of Himalaya, the maximum fortnightly discharge occurs in the second fortnight of July or in first fortnight of August. Therefore, it registers a decline upto the end of September. The topography, forest canopy, soil characteristics, geology, altitude and latitude influence the run-off in several ways.

The glaciers vary in extent in response to change in the prevailing climate. But behaviours of all the glaciers in a region are by no means synchronous. At any given time, it is often found that some are advancing while others are retreating.

Year to year variation of snow cover has a direct effect on the climate of the northern hemisphere through snow surface air interaction. The large expanses of snow-covered areas of Himalayas in winter and spring, suppress the heating of atmosphere which weakens the monsoon circulation in the succeeding summer.

Glaciers have retreated over the past century in the mountainous region of the globe and in some cases glaciers retreated over several kilometres. This is due to the 'global warming' i.e. the increasing of temperature. It is said that, there has been a rise in temperature by one and a half degree celsius during the past century.

The cause of increasing temperature is due to the increasing concentration of different types of gases in the atmosphere. Apart from water vapour and carbon dioxide, other gases present in the atmosphere like methane, nitrous oxide, chlorofluoro carbons and troposphere ozone, have heat absorping potentiality. The concentration of infra-red absorbing gases in the atmosphere has grown significantly since pre-industrial times. Today, the CO_2 concentration of 350 ppm are 20-25 per cent higher than at any time in the past 1,60,000 years. In the very warm interglacial period of 1,30,000 years ago CO_2 concentration was just under 300 ppm, while during the last great ice age it had dropped to around 200 ppm. By the beginning of the Industrial Revolution (20,000 years ago) this concentration had increased upto the 270-280 ppm. level. During the last 100 years, atmospheric CO_2 concentration has risen by 70-80 ppm and attained the present day level. If current trends continue the earth may turn into a "heat trap".

The Himalayan glaciers' recession was more prominent during the seventies when the Gangotri glacier (1966-71) of Uttarakhand (Uttaranchal) had recorded a recession of the order of 27.33 metres per year and the Zemu glacier of Sikkim (1965-75) recorded a recession of 32.0 m/y. The rate of recession declined for a short period which may be due to steady state attained by the glacier or a reflection of positive balance. The rate of recession again increased during the late eighties when Gangotri glacier (1977-1990) and Zemu glacier (1977-1984) recorded a recession of 28.0 m/y and 27.7 m/y respectively.

Glacial landscape is related to the landforms that result from the invasion and subsequent wastage of glaciers and ice sheets on an area of the earth's surface. During the Quaternary era, the extent of ice cover was much more and the maximum quaternary ice sheet spread covered over 30 per cent of the land area of the globe. An explanation of the origin of landforms and deposits occurring on 20 per cent of the earth surface can be found in the present area, occupied by ice mass (i.e. 10 per cent of the earth surface). Glaciers in the Himalayas, by and large exhibit a thick cover of morainic material in the lower reaches of the glacier, which is not always evenly distributed. Glacial troughs, Hanging valleys, Cirques, Aretes, Horns, Tors, Patterned ground, Drumlins, Mountonnee, ground morain, end morain and medial moraine are the main landscape features of Himalayas, which are produced by glacial erosional and depositional processes.

The plant wealth of high altitudinal zones which occur above 3,000 m., around the glacial zone are mainly Brahma-kamal, Archa, Atees, Bankakri, Barmoola, Hatajari, Jatamansi, Laljari, Nelkanthi, Ratanjot, Fankamal etc., which have medicinal and aromatic values and are known as Bugyal in Garhwal Himalayas and Margs in Kashmir Himalayas.

The snow-ice and glacier regime influences the climate of the region and hence vegetation cover of the area. The researches on the snow-ice and glacier regime have appreciability in water resources management, environmental appraisal and hazards like avalanches, lakebursts, and flood settlements in high altitude area management.

The significant of snow cover studies is now increasingly being felt for understanding the cryogenic environment of the Himalayas. The role of snow has a far reaching significance in the development of winter tourism, protection of villages in the higher reaches, safety of road as well as railway constructions, and defence installation in strategic areas. There is a growing awareness of laying more stress on hydroelectric power projects and irrigation schemes in the higher reaches of Himalayan rivers. Glacierised areas in the Himalayas are being considered for future hydel power production as these areas have favourable hydrological conditions.

In these days of environmental concern, glacial geomorphology acquires practical importance in land use planning. It is being generally recognised that soil mechanics must be used against a background knowledge of glacial landforms, for civil engineering projects.

In India, we are still at the fringes of glaciological studies, through a sound base is existent for its furtherance. The glaciological research in India has remained neglected because it is a comparatively expensive activity, involving inhospitable high altitude terrain and short work periods, together with lack of trained out willing manpower.

The Khatling Glacier

Away from the torrid, polluted, crowded atmoshpere of the plains, it is just not the fresh air, virgin forest or the crystal clear water falls that enthrall. But also the ineffable ubiquitous beauty of Khatling valley in the Garhwal Hills, covered with its impenetrable verdant forest, coruscating snow peaked mountains and idyllic hill slopes that allure trekkers, mountain lovers, anchorites, contemplators and perhaps also God.

There is an ancient story regarding the emanation of the ebulliently flowing Bhilangana river which, dancing down from the Khatling glacier (12,200 ft.) embellishing the valley below, joins Bhagirathi river at Ganesh Prayag, near the Garhwal town of Tehri. Legend has that a celestial nymph tried to lure Lord Shiva while he was meditating. She was spruned by him and was converted to a liquid form. Thus, originates the river Bhilangana.

Khatling glacier is surrounded by august peaks of Jogin (6,460 m.), Thalay Sagar (6,905 m.), Bharat Kantha (6,379 m.), Kirti Stambha (6,906 m.) and Meru. From here one can trek to Gangotri and Kedarnath. The trans of Gangotri is about 50 kms. from Khatling that requires mountaineering skills to negotiate. The Kedarnath trek is about 35 kms.

The passion of trekking is inevitable, just as the closeness of a snowclad mountain is ineluctable and culminating. This trek was difficult and challenging. Make all the required arrangements in advance including information about the route from the Garhwal Mandal Office, Rishikesh, early June. is not the right time for your proposed trip from Khatling to Kedarnath.

It takes you 4 hours by bus to reach Guttu (1,524 m.) from Tehri. This was the place from where your trek begins. March without resting towards your first camping place Reeh (12 kms.). You will passed through large terraces flung down from high mountains in green steps of cultivation, maintaining their verdancy and exhilarating thick forest bands, embracing the cool mountain air. The realm of Bhilangana not only nourishes forests but also wildlife of various kinds and is famous for the 'Kasturi Mrig'.

Your next camping place is Kalyani, 16 kms. ahead, via Gangi which is the last village where rations is available. After an arduous climb of one and a half-hours, you reach a place called "Buranschauri" which is famous for its Rhododendron shrubs which largely occupy this area. In March and April these red flowers are in full bloom.

Gangi is a small panoramically located village. During marriage festivities, the local Gangi people kill the 'Barasingha' in front of their holy deity in the temple and enjoy a strong rice beer sweetened with fermented jaggery. Another winter settlement Deokhuri Channi is famous for its fields of 'charas'.

Kalyani is a place with just a cave, near the banks of the Bhilangana. Here one can find bears, which are very mischievous according to the local people. From here a trail bifurcates for Sahastratal lake (16 kms.). The calm beauty and tranquility of Kalyani is unrivalled.

Next morning you commence towards 'Tama Kund' about 17 kms. away. The trail between Kalyani and Birock is through dense forests where numerous untouched waterfalls, small streams, giant conifers, oaks, Bhojpatra and Chandan saplings add to the beauty of this area. The innate tranquility of these forests is unforgettable. Via Birock you reach Kharsoli—a large meadow surrounded by conifers and oak. Upstream is the sublime view of snow clad Rudigera peaks. Here you meet *Gaddi* sheperds on their long migration from Kangra.

The veritable adventure of trekking enhanced after Bhelbagi as you have to cross a steep slippery glacier, extending from the cap of the hill. In the middle of the glacier, due to the heavy weight of the rucksack you are terribly exhausted and unable to walk further. Your legs may be trembling and the trepidation of falling into a crevice or the Bhilangana (galvanizing the adventure) punctured my confidence.

After crossing three more glaciers, you reach Tama Kund famous for its wild flowers. If luck you may see a pair of the famous 'Kasturi Mrig'. You may pitch your tent near the Tama Kund cave. From the camping place the hill in front called 'Devishila' reveals a carved face which was formed due to the wind and snow erosion.

In the morning, you may leave the place for Khatling which was 4 kms. ahead. The trail is much more adventurous and difficult as you crossed 12 small and big glaciers but fortunately without any major mishap, you may see foot prints of tigers and bears on the glacier going down right up to the river. The salutary weather of Khatling glacier make you magically fresh. The invigorating mountainscape is rejuvenating. You proceed towards 'Dudh Ganga Gufa' (3 kms.) just opposite to the Khatling glacier across the river Bhilangana.

As the wooden bridge over Bhilangana is broken, you

cross the river through an ice bridge which is an extension of a glacier full of dangerous crevices. The kilometre long glacier takes you to the top of the mountain from where you have a spectacular view of the muddy origin of the Bhilangana from its shiny glacier. You may bypassed the Dudh Ganga river by crossing another big glacier and reached the 'Gufa'.

From the Gufa a trail bifurcates for Kedarnath, but due to the heavy snow it may be intractable. That night you spent at the Gufa. One is in a state of trance when one sees the full moon rise. The peaks becomes luminous and the valley is bathed in lusturous moonlight.

28

Antarctica Expedition and North-South Pole

Antarctica, the last continent explored by man, lay undiscovered and unsought until 1772. That year, a British explorer, Captain James Cook, began a three-year voyage to look for the southern continent. Men had long wondered whether such a continent existed.

Cook sailed completely round the Antarctic without actually sighting land. His wooden ship, Resolution, was too fragile to smash its way through the ice-pack. The expedition gave up when it was unknowingly only 241 kms. from shore.

A frustrated Captain Cook airly dismissed whatever lay beyond the frozen mass. He loftily declared, "the world would derive no benefit from it". For more than a century his evaluation remained true. Except for the whales, which were hunted to near extinction, the "white desert" seemed to *offer* nothing of commercial value and so the frozen land was left to the gulls, the penguins and the seals.

Man first set foot on the Continent when Captain John Davis, an American meal hunter, sent crewmen ashore on February 7, 1921. They landed at Hughes Bay, near the tip of the Antarctic Peninsula. At the time, however, men did not know whether they had landed on the mainland or on as island. British explorer, James Clark Ross arrived in 1841.

He named-the region he explored Victoria Land in honour of the then Queen of England.

The early Greeks wrote of the Continent and Roman scholars called it *terra icognita australis* (unknown southern land). Tribes of New Zealand told legends about a great white land to the South. In the early 1800's sealers and whalers hunted in Antarctic waters. They guarded the secret of their hunting ground and said little of their voyages.

As more and more got to be known about this largest no man's land nations started staking their claims. Argentina and Chile being close to the region were the first to demand exclusive rights to explore and exploit the continent. Britain had made a similar claim earlier. Around 1940 the situation became hot and hostile on the frozen continent. And in 1948 Antarctica witnessed its first war of sorts. Hostile Chileans, Argentinians and Britons set upon each other and a number of stations were burnt. The following year they signed a peace treaty to avoid clashes but the dispute remained unresolved.

Robert E. Byrd, a U.S. Navy officer, was the first to fly over the South Pole. Before his death in 1957 he had led four more expeditions which added to the knowledge of the continent.

During the 50's and 60's scientists established permanent bases in Antarctica to solve such mysteries as the depth and movement of the polar ice and its effect on world weather. They also wanted to find out more about the land beneath, the ice and whether it had valuable natural resources.

Antarctic exploration had become far too complex and expensive for small privately financed efforts. During the International Geophysical Year (IGY July 1, 1957–Dec. 31, 1958) 12 nations began a gigantic co-operative research and exploration programme. Expeditions were sent by Argentina, Australia, Belgium, Chile, France, Great Britain, Japan, New Zealand, Norway, Russia, Africa, U.S.S.R. and U.S.A. As a result about 40 stations dotted the ice-cap. Over 10,000 then took part. They combined exploration with studies of weather magnetism, gravity, cosmic radiation, earthquakes, sun-spots and oceanography.

By and by other nations also got actively interested in

grabbing the yet unexplored and unexploited frozen wealth
of the only continent which todate belongs to no nation. The
situation was reminiscent of the California gold rush. But
for the Security Council's intervention disputes might have
cropped over the continent which Cook had thought was
good only for penguins and seagulls.

In 1959 the Security Council made the 12 nations, active
on continent, sign the Antarctic Treaty under which they
were free to carry out scientific research on the continent
but ownership disputes were put in cold storage for 30 years.
Political and racial differences were conveniently overlooked
by the signatories. Poland was allowed a late entry.

The Frozen Continent

While the territorial claim of the seven claimant nations
remains frozen as per the Antarctica Treaty of 1959, a totally
different lobby gained momentum on the environmental
threats facing the continent because of the various proposed
industrial activities, particularly that of mining.

France and Australia, the two of the claimant States
spearheaded the convention and India was one of the 25
consultative parties of the 39 strong Antarctica Treaty. The
meeting decided to continue with the *ad hoc* approach to
general environmental protection of the region and to drew
an effective new legal instrument to protect and preserve
the surroundings of the continent. However, most members
were inclined to opt for a long-term moratorium on mining
and other related activities including prospecting.

The huge continent, which is more than the size of India
and China put together, has been constantly luring explorers
and scientists from all over the world ever since the first
major expedition to the continent by Captain James Clarke
Ross, a British, in 1841. And C.E. Borchgrevink, a Norwegian
was the first to winter there. Following these pioneering
attempts, a plethora of nations vying to establish a base in
the new continent proliferated.

Today, you find no less than 39 countries having their

flags fluttering in the Antarctican gales. USSR alone has about seven bases and close on its heels is Argentina with five, while U.K., Chile, Australia and Japan have three each. U.S.A. has four stations. The Antarctica Treaty, however, has identified the region as a zone of peace and no country has any claim over the territory. Arms of any kind are banned entry too, though the skills of armed forces can be utilised for constructive purposes.

Best described as a cold desert, the polar continent holds the key to many geophysical mysteries. Most of the researches carried out here centre around geo-magnetism, meteorology and environmental studies. The observatories here are trying to unravel the mystery behind the spectacular geomagnetic phenomenon occurring during polar nights, when the whole sky is brightly illuminated with rays of colours in quick transformation. Known as *Aurora Australis*, this breathtaking phenomenon has always fascinated and puzzled the scientists. The atmospheric studies include analyses about alarming ozone depletion too.

There is a feeling among the meteorologists that the Antarctican climate has a direct bearing on the Indian weather. Our permanent station *Maitri*, keeps a meteorological recording every six hours and despatches constant data every 24 hours. Radio sound balloons filled with hydrogen gas are floated to analyse the upper layers of the atmosphere. Experiments on air samples are also carried out since the region remains totally unpolluted. Contents of canned foods buried in the ice years ago and found strewn here and there have remained absolutely fresh.

Now with the possibilities of industrial ventures too entering the fray of activities, environmentalists, like the noted French underwater explorer Jacques Cousteau, have been persuading a ban on all activities in Antarctica except the research-oriented ones.

Entering the Antarctica Treaty in August 1983 and becoming a consultative member a month later, India has joined the band-wagon of countries exercising their scientific visions on the unexplored frontiers of the frozen continent. Every

November, an Indian expedition team leaves the shores of Goa to sail across 13,000 km. to Antarctica and reaches there by December. The summer team returns back in February leaving behind a skeleton staff known as the winter team, to man the station.

Speculations about its natural resources are manifold. The major rock exposures in the 2 per cent ice-free area of the continent have revealed that the cratonic nature of these areas bears a similarity to that of the Precambrian Shield areas of South India, thereby lending credence to the geographical theory that Antarctica and peninsular India were one huge land mass eons ago.

Environmentalists argue that the benefits to be derived from the ventures don't outweigh the environmental hazards. On the other hand they might prove futile under the extraordinary climatical circumstances.

The flora and fauna found in the small ice-free area face the threat of extinction, since most of the industrial activities will also take place in these regions only. The depletion of ozone layer which already requires immediate global attention will increase further if these ventures are allowed in the Antarctican region. Moreover Antarctica remains a unique location for taking baseline scientific measurements like those relevant to the study of climate change.

Atmospherically, the region has great global influence. Therefore, the fragile environment of the continent should not be allowed to be jeopardised on any account for mere economic enrichment. Experience on the Alaskan oil fields on the Arctic Circle has already suggested the irreparable damages caused to the atmosphere.

The series of expeditions do cost exchequer crores of rupees, considering the highly harsh nature of the hazards involved. Could a developing country like ours afford this luxury? For, even if minerals are found, it will not be a feasible venture for India, considering the lack of technology and the unprofitable expenses involved.

Even as our image is enhanced on the international scene, we also hope to carve a niche in the realm of science. We may not strike gold, figuratively or literally, but scientific pursuits so far in history have never proved futile.

The Indian Expedition

It was a cold, windy, endless day when a 21-members team from India set foot on Antarctica on Jan. 9, 1982. India thus became the first major Third World country and only the second in Asia, after Japan, to have reached the inhospitable shores of the frozen continent. It also dug up interesting facts about the yet unexploited frozen wealth of the "white desert" and the growing global interest in the land of the penguins.

It was not exactly a red letter day for the country but scientifically a very significant one, for on that day a 21-members Indian team had touched the fringe of the frozen continent—Antarctica.

It was not a red letter day because other nations had already established stations on Antarctica but significant because India too would now be in the exclusive company of those few nations carrying out scientific experiments there.

The hazards encountered on the Antarctica expedition were more psychological than physical. For once you are out on sea you quickly loose track of time. Especially so when it is just one unending chilly day with no night to provide respite.

Such conditions lead to lack of sleep and restlessness. And once the biological clock is disturbed other secondary problems, crop up.

The Indian team had undergone rigorous training in the Kashmir Valley prior to embarking for Antarctica. It had taken into account all possible hurdles and prepared itself both physically and mentally. Most of its gear for use in Antarctica was obtained from Norway. The 550 ton ship *Polar Circle*, in which the team sailed to the South Pole, too was chartered from Norway. The India-made articles in the expedition included HMT watches, walkie-talkie from the Punjab Wireless, frozen food prepared by the Defence Research Laboratories, two Indian Navy helicopters and two ice scooters. In all they carried 12 truck-loads of gear with them.

The team had eight members from the Indian Navy, seven from the National Institute of Oceanography, two from the Department of Meteorology, and one each from the Department of Environment, Geological Survey of India, National Physical Laboratory and the Indian Institute of Geo-Magnetism.

The expedition set out on its arduous journey to the frozen continent from Goa on December 6—in between they took a five-day break at Mauritius to refuel and replenish their stocks. It was also at Mauritius that they got their first jolt—a German expedition to the South Pole lost a ship and abandoned the trip.

Still when the *Polar Circle* set sail from Mauritius morale on board was high. Came the 55° latitude and then began a day which was to last well over a month—nights ceased to exist.

The people on board the *Polar Circle* slept when they wanted to and ate when they felt hungry. There was no breakfast, lunch or dinner in the conventional sense. Men had breakfast, if they felt like, even when the clock showed 10 p.m. and dinner at 10 a.m.

As the ship moved further South the sea became rougher and rougher. In the region of the Roaring Forties (40° latitude), reputed to be the world's most roughest and dangerous of the high seas, it became almost impossible to sleep.

The New Year heralded the beginning of the ice journey of the *Polar Circle*. The starboard of the ship kept rising and falling as the aft went up. Often the ships fore rose 60° in negotiating high walls of ice. Occasionally the ship would get stuck in a steep climb over, say, a three-metre high icecap. At such moments water had to be pumped from the rear to the front and thus melt the ice barrier by the application of heat. Suddenly the ice wall would give way and the front of the ship would go down and the rear up. For seven consecutive days the crew, without a moment's sleep, kept on breaking through the packed ice. It made three attempts to land—all in vain.